"Dr John Vervaeke is an excep[...] not only because he asks and [...]lly answers questions o[...] crucial existential importance, but does so in a manner that makes him a cutting edge cognitive scientist and philosopher. This rare blend of cultural relevance and academic sophistication is on evidence in every page of *Awakening from the Meaning Crisis*, elegantly and clearly co-authored with another rising star, Christopher Mastropietro. The situation is dire but promising, the malaise real but the cure at hand. John and Chris diagnose it effectively and address it brilliantly."

— Jordan Peterson, *New York Times* bestselling author of *12 Rules for Life*

~

"*Awakening From the Meaning Crisis* provides a frame for lost souls to productively engage the malaise in which we collectively find ourselves as we navigate a civilizational crisis. Through a masterful joining of history, philosophy and psychology, Vervaeke and Mastropietro offer powerful insight and guidance for those looking to find their way out of the dark woods of modern nihilism."

— Jonathan Pageau, renowned liturgical artist, writer, and public speaker

AWAKENING FROM THE MEANING CRISIS

PART 1: ORIGINS

JOHN VERVAEKE

CHRISTOPHER MASTROPIETRO

STORY GRID

STORY GRID

Story Grid Publishing LLC
Nashville, TN

Cover Design by Timothy Hsu
Edited by Shawn Coyne

First Story Grid Publishing Paperback Edition
September 2024

For Information About Special Discount for Bulk Purchases,

Please visit www.storygridpublishing.com

Paperback ISBN: 978-1-64501-100-2
Ebook ISBN: 978-1-64501-099-9

To Sara, within whom wisdom and love dwell in beauty; your support is so deeply appreciated.

And to my friends, my brothers. You have carried me across many thresholds.

CONTENTS

1

THE QUESTION OF MEANING

Welcome to *Awakening from the Meaning Crisis*. This is the first in a two-book set, adapted from a lecture series of the same name, that summarizes my lifelong project to understand the nature and function of meaning in life.

As a cognitive scientist, I am keenly interested in how naturalistic accounts of human cognition inform our understanding of intelligence, sacredness, and the cultivation of wisdom. Over many years, I have closely monitored and dialogued with a tradition of thinkers, researchers, and writers who have identified a nebulous problem in our modern epoch. If we could describe this problem simply, there would be no need for this book to exist. However, your intuition may already be filling the gaps; it has something to do with the decentering of human life from its cosmic significance, a decline in our sense of purpose, and a sensation of having lost the soul that gave earlier human societies their adaptiveness and vitality. It seems we are left with a feeling of having lost our place in the world along with a sense of who we are and what we ought to do with ourselves.

After dedicating my personal and professional energies to this problem, I am convinced that it, like meaning itself, operates at many scales of personal and communal life. It is the culmination of a sequence of historical forces that can only be understood through careful, long-form inquiry. My intention in these books is to undertake this inquiry, to draw together an argument that integrates various observations and insights about the nature of human meaning across time. The purpose in presenting such an argument is not simply to exposit a problem but to yield a deeper understanding of ourselves as cognitive agents and help to pave the way for an intelligent response.

This lifelong project began many years ago when, at the University of Toronto, I began to notice a growing confluence between people who were interested in Buddhism and people who were interested in cognitive science. As you read on, we will explore what cognitive science is and why it is so important to the project of this book. Buddhism, of course, is well-known, even to those who don't practice it, but it too will require some careful reintroduction. In the forthcoming chapters, we will explain why this ancient religious tradition, when placed in dialogue with cognitive science, takes on a new kind of meaning. In time, you may discover—as I did many years ago—that this connection was not only possible but tremendously fruitful; it has created a new source of understanding to all who might practice the project of wisdom.

For most people, mindfulness is a much more familiar term in our contemporary culture. Indeed, we seem to be going through what has been called the *Mindfulness Revolution*. Mindfulness is now spoken of everywhere in mainstream media. Bookstores are devoting entire sections to the topic, and it has been invited into schools, universities, governments and corporate culture. We see evidence of its presence in many different sectors of life. Why, though? Why is this Mindfulness Revolution occurring?

As you may guess, this revolution is emerging from the very confluence I began noticing many years ago. As cognitive science comes into maturity, more people are trying to integrate the theory of this discipline with the wisdom-cultivating practices found within Buddhism. Still, we may well ask: Why is this happening now, and why is it so prolific? What do we mean by *mindfulness*? Some of my work tries to answer this question, and this book will describe it step by step.

In order to better understand the confluence between Buddhism and cognitive science, we must also take notice of how it converges with other important movements. Both academically and in the public sphere, people are becoming more interested in the topic of *wisdom*. This is something people did not talk about very much a few decades ago, but wisdom is now a hot topic within psychology and cognitive science, and books offering instruction in wisdom are becoming popular again. For example, I recently bought my son a book called *How to Be a Stoic* by Massimo Pigliucci.[1] Consider this novelty: How is it that a philosophical practice over two thousand years old is once again in demand? Why is there such hunger for wisdom? Why are people meeting this hunger by looking into philosophies of the Hellenistic period? As we'll soon discover, I think there are compelling answers behind all of these questions.

Another important movement we cannot ignore is the growing interest in psychedelics and psychedelic experience. Academic interest in this topic dates back several decades, of course, and its influence in human culture has persisted for millennia. Yet as our knowledge of the brain transforms, so does our understanding of these mysterious substances, their capacity to radically alter our perspectives, our sense of meaning, and the way we participate in the world. For example, clinical evidence now suggests that psychedelics assist in releasing people from treatment-resistant addiction and overcoming post-traumatic stress disorder. The normal recovery rate for individuals suffering from post-traumatic stress disorder undergoing therapy is around 20 percent. When psychedelics are introduced into the therapy, the healing rate increases up to 80 percent.[2] What accounts for this dramatic effect? What prompted this interest in using psychedelics in the therapeutic context?

---

1. Massimo Pigliucci, *How to Be a Stoic: Using Ancient Philosophy to Live a Modern Life* (Basic Books, 2017).
2. Peter Oehen, Rafael Traber, Verena Widmer, and Ulrich Schnyder, "A Randomized, Controlled Pilot Study of MDMA (±3,4-Methylenedioxymethamphetamine)-Assisted Psychotherapy for Treatment of Resistant, Chronic Post-Traumatic Stress Disorder (PTSD)," *Journal of Psychopharmacology*, 27, no. 1 (2013): 40–52.

Finally, there is a renewed public interest, matched by a huge academic interest in the subject of happiness and meaning in life. In some ways, this isn't a new phenomenon; we have always been a happiness-oriented culture, and the American ethos has encoded this value into our society. The American Declaration of Independence famously states that humans have inalienable rights, including "Life, Liberty and the pursuit of Happiness." Yet this pursuit of happiness has taken an interesting turn in recent years; the topic of *meaning* is coming back to the fore. More and more, people are becoming preoccupied about not just material success or contentment but what it means for a human life to be meaningful. As it turns out, this is quite a fundamental question, and it appears to reach so deeply into our experience as human beings that we have a very difficult time accounting for it.

Thanks to this convergence of cognitive science and Buddhism along with the renewed interest in wisdom, we have more adequate explanations to instruct our intuition and to explain the primacy of meaning in human life. We are beginning to understand again that meaning in life, rather than simply an accessory to survival, is essential to human flourishing, predictive of well-being in every sense of the term. It is little wonder that people seek it so voraciously. Nor is it a coincidence that all of these movements are happening right now: the confluence between Buddhism and the Mindfulness Revolution, an interest in wisdom and ancient philosophies like *Stoicism*, a burgeoning interest in psychedelics, and an uptick in transformative and mystical experiences.

There is a pattern to all of these efforts, a certain hunger in the human spirit, a depth of need that has not been fully understood. When we begin to recognize this need as a feature of our spiritual condition, we can begin to piece together a unifying account for why all of this is happening. Each of these movements is responding to a crisis of meaning, a disorienting sense that we have forgotten some essential dimension to reality and lost our relationship to what is good, true, and beautiful. This crisis has deprived us of something essential at the center of our lives. It has been described in many ways by many thoughtful people across time, but we might think of it quite simply as a famine of the spirit, an existential illness that has taken shape in the human brain, body, culture, and soul.

The Dark Side of the Meaning Crisis

In the first section, we discussed what might be called the brighter side of the Meaning Crisis, all of those practices and traditions that are attempting to reacquire our relationship with a meaningful life. However, a darker set of factors exists that seems to be converging as well. Although some people dispute it, the evidence is becoming clearer that we are going through a mental health crisis.[3]

Suicide is spiking, and while some socioeconomic factors account for this, other influences are clearly at work as well. In April 2020, the National Center for Health Statistics published a data brief reporting increased suicide rates between 1999 and 2018.[4] These "deaths of despair" cannot be easily sourced to material conditions any more than depression can be reduced to chemical imbalances in the brain.[5] Instead, many people are expressing an acute sense of having lost touch with reality.

More and more often, in both individuals and groups, we encounter expressions of nihilism and cynicism as well as deep frustration and futility. We no longer trust in our public institutions. We have completely lost faith in our political and judicial systems. Religious affiliation is receding consistently, and participation in community organizations is in decline. If this cultural disintegration was true before, it has only been amplified in the wake of the COVID-19 pandemic.

When these systems of culture become unglued, it becomes increasingly difficult to keep a coherent model of the world. The

---

3. I discuss this evidence at length in my talk entitled, "The Meaning Crisis, Religio, and Religion in the Twenty-First Century," which you can watch here: https://www.youtube.com/watch?v=YoJxL-acvuM.
4. NCHS Data Brief 362, 2020: https://www.cdc.gov/nchs/data/databriefs/db362-h.pdf.
5. Though much debate remains on this topic, this reductive view of depression has generally been discredited.

world itself begins to feel untrustworthy, as though we can no longer feel the ground beneath our feet. In our book on *Zombies in Western Culture: A Twenty-First Century Crisis,* my coauthors—Christopher Mastropietro and Filip Miscevic—and I argue that the sense of being out of touch has intensified the prevalence of *bullshit,*[6] a term inspired by the work of Harry Frankfurt.

Bullshit, unlike lying, works by making you unconcerned with whether speech is true or false. The bullshitter, like the sophists of antiquity, does not appeal to any measure of truth outside of the needs of the moment. Instead, he tries to capture your attention with the *catchiness* of his claim and how much it provokes something inside of you: some desire, belief, or association that may not be fully conscious. In other words, the bullshitter has no love or relationship with reality, only with appearance. For him, *man is the measure of all things.* His goal is to overpower you with the force of subjective conviction.[7] We already see plenty of evidence for this kind of relativism in the public media of course, but it also afflicts the academic world.

In *Zombies in Western Culture,* my coauthors and I observed that the intensification of bullshit seems concordant with increases in several of these other dark factors—the decline in religious participation, the decay of familial and social systems, and the ideological inflation of political discourse. Consequently, we are spending far more time in our virtual environments, and there seems to be increasing evidence of a connection between various social media outlets and depression as well as loneliness.[8] We are dealing with a loss of social community but also the sense of company we keep within ourselves. The loss of these relationships, inward and

---

6. I am using this term technically, as put forth by Harry G. Frankfurt. See Harry Frankfurt, *On Bullshit* (Princeton University Press, 2005).

7. For those interested, this phenomenon—called *misology*—is also examined at length by D.C. Schindler in his book, *Plato's Critique of Impure Reason: On Goodness and Truth in the Republic,* 2015.

8. Daria Kuss and Mark Griffiths, "Online Social Networking and Addiction—A Review of the Psychological Literature," *International Journal of Environmental Research and Public Health,* 8 no. 9 (2011), 3528–3552, https://doi.org/10.3390/ijerph8093528.

outward, somehow seems connected to the loss of our relationship to reality itself, our ability to resist the blandishments of bullshit, and to keep in touch with some more ultimate value.[9]

For many people, the notion that we thirst for transcendent value can seem abstract and academic, perhaps even imaginary. But we are often acting it out when we least suspect it. This trend toward the erosion of meaning shows up implicitly in the entertainment we seek as well as the mythologies we elevate. Why, for instance, are zombies so ubiquitous? Why are superheroes so popular? Why is *Star Wars* nearer and dearer to us than the religious traditions that influenced it?

These mythological forms are expressions of an intuition that we have reached a dead end in our cultural worldview and are, in turns, despairing over its loss and attempting, nostalgically, to revive it. Notice how references to "crisis" and "collapse" have—like the zombie apocalypse—become constant factors in our discourse. All of these symptoms, which indicate that meaning is under threat, are now so pervasive that we take them for granted. Several decades ago, movies depicting apocalypse and collapse were considered radical science fiction. But now, these themes have become part of our cultural ambience. The modern world seems chaotic and impersonal, yet at the same time scarce, finite, even boring. When unforeseen events in the world force us to keep company with ourselves, we find the same malaise[10] in our interior lives. A vacuum opens beneath us, a grief for something lost. But we struggle to remember exactly what is lost, and this spiritual amnesia only intensifies the feeling of hopelessness. It becomes difficult to diagnose, let alone to treat, a problem that we cannot see or feel, precisely because it is behind *how* we see and feel.

Just like their positive counterparts, there is a pattern to these dark factors that points us to a unified explanation. This book will argue that they are all interconnected, variations on a theme,

---

9. Mary Eberstadt cogently argues for the connection between the dissolution of family systems and the spiritual crisis of the West. See *How the West Really Lost God: A New Theory of Secularization,* 2014.

10. See Charles Taylor, *The Malaise of Modernity, 1991.*

symptoms of a profound crisis in meaning that we shall call the *Meaning Crisis*. This is not the only crisis we face; the Meaning Crisis is interacting with other crises, such as the environmental crisis and the socioeconomic crisis. It plays the role of a silent catalyst, undermining our ability to solve problems by inhibiting the perspectives we are able to take on ourselves as individuals and as a species. But while these other crises are discussed at length in the public sphere, the Meaning Crisis is generally unmentioned. It is difficult to diagnose a problem that is so fundamental and that operates at every scale of culture. It is complicated enough to require a genealogy, an account of how and why it came to be, and what it tells us about our nature as human beings. That is the task of this book. To begin understanding the Meaning Crisis, we must first understand what *meaning* actually means.

What is this meaning that is coming to crisis?

Why do we hunger for meaning? How do we seek to cultivate wisdom? As you will discover in this book, these two concepts form a call and response with one another, and it is crucial to understand how deeply they are connected. Wisdom is ultimately about how to generate and enhance this meaning. Wisdom is about *realizing*. This means that cultivating wisdom generates realization in both senses of the word: becoming aware and making real. Wisdom is about realizing meaning in life in a profound way.

How do we cultivate this wisdom? What does it mean? This book will talk about wisdom cultivation not just theoretically but practically as well. What are some practices, for example, that people are engaging in to address this need for the cultivation of wisdom? What role, for example, do mindfulness practices play in this cultivation?

Throughout this book, we will keep coming back to these three questions:

- What is this meaning?
- Why do we hunger for it?

- How do we cultivate the wisdom to realize it?

To answer these questions adequately, this book will attempt to trace the evolution of meaning in our culture. What is it? Why is it so important to the development of our humanity? Then, more specifically, this book will focus on the history of the Meaning Crisis. Why did it arise? What were the historical factors? By tracing this closely, we will get a historical account of meaning that makes sense of our predicament. We will see how perennial parts of our nature—features of human experience that are consistent across time—have interacted with this historical evolution. We will discuss how they have collided to produce profound traditions of wisdom while also laying the conditions for their collapse.

As we progress, I will address and explicate the connections between meaning, wisdom, and a third related concept—self-transcendence. It may sound high-minded and mystical, but self-transcendence is an essential need for human beings. It performs core functions for our cognition. For instance, deep connections exist between meaning, wisdom and *altered states of consciousness* (ASC). Throughout our history, human beings have consistently sought ways to alter the quality of our conscious experience by manipulating our physiology and behavior. Other intelligent organisms also engage in this; New Caledonian crows will tumble down roofs in order to make themselves dizzy, for no other apparent purpose than to alter their state of consciousness.

What is going on here? Why would intelligence need to be conjoined to an ASC? Why in particular have human beings developed such sophisticated processes for generating, harnessing, and interpreting these ASCs? We will consider this in connection with shamanism and ritual, but first we will talk about how it relates to *flow*,[11] a state of heightened attention that sharpens our consciousness and competence while deepening our participation in the world—the feeling of "being in the zone."

---

11. Mihaly Csikszentmihalyi, *Flow: The Psychology of Optimal Experience* (Harper & Row, 1990).

9

We will explore why people seek the flow state, and why it is so powerful. We will explore the connection between the flow state and psychedelic experiences and, more importantly, the mystical experiences that can occur within some of these psychedelic experiences. Mystical experiences, as it turns out, are more important and transformative than the merely psychedelic ones, and a subset of those experiences is crucial to transforming people's lives.

These are *awakening experiences*, wherein people return from the mystical experience feeling it was somehow more real than reality. They feel a compelling need to change their world and themselves to fit that new reality. They engage in what philosopher L. A. Paul has called a *transformative experience,*[12] a kind of quantum change that causes a radical transformation of their lives. We now have good research to complement these subjective accounts.[13] People's lives seem to get better after these awakening experiences, and we will explore why this might be true. Eventually, we can bring all of this together to propose a cognitive scientific account of enlightenment— what it is and why it alleviates the suffering caused by this lack of meaning. This form of suffering might feel particularly urgent for us today, but it has always been a perennial threat to human beings, at least as far back as the *Axial Revolution.*

In order to properly address enlightenment and the question of meaning, we must also interrogate the darker aspects of meaning-making. What are the deep, profound connections between this meaning-making, which is so central to our cognitive agency, and our endemic capacity for self-deception and self-destruction? Something about human consciousness, it seems, elicits a special kind of suffering, just like the daytime sun has its shadow in the night. This is one of the tenets of Buddhist thought and wisdom found in many religious traditions; something about our capacity for meaning draws

12. L. A. Paul, *Transformative Experience* (Oxford University Press, 2014).
13. See D. B. Yaden, K. D. Le Nguyen, M. L. Kern, N.A. Wintering, J. C. Eichstaedt, H.A. Schwartz, A. E. K. Buffone, L. K. Smith, M. R. Waldman, R. W. Hood, and A. B. Newberg, "The Noetic Quality: A Multimethod Exploratory Study." *Psychology of Consciousness: Theory, Research, and Practice, 4,* no. 1 (2017), 54–62. https://doi.org/10. 1037/cns0000098.

the threat of meaninglessness, and we must learn to live within this paradox if we hope to summit our human potential. As C. G. Jung once wrote, one of the perils of having a soul is the risk of losing it.[14]

When we consider this human complexity, we can begin to see why we are so awash in bullshit; self-deception is endemic. To properly understand it, we must make an important distinction between foolishness and ignorance. Ignorance is a lack of knowledge, whereas foolishness is a lack of wisdom. Foolishness occurs when your capacity to engage your agency or pursue your goals is undermined by self-deceptive and self-destructive behavior. This behavior is a perennial vulnerability in your cognition.

As I will argue, the machinery that makes you so adaptively intelligent is the same machinery that makes you susceptible to foolishness. It is important not to underestimate this foolishness or to think of it as belonging to a few hapless people. We are all susceptible to this behavior when we confront, or are confronted by, the dark features of our existence: life's finite nature, the presence of fatalism, the constancy of change, the erosion of life by time, and the tension between our lofty aspiration and life's unpredictable fatalities.

These confrontations induce in us experiences of absurdity, alienation, futility and horror. They undermine our grip on reality and our ability to make sense of the world. Yet there is often a deep meaningfulness on the other side of these experiences. When we lose the capacity to confront them, we begin to avoid some essential part of our humanity. In doing so, we become less than ourselves. Life takes on a feeling of weightlessness and seems to lose its substance altogether. This despair that is so endemic to life, if we do not have the wisdom to converse with it, turns into nihilism. This, it seems, is what has happened in modernity.

In the forthcoming chapters, we will discuss these various dimensions of meaninglessness and why more people, compared to the past, appear to succumb to this state of despair. This book will address the historical account of the origin of the Meaning Crisis, giving us some sense of what meaning is and why it is so important.

---

14. C. G. Jung, *Psychology and Religion* (New Haven: Yale University Press, 1927), 18.

In the second book, we will delve further into the scientific study of cognition and the investigation of meaning and meaning-making. This study will serve as a basis for recommending practices to better enhance and enact meaning and wisdom in your life. This order is deliberate; cultivating these practices most effectively depends on having a deep understanding of our longstanding relationship with meaning.

When people use this word "meaning," it is a metaphor. They mean that the way life becomes significant is somehow analogous to the way a sentence has semantic meaning. The pieces fit together in some way that impacts our cognition and connects us to the world. When words become a sentence, we no longer see the words, but see *through* them. They become transparent and give us access to participate in reality, allowing us a chance to grasp it, to have contact with it. We have to unpack this metaphor. Why do we use it, and what does it reveal when we talk about the meaning of our lives? How is it that some of the most meaningful experiences people have are precisely the ones that are completely ineffable to them, that they cannot put into words?

To answer that question, we will have to broaden many of our definitions, beginning with the concept of *knowing*. There are different kinds of knowing, different ways in which a human being is able to know. Some of these ways have fallen off our cultural radar in the wake of the Meaning Crisis. When we read the ancients talk about knowing, we think of it now as a special kind of belief that something is true or false. But there is much more to knowing than having justified true beliefs.[15]

Trapping ourselves in this mode of factuality has made us more susceptible to bullshit and ideology because it has caused us to ignore several dimensions of experience that are essential to being rational. In this book, we will begin to reacquaint ourselves with these other ways of knowing: *knowing how* to catch a baseball,

---

15. In the recent history of epistemology, the discipline of philosophy that deals with human knowing, many philosophers have proposed "justified true belief" as a sufficient criterion for knowledge.

knowing what it is like to sit in your room and read this chapter, and *knowing what it means to participate* in a relationship. Consider that your relationship is not something you believe to be true or false. It is something you *believe in*.

These other kinds of knowing, when they are addressed at all, are usually encountered in the therapeutic context. Therapy is another cultural practice that seems to have surged in response to the Meaning Crisis. Many people who seek therapy are trying, among other things, to recover these lost kinds of knowing, to retrieve the kind of insight that can transform them—not just change their beliefs but change the perspective they take on their lives, the procedure of how they interact with it, and the way they participate in themselves. That is why psychedelics can play a key role in therapeutic success; they help reactivate these different kinds of knowing.

Connecting these different elements will give us an account of meaning that allows us to see both its structure and function. What are its cognitive processes? What are its cognitive mechanisms? How do they work? What happens when they cease to work properly?

Our historical account of the Meaning Crisis will prepare us for this structural-functional understanding of meaning. The two accounts will inform, constrain, and enable one other. From their dialogue, I will endeavor not just to explain this crisis, but to offer a response to it.

This book is entitled *Awakening from the Meaning Crisis*; awakening invokes the tradition—and etymology—of Buddhist practice (Buddha means "the awakened one"). But it also invokes the Socratic way of life and the original purpose of philosophy. I will call upon many traditions of wisdom to educate and prepare us for this task. This book is not simply a diagnostic project but an attempt to confront this crisis with wisdom—not in some ideological fashion, but in a profoundly transformative and existential manner.

There are no simplistic answers to this crisis, and any claim that suggests otherwise should be treated with great suspicion. Awakening from the Meaning Crisis is a complex and difficult undertaking. This is the first of two books that will carefully build our argument for the existence of this crisis, for its interaction with the other crises in our world, and eventually, for the possibility of overcoming it.

Throughout, I will maintain a commitment to rational argumentation and give proper scholastic credit to other people whose work has contributed to my understanding. I do not—and nobody should—claim to offer you the absolute truth. The Meaning Crisis exceeds the capacity of any one person to fully understand it, and an inquiry like this requires rigor and intellectual integrity. However, this is not an academic book or an academic project. It is a project for anyone who is drawn to this problem out of a genuine personal and existential interest.

I will try to keep jargon and technicalities to a minimum. New terms and concepts will be italicized and carefully explained along the way. You can also use the glossary to assist your reading. I cannot be unbiased; that is not possible. But I will present my viewpoints as methodically as I can to demonstrate the scope of this situation. We cannot just treat the Meaning Crisis as a scientific problem, but we can certainly argue for it in a highly plausible way.

The Upper Paleolithic Transition: The Birth of Humanity

Meaning is such a deep part of our nature that it seems to define, at least in part, what it means to be human in the first place. It plays a formative role in many of the uniquely human attributes that seem to distinguish us from other species—like language, religiousness, or even reflective self consciousness. So many human endeavors, especially artistic ones, seem to have no other function than to celebrate our meaning-making abilities. It seems beside the point to ask why the poet writes, the dancer dances, or the rock climber puts herself in danger to scale a thousand-foot cliff.

It is difficult to know where to start. In the words of my colleague, Filip Miscevic, the beginning of meaning is a continuum question. The deep connections between meaning-making and cognition go far back into our evolutionary heritage, well before we were recognizably human. There is no absolute or definitive starting point for this evolution. We simply have to pick a point on the continuum and decide where the story will start.

We will begin with the Upper Paleolithic transition, which occurred around 40,000 BCE. Many people think of this period as the time when humanity—as we now define it—came into form. While we wouldn't be able to relate to these ancestors culturally or linguistically, we would nevertheless recognize their kind of humanity as akin to ours, a humanity that is bound up with the same meaning-making characteristics that I have been exploring with you in the previous sections.

There is some controversy about dating Homo sapiens, but conservatively we have existed since at least 200,000 BCE. Around 40,000 BCE a radical change occurred within this evolutionary continuum. We have come to call it the Upper Paleolithic transition. Human beings began doing things they were not doing before. They began to make representational art, like sculptures and cave paintings. We have good evidence to suggest that they also started making music.

Figure 1.1: Example of the representational sculptures made during the Upper Paleolithic transition. Image obtained from Wikimedia Commons entitled Venus of Willendorf, on display at the Naturhistorisches Museum, Vienna, by Captmondo.

During this transition, human beings seem to have undergone a significant enhancement in cognition. How do we know this? We see the first use of calendars, not with numbers and dates (numeracy had not yet been invented) but with symbolic representations of the phases of the moon and the passage of the days. Human beings were keeping track of time across abstract patterns so they could enhance their hunting abilities. Something else began to happen, intrinsic to our humanity and deceptively important even to our modern nature. They began developing projectile weapons.

The Neanderthals, who were contemporaneous with Homo sapiens at this time, did not have long-range weapons. Their spears were thick-shafted with heavy stone, and they had thrusting tools. We know they got close to their quarry because their remains have bone damage similar to the kind we see in human beings involved in rodeos, where people contend with large, thrashing mammals.

Figure 1.2: Bone spear heads from the Upper Paleolithic period. Image obtained from Wikimedia Commons entitled Museum of Prehistory: Paleolithic bone spear heads (25,000 BCE) from Wartberg, by Wolfgang Sauber.

The Homo sapiens did something different. They started to develop very thin spears, not with stone tips but with bone tips. Bone is much harder to work with, but it is also very light and more effective as a projectile weapon. The early humans also procured two related inventions: the spear thrower and the sling. They developed the ability to carry multiple missiles at a time and project them over a long distance. These skills required increased development of the frontal lobe area of the brain, which, as we will see, is very important for enhancing intelligence.

We need to abstract for a moment to realize the momentousness of this evolutionary development. Think about how deep this idea of *throwing* is in our cognition. Think of a project you are working on —*project,* like throwing to strike a moving target. Or consider the word *object,* which means "thrown against." *Subject,* meaning "thrown under." All day long, cognitively, you are throwing at moving targets. This is a deceptively complex task. As the military has discovered, trying to build artificial intelligence to project at moving targets turns out to be a very tall order.

In time, the advent of long-range weapons was accompanied by other seminal human *projects,* such as calendrics, music, sculpture, and paintings. Notice how all of these activities are associated with different aspects of meaning. They extend our attention into different domains of experience and multiply our ways of knowing ourselves and our environment. They are playful, explorative, and experimental. They augment the world by repurposing it, turning it into an arena for our imagination. These artistic undertakings have the uncanny effect of discovering part of reality and appearing to invent it, all at the same time. The ancient Latin term for this, *inventio*, should remind us of our earlier term, realization—bringing some ineffable pattern more directly into our conscious experience, and in doing so, making it more real. If we begin to think of this in relation to this book's central "project," *awakening*, we can begin to anticipate where this profound human evolution, and indeed this argument, will lead.

It is remarkable to think that the dawning capacity to realize our environment, to change the role we play within it, to develop more participatory relationships with the world, is all awakened by our use of projectile weaponry. This is even more astonishing when we consider how it changed our relationship to fundamental aspects of reality—like time.

During this period, time becomes a more distinct entity in our experience, capable of being known, measured, and related to in more dynamic ways. It becomes a kind of character. This characterization of time doesn't just change reality, but it also characterizes us—who we are, what defines us, and what we ought to do with ourselves. In short, our relationship to time becomes meaningful by becoming *symbolic*.

I will explain the connection between meaning and symbols in forthcoming chapters. For now, it is enough to observe that this new human capacity that emerged in the Upper Paleolithic transition— the capacity to internalize and map movement, to abstract our spatial awareness as a way of representing and reimagining the world—is formative for human cognition, and it is the precursor to our facility for metaphor and symbolic thought. As our early ancestors discovered, it is our capacity to intervene and participate in the world.

Through our ability to project ourselves, we somehow became more present in the world and present to ourselves. The "meaning" of this project was not a principle but a pattern for relating to life and existence, guided by transformations in our attention. It was a pattern we realized, lived in, and evolved through. Eventually, our symbolic reinvention of space and time began to reinvent humanity itself.

At this juncture, you may understandably be waiting for a causal explanation. How and why did this seismic change occur? It is impossible to know such a thing definitively, but excellent anthropology has been devoted to the subject, especially by David Lewis-Williams,[16] Matt Rossano,[17] and Michael Winkelman,[18] trying to explain this radical change in human cognition. It seems evident that sometime before the Upper Paleolithic transition—between 70,000 BCE and 30,000 BCE—human beings went through a near extinction event. Human population was reduced significantly, maybe to a maximum of ten thousand individuals. The cause of this cataclysm is debatable; it may have been the climatic change of the end of the last Ice Age in Africa, or the existence of a supervolcano that erupted around seventy thousand years ago. Whatever the direct cause, tremendous pressure was put on human populations to adopt different survival strategies. They moved to the coasts of Africa and diversified their diet. But the most meaningful response was not technological—the climate inhibited most innovation—but sociocognitive. These early humans started to create broader trading networks. This helped to reduce some of their vulnerability to environmental variation. It also made them more resourceful—materially, and in their capacity for discovery.

Forming these broader trading relationships was seminal because it changed the scale at which human cognition could operate. Your cognition is very participatory; you partake in large, distributed networks of cognition. Before the internet networked computers together, culture networked brains together to provide some of our most powerful problem-solving abilities. This is how human beings

---

16. See David Lewis-Williams, *The Mind in the Cave: Consciousness and the Origins of Art* (Thames & Hudson, 2002).

17. See Matt Rossano, *Supernatural Selection: How Religion Evolved* (Oxford University Press, 2010).

18. See Michael Winkelman, "Shamanism and Cognitive Evolution," *Cambridge Archaeological Journal*, 12, no. 1 (2002), 71–101. https://doi.org/10.1017/S0959774302000045.

responded to an impossible predicament. They formed a social network. These networks were managed with a form of pattern-oriented activity that became so fundamental to human culture that its influence pervades nearly all of our behavior. We call it *ritual*.

Ritual is a deeply complex phenomenon, and I will devote considerable discussion to it in the coming chapters. If you sit at a cafe for a few hours and let your attention wash over the street, you may find yourself marveling at the silent patterns of communal life. Consider, for example, how much time we spend with strangers. It is a rare thing for species to engage in or form relationships with other members that are not kin, outside the hunter-gatherer group. This is one of the legacies of the Upper Paleolithic transition. Our tolerance of strangers distinguishes human beings. Ritual provided the unconscious choreography for engaging with our own species; it allowed us to communicate and foster trust with individuals we did not personally know.

This choreography is still present in many of our complex behaviors. We arrange ourselves in an elevator to look in the same direction. We fall into lines at the bus stop. We form circles around street performers. We clink our glasses together to share trust and felicitations. When you meet somebody, you stick out your hand. The other person grips it, and moves it. Many silent signals are exchanged in this evaluative motion: You show that you have no weapons. You allow the person to touch you, to sense tension, to feel if your hands are clammy.

The same is true in the familiar refrain, "How are you?" It is a famously trivial question; most of us neither welcome nor offer an honest answer. But the semantic response is incidental. The communication does not consist of what a person says but how they respond, how they intone their reaction, and how you intone yours. When it seems you are talking about nothing, you are in fact talking about your relationship, subtly negotiating it the same way your hands are measuring and fitting to each other's grip.

Ritual is guiding your interaction without you noticing. It is the groundwater beneath these cultural forms. If you dig into your own behavior, social or otherwise, you will find it. Even when our interactions seem empty, they continue to convey—and convey us through—these patterns of meaning. In the minutest of gestures, in the smallest of small talk, ancient rituals are at work.

However simple it might seem, following the choreography of ritual requires more than memory or observation. It requires certain cognitive aptitudes. To engage with you, I need to be able to anticipate your actions. I need to have some sense of how you feel. I need to have some idea of what is going on in your mind. In short, I must be able to take your perspective. If I cannot do that, I am not going to be able to trade with you.

The ability to take the perspective of others also means taking perspectives *on* others, especially those you do not know. To do this, you must develop what Daniel Siegel calls *mindsight,*[19] the ability to gain insight into other people's mental states. As you improve mindsight, you also gain a different kind of access to yourself: reflection and insight into your own mental states.

This prototypical form of self-knowledge is the beginning of a development circle; your perspective on yourself perceives and corrects how you take perspectives on others, which in turn affords better mindsight. As this capacity evolves, you begin to take perspective on perspective itself, i.e., know what it *means* to take a perspective. As you may guess, the ability to migrate our attention from first-person perspective to second- and third-person perspectives is critical to the project of *realization* and lies at the origin of processes like metacognition and mindfulness.

Rituals that acquaint and entrust human beings to one another must also have ways of maintaining that trust. If we had to redraw our relationships every time we traded with a new stranger, it would be difficult to maintain the bond of our distributed networks. Loyalty to one's group was taken for granted when the community was always present. When one begins to interact with strangers, this loyalty is called into question. Strangers present temptation. It is a very old motif in our myths.

---

19. Daniel J. Siegel, *Mindsight: The New Science of Personal Transformation* (Random House Publishing, 2010).

This is why we had trade rituals, rites of initiation designed to bind an individual's commitment to the group and hold fast against the incursive threats of outsiders. Proportionately, these rituals needed to test and affirm the resolution of the member against the possibility of temptation. Therefore, they often included great risk, threat, and sacrifice. Our initiation rituals now have been tamed, but if you look back in time, they were often traumatic. People were put into situations wherein they might experience tremendous pain, fear, or even death. If they endured it and came out the other side, they had proven their commitment to the group.

What do these demonstrations mean to a cognitive scientist, and what do they do to the mind? Ritual trains your ability to regulate your emotion and to undertake a process called *decentering:* adopting a non-egoic perspective by redirecting your attention to something real outside of you. Undertaking a ritual often means placing yourself in the hands of other people. In the initiation rituals, the entire group is, so to speak, shaking hands with the new member. The third-person perspective of the group becomes the first-person perspective of each participant. The ritual is centered on you, but through the ritual, your attention and identity become centered on the group. This has a tremendous impact on your cognition.

The cognitive enhancements that emerge from these trade and initiation rites seem to produce a third kind of ritual. To understand how this ritual works, I need to introduce a new concept—that of *exaptation.* This concept originated in biology, but the work of cognitive scientist Michael Anderson has repurposed it to show how the brain and cognition operate.[20] This seems fitting because exaptation, in biological terms, is an evolutionary mechanism whereby our natural instruments become repurposed to develop new kinds of functions. For example, I use my tongue to speak, but tongues did not evolve for speech. If they did, your cat or dog may very well be speaking to you.

Why, then, did the tongue evolve? Consider its other properties. It

20. Michael L. Anderson, *After Phrenology: Neural Reuse and the Interactive Brain* (The MIT Press, 2014).

has the flexibility to maneuver food in your mouth, and it contains a constellation of nerve endings with the sensitivity to detect poison. However, because of the way we evolved, this highly sensitive, highly flexible muscle also rests over in the air passageway.

Evolution is not an intelligent designer; we use the same passage for breathing as we do for food. Your tongue can therefore interrupt your airflow and punctuate the sounds that issue from your vocal tract. With these conditions, this tasting muscle was exapted to produce speech. Evolution did not make a speaking machine from scratch; it took something that evolved for one purpose and exapted it for an entirely new one.

According to Anderson and others, this kind of exaptation is exactly what the brain does. The brain will develop a mechanism—a little machine, a set of cognitive processes for doing one thing—and then it will adaptively apply that mechanism to solve some other order of problem. This is what happened in the Upper Paleolithic transition. The enhanced mental abilities that came out of the adaptive trading and initiation rites were exapted into *shamanic rituals*. The capacity to decenter one's attention, to become aware of one's own cognition, to adopt a foreign perspective... all of these presaged the advent of *shamanism*, a practice for exapting this enhanced mindsight to alter and refine the state of human consciousness, to manipulate our mental and emotional state, and to transform the very character of our humanness.

Anthropologist Michael Winkelman's[21] work shows how historically pervasive shamanic figures are in early hunter-gatherer groups. This historical—or *phylogenetic*— account interacts with a prolific psychological motif. The shaman is the prototypical appearance of an archetypal figure that Carl Jung called the *Magician*, a numinous figure of self-transcendence and transformation, a bridge between the unsteady human ego and the "Self" that is the totality of each individual's potential.

This motif has been endlessly recreated in our cultural myths,

21. See Michael Winkelman, *Shamanism: A Biopsychosocial Paradigm of Consciousness and Healing* (Praeger Publishers, 2010).

notably in the Arthurian figure of Merlin or in the more recent characters of Gandalf and Yoda. Their presence is associated with luminosity, an elevated consciousness, and a capacity for healing. Shamans were the health-care providers of early humanity and the fonts of wisdom in communal life. If you had a shaman in your midst, it helped to reduce discord and enhance the hunting abilities of the group. The shamans were believed to have a foothold in the spirit world, from which they could draw otherworldly knowledge and skillfulness. As a naturalist, my prerogative is not to take these beliefs at face value but to develop a cognitive scientific account of shamanism that makes sense of its excellence and adaptiveness.

By the accounts of Rossano, Winkelman, and Williams, among others, the advent of shamanism can plausibly account for the sudden explosion in cognition that took place during the Upper Paleolithic transition. Critically, this was not a "hardware" change. The human brain had already existed for 160,000 years, and it did not undergo significant physiological changes during the Upper Paleolithic transition. This was more akin to a software update, an exaptation that changed how human beings *used* their brains. As I will argue in later chapters, shamanism likely played a significant role in that software change.

If shamanism was like a software update, we can conceptualize it as a form of technology for the brain—or a *psychotechnology*. As the cognitive scientist Andy Clark wrote, you are a natural-born cyborg.[22] Your brain has evolved across several species to use and integrate tools into its everyday functionality. When you start using a tool, even for a very short period of time, your brain will begin to model it as part of your body. When you are parking your car, for example, you can sense where the edge of your car is. The car turns invisible; it becomes an extension of your person. This spatial co-identification also allows a tool to work so effectively. The same is true of your clothes, which modify your mobility and dexterity through various environments. Your eyeglasses or contact lenses disappear from your

---

22. See Andy Clark, *Natural-Born Cyborgs: Minds, Technologies, and the Future of Human Intelligence* (Oxford University Press, 2003).

vision even while enhancing it. Cutlery, writing implements, weapons, wristwatches—the list goes on.

When we add smartphones and Bluetooth technology to this pattern, we see just how penetrative our technology has become, how coextensive it is with our identities and experience. This technologization can become a problem, as Martin Heidegger famously observed, when it monopolizes our mode of participation and turns the entire world into a tool waiting to be optimized. But there is little doubt that it has made human beings tremendously adaptive.

Yet this is not the end of the story; your ability to internalize a tool can be exapted into a cognitive process, and this is how psychotechnologies become possible. A physical tool fits into your biology, extending its capacity. A psychotechnology fits into your brain and enhances how it operates. To find an example, consider that you are using a psychotechnology right now: literacy. This tool does not come naturally to you. You may have been born linguistic—as Noam Chomsky has argued[23]—but you were not born literate. In fact, human beings were completely illiterate for most of our history.

Literacy is now so embedded in our culture that it is difficult to account for its many functions. This set of tools standardizes how you process information and allows you to share, remember, develop, and transform that information. I do not have to retain all of my knowledge in mind; I can write it down and return to it later. I can see patterns in it that I didn't see before, and I can adjust and add to it across time. This also means I can see and adjust *myself* across time. I can link my brain to its counterparts in the past and future and network all of these moments of problem-solving together. I can also network my brain with your brain and mutually improve our ability to solve problems. Think of the effect on mindsight and the distributed networks we discussed above. Literacy allows me to know you better, know myself better, and know what it means to know better. It therefore gives me the capacity for what we call *second-order thinking*.

---

23. Noam Chomsky, *Language and Mind* (Cambridge University Press, 2006).

The effects of indispensable technologies become most conspicuous in periods of dysfunction or privation. When the electricity grid shorts or mobile networks lose service, we become aware of how dependent we are on their functionality. This dependency is even more dramatic in the case of psychotechnologies. If I took literacy out of your brain right now, the effect would be catastrophic. Our distributed networks would founder. Your cognitive hardware would be no different, yet you would experience a profound loss of memory, self-reflection, and cognitive organization. The volume and types of problems you can solve would decrease dramatically. That is what psychotechnologies do. They enhance the software of your cognitive machinery.

Shamanism, as the first psychotechnology, is a kind of anthropological origin story for the project of meaning in life and therefore also for the Meaning Crisis. The way it altered our state of consciousness and cognition led to the philosophical and scientific enterprise, the capacity to turn scrutinous inquiry on worldly phenomena and take a perspective on our existence. We see evidence of sacred and symbolic activity in shamanic cultivation, which continues to be present in human society.

Shamans often engaged in sleep deprivation and long, intense periods of singing, dancing, or chanting. The shaman cultivated mimesis (imitation), putting on clothing and masks to take on the character of other figures or animals. Sometimes the shaman would go into periods of social isolation and withdraw into the wilderness. The use of psychedelics, though not necessary, would complement these other practices to help bring about an ASC.

It is quite evident that these ritual enactments were not simply for dramatic effect. The shamans discovered an important connection between cognitive disruptions—breaks in the ordinary continuity of consciousness and physiology—and the capacity for insight. This connection has survived well into the modern world. In his book *Waking from Sleep,* Steve Taylor, a psychology lecturer at Leeds Beckett University, discusses the *disruptive strategies* that people still use to provoke awakening experiences and effect transformation in their sense of self and reality.[24]

The shaman essentially tried to disrupt the normal ways of detecting patterns in the world. Why would this be useful? The very thing that makes you adaptive also makes you subject to self-deception, just like your use of technology. The ability to pick up patterns is a profound human aptitude, and repeating these patterns allows us to sustain many systems in our culture, including communal ritual. However, if we become locked into these patterns, we risk losing the cognitive flexibility that allowed us to be so adaptive in the first place. Maintaining this flexibility is the purpose of shamanic deprivation and the disruptive strategies that followed.

A few classic experiments in psychology show how our ability to detect and predict patterns can close a frame around our thinking and prevent us from solving problems. Perhaps the best and simplest example is the *nine-dot problem,* presented below:

Figure 1.3: The nine-dot problem.

The nine-dot problem as it is presented to subjects in an experiment. Subjects are told to join all the dots together using four straight lines.

---

24. Steve Taylor. *Waking from Sleep: Why Awakening Experiences Occur and How to Make Them Permanent* (Hay House, 2010).

The problem-solver is told to join all nine dots with four straight lines, with each new line beginning from the terminus of the previous one. When people see this task, they are relatively confident. The first attempts usually resemble these patterns:

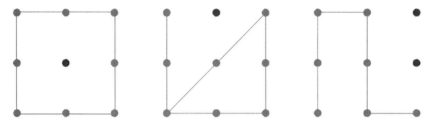

Figure 1.4: Common first attempts to solve the nine-dot problem.

After these early attempts, the subjects often become puzzled. A problem that seemed very recognizable turns out to be difficult to solve. However, when someone demonstrates the solution, it seems exceedingly simple:

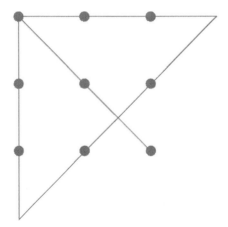

Figure 1.5: The solution to the nine-dot problem.

Subjects are required to break the frame of the invisible square and extend the lines outside of the square to connect all the dots.

When they are finally shown the solution, the subjects of this experiment become indignant. They will sometimes accuse the solver of cheating, of going *outside the box*. This, in fact, is the origin of our common expression, "think outside the box." The problem appears insoluble at first because the subjects project a pattern into these nine dots. They project a square. Unconsciously, they engage a set of well-worn skills learned from prior exercises and experiences.

When you were a kid, for instance, you would connect the dots to create images, and by following these outlines faithfully, you would refine your craft for geometry and illustration. Yet the square is not an essential or necessary feature of these nine dots. It is a product of how we have *framed* them. Unconsciously, we project a pattern and then activate the appropriate skills. This results in us becoming locked and blocked. To solve the problem, you have to disrupt your framing of it. You must achieve an *insight.*

It is well and good to be told, "be insightful," but a key finding of the experimental work related to the nine-dot problem indicates that telling participants to "think outside the box" does not, in fact, help them to do so. The proposition that a person needs insight does not magically produce it, nor does it change the subject's relationship to the problem—except perhaps to frustrate it. In addition to this *propositional* knowledge, they need to know *how* to go outside the box; they need the requisite skills of attention and perception to enact the solution. This is what I call *procedural knowing.*

Knowing how to go outside the box requires you to change where you stand in relation to the problem, how you apply your attention, and what is salient, important, relevant, and real. This emergence of new perspective, facilitated by your procedural knowing, is called *perspectival knowing.* Undergoing an insight is a prototypical example of perspectival knowing.

When one way of knowing is mistaken for another, when we use a proposition to substitute for a procedural intervention, the result is frustration, anxiety, and a feeling of being stuck. The nine dots are a low stakes problem, but they represent a dynamic that can be found at every scale, right up to the Meaning Crisis. This is why *Awakening from the Meaning Crisis* begins with shamanism, this set of attentional practices designed to disrupt everyday framing.

These practices are meant to gain insight into patterns in the environment that other people might not be picking up on. When the shaman is enacting the animal, he is not having beliefs about that animal. He is developing mindsight. He is becoming the animal, not metaphysically, but *imaginally*.

The shaman is gathering a lived sense of the animal's skills, the kind of perspective the animal has, the way the animal thinks, and the kind of world it lives in. By becoming the animal, by having this *participatory knowing* of what it is to be the animal, the shaman enhances his ability to track it, to find it, and when he hunts it, to strike it true.

Participatory knowing allows the shaman to combine many attributes that, in the modern epoch, are sequestered into separate roles and offices. The shaman is antecedent to the sage, highly charismatic and multifarious. Imagine combining a prodigious rock star, therapist, and artist into one individual and being visited by this individual when you are sick and indisposed.

The shaman does not simply mete out advice but induces changes in your participatory, perspectival, and procedural knowing. Their presence can therefore enhance your ability to trigger your own placebo effect.[25] All medication has to surpass the placebo effect in order to be considered real and efficacious. In the absence of modern pharmacology, an individual who can trigger this effect is the best possible advantage for a community. It is little wonder that the potency of the shaman elicits belief in magical ability.

It is important not to understand the shaman's pretense of magical ability as a form of charlatanism. This would be an anachronistic mistake. The shamans are not trying to pretend at knowledge they do not possess. They are engaging in a process of *realization*: playing with meaning, recasting perspective, enacting a role to access insights that were previously inaccessible. There is great pragmatism to this cognitive strategy. In the next chapter, we will talk more about what the shamans are doing, how they are enhancing their cognition, and why this played such an important

---

25. For further reading on the placebo effect, see Norman Doidge, *The Brain's Way of Healing: Remarkable Discoveries and Recoveries from the Frontiers of Neuroplasticity* (Penguin Random House, 2015).

role in transforming human beings into the kind of meaning-makers we are. The word *shaman* means one who knows, one who sees, one who has insight. The shaman is the "wizard," the wise person.

You may see now how we are going to proceed. If we are to awaken from the Meaning Crisis, we need the tutelage of ritual, of psychotechnologies, of all our ways of knowing. This journey will lead us back—and forward—to the tradition of wisdom cultivation that the Greeks called *philia sophia*. Like the shaman, we must reunite roles that have become estranged across time and disabuse ourselves of many modern conceits: the idea that knowing is separate from virtue, that a naturalistic worldview cannot include sacredness, that myths and symbols are set apart from reality. To do this, we need to venture outside the imagined frame that keeps the nine dots captive in their square, static formation. As we continue on our journey, we will need to gather a cognitive account of the human being that supports a new understanding of meaning. To accomplish this, we need the companionship of both science and the sage.

2

FLOW, METAPHOR AND THE AXIAL REVOLUTION

In the previous chapter, we began to examine the historical origin of our human capacity for meaning. We explored connections between early ritual and the evolution that took place in the Upper Paleolithic transition. We discussed how these prototypical forms of human networking did not result from biological change but from radical transformations in how human beings were using their cognition.

It seems likely that this evolution was made possible by the advent of psychotechnologies—distributed systems of identification, communication, or representation—that became prostheses for the brain, enhancing the scope and function of human cognition. Shamanism was a set of psychotechnologies for altering states of consciousness that could cognitively exapt the enhanced abilities created by trade rituals, initiation rituals, and healing rituals.

The Flow State

As I have described, the shamans' disruptive strategies could alter their framing of reality. "Framing" is the source of our adaptability— our ability to detect and track patterns—but it makes us maladaptive when we misframe reality and become locked into patterns of perception that ignore significant details. When this occurs, we need a moment of insight to break the maladaptive frame, like going "outside the box" of the nine-dot problem.

Attaining these moments of insight depends on our ability to cultivate kinds of knowing that are independent from mere statements of belief: knowing *how to do something*, knowing *what it is like to have a certain perspective* and what it is to know something by *identifying with it and participating in it*. The shaman's ASC allowed for these different kinds of knowing to become more integrated, and the consequent insight improved the shaman's ability to innovate hunting and healthcare, two activities that would radically improve human survival.

Typically, the shaman would provoke an altered state by undertaking practices that effect dramatic changes in attention and in the way the brain is operating. Winkelman has observed that the shaman's practices facilitated a process of cross-modular and neuroaxial integration inside the brain, a powerful complexification of his cognition.[1] These activities—which included sleep deprivation, sex deprivation, social isolation, the use of psychedelics, and extended chanting and dancing—created conditions that induced the flow state, a mode of heightened attention and performance that increases our general competence and problem-solving. As I described in the previous chapter, the flow state was first made famous in the work of Mihaly Csikszentmihalyi.[2] People often describe it as "being in the zone." The flow state occurs when the demands of the situation slightly exceed your skill level, provoking an intense form of focus that allows for more cognitive flexibility in the way you detect and track patterns. Csikszentmihalyi often represents this dynamic as the *flow channel*.

---

1. Winkelman, *Shamanism: A Biopsychosocial Paradigm of Consciousness and Healing* (Praeger Publishers, 2010).
2. Mihaly Csikszentmihalyi, *Finding Flow: The Psychology of Optimal Experience.* (Harper Perennial, 1990).

Figure 2.1: This figure depiction of the flow channel was taken from Flow and the Foundations of Positive Psychology: The Collected Works of Mihaly Csikszentmihalyi, *chapter 10.*

According to Csikszentmihalyi, when the level of challenge or degree of difficulty (represented by the vertical axis) is far greater than the individual's capabilities (represented by the horizontal axis), the individual experiences anxiety. When the level of challenge is greater than an individual's skill set, but to a lesser extent, the individual experiences worry. Conversely, if our skills slightly exceed the challenge of the task, we experience boredom, and when our skills are far greater than the challenge of the task, we experience anxiety.[3]

In order to get into the flow channel, I must extend myself to meet the demands of a task that slightly exceeds my capacity. This requires me, through insight, to restructure my attention and change something about the way I am approaching the problem. This restructuring may be prolonged and methodical or sudden and spontaneous. Either way, it requires me to put everything I have into the task. If my skills exceed the demands, I lapse into boredom. If the

---

3. There may be some phenomenological confusion in this account and ambiguity as to whether the anxiety is psychological or existential. Csikszentmihalyi might be referring to a deep existential ennui or sense of futility, perhaps not unlike the state that Camus depicts in *The Myth of Sisyphus,* which arises in the confrontation with absurdity.

demands exceed my skills, I lapse into anxiety. The key to the flow state is a dynamic coupling between the individual and the environment as well as a closed feedback loop running between them; as your skills improve, your environment responds and yields additional pathways and opportunities for action.

Now that we have outlined the conditions for flow, it becomes clear that the flow state is not the result of some mysterious alchemy; we can consciously reverse engineer those conditions that activate it. Shamanic rituals, with their various deprivation and feats of danger, are designed to do just that. While most of these rituals have faded from popular practice, elements of them remain in athletics, the arts, and in ascetic religious traditions.

We undertake many activities precisely to get into flow. We dance, play jazz, or practice martial arts. Consider an activity like rock climbing. You climb precariously up a vertical rock face. The task is extremely physically demanding and carries the risk of injury, exhaustion, and even death. Once you get to the top, you come back down and eventually repeat the climb. This exercise might seem like a Sisyphean torture were it not for the experience it conduces.

Experienced rock climbers attain a very profound flow state. This is not the same thing as physical pleasure, but it is a deeply positive experience, a sense of connectedness to the world and to oneself that makes a person feel somehow more alive, more present to existence. It seems to silence the nattering voices of discontent that are often intruding in everyday moments of waking consciousness.

Even in the absence of a climbing wall, our culture has created flow induction machines that produce this state very reliably: systems of interactive problem-solving whereby your skills must constantly improve to meet the demands of an environment whose level of difficulty is steadily escalating. These flow induction machines are immersive and participatory. They require an individual to change identities to fit into an augmented world, take on a character's perspective, acquire a depth of procedural know-how to perform many different skills in conjunction, all within a mythic structure that dramatizes the shaman's facility in hunting, healing and projectile weaponry. In these systems, there is a clear, tight feedback loop between what you do as a character and how the environment responds. Though it does not carry the peril of scaling a vertical cliff, it simulates similar stakes; if you fail, your character will die.

You may have realized that I am talking about video games. Game consoles are among our most reliable tools for inducing the flow state, and this accounts—at least in part—for why they are so absorbing, often in spite of their users. Consequently, video gaming is now recognized as an addiction by the World Health Organization. Any activity or substance that engenders the flow state can become addictive, precisely because addictions run off the same cognitive machinery that makes us evolutionarily adaptive. We will discuss this dynamic more in subsequent chapters. For the same reason, the flow state seems significantly connected to our experience of meaning in life. The more often you get into the flow state, the more likely you are to consider your life meaningful.[4]

The flow state appears universal. It is experienced by people across cultures in all kinds of socioeconomic groups, genders, languages, environments and age groups. In every case, it is described in almost exactly the same way. Universals are important in cognitive science. We pay close attention to them because they yield important insights into the nature of our cognitive machinery and our evolutionary history.

Understanding the flow state leads us back to shamanism, but it also helps us understand many timeless human experiences that are otherwise difficult to describe. When you are in the flow state, you feel deeply at one with things, as though you are being acted upon by an outside force that lends timing and fluidity to your movements. I am a martial artist, and when I am sparring, I feel a sense of connectedness to my opponent, a heightened spontaneity, readiness and anticipation of his movement. When his strike comes toward me,

---

4. See Laura A. King, Joshua A. Hicks, Jennifer L. Krull, and A. K. Del Gaiso, "Positive Affect and the Experience of Meaning in Life," *Journal of Personality and Social Psychology* 90, no. 1 (2006): 179–196, https://doi.org/10.1037/0022-3514.90.1.179.

See Todd B. Kashdan and Michael F. Steger, "Curiosity and Pathways to Well-Being and Meaning in Life: Traits, States, and Everyday Behaviors," *Motivation and Emotion* 31, no. 3 (2007): 159–173, https://doi.org/10.1007/s11031-007-9068-7.

my hand rises to block it without any conscious or premeditated thought. The block simply flows out of me.

The same thing happens to a hockey goaltender as her glove hand darts out to meet an oncoming puck. Each sport has an equivalent kind of excellence that corresponds to the flow state. There is a tremendous sense of *at-onement,* a state of mind and body by which a person experiences a deep conformity with the world, a sense of connectedness between oneself and some other thing, situation, person or even reality as a whole. In this state, time appears to slow down, and the world seems more vulnerable and receptive to your actions. At one level, you are aware—like the shaman dancing or chanting—that tremendous metabolic energy is being spent. But on another level, the flow feels effortless.

It is not simply time that seems to change in the flow state. It is also your presence and sense of self. When people are in the flow state, their self-consciousness disappears into the background. This doesn't mean they become oblivious or obtuse, but they are temporarily relieved of that nattering, autobiographical voice that is constantly evaluating their presentation: *How am I doing? What am I doing? Who am I? How am I perceived? How do I look? What are people thinking of me? Am I under threat?*

The presence of that authorial voice—though important for its own reasons—can overstay its usefulness. It can keep you at a distance from the world, interrupt your focus, elide the quality of attention you bring to bear on your activities. In depressive states, this kind of rumination can be paralytic, but in the flow state, it retreats into the margins of your concentration.

The flow state brings salience to experience, a certain intensity to the world, and a brightness and vividness you might associate with a video game. It draws forth your attention and begets your participation. The flow state is rewarding, not simply because it is enjoyable and stimulating but because it creates the conditions wherein people do their best work. It excels our performance, whether that performance be physical or cerebral, athletic or artistic. That is why it motivates us to seek and cultivate it.

Understanding this excellence requires an account of flow that includes its cognitive functions and properties. In 2018, I published work with Arianne Herrera-Bennett and Leo Ferraro undertaking precisely this study.[5] Csikszentmihalyi understood that the flow state requires very specific environmental conditions. Skills and demand must be matched. A tight coupling must occur between you and your environment. Information must be clear and legible, and the stakes must be consequential.

In other words, failure must be costly: a fall from the rockface, shame before an audience, or defeat at the hands of an opponent. Csikszentmihalyi observed, as I and my coauthors did, that certain kinds of training, like mindfulness, help people to confront these conditions more forthrightly by managing their responses to stress and anxiety to produce the flow state more reliably.

Given its central role in ritual and shamanic practice, a unified explanation for flow can help us interpret the prototypical forms of meaning-making. Our project is to account both for its phenomenology—the felt character of its experience—and the measurable effects it has on our cognition. We must understand what it felt like to the shaman, what made his consciousness so submersible, and what was happening to him in terms that are appreciable to a scientific instrument.

Recall that the patterns you frame and find in the world are not just patterns in your mind. They are more like sensible impressions of a relationship you negotiate with your experience, a handshake with the world that adapts its grip from one moment to the next. Consider the rock climber again. If your ability to see patterns breaks down while scaling a cliff, you reach an impasse, a physical and cognitive stuckness. If you want to recover, you must refresh the framing that led to the impasse. You have to train yourself to break the frame, restructure your attention, change what you are finding relevant, and then change *yourself* to fit the new relationship. Then, you refit yourself to the rock face. You do this again and again to avoid

5. John Vervaeke, Leo Ferraro, and Arianne Herrera-Bennett, "Flow as Spontaneous Thought: Insight and Implicit Learning," *The Oxford Handbook of Spontaneous Thought: Mind-Wandering, Creativity, and Dreaming* (Oxford University Press, 2018).

getting stuck. Jazz musicians practice the same game with their instruments; they pick up a pattern, play with it, but do not remain with it. They shift and restructure their play continuously. They refresh it again and again.

When they activate the flow state, the rock climber, the jazz musician, and the martial artist all become more adept at detecting, playing, breaking, and regathering patterns in their environment. This dexterity of attention gives them insight, and therefore access, to new actions. It is important to remember that the "aha!" of insight is not only a cerebral event but also a metabolic one. That is why we represent it pictorially with a lightbulb overhead; it illuminates (gives intelligibility) and energizes (adds force) at the same time.

Imagine taking that single "aha!" moment and extending it through time: one insight leads to another insight, which leads to another insight, which leads to another. The process begins to cascade. The more you flow, the more you are training your ability to read and reread your environment, to develop a discerning relationship with it just as you would another person. By this analogy, the shaman's flow is a communion with the world, socially and ecologically. The world is more legible to the shaman. It is therefore more real and more vulnerable to his touch.

Intuition and Implicit Learning

Something else is going on in flow that is just as important as the insight cascade. It has to do with your capacity for *implicit learning*, a concept refined in the 1960s by Arthur Reber among others. Reber was trying to understand how people learn language, and he designed an experiment that showed how human beings could detect subtle patterns beneath their conscious recognition.[6]

First, Reber generated an arbitrary set of rules for linking strings of letters and numbers together (for example, one rule may stipulate that you cannot have more than three vowels in a row). Then, he

---

6. Arthur Reber, "Implicit Learning and Tacit Knowledge," *Journal of Experimental Psychology: General* 118 no. 3 (1989): 219–235, https://doi.org/10.1037/0096-3445.118.3.219.

generated letter strings according to these rules, which were approximately eight or nine letters long. Each string had to be long enough that participants in the experiment could not easily hold it in *working memory*. The first part of the experiment consisted of showing participants multiple eight- or nine-letter strings, one after another, all of which followed the arbitrary rules. In the second part of the experiment, participants were shown two kinds of letter strings: one that complied with the first set of rules, and one that followed a new, second set of rules. These two kinds of strings were mixed together. Participants were asked to identify whether or not the strings shown in the second part of the experiment corresponded to the strings they were shown in the first part of the experiment.

Figure 2.2: A schematic outlining Reber's experiment.

Originally, Reber hypothesized that because they were generated so randomly, people would not be able to tell the difference between these two sets of strings. However, he found that the participants in the experiment scored well above chance. They could reliably identify which strings in the second part of the experiment corresponded to the strings shown in the first part. When the participants were asked how they did it, the answers varied. They simply had a feeling, guessed at random, or offered a rule they felt had helped discriminate between the strings. In each case, their rule was incorrect and could not have been used to predict their success.

Without knowing it, these participants were demonstrating implicit learning. Reber's experiment uncovered an unconscious capacity to pick up on very complex patterns in the environment, and this capacity seems to account for certain feats of human perception that are usually thought to be uncanny or mysterious, like those associated with psychic abilities. Many people, for instance, report feeling a curious sensation when someone is watching them from behind their back, and they claim to perceive the action even in the absence of sensory confirmation.

A different experiment[7] explored this sensation: participants were put in the center of a room and deprived of sensory input (e.g., blindfold, ear plugs, and a scent-free environment). Various people would enter the room and stare at the participants without them knowing. The person in the center of the room had to guess whether or not someone was staring at them. Remarkably, the participants were able to report the correct answer well above probability.

This extrasensory perception seemed miraculous until a modification was made to the experiment. The first time the experimenter brought people into the room, researchers would tell the participants whether or not their guesses were correct. This feedback turned out to be decisive for the outcome. The researchers thought they were introducing people into the room randomly, but as it turns out, it is very difficult to randomize our behavior. We act in patterns without realizing it, and unbeknownst to the researchers, they were actually introducing people into the room in a complex pattern. The person who was blindfolded and ear-plugged was implicitly learning the pattern based on the feedback they were given. When the feedback was withdrawn, the performance dropped to chance.

Our tacit ability to detect complex patterns is what we often refer to as *intuition*. Robin M. Hogarth makes this argument in his book entitled *Educating Intuition*[8] and Peter T. Struck has reevaluated the divination traditions of antiquity through this cognitive scientific idea.[9] Intuition is real but not magical. It is the result of your implicit learning.

---

7. See Eva Lobach and Dick Jan Bierman, "The Invisible Gaze: Three Attempts to Replicate Sheldrake's Staring Effects," *The Parapsychological Association Convention*, 2004 and John Colwell, Sadi Schröder, and David Sladen, "The Ability to Detect Unseen Staring: A Literature Review and Empirical Tests," *British Journal of Psychology* 91 no. 1 (2000): 71–85, https://doi.org/10.1348/000712600161682.
8. Robin M. Hogarth, *Educating Intuition* (University of Chicago Press, 2010).
9. Peter T. Struck, *Divination and Human Nature: A Cognitive History of Intuition in Classical Antiquity* (New Jersey: Princeton University Press, 2016).

Recall our discussion of everyday rituals from the previous chapter, those unspoken formations that govern social norms; you know how far to stand from somebody, where you should stand, and how to reposition yourself as the conversation changes. If I were to ask you how you know this, you would not likely have an answer. When we encounter someone who seems not to follow these patterns, who stands too close or does not adjust for the proper space, we usually become uncomfortable or even defensive.

As a ritual form of perception, our implicit learning is a powerful cognitive instrument. However, it is not infallible. When it fails to adapt, it can lead us astray. This is why, as Hogarth points out, we have two different terms for talking about implicit learning, each with a different connotation. When it is revealing the most relevant and useful patterns and gives us access to insight, we call it *intuition*. When our implicit learning locks us into a framing problem and inhibits our insight, we call it *bias*.

We can track the wrong kind of pattern, or confuse one kind for another. For instance, there are two kinds of patterns in your environment: correlational patterns and causal patterns. *Correlations* merely refer to a relationship between two factors. Take the following statement: the bigger your wedding, the longer your marriage is likely to last. This statement is statistically true, yet one would be a fool to think you should stage a larger wedding to create a longer marriage. Bigger weddings predict longer marriages, but they do not cause them; they reflect a bigger social network and more financial resources, both of which are factors that actually cause a marriage to last longer.

Many patterns in the world are illusory because they are only *correlational*, not *causal*. When training intuition, you want to train your implicit learning to pick up on the causal patterns that are real rather than the correlational patterns that are illusory.

This is more difficult than it may seem. These real patterns are elusive to our conscious attention, and they do not avail themselves simply because we look for them. Recall Reber's experiment. If the participants looking at the letter strings were instructed to figure out the rules consciously and deliberately, their performance would not improve. It would worsen. By definition, we cannot replace implicit learning with explicit learning; implicitness is key to its form and function.

Explicit learning is aware and directed to a purpose. Cultivating our implicit learning instead depends on setting up the right context, selecting and arranging the environmental factors to make causal patterns more salient. You do not force the process but condition it, and conduct it. You do not get into the flow state by screwing up your concentration but by matching effort, activity, and attitude. To use an ancient analogy: you can set the logs and lay the kindling, but you cannot create a self-sustaining fire by force of will.

How, then, do we cultivate implicit learning and distinguish causal patterns from correlational ones? Much the way we do experimental science, as Hogarth reminds us. We set up an environmental situation and make sure everything is clearly measured. We track the change in one variable to see if it is closely followed by a change in another variable. If I change your drug dosage, do your symptoms improve? I look for clear information and clear feedback.

Error and failure matter in science; disconfirmation has to be possible when testing a hypothesis and when training implicit learning. We must put ourselves in a situation where we have access to clear feedback and where a tight coupling exists between what you do and how the environment responds. Hogarth says we should try to practice implicit learning in these kinds of contexts.

In our 2018 study, Herrera-Bennett, Ferraro, and I argued that the very criteria that develop good implicit learning are exactly the conditions for flow: clear information, tightly coupled feedback, and the relevance of failure. These factors provide a much greater chance that the implicit learning machinery will pick up on complex causal patterns rather than correlational ones. The shaman is harnessing these exact conditions for flow, and something very interesting is happening at the level of his intuition: the insight cascade and the enhanced implicit learning are reinforcing each other. Insight moves cognition to explore new patterns, and the implicit learning picks up on those new patterns. This enhances the shaman's ability to restructure his frame of attention and continually ratchet his skills. This is certainly someone you will want to have around.

It is important to understand that these insights are not related to words or beliefs. The shaman does not know how she is getting these insights and information. Getting into the flow state is almost like a mystical experience, a powerful ASC. As the shaman moves to enact the animal, she experiences a radical sense of at-onement with the world, and she loses her sense of self in the mimetic exercise. The animal's way of moving, seeing, and thinking—in short, the new identity—gives the shaman access to new ways of perceiving and interacting with the tribe. This allows her to trigger the placebo effect and alter her tribe's sense of identity through singing, dancing, and storytelling.

The World of Metaphor

The work of Michael Winkelman and Matt Rossano[10] has shown that the shaman's flow is a significant part of what powered the Upper Paleolithic transition. The ASC—especially during a massive disruption strategy like fasting, social isolation, or the influence of psychedelics—creates a kind of dialogue within the brain. If you look at a brain scan of somebody who is having a psychedelic experience, areas of the brain that normally do not talk to each other are talking to each other. We now take for granted this ability to coordinate our brain and to bridge areas within ourselves and connect the world through insight. We depend on it so comprehensively that it is easy to dismiss it as a normal part of our cognition. Now, we call it *metaphor*.

The word metaphor is itself a metaphor. It means to bridge, to carry over, to connect things that are normally not connected. Remember our word "project" from the previous chapter. Reflect on it. Now, notice the word "reflect" is also a metaphor. Do you *see* what I am saying? Do you *get* my point? Can you *grasp* it? I hope the exercise is not too *hard* to undertake. These statements are all metaphors.

---

10. Matthew J. Rossano, *Supernatural Selection: How Religion Evolved* (Oxford: Oxford University Press, 2010).

Take the following sentence: the weather *feels moody* as you *have* your breakfast, *wondering* how to *broach* a *delicate* topic *on the way* to work with a colleague who is *touchy* about *taking* your criticism.

Our phrases are composed of these molecular metaphoric compounds. Even the most rigorous analytical thinker does not speak literally. The psychotechnology of metaphor is as pervasive as it is profound, and it is so essential to our thinking as to be invisible in our everyday language. To adapt Heraclitus's words, metaphor is a hidden harmony that undergirds our speech.

As you read on, you will encounter tacit metaphors over and over again. As I will explain in later chapters, learning to dwell in the poesis of these metaphors allows us to participate more deeply in the texts we read, to play and participate in this harmony, and to open new ways of understanding its meaning.

Many studies have now been completed on metaphor, most famously by Lakoff and Johnson.[11] Most of these studies converge on the idea that our cognition functions in large part through metaphorical enhancement. The power of metaphor lies in its poetic capacity to create connections between ideas and to fit things together that did not originally belong together. When two independent domains of thought or experience are made to belong together, they create a kind of third identity, a new region of imagination that expresses and explores parts of our experience that were not expressible or explorable.

As I explained in the previous chapter, this is why we describe the shaman's world as *imaginal*; it is a way to create and discover at the same time, such that creation and discovery seem like identical acts.

---

11. See George Lakoff and Mark Johnson, *Metaphors We Live By* (Chicago: University of Chicago Press, 1980).

I have some criticisms of some of Lakoff and Johnson's theory, and I have published work of my own on this subject:

John Vervaeke and John M. Kennedy, "Metaphors in Language and Thought: Falsification and Multiple Meanings," *Metaphor and Symbolic Activity 11* no. 4 (1996): 273–284, https://doi.org/10.1207/s15327868ms1104_3; and

John Vervaeke and John M. Kennedy, "Conceptual Metaphor and Abstract Thought." *Metaphor and Symbol 19* no. 3 (2004): 213–231, https://doi.org/10.1207/s15327868ms1903_3.

As with flow, metaphor is a way of reaching into the world so it seems to reach back. The word *inventio* becomes useful again here because metaphor is an instrument for both intelligibility and realization, and thus at the heart of both science and art.

As the shaman prototyped this machinery, he was teaching his brain how to relate to itself, how to talk to itself. Metaphor puts parts together to make a new whole, but it also allows a whole—e.g., the brain—to relate its own parts. These parts now belong more with one another, and so the shaman seems to belong more in himself. Metaphor plays a decisive role in how we gather ourselves together, gather to the world, and gather the world to order. There is a deep connection, therefore, between metaphorical thought and insight, your ability to solve problems.

When someone is facing a problem, and they need to restructure their perspective, we often tell them to use an analogy, to keep one foot inside the problem frame while stepping tentatively outside of it. By joining domains together, we come upon a covert likeness between things, a new pattern, an instance of "hidden harmony" we can use to retune our perspective and mode of participation. This retuning has the effect not simply of solving a problem but changing its relevance entirely. The world somehow transforms by effect of the metaphor or symbol; a new entity or idea is carried into consciousness by the novel compound of identities.

Metaphor is a carrier of insight and intuition generated by the shaman's inventive consciousness and trained in the psychotechnology of flow, ritual and ASC. Through metaphor, the shaman wed various features of the world into new participatory relationships, and she found ways of codifying these relationships in concrete tools—objects that could contain and re-present her insight.

She inscribed a piece of bone to track the movements of the moon, or carved a figurine to personify fertility. These creations are not simply works of art, but the human hand extending itself symbolically into complex patterns—harmonies—that are too hidden to be described and must somehow be enacted in order to be known. With this, we can begin to see the emergence of our prevailing theme. The shaman is literally—or rather, metaphorically

—making more meaning, not arbitrarily, but in an intimate and evolving dialogue with reality. It is little wonder that hunter-gatherer groups with a shaman in tow could outperform their competitors or why these technologies have become so universal; they exapt some of our most basic cognitive machinery and enhance it in a remarkably powerful way.

The shaman's meaning-making power yielded access to an uncanny array of experiences. These experiences redrew the boundaries of human potential and made the psychic feats of modern intuition—like knowing when you're being watched—seem mild by comparison. One of the most transformative of these experiences was *soulflight,* an out-of-body sensation of traveling to another world. This ancient phenomenon is the origin of a common metaphor: "getting high."

The shaman experienced himself as flying above the world, not in a dissociated dream, but in waking, conscious reality. How would the brain generate such an experience? This is where the imaginal world of metaphor, ratcheted by the flow state, stimulated by disruptive strategies and psychedelics, unfolds into a kind of immersive myth, a symbolic arena for the shaman's insight.

The shaman is acquiring a more comprehensive grasp of complex patterns, but his experience is mostly intuitive. Where are you when you seem to get a bigger picture of things? You are above them. We often use the term *oversight.* Somebody who oversees has *supervision.* Consider these two metaphors closely; they are the distant echoes of shamanic flight. The shaman's insight earns him his role as the overseer of the group. As the maker of meaning, his authority mediates the relationship between seen and unseen realities.

The Bronze Age, the Dark Age, and the Axial Revolution

With the Upper Paleolithic transition—the exaptation of our meaning-making machinery through flow and ritual, altered states of consciousness, and the self-transcendence of soulflight—we see the emergence of a prototypical spirituality as well as the beginnings of religiousness and wisdom cultivation. These transformations were irrigated, so to speak, by another sprawling change that took place around 10,000 BCE—the *Neolithic Revolution.*

The Neolithic Revolution brought the invention of agriculture. This was a profound apparatus for supporting complex structures and societies. For the first time, populations could stay in one place for significant amounts of time and develop long-form and lasting relationships to their environment. This also meant they could develop more lasting relationships with one another, and larger groups of strangers expanded ritual to more complex scales. This became the ancient world we recognize; as stone gave way to metal, the Bronze Age came into existence, along with the first great civilizations in Mesopotamia and Egypt.

The Bronze Age inherited and developed all of the important shamanic features of the Upper Paleolithic transition. This new world lasted for a very long time, but our connection to it is somehow distant. If I were to ask: Have you read anything from the Bronze Age? Have you read the Epic of Gilgamesh, or the Egyptian Book of the Dead? The Sumerian, Mesopotamian and Egyptian civilizations were colossal in their scale and influence, but most of us have not retained a direct relationship to their mythology.

Alternatively, if I ask the same question of the Bible, or Plato, or the teachings of the Buddha, chances are you have read them, or at least assimilated a relationship to them. We somehow feel that these figures are relevant to us in a way that the Bronze Age figures are not. We don't see ourselves in the Bronze Age; there is a discontinuity of identity between the kind of human beings we are now and the kind of human beings we observe in these earlier incarnations of our species.

Our distance from the Bronze Age is not just measured by time. There appears to have been another great change in the human complexion, comparable to the one that took place in the Upper Paleolithic transition. Between 800 and 300 BCE, there was a seismic shift in human cognitive activity, and this change seems responsible for introducing many of the ideas, beliefs and value systems that define modern humanity.

In *The Origin and Goal of History,* the philosopher Karl Jaspers referred to this period as the *Axial Age*. Karen Armstrong has since made the term famous with her own book, *The Great Transformation*. The Axial Age is a decisive time in the development of human meaning, and the project of explaining the Meaning Crisis depends largely on how we understand our relationship with its legacy. The canvas of human civilization was threaded by this transformation: our concepts of what is real, of what is good, of who we are, and how we ought to be. Though refracted through many traditions, the forms of the Axial Age persist, and we share an identity with them and their luminaries that we do not share with the Bronze Age.

The causes of the Axial Age are a matter of debate, but any account must begin with the collapse of the Bronze Age in approximately 1200 BCE.[12] There are many different theories about why this collapse occurred—the failure of general systems, changes in chariot warfare, and military technology. For our purposes, the cause of this event is far less relevant than its gravity; it was the greatest collapse in civilization the world has ever known. Trade ceased, literacy was lost, cities faded from existence, and more cultures disappeared than any other time in recorded history. This was the closest thing to an apocalypse that humankind has ever experienced—an end to the world as we knew it.

Figure 2.3: A timeline outlining the collapse of the Bronze Age, the Dark Age and the Axial Age.

It is difficult to imagine the scope of this collapse. The Egyptian and Mesopotamian Empires were vast and titanic. They lasted for centuries. Then, all of a sudden, they faced disappearance.[13] We

---

12. Robert Drews and Eric Cline respectively provide thorough accounts of this Bronze Age Collapse. For further reading, see Drew's *The End of the Bronze Age*, and Cline's *1177 BC: The Year Civilization Collapsed*.

13. The Egyptian empire arguably survived only because of the military brilliance of Ramesses III.

might compare this event to the extinction of the dinosaurs; their departure allowed for many smaller mammals to evolve. When these dinosaur empires passed out of existence, they left many straggling, small-scale societies clinging to survival.

This diffuse cultural vacuum became known as *The Dark Age,* a time that placed a great adaptive demand on human cognition and resembled the kind of bottleneck that preceded the Upper Paleolithic transition in Africa. Once again, human beings were now more willing to experiment and try new forms of social organization. They began inventing new psychotechnologies, standardized ways of processing information, and new rituals and practices that could improve cognition by linking brains together.

One of these new psychotechnologies emerged in the land of Canaan, the region of Palestine that is now modern Israel and Jordan. Here was the birthplace of alphabetic literacy. The Bronze Age empires already had idiographic literacy; the Egyptians had hieroglyphics and the Sumerians had cuneiform. However, these forms were very difficult to learn, and they required extensive study and skill to use effectively. Literacy was a distinguished profession in the ancient world because it was so rare and valuable. It was not easy to learn nor to transmit.

Alphabetic literacy was more powerful because it was learnable. This much was evidenced by its rapid transmission across the region. After emerging in Canaan, it was adopted by Phoenicians, who conferred it to the Greeks. From there, the Canaanite alphabet merged imperceptibly into archaic Hebrew. It spread like a fire, alighting from place to place.

In the previous chapter, I explained how literacy enhances cognition, and with alphabetic literacy the quality of this enhancement is magnified by its dissemination. When more people learn it, its capacity to transform cognition operates at a new scale, and it turns into a tool for transforming culture. Literacy has a profound effect on your sense of self. Human beings have a natural capacity for metacognition, an awareness of our own minds.

By bringing attention to your thinking, you can observe its patterns. You can reflect on whether you have a good memory or where your thoughts appear to stray. Alphabetic literacy, when we internalize it, becomes a powerful prosthetic for this reflective activity. I can record my thoughts, reflect on them, and become aware of them. Most importantly, I can correct them. Literacy allows me to extend my thinking beyond my memory, to externalize it and examine it. Through literacy, human beings acquire a sapiential ability that sociologist Robert Bellah calls *second-order thinking*.[14]

Another powerful psychotechnology was emerging at this time, another profound catalyst for disseminating and transforming culture—*coinage*. There were many roving armies during this period as societies competed and rebuilt, most famously the Assyrian Empire in the Middle East. These itinerant conditions required an agile form of commerce, a more transmissible means of conveying resources.

Coinage became a practical physical technology, but its enduring legacy—especially in our time of coinless and paperless transactions—is its representational nature. Money is a semiotic entity: something that stands for something else. The use of money taught human beings to think and function in abstraction, in systems of signs and symbols. It also gave us something else of inestimable value—*numeracy*. We were required to think arithmetically, to use abstract and logically rigorous thought for practical purposes.

Once again, these skills became candidates for exaptation, the repurposing of one capacity to meet a novel cognitive demand. The psychotechnologies of alphabetic literacy and coinage trained our capacity for representation, which exapted into second-order thinking. Our second-order thinking was then exapted to serve many feats of engineering and erudition, and it distributed itself into sprawling projects of civilization-building.

These psychotechnologies were the building blocks of the Axial Revolution. If we connect their two greatest endowments together—second-order thinking and symbolic, logically rigorous thought—we find humanity regathering itself into a new form of humanness. It

---

14. See Robert Bellah, "What Is Axial about the Axial Age?" *European Journal of Sociology* 46 no. 1 (2005): 69–89, https://doi.org/10.1017/S0003975605000032.

was a rebirth of our cognition, a re-*inventio*. The ability to correct that cognition gave us access to self-transcendence.

We became aware of self-deception. We could invoke the shaman's ability to break the frame of an ill-adapted pattern and apply insight to our representational thinking. Human beings could search themselves for error and find fallibility in perception and belief—not just in a moment, but also over time. This realization changed the dimensions of the human project. In culture, it allowed for more deliberate progression across time. However, it also revealed something about the nature of mind that altered our sense of self.

We started to perceive the mind not simply as a passive instrument but as an active agent in framing our perception, one that could improve or inhibit our access to reality, depending on how we managed it. Our second-order relationship with mind—and with our own selves—became a decisive element in creating reality, *in making meaning*. It opened an inward, existential space, a gap between who we were in this moment and a possible version of ourselves that was more cultivated, more excellent.

This gap was the beginning of an axial normativity, a *personal* responsibility that we find in subsequent moral systems. There was now a standard of reality, a good or truth by whose measure we could personally succeed or fail. We could be rational or irrational, think well or think poorly. We were able to sin. This was the beginning of the individual person, the axial "self" as we now understand it.[15]

Before the Axial Revolution, chaos, warfare and violence were part of the natural order. Human beings were merely the vassals of greater powers. With the advent of second-order thinking, people began to realize they had a hand in their own misfortune. We too were responsible for violence and chaos. They were consequences of meaning-making. This axial insight is captured in *The Dhammapada*: "the mind is the chief thing... there is no enemy greater than your own mind, but there is no ally greater than your own mind." Cognition is a double-edged sword. If it goes undisciplined, it leads

---

15. See also: Robert Bellah and Hans Joas, *The Axial Age and Its Consequences* (Harvard University Press, 2012).

us to illusion, self-deception, and violence. If we discipline it through self-correction, our cognition becomes a greater power of its own, and it can alleviate unnecessary suffering. Thus was the gauntlet thrown at the foot of humanity. Wisdom was not a luxury but somehow a necessity. This insight was the beginning of antiquity as we now remember it.

3

THE CONTINUOUS COSMOS AND MODERN WORLD GRAMMAR

In the previous chapter, we explored how the evolution of meaning had much to do with the process of exaptation: the way our species responded to the demanding conditions imposed by our environment and by the inner space of awareness that emerged from our use of psychotechnologies. Exaptation, the repurposing of one cognitive capacity to produce another, has been one of our most powerful tools. These moments of evolution not only solved vexing problems but created new ways of interacting with the world and, eventually, new ways of reconceiving it.

The shamanic integration of flow with altered states of consciousness (ASC), the insight and refinement of intuition, the capacity for metaphorical thought—all of these expanded human cognition by making it much more creative, capable of reading patterns and generating connections between different scales and categories of the world. This allowed our ancestors to gather the world together and unite different parts of experience to create working models of reality as well as the structures that seemed to exist beneath us, around us, and within us. These symbolic unities, or *mythologies*, gave us a new kind of agency in the world and an idea of who we were within it. This was the beginning of what we would later call a *worldview*.

This new human agency drove the explosion of culture and technology in the Upper Paleolithic transition (occurring around 40,000 BCE). When combined with agriculture in the Neolithic Revolution, it made the Bronze Age civilization possible. In the wake of the Bronze Age collapse, alphabetic literacy and coinage became new ways of exapting this symbolic capacity. They made both literacy and numeracy more effective, more efficiently learnable.

This had an exponentiating effect on distributed cognition. We could link ourselves together faster and in more complex ways as well as coordinate to solve more intricate problems. As I explained in the previous chapter, these psychotechnologies internalized into our metacognition, and this second-order thought provided a heightened awareness of our own cognition—of both its power and its peril.

We were alerted to our own meaning-making nature and its capacity to generate illusion and self-deception but also to break these patterns of illusion and make contact with something real. Axial culture became aware that the transformation of mind, or *mind and heart,*[1] was the way to alleviate suffering. This dawning of personal responsibility was a deep and profound change in the mythological framework that began in the shamanic world.

It is important to explain how I am using this word—*myth.* It is often used now for something spurious or unreal, a falsehood that is widely believed. I am not using it this way. When I speak of myth in this book, I am continuing from the shamanic context, using it in the tradition of thinkers like Carl Jung, Paul Tillich, and Victor Turner, among others. Myths are not false stories about the ancient past. They are symbolic motifs that represent and dramatize perennial patterns, the structures of meaning that are always with us. Myths allow us to bring these intuitive, implicit patterns into consciousness to make them shareable and allow us to internalize, ritualize, and apprehend them in more revealing ways.

---

1. In the Axial Age, these terms are often referred to in a singular manner.

The Continuous Cosmos, and the Great Disembedding

Epochs of humanity are in part defined by their mythic character, the way they have understood and depicted the structures of reality. It can be very difficult to take the perspective of mythology that is not native to our time or culture. It requires a generous imagination. Attempting to take this perspective is essential, however, to understand the works and deeds that emerge from a particular epoch. We have to change the categories of our thinking to access a foreign phenomenology.

This is a demanding task, but one we must undertake to understand how meaning evolves. For instance, in the Upper Paleolithic transition, the spirit world was not separated from the material world in the way we might think. This separation came later. The world of spirit was here with us. It was available if you but knew how to access it, and this was the shaman's specialty. This continuity of what we might call the "mortal" or "natural" world, and the "spiritual" or "supernatural" world carried over into the Bronze Age. Charles Taylor has referred to this mythic structure as a *continuous cosmos*.[2] Taylor's formulation is very helpful for our understanding, though as you will see, I question his use of the word *cosmos*.

In the continuous cosmos, most people feel a deep connection between the natural and the cultural worlds as well as between the cultural world and the world of the gods. In fact, these were so bound together in the Bronze Age that it is not accurate to call these worlds distinct—hence the idea of continuity. The differences between these categories were not differences in *kind* as much as differences in *power* or degree. It was not odd to imagine that animals might speak or conceal their own societies. It was also not odd for certain human beings to think themselves divine.

In the Egyptian Empire, for instance, the Pharaoh was a god-king. Godship was not a metaphor for the ancient Egyptians; the

---

2. Charles Taylor, "What Was the Axial Revolution?" *The Axial Age and Its Consequences* (Cambridge, MA and London, England: Harvard University Press, 2012): 30–46.

differences between human beings and the gods were differences in power. This is what stratified the reality of the continuous cosmos. The gods were not distinguished by a transcendent moral nature. They were just more powerful than us, more glorious than us.

The word most often used for describing God in the Old Testament is "glorious," shining with power. This is also true of the Greek Pantheon; they are not moral exemplars at all. The Greek Gods, like the Egyptian Pharaoh, were distinguished from mere mortals by the way they embodied and wielded their colossal potency.

The continuous cosmos bound all beings into the same order of reality, the same hierarchy of power. But it was also continuous in a temporal sense. It was cyclical. Like day into night or winter into spring, the movement of time was perceived in large cycles, repeating endlessly through eternity. Ritual behavior in the Bronze Age was often attempting to access this cycle, to tap into its continuity and return us to that original power of creation.

By enacting the metaphor, the myth of the universe's creation, we could draw from its font, its vitality. The myth was guided by nostalgia, a yearning for return, a longing to regain harmony with the movements of these cycles. A person's goal was not to change or break the cycles; if you changed your future, you would undermine your past. The continuum from the natural world, to the social world, to the divine world was blended with the continuum of time, which wrapped and recurred on itself.

Continuous Cosmos

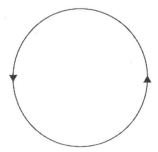

Figure 3.1: The flow of the continuous cosmos. There is no given point of origin, but rather a cyclical progression; time is wrapped and turns on itself. Past and the future feed into each other.

With the Axial Age, the continuity of time and power was interrupted. It did not disappear altogether—some aspects of the cyclicality persisted—but a new worldview was overlaid, a different mythology for understanding the connection between self and world. Charles Taylor calls this *the great disembedding,* in which the world of the continuous cosmos was replaced by a different mythological structure.[3]

The mythological disembedding was another seismic shift in the human species, but this one seems more recognizable because its roots are discernible in modern mythology. Remember that to speak "mythologically" is not merely to speak literally, scientifically, or even metaphorically. I do not mean that the materiality of the earth changed in the Axial Revolution. Rather, human beings changed their relationship with reality. We came into a new way of seeing, of knowing, and of being. The world changed because *we* changed, because the meaning of things changed.

In the great disembedding, one world became two. The everyday world was that of the untrained mind, a world beset by self-deception, self-destruction, illusion, violence, and chaos. To live in this world was to be out of touch with reality. The real world lay behind this world of illusion. This was how the trained mind, the wise mind, saw the world.

---

3. Ibid.

The contact with reality did not yield a descriptive knowledge, like the kind that science pursues. It is more useful to think of this contact in the analogy of a personal relationship, moving from an acquaintance defined by pretense to one defined by genuine, mutual understanding.

Contact with reality was somehow also contact with yourself. Understanding was the restoration of your agency, and the reduction of suffering—not physical pain, but the anxiety and despair that come from chafing against the flow of the world, and being out of touch with its fundamental structures. In other words, attaining contact with reality required a person to turn her mind from enemy to ally; befriending herself—becoming herself—was a way of becoming real.

Once again, wisdom was understood as an integrating movement from being "apart" to being "together." And as we will explore, using a personal relationship to analogize the movement toward reality is one of the most enduring symbolic legacies of the Axial Age.

Two Worlds Mythology

Figure 3.2: Depicting the two-worlds mythology: transcendence from the everyday world, beset by illusion and self-destruction, to the real world, wherein the trained and wise mind sees the world for how it truly is.

In the continuous cosmos, wisdom was power-oriented. A wise individual learned how to acquire the power of cycles, to tap into the energy imbued at their creation. The aim of this acquisition is perhaps best expressed by the Vulcan motto: "live long and prosper." This is an idea of wisdom still captured in the word *prudence*. Being prudential is knowing how to fit into the power structures of society, knowing how to make things work for you, and getting the most power and prosperity you can to ensure security for your offspring.

In the two-worlds mythology, wisdom is not the acquisition of power or prosperity. It is the emancipation from a lesser reality. The axial hero did not want to conquer the everyday world. He wanted to be transformed out of it. Notice the powerful instance of exaptation here. The shamanic myth of *soulflight* was adapted into the Axial context, and wisdom was now the ability to make that transformative leap.

In the two-worlds mythology, meaning was not just about connectedness as it was in the continuous cosmos but specifically connectedness to the real world. This also changed the idea of the self. In the continuous cosmos, you were defined largely by how you fit into the world. In the two-worlds mythology, you were defined more by self-transcendence, how you transformed and grew as a person.

This idea persists to this day with the same metaphoric language. When we refer to maturing, we refer to growing *up* and getting more in touch with oneself and reality. This transition from the continuous cosmos to the two-worlds mythology is called the great disembedding because we are somehow uprooted from the everyday world. We are now strangers, pilgrims in this everyday world. We do not belong in it.

This idea is interpreted in a variety of ways: Some people literalize the two-worlds mythology and consider the everyday world as separate and independent from the real world. Others understand this division as mythological representation, symbolizing the process of self-transcendence and self-transformation. One of the most famous depictions of this process is the myth of the cave found in Plato's *Republic*.

The Axial Revolution was not simply a Western phenomenon. It occurred in many places, and it precipitated the emergence of most religious and philosophical traditions we recognize around the world. I cannot account exhaustively for these traditions, but I will focus on a few specific exemplars, cultures that played host to this transformation in both East and West. These include the ancient worlds of Greece, Israel, India, and China. Each of these places developed particular psychotechnologies that became so internalized in our cognition that we mistake them for being natural features of mind.

It is very difficult, for instance, to remember life before literacy, to imagine how it was to think without the ability to imagine words. Many Axial psychotechnologies are now so second nature to us that we have long since forgotten their historical origin. This historical forgetfulness is a problem; it makes us ignorant of those crucial historical factors that have propelled the Meaning Crisis.

Anticipating the Crisis of Re-Embedding

The two-worlds Mythology is a mythological form of thinking that allows us to articulate and train the psychotechnologies of the Axial Revolution, the projects of self-transcendence and wisdom. It took the meaning-making of the shaman and refined it into a more precise way of cultivating human cognition. However, this mythology is failing us now. The scientific worldview, with its materialist and physicalist metaphysics, is gradually eroding the Axial project.

It is a cosmic irony, perhaps, that the scientific worldview is returning us to a continuous cosmos. Its naturalism is retracting the movement of self-transcendence. There is no radical difference in kind between you and the primates you evolved from. There is no radical difference in kind between your mind and your embodied existence. Science is leveling the world again. It is bringing us back to the world of the everyday and containing us here. While many of us still claim to believe the two-worlds mythology and speak in commensurate ways, it does not feel livable or practicable anymore, at least for a great many people.

This is one of the great problems of the Meaning Crisis. Since the shaman, human beings have depended on mythology for meaning-making. It has become inseparable from humanness itself. The Axial worldview still holds up our idea of the sovereign person, the individual who has agency, freedom, and responsibility. However, a mythology must be livable in order to perform its function.

The meaning of a mythology is like an atmosphere, and it gives oxygen to our idea of humanness. This atmospheric property of meaning—symbolized by the shaman's soulflight—refers to human "spirit," the idea that something about human beings is not confined to body and world but also extends beyond it. Paolo Costa, among others, has observed this atmospheric quality in the attitudes and phenomena of religious experience, "as if we were immersed in a sort of bubble of meaningfulness, or, better, in an atmosphere of significance that we do not create from scratch but are absorbed by."[4]

When this symbolic reality begins to decline, it is like the thinning or pollution of that atmosphere. Our meaning-making is asphyxiated, and we are barred from accessing the spirit of soulflight. Human beings become homeless in the universe, as though the soil from which we have grown meaning, and grown ourselves, is no longer fertile.

With this comes an impossible kind of dilemma that we will discuss at length in later chapters: How do we regrow ourselves? How do we salvage the ability to cultivate wisdom, meaning, and self-transcendence—to *realize* ourselves and the world—when we can no longer use the mythological structure that is native to these abilities? We seem to be undergoing a kind of re-embedding, and it has accelerated over the last few centuries with the pivotal revolutions of Copernicus, Galileo, Darwin, and Einstein. As many have observed, these revolutions have gradually displaced us from our privileged position at the center of reality and created a taxonomic world in which meaningful human consciousness is no longer relevant.

We have collapsed back into the physical world. Much of our recent cultural history depicts a violent thrashing against this confinement, this loss of human possibility. As Nietzsche famously observed, if we live only for the next world, and the next world is

---

4. Paolo Costa, "A Secular Wonder," The Joy of Secularism: 11 Essays for How We Live Now 11 (2011): 138

taken from us, precious little is left for the project of meaning, and the consequences are nihilism and profound self-destruction[5]. We do not want to lose all that we gained through the great disembedding, but how do we live with this legacy when we can no longer inhabit its worldview? To begin answering this question, we must gain a fuller understanding of what this world bequeathed us.

The Transformation of Time and the Invention of Story

To retrace the steps of the Axial Revolution, I will begin in ancient Israel. It is difficult for many modern people to fathom the scope of influence of the Bible—not just for practicing Jews and Christians but for all who grew up and live in the West. Biblical illiteracy has been steadily rising in tandem with our secularization, and this a thwarting problem for our culture—not because people should be Christians or Jews but because failure to grasp the grammar of the Bible is also the failure to grasp the grammar of your own cognition.

You may well profess to be an atheist and disbelieve the doctrines of these traditions. However, this kind of belief—in other words, the *propositional* belief—is irrelevant in this context. I am not referring to what you profess but how you think and behave. Defining belief only by creed and proposition is analogous to defining the democratic sensibility by whether or not you cast a ballot on voting day; you still participate, however unconsciously, in the ethics, rituals, and institutions that structure this form of society.

In the same way, we in the West all participate in the cognitive structures endowed by the Bible's influence. Grammar is how you put thoughts together, how you frame and convey the world in front of you. As Mark Taylor wrote, religion "is often most influential when it is least obvious."[6]

Nietzsche also made this point quite famously: *I am afraid we are not rid of God because we still have faith in grammar.* We still talk in the

---

5. See Friedrich W. Nietzsche, *The Twilight of the Idols and the Anti-Christ: How to Philosophize with a Hammer*, trans. R. J. Hollingdale and Michael Tanner (London: Penguin Books, 2003).
6. See Mark Taylor, *After God* (University of Chicago Press, 2009), xi.

two-worlds mythology way, and we are still filled with the God grammar of the Bible.[7] For example, when you go to a movie and track the protagonist, you notice many of the same narrative patterns and motifs, not invariably, but with great frequency.

The protagonist begins with promise but usually succumbs to foolishness, greed or temptation. The fall leads to disillusionment and reflection. Then they have an insight; they are drawn back by a glimpse or vision of what is more real, and good, and they surrender or sacrifice themselves to this good. In so doing, they redeem and restore the world around them.

Our most celebrated modern myths—like *Harry Potter*, *The Lord of the Rings*, or our multitude of superhero mythologies—are all suffused with patterns drawn from biblical grammar, sometimes alloyed with elements of shamanic and Bronze Age mythology. These stories continue to move us, to exert a powerful hold over our nerves and imagination. We still want to be saturated in these universes, to expand them and live inside of them. Departures from these symbolic structures—like the unredemptive deterioration depicted in zombie myths[8]—are striking for precisely this reason. It is not only fiction that recreates these patterns; many secular therapeutic methods and addiction treatments, like Alcoholics Anonymous, are also structured around these motifs.

In describing the pervasiveness of religious mythology, it is important to emphasize that I am not advocating for a particular religion. Rather, I am explaining how the Axial psychotechnologies have naturalized into our cognition, our existential sense of being. The mythology of the Judeo-Christian heritage, for instance, has become an invisible architecture for our thinking, a meaning we live in, furnish, and refurnish over time.

One of the psychotechnological inventions that undergirds this architecture appears so obvious that we do not stop to consider its

---

7.   Tom Holland provides a compelling argument for the ubiquity of the Christian grammar, even in this supposedly secular age. See Tom Holland, *Dominion: How the Christian Revolution Remade the World* (New York: Basic Books, 2019).
8.   See John Vervaeke, Christopher Mastropietro, and Filip Miscevic, *Zombies in Western Culture: A Twenty-First Century Crisis* (Open Book Publishers, 2017).

novelty: the understanding of time as a cosmic narrative, as a *story*. All cultures tell stories, and we will unpack the cognitive science of story in later chapters. Yet the Continuous Cosmos was not a story. It was a cycle. The story has a beginning, a crucial turning point that forces a crisis and leads the protagonist to act, and a resolution. There is a direction to a story. There is a purpose to it.

Figure 3.3: Depiction of the linear progression of the storyline. Directionality establishes a progression, which involves a series of events leading to a turning point, eventually followed by a resolution. The creation of a storyline concept of time with a linear direction as opposed to the cyclical pattern of the continuous cosmos facilitates the ability to focus on one's progression in life toward an open future.

Since the Axial Revolution, the West has expressed the passage of time through the pattern of story, the unfolding of a narrative in a single, linear direction. Yet this was a radical reinvention of time. The cyclical continuous cosmos was not an open future. It was an endless recurrence. The Eastern cultures of the Axial Revolution began to regard this temporal repetition—like the *saṃsāra* in Buddhism, Jainism and Hinduism—as a form of suffering, something aimless and illusory that tethered us to the lesser world.

It is common for the Western mind to regard reincarnation as an adventure, but this is a misapprehension. The object of these Eastern traditions is to be released from those cycles, not to indulge them. *Moksha* refers to freedom. *Nirvana* refers to cessation. In each case, a transcendent objective draws the individual beyond the cycle of time.

This linear concept of time was invented—or at least significantly developed—in ancient Israel, perhaps influenced from Persia through Zarathustra. This concept of time was revealed in the God of ancient Israel. Gods of the pre-Axial world were generally gods of a place or function. There was a god of wisdom, of weaving, and of hunting. There was a god of ancient Thebes. Gods were local entities, embodiments of those patterns that vectored significant aspects of human life and activity.

However, they had no significant moral arc; they were unchanging features of the universe, like the celestial bodies in the sky. The God of the Old Testament broke this pattern. This new God was summative but indefinable. He was like all of the other gods yet like none of them. This God was not bound to time and place but moved through both. His novelty is dramatized in the Book of Exodus, which also depicts the birth of the Axial Revolution from the Bronze Age world. God appears and liberates the Israelites imprisoned in Egypt and sets them on a journey toward an open future, a promised land. The cycle of repetition is thus broken. The narrative begins.

The God of the Old Testament is the God of the open future. It is significant that he first appears nameless; to name something is to locate it, specify it, and tie it down. When He reveals His name to Moses, it is often translated as "I am that I am," but a closer translation reads, "I will be what I will be." I am the God of the open future, and you can participate with me in the ongoing creation of that future. You can shape it, reveal it, bring it to resolution, or steer it off course.

Here again we see the emphasis on human agency that becomes so central to the Axial Revolution. Human beings are called to coauthor their fate, to bind themselves to this God of the open future, not by coercion, but by will. In her book *The Gnostic New Age,* April DeConick has described this transformation as a turn from "servant spirituality" to "covenant spirituality."[9] Creation is not simply given but continues to unfold. Human beings, with our moral action and meaning-making, are called to participate in the course of its unfolding.

---

9. See April D. DeConick, *The Gnostic New Age: How a Countercultural Spirituality Revolutionized Religion from Antiquity to Today* (New York: Columbia University Press, 2019).

We still hold fast to this idea of time as a *course*, a story with forward momentum. A story does not simply flow. It turns. It brings decisive moments of revelation and transformation, wherein one nature or reality yields to another that is more complete. The idea of character is rooted in this kind of revelation. The most classical works of narrative are those wherein the turn of the story reveals character in such a way that the revelation is both creation and recollection —*realization*.

The turn surprises us yet could not have been otherwise. Though we understand that the events of life do not always seem to follow these structures, something nevertheless seems true about them. We seek them out with religious ardor; we are moved by them, find ourselves in them, feel ourselves known by them. We celebrate great novels, plays, and films for precisely this reason. By participating in them, their turning seems to turn us. They bring us closer to ourselves and closer to what is real.

As with most historical transitions, the cross-fade from continuous cosmos to Axial mythology was gradual rather than immediate. You can detect many aspects of a Bronze Age god in the Old Testament, but He becomes more Axial as He becomes the force of *progress*, the idea that history, when directed to its proper course, is moving closer to its purpose, gathering together across time, perfecting and refining, becoming more real. This gathering is happening on a cosmic scale but also on an individual scale, and God becomes the correspondence between these scales, whose revelations collapse together—like the character and the world of a narrative— when the narrative reaches a pivotal turning point.

The turning point of the story is called *kairos*. In common parlance, kairos refers to a critical or opportune moment, an opening in time that allows us to see, access or intervene in something that was once invisible or obscure. In the two-worlds mythology, kairos is a revelation of the real world from within the mirage. Our readiness for the opportunity is prepared by the state of heightened participation—or *flow*—wherein we are more attentive, more perceptive to patterns, and more prepared to act nimbly.

The etymology of the term invokes the skills of incisiveness and accuracy; in the ancient Greek tradition, "kairos" was used in archery and weaving, referring to the narrow passage through which the arrow or yarn must pass in order to meet its aim. The archery analogy is very significant. The idea of striking the target—recall the *project* of the shaman—exapted to symbolize the penetration of illusion, the direction of attention to the greatest order of reality.

A famous phrase from the Upanishads reflects a similar idea: *Om is the bow, Self is the arrow, Brahman is the target.* As I will explain in later chapters, the idea of kairos also becomes a significant feature of the Christian tradition, a crucial turning point and culmination in time that brings the cosmic story back on course and restores an eternal pattern. The ignorance or denial of the kairos is closely related to the idea of sin, which, as many have observed, originally means "missing the mark."

As we progress, we will discover that ritual and religious participation are embedded in these symbolic exaptations, the internalized movements of ancient crafts, like those of archery and weaving. Each involves a rejoining of our attention to the center of reality, gathering it back together, discovering it by creating it anew. Kairos requires a shamanic synonymy of knowing and participating. This synonymy is captured in the idea of *Da'ath*, an ancient term for *knowing,* used in the Bible to refer to sexual intercourse (e.g., Adam *knew* his wife Eve). Modern Westerners may find this confusing; we do not often use sex as a metaphor for knowledge. Yet many cultures do.

The identity relationship between knowing and participating is a fundamental Axial idea, and it is central to understanding the religious nature of the ancients and their symbolic way of experiencing the world. "Knowing" is not the apprehension of facts, seen dispassionately from the outside. It is nothing you could acquire from a distance. You know something by assuming its identity, by becoming it. Your becoming it somehow changes it, reveals it, makes it real.

The sexual metaphor, and this process of realization, recalls Heraclitus's "hidden unity," and the symbolic joining of the world we discussed in the previous chapter. As one of his famous fragments reminds us: *the river I step in is not the river I stand in*. Knowing is like being immersed in the flowing course of the river. You cannot know this river without also being known by it, and you cannot know it without being changed by that knowing.

When you are making love with someone, you are participating in them, identifying with them, empathizing and resonating with them. You are changing them as they are changing you, and this process of change rises—forgive me the pun—to a climax, after a turning point and before the resolution. You may begin to see why, in so many religious traditions, sexuality is a perennial symbol for our sacred union with reality. *Da'ath* describes our participatory knowing in the course of its unfolding.

This idea of knowing is critical for our project because it changes the way we interpret religious ideas of faith and belief. In ancient Israel, faith did not mean having incredible beliefs without evidence. That is a recent, very modern idea. Faith was Da'ath. It described this symbolic relationship you had with the world and with your existence. It was your sense of living in this reciprocal realization. You were on an unfolding course. You were involved and evolving with how the world was occurring. You reached a turning point and realized that you must change in order to maneuver it and remain on the right path.

In order to be more of yourself, you had to transform yourself to match the widening frame of the world. Faith is relational expression; it describes your relationship with reality, with its identity, participation and evolution. This is much like the relationships you have with your family, friends, and intimates. You may often ask yourself: How is this relationship going? Is it on course? Is it progressing, and growing? Is this the kind of person I want to be with? What is my sense of how I am changing? Is this all going well? Using personal relationships to symbolize this connection with reality is a profound cognitive shift. It means that we participate in—

but do not singularly produce—the meanings we live. That is what we mean by Da'ath.

Understanding faith in relational terms is helpful for showing us how it can be distorted. You can mistake a relationship. You can force it, try to dominate it, or fail to act decisively. The relationship can be characterized by fear, avoidance, or anxiety rather than courage and reciprocity. It can suffer illusions and misapprehensions. You can think you are on course when you are, in fact, dramatically off course. When you find yourself veering from the path and misplacing your attention, we might say you have *trespassed* on the relationship.

This kind of language returns us to the idea of sin, but our biblical illiteracy inhibits us; we are tempted to understand sin as doing something immoral, committing a particular act of transgression. This is much more a symptom than a definition. Sin is better understood as being in a distorted relationship with reality. It is the misdirection of love and attention.

Recall the archery analogy that sources the term's meaning; you cannot shoot for where your eye tells you to look. If you do, you will miss the bull's-eye. The true arrow is guided by Da'ath, the kind of knowing that conforms the attention of the archer with the proper target. The archer and her target seem to share the same body, the same identity. Their craft is a movement toward connectedness and participation. When she lands the target, it becomes real to her. She stakes herself in its reality. She is binding herself to the world and the world to herself. One way of understanding sin is as the failure to effect that binding.

It is important to understand that the kind of knowing I describe in Da'ath is not passive. It is both generative and consequential. This act of relating shows forth the world and brings it into consciousness. Just as sexual union can result in childbirth, so our union with reality helps to create—or reveal—the meanings we live in. To mistreat this relationship does not simply mean mistaking reality but refracting and distorting the way that reality occurs.

Self-deception is not an isolated error. It draws us away from reality, and because our actions are consequential, it draws reality away from itself. This is why the Axial world was so determined to awaken from it. The future was now open, and human beings were thrown into a universe in which they had the opportunity of participating in the creation of that future.

This freedom of participation and the responsibility of drawing forth this meaning (as the archer draws her bow) can also produce a powerful kind of anxiety. The possibility of sin was now implicit in every perception we made and every action we took. The anxiousness of this responsibility has been amplified in the modern existential tradition, where we lack the two-worlds mythology to give us an orienting marker for reality. This, as I will discuss in later chapters, is among the more powerful and features of the Meaning Crisis.

Notice what the Hebrews were doing. They took this movement from the everyday world to the real world and turned it into a story, into a *history*. This movement was their journey to a promised land. But their own sins could intervene in this story; they could make decisions that steered the course of history away from its proper culmination. God's intervention was required periodically to correct for their error, to wake people up, and to remind them of the proper course.

In the Old Testament, this intervention came in the creation of the prophetic tradition. Like sin, prophecy is a concept that has been refracted by modern misunderstandings. A prophet is not merely someone who foretells the future. Prophecy means *telling forth*. Like the shaman, the prophet sees more deeply into the patterns of reality and can understand how human beings are affecting the unfolding of history.

The prophet can therefore perceive future consequences of our foolishness by seeing into the present. He tells us how we have mistaken reality and exhorts us to wake up to our moral responsibility and return to the path of the promised land. Ideas of justice, righteousness, and moral decision-making are all taking shape in the Old Testament prophet, though they are still mixed with many pre-Axial elements.

The tradition of prophecy helped to enshrine the idea of the metanarrative, a cosmic story that is played out on the most intimate and personal scales of reality and relies on our minute actions and decisions in order to be realized. This is a highly radical idea, that we participate in this colossal dimension of reality, that our own narratives somehow connect to it and share in its identity.

When we veer from the right path, the entire story veers with us. We perceive our own stories as having precisely this kind of cosmic importance. You think of yourself as somebody who is on a journey, trying to make a better self, trying to make the right decisions, and trying to steer things toward something truer and more meaningful. You want to progress. You want your culture to progress. The wisdom of the prophets is the practice of remembering that our paths fit into a more encompassing path. This is the practice of remembering God, not by reciting beliefs but by participating in the ongoing creation of the world: shaping the future, helping yourself, your neighbors, and your society to progress. Progress is measured by moral improvement, justice, and flourishing. It means living up to our promise, both individually and collectively.

Try to imagine how you would understand and judge yourself without this notion of progress. The very idea of living up to our potential, of fulfilling our promise, is part of the grammar we inherited from the Hebrews. It is now part of the very way we think, part of the warp and woof of our cognition. Later in the book, we are going to return to the idea of kairos as the fulfillment of this promise.

Birth of the Greek Cosmos: Cognitive Fluency, Democracy, and Philia Sophia

As the Hebrew metanarrative unfolded a new kind of cognitive grammar, another cognitive transformation was taking place in ancient Greece. As I will discuss in later chapters, the evolution of meaning and kairos has much to do with how the Hebrew and Greek cultures, along with their distinct symbolic forms, came into penetrating dialogue—or *Da'ath*—with one another.

When the Greeks inherited the psychotechnology of alphabetic literacy, they did something deceptively radical. They added vowels to the alphabet. In doing so, they made it easier for human beings to process information. To explain the importance of this development and how it works, I need to introduce you to another important idea from cognitive science—the concept of *cognitive fluency*.

We have increasing experimental evidence for the following fact: when you increase the ease at which people can process information —regardless of what that information is—they come to believe it is more real and have more confidence in it. This ease can be effected by something very simple like changing the color contrast between the letter font and the page. If the contrast is cleaner, and the font is easier to read, it will significantly improve the reader's contact with the information. This contact is not simply a matter of comfort; if two people read the same text with different contrasts, the person with the better contrast will have more confidence in the content and is more likely to believe it true.

Fluency of processing increases your confidence in the processing itself and the image of reality that takes shape through its medium. The ease does not just remove strain on your senses. It changes the way your brain is accessing and applying the information it perceives. When your cognitive fluency improves, your brain generates an enhanced sense of being in touch with things. This is not an arbitrary correlation. There is great effectiveness in taking the ease of processing as a measure of our contact with reality. Cognitive fluency helps to generate the flow state, and is therefore a contributing factor in our capacity to pick up on real and relevant patterns.

So when the Greeks introduced vowels, they improved the fluency of alphabetic literacy and made it much more powerful. For example, tr rdng ths sntnc. Now, try reading it again. With vowels, reading became considerably more fluid. The Greeks also introduced a standardized reading format from left to right, which we now take for granted.[10]

Standardizing the format helped to make literacy more consistent, predictable, and easier for cognition to automate. This meant that, in ancient Greece, the power of literacy to enhance cognition—both individual and distributed—was profoundly

---

10. Other languages, of course, like Hebrew, are read from right to left. It is not the particular order, but rather the consistency, that improves the fluency.

ratcheted. This cultural apparatus was also complemented by another social psychotechnology; the Greeks did not form a unified nation state but a number of individual city-states that were all in competition with one another. Athens was the hotbed of the Greek Axial Revolution, but it is perhaps most known for its political innovation. I am referring, of course, to the invention of democracy.

Ancient Greek democracy is a prototype of our modern equivalent but differs from it in many ways. For our purposes, it is important to understand that the direct form of democracy placed a premium on argument and debate. This practice gathered together and exapted many of the other psychotechnological innovations of the time like alphabetic literacy and second-order thinking. The simultaneous constellation and distribution of these technologies worked to accelerate the Axial Revolution, and it multiplied the variety of abstract symbolic tools, such as mathematics and geometry, that could be used to perceive patterns, measure truth claims, and generally make sense of the world.

Our capacity for individual reason and reflection was being extended into more social and organized forms. At the center of these innovations, a new capacity was taking shape: the cultivation and training of rational argumentation. This is justly known as the most radical invention of the ancient Greeks, and it had profoundly meaningful consequences for everything that followed.[11]

The legacy of the shaman was key to these innovations. Just like their forebears, the inventions of the ancient Greeks were embodied in certain exceptional individuals. Their capacities were exemplary of the Axial Age, and their examples reorganized the imagination of their epochs. These individuals became known as "lovers of wisdom" (philia sophia) or *philosophers*.

Some of these Axial philosophers are still well-known to popular consciousness while others have been relegated to niche scholarship.

---

11. This is not an ethnocentric claim. The emergence of rational argumentation in ancient Greece does not privilege the cognitive capacity of this region or mean that other groups or cultures are comparatively irrational. It simply means that, due to a combination of historical forces and circumstances, this was the place where the innovation occurred.

One of the most influential philosophers of the period is still recognized primarily for the mathematical theorem that bears his name. Pythagoras belonged to a group of individuals that emerged from the end of the Dark Age around 600 BCE. These individuals would be called the *Divine Men*, and they seemed to represent a rediscovery of shamanic psychotechnologies.[12]

These liminal figures straddled the mythological and rational forms that characterized the Bronze and Axial Ages. Though Pythagoras was a real person, and associated with the inventions of mathematics and argumentation, his legend is also suffused with shamanic abilities of healing and flight. These legends retained important mythic elements that would later fade from the philosophical tradition, specifically the emphasis on self-transformation. Pythagoras seems to have undergone a form of shamanic training. He engaged in a ritual called the *Thunderstone Ceremony,* which involved isolating himself in a cave for a length of time and reemerging after a radical transformation. He even seems to have experienced soulflight. Pythagoras became known as one of the earliest proponents of *metempsychosis*, the idea that the human psyche can migrate away from the body.

Pythagoras was a pivotal figure, and he stands as a bridge between the ages. He was tall, and dressed as a god. He had the mien of a Bronze Age deity, just like the ancient pharaohs. He reintroduced shamanic meaning-making and self-transcendence into the two-worlds mythology, and refined these powers with rational argumentation. He enhanced the symbolic ability to commune more closely with the world and to catch hidden patterns that were outside human awareness. His insights and discoveries were instrumental in uncovering many principles we now take for granted: the discovery of the octave and ratios as well as the presence of mathematical proportions in the world. Pythagoras embodied the idea that human beings are trapped in this world but, with training and cultivation, can learn to fly above it.

---

12. See Francis McDonald Cornford, *From Religion to Philosophy: A Study in the Origins of Western Speculation* (Princeton University Press, 1992).

At the beginning of the chapter, I noted that I do not like calling the pre-Axial world a *cosmos*. This term began with Pythagoras. Cosmos is not simply a synonym for the universe. This unifying principle or form of order gives reality its elegance, coherence, and arrangement. To understand its meaning, consider the word *cosmetics*. Pythagoras had the idea that we could use music, mathematical thinking, and ASCs to trace the contours of this supernal order. This order was perceived in the aspect of beauty.

As I will discuss in the next chapter, Pythagoras's cosmos anticipated the relationship between beauty, order, and realness that would become essential to the Greek philosophical tradition. When people report awakening experiences, they often rediscover these Pythagorean affinities. They suddenly perceive the world as a cosmos, and their perception of order and coherence is suffused with beauty.

The notion of cosmos created a powerful model for how we understood meaning and wisdom—what a self was, how it perceived and grew, how we fit into the universe, and how we made contact with reality. It draws a striking contrast with the modern worldview. Though we continue to use his word, it has been largely emptied of its shamanic and shimmering qualities.

4

SOCRATES AND THE QUEST FOR
WISDOM

In the previous chapter, we discussed the transformative influence of
the Axial Revolution and the features that distinguished it from the
antecedent Bronze Age. This revolution produced a profound change
in the mythic structure of the world, turning it from a continuous
cosmos, where deities and human beings lived in coextension
separated only by degrees of power into a two-worlds mythology,
wherein the everyday world was illusory. The transcendent
dimension of reality was made available only by works of human
cultivation, made possible by a dawning capacity for second-order
thinking, an ability to re-present, reflect on, and promulgate our
cognition through psychotechnologies like literacy and coinage.

As the Axial Revolution moved into ancient Israel, it also changed
the nature and direction of time. This was the advent of story, and
history; the universe was now an unfolding narrative that had
direction, propulsion and an open future. The openness of time
called forth a participation from human beings and implicated us in
its history; we had to maintain the course of the story and bring it to
fruition. Human beings, therefore, found themselves in a new
relationship to reality, and within it, a new moral responsibility.

Our decisions and actions, our will, could determine the future,
and we had a role to play alongside God in the creation of that future.

The movement from the lesser world into the real world became a progressive, moral journey through time and space. For the ancient Israelites, God's intervention came only at moments of kairos, decisive turning points where human beings fell into sin, where we strayed from the proper path and needed reawakening by the hands of divine intervention.

The prophets were the heralds of this reawakening, and their Axial vision was the moral redemption of history. The idea of faith described our connection to the rightful path, our participation in the flowing and unfolding of this narrative, and our relationship to God as the highest order of reality. We helped to realize this narrative, to shape it, and we were shaped by it in turn.

In the previous chapter, we also explored how the Axial Revolution began to take shape in ancient Greece and constellated around the figure of Pythagoras. This prototypical philosopher was a bridge between epochs, merging the psychotechnologies of different ages and integrating them together. He exapted the shamanic character and practices of the Upper Paleolithic transition, like cultivating ACSs, and folded them into Axial insights and innovations: rational argumentation, the relationship between music and mathematics, and the discovery of rational patterns in the world.

For Pythagoras, by coming into direct awareness of those patterns through our rational insight, we could transform ourselves in the likeness of those patterns and be in greater conformity with reality. In his carriage, shamanic soulflight became a form of self-transcendence, a migration away from the lesser world of illusion and the fragile body that composed its prison.

Though his name still appears in philosophy and mathematics, Pythagoras's contribution to the Western tradition is often overlooked. His idea that mathematical patterns underpin the structure of reality married to the ideas of his contemporaries, like Heraclitus, Thales, and Parmenides, who proposed a rational structure to the world, an ordering principle of arrangement, or *logos*, that gathered the world into coherence and could be known by the soul when it learned to move its attention in those same patterns.

Pythagoras is generally credited with inventing the word

philosophy, which is a combination of two Greek words: *philia* (the love of friendship) and *sophia* (wisdom). Pythagoras's "love of wisdom" became the virtual conductor in a concert of new relationships, a network of distributed cognition that was dedicated to the cultivation of wisdom. A philosopher, simply put, was a lover of wisdom.

The fact that Pythagoras and his philosophical contemporaries are now distinguished as "Presocratics" gives us a clue as to their historical import; of course, another figure features even more prominently in the Axial Revolution of ancient Greece. The name of Socrates is a revolution of its own, and Socrates and Pythagoras would become the two most important influences on Plato and the Western philosophical tradition. This means their contributions are among the building blocks of our worldview. If you were to put Western Civilization on two feet, one foot would be the Bible, and the other would be the works of Plato.

Socrates is a very unusual figure. Nearly as many interpretations of him exist as do interpretations of Jesus of Nazareth. His existence is historical, but his cultural presence is mythical. His words come to us indirectly, interpreted through his depictions in Plato's dialogues and other texts of the same period. These depictions, depending on how we read them, tell of very different creatures: one is a man of ordinary means, humble and homely, who roams the streets of Athens as a glorified gadabout. He engages his peers in heady conversations about abstract ideas, and has an exceptional—if imperfect—command of argumentation. On the other hand, he is a man with a mysterious and uncanny nature along with almost preternatural capacities. Under this aspect, he resembles the Axial shaman, much like Pythagoras. He is famed for courage and prowess on the battlefield, can stand in reverie for hours uninterrupted, and is erotically desired, despite his homeliness.

His character in these texts varies as much as his naturalism. He is a profoundly difficult figure to size up, and he defies a clear, definitive reading. He is brilliant, rigorous, and persistent but also impish, lilting, and maddeningly frustrating. He lives sociably among his peers but remains profoundly apart from them. The term *atopos* is sometimes used to describe him—a kind unto himself, so unlike most people in the texture of his thought that his inward life is scarcely knowable. His behavior defies the recognizable patterns that we use to classify human beings as one kind of person or another.

Many of Socrates's ideas and observations are beautiful. However, his arguments vary in strength, and he frequently contradicts himself. Sometimes these contradictions seem deliberate, as if he lives in an augmented place and uses the entire world of men as a playing field for a higher kind of game. This was the famed Socratic irony; something of him always remained concealed. The truth of the matter was always beyond the words he used or the perspective he took. He was so committed to this mysterious game that he played it in defiance of the laws of Athens and the prevailing ethic of his day.

He was, to use a term from Plato's *Symposium*, a kind of *metaxu*, an entity that traveled between worlds, much like Pythagoras had. He seemed to have access to both realms in the two-worlds mythology, and so committed was he to this second world, so betrothed to what was most real, that he unhesitatingly gave himself to it, even when his commitment consigned him to death. The trial of Socrates is a pivotal drama in the soul of Western history. The fact that Socrates—historically or mythically—followed this sun unfalteringly below the horizon speaks to the power of the Axial worldview, and to the spring of wisdom that was to follow in its wake.

When I discuss Socrates in this chapter, and throughout this book, I am speaking of a particular interpretation. Many scholars could contest its historical reality; however, that "historical reality" is not the only criteria for appreciating Socrates or his tradition. It is helpful for us to think back again to the mythic world of the shaman, to the way symbols and psychotechnologies can gather the world together by playing host to different parts of reality, especially those that are contradictory.

The Socratic tradition is like one of these symbols. Yet Socrates is not simply a technology but an agent, someone who discovers and uses these symbols, creating new patterns of participating in the world. The historical accuracy is irrelevant to the impact that these patterns have on our cognition.

Many scholars think of Socrates as a mouthpiece for ideas and arguments. While this is not entirely incorrect, it misses the import of his *character*, which is not just relegated to the propositional kind of knowing.[1] Socrates has become part of the cognitive and existential grammar of the West. His reality is a structure of agency itself, a new relationship with existence, real for the sum of consequences it has generated in the evolution of our thinking, perception, disposition and behavior. For this reason alone, it could be said that Socrates is more real to us than most men who have ever lived. To understand his myth is to understand something crucial about ourselves.

One story from this tradition captures the enigma of the Socratic character. In the beliefs of ancient Greece, the voice of the gods was conveyed through the oracular tradition. Oracles spoke in ways that were elusive, indirect, and carried powerful force of suggestion. One of the most important and famous oracles in the ancient world was seated at Delphi, where the mountainous landscape inspired sensations of celestial presence.

The oracle, also called the Pythia, would sit in a cave or stone temple, and her bearing was a kind of shamanic trance, an altered state of consciousness. She sat on a tripod, augmented by intoxicating vapors or eucalyptus leaves. People would come from afar and pose questions to the Pythia. From her trance, she would speak on behalf of the gods, and males who surrounded her would interpret her words.

For instance, a man might approach to ask if he should marry into a certain family or invest in a business venture. She would respond with a cryptic verse: "Winds change quickly in a mountain pass." You can imagine why the interpretive role was necessary; an oracle who wished to stay in business avoided giving clear answers.

In the previous chapter, we discussed how prophecy is not the act of seeing into the future but seeing into the present, using insight to perceive meaningful, complex patterns in the world and make these

---

1. Many recent influential thinkers emphasize the dynamic, essential role of the non-propositional in Socrates and the Socratic tradition, including David Schindler, Sara Ahbel-Rappe, Francisco Gonzalez, and Jacob Howland.

patterns accessible to human agency. The oracle's poetic vagueness was not just a sustainable business strategy. It was also a shamanic frame-breaking device. It softened the eye of perception and made it more permeable.

Consciously, you may not have known what to make of her words, but they would stir the waters beneath the surface, provoking intuition or reflection. They could awaken something that was already inside you and open an interior space for it to emerge. There was a strong element of midwifery to this oracular tradition, and whether the events of your life went one way or the other, you could retrospectively interpret them as having been consonant with the Delphic pronouncement.

The ancient story goes something like this. A group of Socrates's friends make a pilgrimage to the Delphic oracle. One of them asks: "*Is there anyone wiser than Socrates?*" They are familiar with the custom, of course. They expect to be greeted by one of her cryptic answers. Instead, she simply replies: "No."

It is jarring for the oracle to be so unambiguous, but her answer must be read carefully; there is no *human being* wiser than Socrates. Unsurprisingly, the most important interpreter of the oracle's pronouncement was Socrates himself. When his friends return and relay the encounter, he faces a great temptation. The oracle spoke on behalf of the gods, and Socrates believed in these gods. He and Plato were instrumental in transforming them from the petty, prurient figures found in the Homeric myths into transcendent moral exemplars.

In the Axial view, the gods became honest, forthright, and trustworthy. They wedded power to truth and divinity to reality. Imagine being crowned by such an authority. Socrates would not presume to contradict them, so it would have been natural to accept the oracle's bestowment. One of the most persistent cognitive biases is to believe we have above-average intelligence, and most of us would indulge in the divine permission to confirm such a bias. Most of us would inflate—"I knew all along!"—or find ourselves so absurdly unequal to the responsibility that we would become anxious and self-effacing.

Socrates does neither. An entire paradigm shift can be read in his response. Rather than giving in to the confirmation bias, he challenges it. The challenge is delicate, though; the gods are sources of truth. They would surely not deceive him. On the other hand, Socrates is profoundly self-aware, and he has a deep appreciation for his own finitude. This makes him particularly receptive to mysteries that elude his understanding. He seems to know where his person ends and where these mysteries begin, and this allows him to participate more authentically in the world around him. This essential feature of the Socratic character is most famously captured by the inscription above the Delphic oracle: *gnôthi sauton, or "Know thyself."*

The idea of "knowing thyself" has become a cliché term in folk culture and psychology, subject to a world of misinterpretations.[2] *Knowing thyself* in the Socratic sense does not refer to your personal autobiography, a store of treasured memories that polish the ego's uniqueness. We can all fall prey to a sense of cosmic exceptionalism, but this is not the meaning of the Delphic inscription. Knowing thyself is a form of *participatory knowing*, the ability to trace the contours of your own thinking and behavior.

Consider a literary analogy. Self-knowledge is not your memoir but more like your owner's manual. It is how you operate, what principles, powers, perils, and constraints are working within you, directing your reactions and decisions. This is the core of Socratic self-knowledge and eventually the entire Axial Revolution: the critical awareness and responsibility for refining your own cognition.

Personal experience and memories can play an important role in this refinement but only if they are used as instruments for symbolic reflection. The *Confessions* of Saint Augustine, arguably the first autobiography of the ancient world, is a good example of personal recollection serving Socratic self-examination. The fact that it was framed as a dialogue seems key to the exercise of this reflective

---

2. Some scholarship has contributed to correcting these misapprehensions. For example, see Christopher Moore, *Socrates and self-knowledge* (Cambridge University Press, 2015).

function, allowing the personal memory to cultivate a deeper memory—i.e., remembering our relationship with the highest order of reality and the responsibility we owe to it. This is known as *anamnesis* in the Platonic tradition.

The gods cannot lie when they say Socrates is wisest; he is pious and faithful to their words. On the other hand, Socrates has deep self-knowledge. He *knows* he is not wise. So while he recognizes the divine pronouncement, he is equally certain of his own ignorance. Neither insight can prevail above the other, it seems, so Socrates holds them in tension. How, though, can the two beliefs coexist? This dilemma becomes a paradox that goes to the core of who and what Socrates is. How can he be the wisest human being when he knows that he is not wise? How can both be true at the same time?

This paradox is a question that Socrates chooses to live in and live out. It is not a logical problem, but an existential one (for it concerns the nature of his existence) and an ontological one (referring to the orders of being). To solve the problem, Socrates seeks the question in a long-form inquiry. He opts to dwell inside of the question, and it becomes the quest depicted in Plato's dialogues.

Socrates would seek people who claimed to be wise—or were thus credited by Athenian society—and engage them in conversation. His questions were the basis for what became known as the *Socratic Method,* or *Elenchus.* He used questions as conductors, means of drawing someone out, not simply to clarify their propositional beliefs but to access the seat of those beliefs and uncover the attitudes that arranged them and gave them agency in the world. In other words, he would attempt to know the person by knowing their ways of knowing, to relate to the whole of the person by tracing out the patterns of their thinking, the geometry of their cognitive structures, the way they related to themselves and to reality.

People responded to Socrates in very different ways. Many of his interlocutors became his friends and followers, hanging on his words. Others felt aggressed by his mode of inquiry and became either avoidant or downright hostile. Of the many people he interacted with, Socrates accredited two groups of people with a reputation for wisdom, and he sought them out as part of his quest. The first of these groups was a cohort of Presocratics known as the *natural philosophers*. These natural philosophers predated Socrates by a couple hundred years and seem to represent the beginning of the fundamental change in human cognition that emerged from the Dark Age. For the same reason, very little of their work remains. One of their greatest exemplars was Thales of Miletus, who is sometimes considered the first philosopher of the Greek tradition. Most of Thales's philosophy can be condensed into three deceptively simple sentences.

Thales's Three Fragment Philosophy: All is the moist.

The loadstone has psyche.[3]
Everything is filled with gods.[4]

These three fragments seem brief, but they contain volumes. What you must pay attention to here is not what Thales is saying but how his statements reveal the process of his thinking. Consider the first fragment: *all is the moist*? Given the age of these fragments, there is some debate about their meaning, but later figures in the ancient world, like Aristotle, have given us a plausible interpretation: *everything is made out of water.*

This statement is false, of course, and not just scientifically. Everything cannot be made out of water or we would not be able to identify water on its own. But if we set aside the metaphysical objection and consider the merits of the observation, we find it to be intelligent and highly refined. Water falls from the sky, surrounds all the land, and pours from the body. Living beings consume it to sustain themselves, and it assumes the shape of any receptacle it fills. Water is nearly always underneath us when we dig far enough into the earth, and even our own evolution originates in water ecosystems.

Without technologies that give us a microscopic, particle view of

---

3. The word "psyche" is important. It is the basis for the word, and discipline, of psychology.
4. This fragment sounds very pre-Axial, almost shamanic.

matter, how unreasonable would this have been as a worldview? Thales's idea may be false, but its cognitive legacy is rich. He was using reason and observation to come up with a plausible explanation about the underlying substance[5] of the cosmos. You may also notice that Thales's proposal is not mythological. He is not attributing the substrate of the universe to Zeus's philandering or Hera's jealousy. There is no story here. No narratives or divine agents are involved to be the moving force or causal mechanism. Instead, Thales is undertaking a rational analysis based on observation. He digs vertically for an explanation. He is inventing how to think scientifically.

Now the second fragment: *the lodestone has psyche*. The lodestone is a natural magnet. The original meaning of psyche is breath or wind, but it ultimately came to refer to anything living and self-moving. I am aware of psyche within me; I can move myself, and therefore I can cause other things to move. The magnet shares these properties, and we may understand how Thales could conclude that he and the magnet both shared psyche. Whether he was right or wrong about this does not matter; it is a plausible and rational argument.

In this second fragment, he is trying to access the animating principle, the force behind things. Psyche becomes the word for the most self-moving part of the human being and the part that sources our capacity to move all other things. It becomes the word for mind. When I move an object, my mind first moves itself, and this drives me to move the object. Thales's pre-scientific inquiry allows us to begin thinking about the psyche in such dynamic terms.

Now the third fragment: *everything is filled with the gods*. While the first two seem relatively scientific, the third seems to invoke the mythological. However, it is better to understand his fragment as an ontological statement, a study of being. Ontological analysis uses reasoning to access the underlying structure of reality and the forces that work within it, using the self-moving mind to see into its depths.

---

5. The word substance is another metaphor, which means "stands under." It became the basis of *understanding* and other related words.

Thales's inquiry into the structure of reality, his *ontological depth perception*, is the beginning of a Scientific Revolution. This is not a dispassionate, calculative exercise but a sacred one. It provokes awe and wonder. It gives him a felt connection to what is most real.

Socrates was influenced by a successor of Thales, another natural philosopher and Athenian named Anaxagoras. Anaxagoras declared that the sun was not a god but a hot rock. As we might imagine, he got into some trouble for this speculation. Socrates seems to have been impressed by Anaxagoras's commitment to accessing the truth. However, Socrates ultimately rejected natural philosophy—not because he rejected reason, rational analysis, or argumentation (he engaged in these himself) but because the natural philosophers did not advance his Axial project.

The Axial philosophers searched for truth without transformation. They presented facts and knowledge but did not indicate how one became wise or overcame self-deception. These criticisms echo in critiques of modern science, which provides a plethora of knowledge without training us for wisdom without telling us how to become good persons. Socrates is perhaps the most important author of this critique.

In natural philosophy, we have truth without relevance. The facts discovered do not have existential import. They do not enable a cultivation of wisdom, the transformation and transcendence of the self. This significant part of the Socratic legacy would evolve through generations of students and successors. The truth is not significant unless it changes you. The transformation of consciousness and character is the Socratic expression of truth, more truthful than any statement one could make about the world, an idea, or even the structure of reality.

While he seemed respectfully disappointed by the project of natural philosophy, Socrates's famous interactions with the sophists —at least as rendered by Plato—were much more antagonistic. The sophists were an outgrowth of the proto-democratic culture.[6] The

---

6. It is important to note that the democracy of ancient Athens, however admirable, was unglamorous by modern standards; it was reserved for Athenian males, and

democracy of ancient Athens was direct democracy, and it placed a premium on debate and argumentation. For a young political aspirant, these were the route to power. The better you were at arguing and persuading other people, the more influential you would be.

In this new arena, a new form of agency develops, and a new psychotechnology emerges—rhetoric. The sophists were its technologists. They observed how language and cognition interacted, and they used this interaction to refine skills of persuasion and influence. The sophists were not concerned with how these skills were applied; they were only concerned with teaching them. They separated the technology from any moral commitment. In the morning, a sophist might tutor an aristocrat to argue that Athens should increase its navy fleet and in the afternoon tutor his opponent to craft the opposite argument. The sophist did not care which argument was true or which action was good. What mattered was winning the argument.

Just like the natural philosophers, the cognitive legacy of sophistry is alive and well in modernity. Sophists know that when we communicate, we are driven not simply by truth, but by salience. The aesthetic forms and features of communication can make things shine, stand out, and adhere to memory. Remember the nine-dot problem: relevance and interest shape how we see things, frame them, and understand them. Rhetoric has a role in every sphere of society, and sophistry is often used to refer to the moral and ontological relativism of its character, the focus on triumph and effectiveness over truth or goodness.

Branding and advertising are perennial forms of rhetorical manipulation; an advertisement co-opts your brain's capacity to associate things and uses this association to nudge your behavior. Think of the following commercials. A man raises a *beer* to his friends around a table, a *car* drives through a stunning mountain range, a *smartphone* sets the playlist for a dance party.

---

excluded women, foreigners, and anyone else who was thought unworthy of participating.

The rhetoric might be linguistic or imagistic, but it puts things together that don't necessarily belong together so one thing takes on the character of the other. The consumer is not oblivious; she *knows* these things don't belong together. But this knowledge scarcely matters. When you see these spots, you place yourself in the drama—into the friendship, into the song, into the scenery. The products just happen to be there.

You know the meaningful elements do not say anything objectively truthful about the products, but that belief is not driving your perception and experience. The product is made to participate in the relevance of these stimuli, in the sensations, familiarity, or longing they evoke. As *Mad Men's* Don Draper famously says to American Tobacco: "Everyone else's tobacco is poisonous. Lucky Strikes'... is *toasted.*"

You might see how the sophist is an antagonist to the Socratic project. Sophistry brings us back to a concept from chapter 1, introduced in Harry Frankfurt's classic essay *On Bullshit.* Frankfurt makes an important distinction between a liar and a bullshit artist. The liar depends on your commitment to the truth. She makes a proposition that knowingly subverts the truth, but to steer your decisions, she relies on you having a relationship to the truth. If she can convince you that something false is something true, she can change your behavior. Lying depends on a concern for the truth; the liar has enough concern for it to subvert it knowingly, and the one she lies to has to care enough about the truth that being convinced of it will change her actions. For this reason, we might even say that the liar speaks *truthfully*, even when she does not speak the truth.

Bullshit is different from lying because it does not refer to the truth, either to seek it or subvert it. The bullshitter is disinterested in truth. He may accidentally say something true or false, but he does not speak truthfully. He does evoke your concern for the truth but attempts to rhetorically access your interests. He captures your attention with catchiness, just like the salient ad. There is a famous example of this in the "Treehouse of Horror" episode of The Simpsons. Two aliens descend to earth and attempt to take power by running for political office. One of the aliens, Kang, gives the following speech to a crowd:

My fellow Americans... as a young boy, I dreamed of being a baseball... But tonight, I say we must move forward, not backward! Upward, not forward! And always twirling, twirling, twirling toward freedom!

The crowd cheers. The speech contains no content but invokes a series of associations that are meaningful to his American audience: youth, baseball, progress, freedom. It reads as if a chatbot tried to reverse engineer meaning from assorted signifiers. It barely exaggerates; candidates saturate their campaigns with mimetic buzzwords, and companies use popular ideological monikers in their advertising ("We're green. We're a positive space. We value diversity and inclusion.") that have nothing to do with the products they sell. Commonplace examples of bullshit are scarcely less absurd than Kang's, and make their mouthpieces seem comparably less human. Humor, of course, can be a helpful Socratic response.

Why is this relevant to the Meaning Crisis? The concept of bullshit provides a way of understanding self-deception, which thwarts the Socratic project. Self-deception is not a lie you tell yourself; you cannot know something is true and tell yourself otherwise. You cannot change your belief by force of will. However, you can bullshit yourself. Your attention can be captured by salience, like something noisy, dangerous, or attractive. You can also choose how and where to direct your attention.

If I say, "Pay attention to your index finger," you can. You can avoid paying attention to one thing, and instead pay attention to another. You can direct your attention to something and make it more salient. Because it is more salient, it will tend to capture your attention. This is the beginning of a circular pattern. I pay more attention to something and it becomes more salient. As it becomes salient, it gathers my attention, and I gather myself around it.

This cycle spins on itself in this self-organizing manner until your attention is attracted and attached to something and loses the desire to notice other things. That is how you bullshit and deceive yourself. The salience of the stimulus overtakes you and overwhelms any concern you have for whether or not it is true, or good, or real.

You can see why Socrates is so antagonistic to the sophists. Their artistry of bullshit stands in contrast to the Axial legacy, the attempt to cultivate rational self-knowledge and overcome self-deception. If the natural philosophers seek *truth without relevance*, the sophists represent *relevance without truth*. They have the technique to direct attention and transform individuals, but they have disconnected this practice from anything real outside themselves. Natural philosophers gave knowledge of facts, but they did not facilitate self-transformation.

Socrates wanted to marry these powers of truth and transformation. He wanted individuals who could cultivate attention properly, such that salience could be used to seek truth, and that truth could train attention to salience. Socrates's search for this wisdom famously brought him into contact with his Athenian contemporaries. His inquiries, reinvented by Plato's dialogues, became sources of great frustration for his discussants. If Socrates approached someone in the marketplace, the conversation might go something like this:

SOCRATES: Good morning! What brings you to the market?

SHOPPER: I came early, Socrates. To purchase goods.

SOCRATES: Very good. And what goods are you purchasing?

SHOPPER: Grain and fish.

SOCRATES: And why do you want these particular goods?

SHOPPER: To eat, of course. To satisfy my hunger.

SOCRATES: And with your hunger satisfied, what will happen?

SHOPPER: I don't know, Socrates. I suppose I will be happy.

SOCRATES: Of course! Is it fair then, to say that you came to the market for happiness?"

SHOPPER: It is fair to say that, Socrates.

Now Socrates is engaged. He has drawn out a claim and begins to probe deeper.

SOCRATES: So what is the happiness you are referring to?

SHOPPER: Happiness is whatever brings pleasure, Socrates. Or relieves pain.

SOCRATES: And the discomfort of your hunger is a kind of pain?

SHOPPER: It certainly seems to be.

SOCRATES: Very sensible. So because these goods will relieve your hunger, they will also relieve your pain?

SHOPPER: They will.

SOCRATES: And will this relief also be a pleasure?

SHOPPER: I believe it will be, Socrates.

SOCRATES: Is it fair to say then that relief from pain is also a kind of pleasure?

SHOPPER: It seems fair.

SOCRATES: And this pleasure is something we call happiness?"

SHOPPER: Yes, Socrates. That seems right.

Now Socrates has a proposal from the shopper, and he begins a proper inquiry.

SOCRATES: This is a good proposal. I see how happiness might in fact be the same as pleasure. But is it possible to find pleasure in grain and fish and meanwhile be unhappy? For example, if you are eating your meal but at the same time quarreling with a friend?

SOCRATES: It does seem possible, yes. In that case, I would be happy about the meal, but unhappy about the friend.

SOCRATES: In that case, it seems you are both happy and unhappy. Is it possible to be both happy and unhappy?

SHOPPER: It seems possible to me, Socrates.

SOCRATES: But surely happiness is not being both happy and unhappy?

SHOPPER: Surely not.

SOCRATES: Which would produce more happiness: to add more fish, or remove the quarrel?

SHOPPER: To take away the quarrel, Socrates.

SOCRATES: So is it better for us to say that happiness is the absence of pain, rather than the addition of pleasure?

SHOPPER: That does seem more precise.

SOCRATES: Does this mean you are happy whenever you are without pain?

SHOPPER: Yes, Socrates.

SOCRATES: And if you are happy, do you need to seek happiness?

SHOPPER: Certainly not.

SOCRATES: Yet would we not say that those who seek wealth or glory are also seeking happiness?

SHOPPER: I suppose we would.

SOCRATES: And in seeking glory or wealth, are they simply seeking relief from pain? Or are they also seeking something else?

SHOPPER: Something else, I think.

SOCRATES: I think so too. And if we are seeking something else when we seek happiness, can happiness simply be the relief from pain?

SHOPPER: I don't see how it can, Socrates.

Socrates has now cast doubt on the shopper's proposal for happiness and provoked a change in the direction of the inquiry.

SOCRATES: And what about the seekers of wealth and glory? What happiness do they seek?

SHOPPER: Perhaps their happiness is simply getting what is most important, Socrates.

SOCRATES: Very good. This already sounds more like happiness. Does getting what is most important first require someone to have knowledge of what is most important?

SHOPPERS: That would seem necessary.

SOCRATES: Do you need knowledge of what is *truly* important, or what *you* think is important?

SHOPPER: What is truly important.

SOCRATES: What do we call knowledge of what is truly important?

SHOPPER: I guess that would be wisdom, Socrates.

SOCRATES: So in order to find happiness, you must first have cultivated wisdom. Now tell me: how do you cultivate wisdom? What is wisdom?

This is the Socratic elenchus at work. The poor shopper cannot respond; he has more than he bargained for in this trip to the market. He loses the plot of his proposal again and again and falls into *aporia*. People compared the state of aporia to being stung by a stingray, or falling under a magician's spell. The shopper suddenly encounters the limits of his knowledge. Not only does his idea of happiness fall into doubt but also his idea of himself as a knower and the possibility that he knows anything at all. Understandably, most of Socrates's interlocutors are looking for the exit signs by this point in a dialogue.

Socrates leads us into our ignorance with his famed sense of irony, the playful pretense that we can use propositions to access the final truth about ourselves and reality, only to find out that this knowledge falls short and leads us to an impasse. It is easy to think of Socratic ignorance as skepticism and his doubt as a rejection of truth and knowledge. But this is a far too simplistic reading.

Socrates is trying to alert us to our own self-deception; each one of us is bullshitting ourselves continually and putting our attention in the wrong place. We find things salient, like happiness and fame. We pursue these long before we understand their meaning. We do not know what powers move and motivate us, but it is scarcely ever what we presume or purport. An encounter with Socrates reveals that we do not know ourselves as well as we think we do.

As I discussed earlier in the chapter, the encounter with Socrates provokes various reactions among his contemporaries, just as it would today. Some become angry and avoidant; they did not like the ignorant reflection that surfaced in the Socratic mirror. In others, he provoked insight. They realized they were self-deceived and saw the need to transform themselves. They sought a way to connect their attraction to what was attractive in itself to develop a relation between relevance and truth.

When Socrates realized he was having this effect on people, he had his answer to the dilemma placed upon him by the oracle at Delphi. The gods were not lying. He was indeed the wisest of human beings. His answer was this: *he knew what he did not know*. This did not refer to knowledge of the world but to the errors of human thinking: the way people behaved, valued things, proclaimed truths, pursued goals, all without understanding why. This foolishness caused much suffering and put people at variance with themselves. Socrates saw this deep human capacity for self-deception and endeavored to bring it into consciousness.

For obvious reasons, the consciousness that Socrates stirred was often unwelcome, and he was famously put on trial in ancient Athens, brought before a jury of some five hundred men. One of his accusers, Meletus, presented a charge of atheism—corrupting the youth of Athens by teaching strange gods and showing impiety toward the Athenian pantheon.

Socrates's response is depicted in Plato's *Apology*. During the trial, it becomes clear that the state will release Socrates if he ends his disruptive behavior and ceases doing philosophy. His response is one of history's most famous utterances: "The unexamined life is not worth living." A life that lacks both truth and transformation is a life awash in bullshit, filled with unnecessary suffering and moral failure, beset by self-deception and self-destructive behavior. For Socrates, this is an uncultivated life, an intolerable one. It is a life without wisdom.

Contrary to popular opinion, Socrates did not claim to know nothing. He famously claimed to know *Ta Erotika*. "Eros" in ancient Greece did not refer to sexuality or romantic love. Socrates meant that he knew how to love well, knew what to love, knew what to care about. He might walk through the marketplace and say: "look at all these things I do not need." He would ask someone how much time they spend on fixing their hair in the morning and then ask how much time they spent on fixing themselves.

Socrates compared himself to a midwife. He cared about the part of the person that was most real, and helped the person to draw it out, to give birth to their better self. The insecurities and aggravations of philosophizing with Socrates were the labor pains of this midwifery. For him, reason and love were not antithetical, as moderns might insist. They were deeply related, and mutually reliant. We needed love to power our reason, and we needed reason to tutor our love.[7]

Socrates was found guilty, of course. He lost narrowly, and for largely political reasons; he put off many powerful people. After the verdict is rendered in the *Apology*, each side proposes a penalty. The accusers proposed that Socrates be killed, and Socrates makes the following reply:

"He assesses the penalty at death. So be it. What counter assessment should I propose to you, men of Athens? Clearly it should be a penalty I deserve, and what do I deserve to suffer or to pay because I have deliberately not led a quiet life but have neglected what occupies most people: wealth, household affairs, the position of general or public orator or the other offices, the political clubs and factions that exist in the city? I thought myself too honest to survive if I occupied myself with those things. I did not follow that path that would have made me of no use either to you or to myself, but I went to each of you privately and conferred upon him what I say is the greatest benefit, by trying to persuade him not to care for any of his belongings before caring that he himself should be as good and wise as possible...What do I deserve for being such a man? Some good, men of Athens, if I must truly make an assessment according to my deserts, and something suitable. What is suitable for a poor

---

7. See also: Harry Frankfurt, *The Reasons for Love* and D. C. Schindler, *Plato's Critique of Impure Reason.*

benefactor who needs leisure to exhort you? Nothing is more suitable, gentlemen, than for such a man to be fed in the Prytaneum, much more suitable for him than for any one of you who has won a victory at Olympia with a pair or a team of horses. The Olympian victor makes you think yourself happy; I make you be happy. Besides, he does not need food, but I do. So if I must make a just assessment of what I deserve, I assess it at this: free meals in the Prytaneum." (36b–37a)[8]

Note the irony and humor in this retort. It is absurd when held against the accusation, yet quite reasonable when Socrates reframes the charge into a service rendered, and rendered at great cost. But in doing this, Socrates colors outside the lines of the state, and his "nine-dot" solution does nothing to ingratiate the crowd. So he is condemned to death.

We must not just think of Socrates as a thinker. He is a *lover* of wisdom. This love prevails over other loves and endows him with a mysterious and mythic kind of resolve. It strains credulity perhaps, but remains plausible. Socrates knows who he is; he knows how his own mind works. This knowledge seems to give him certainty and serenity in dire circumstances. This is his part of his shamanic atopy: his hours of standing in meditation, his command over his physiology, his resistance to the elements, his courage in battle, and most of all, his *daimonion.* He had a divine voice to guide his attention to maintain the tension between relevance and truth. Whenever he was about to do something wrong, this voice would intercede and tell him not to do it.

Despite his political opponents, Socrates has many followers, past and present. He is known now by the fruits of his teaching, by the attention he gave to the lovers of wisdom, by those he exhorted to care for their souls more than the incidental successes they acquired. His legacy runs through the entire Axial Age and well into modernity. Much of this is owed to his most important follower, who was present

---

8. Plato's "Apology" in *Plato: Complete Works,* trans. G.M.A Grube, eds. Cooper and Hutchinson (Hackett Publishing Company, 1997).

at the trial and gave us access to his voice. Plato became the custodian of the Socratic spirit and provided a dynamic form for its amplification. As I have foreshadowed, Plato's integration of Pythagoras and Socrates would become the formative tradition of meaning and self-transformation in the West.[9]

---

9. For those who desire a more concentrated, practical guide to the Socratic tradition and way of life, I recommend *After Socrates,* my video lecture and dialogue series published in 2023.

5

PLATO AND THE CAVE

In the previous chapter, we explored how the Axial Revolution came into Greece, carrying with it the complement of shamanic psychotechnologies. First in the figure of Pythagoras and then in the figure of Socrates, it bound together the questions of meaning, wisdom, and self-transcendence. Socrates's particular conception of wisdom attempted to bind the salience of the sophists to the proto-scientific truth of the natural philosophers. The latter threatened disinterest before an impersonal objective truth, and the former threatened the self-deception that comes with purely subjective and relativistic interests. Socrates had developed the skill to hold himself in tension between these alternatives. Succumbing to either meant a life not worth living.

We are still in the midst of a historical journey, but it is important to consider these alternatives to the Socratic project. These are not just historical perils but also perennial ones. They represent two dimensions of the modern Meaning Crisis: (1) the nihilism that descends on us when the relevance of our subjective experience vanishes before an objective, scientific worldview, and (2) the existential anxiety that arises when our normativity is endless variable and fluctuating, and our freedom of action is unmoored from any objective reality. We must keep both of these pathologies in mind as our discussion progresses.

Plato and the Centers of the Psyche

If Socrates was controversial, Plato has long since surpassed him. His foundational influence in Western philosophy and spirituality cannot be overestimated, and every year hundreds of books are written about him. Plato's dialogues and letters do not just present a series of ideas but an immersive drama. Their literary, theatrical texture communicates the Socratic character in an embodied and animate way.

Plato preserved his teacher and made him evergreen; his works dialogue with us. They challenge us. They invite us back at different times to see the things we could not see before. You can return to Plato over the course of your life and find that he speaks to you in different voices. You find new things intelligible. You happen upon new insights. The Socratic mirror recognizes and reflects new aspects of you as the years wear on.

This quality of inexhaustibleness is a core feature that defines a sacred text. Many people in the ancient world read Plato mystically, just as they would religious scripture. I would join Arthur Versluis[1] and others in claiming that Platonism, or Neoplatonism, is the bedrock of Western spirituality. This is, of course, a significant claim and requires a Socratic apology. I will return to Neoplatonism in due course.

Plato was not present for the death of Socrates, but he was deeply affected and disturbed by it. He returned to it again and again in his writing. He wanted to understand how the city he loved, Athens, could have killed the man that he admired and loved so deeply. Where Socrates had a dilemma apparently given to him by the gods, Plato had his own dilemma given to him by the death of Socrates. Plato wanted to understand how people could be so foolish.

---

1. Arthur Versluis, *Platonic Mysticism: Contemplative Science, Philosophy, Literature, and Art* (State University of New York, 2017).

Plato also adopted the two-worlds mythology we discussed in the previous chapter, but he treated it differently than the Hebrews did. Recall that the Hebrews considered the everyday world to be a fallen state but also a progressive movement toward a future and the real world. They gave a historical answer for human foolishness and suffering as well as a temporal journey to chart the ascent from illusion to reality. Plato's answer was not historical. It resembled the proto-scientific inquiries of the natural philosophers. To solve the riddle of how Athens could have killed Socrates, Plato created the first psychological theory in history.

Remember that Plato is ultimately influenced not just by Socrates but also by Pythagoras. He spent some time with a Pythagorean community, and he seems to have undergone some kind of training there. Plato's theory of foolishness is informed by this training, and it addresses one of the most universal existential conditions—the experience of inner conflict. We have all felt this tension, when two strong motives seem to be working against one another, each pulling us in a different direction, each as a separate force of personality.

The first existential philosopher, Soren Kierkegaard, who was also a student of Socrates, would call it the "double-mindedness" of despair. It is perhaps our nearest enemy to meaning in life. It fouls our relationships and fogs the glass of perception. We feel most distraught, most anxious, most dreadful when we are divided against ourselves. It was, therefore, one of the central Axial motifs, captured in scripture, sacred texts, and wisdom literature across both East and West.

Examples of inner conflict range in stakes and severity, but they often follow similar patterns. Procrastination is a classic. A student has two weeks to write a paper—plenty of time for reading, research, and rewriting. But she also has two weeks' worth of social calls. She goes out for drinks on several evenings and writes the paper the night before.

I face similar temptations even as an older adult. For instance, I'm a great lover of chocolate. It has a deep and unfailing attraction for me. Recently, I went on a diet and lost twenty pounds. I knew that maintaining this achievement depended on committing to a strict regimen. Then I went home one night to a leftover chocolate birthday cake, sitting in the fridge and humming its chocolatey goodness. I ate almost the entire cake. It is little wonder that dieting is one of the most unsuccessful human endeavors. The recidivism rate is 95 percent. Within a year, almost all dieters regress to their pre-diet weight. Many industries benefit from our inner conflict, just as they do from bullshit. I know I should lose weight; there is a technique to follow, many rational arguments, and clear and foreseeable consequences. None of these factors could overcome the salience of the cake.

Plato had a brilliant insight about this problem. He saw a deep connection between inner conflict, self-deception, and self-destructive behavior. He proposed a paradigm-shifting idea, one of those conceptual revolutions that seems obvious to everyone who inherits it. Plato posited the idea that human beings have different centers in the psyche, or parts within the soul. Each center has a different cognitive relationship to the world and motivates us in different ways. Plato, through Socrates, explores this theory in detailed arguments, but he also represents it mythologically. The idea of the tripartite soul became one of his most famous inventions. It is one of the central themes of the *Republic,* which uses the city as an allegory for the soul.

For Plato, the highest part of us is "man."[2] It represents reason. It is motivated by truth. It cares about truth and falsity. It can deal with very abstract entities and pursue long-term goals, like preparing an essay or planning for your health. Plato situated the man in the head. In the city, it is the ruler of the state.

The opponent of man was the "monster," the part of my soul seduced by the chocolate cake. This part has a different normativity. It is not moved by truth or falsity, but by pleasure and pain. The

---

2. As I noted in the last chapter, Athenian democracy was highly sexist. However, Plato rose above it by the standards of his day. He argued that women should rule as well as men and should also serve in the army. This would not perfectly absolve him by our standards, of course, but it remains an admirable example of his independent mindedness.

monster dwells in the stomach and genitals. It represents appetite. In the city, it is the common citizenry.

Plato does not hold that appetite is evil. The monster operates according to different principles than man, but it has an essential function. In life and death situations, a superficial appraisal is often the most adaptive. It allows us to avoid a predator or a hot stovetop. If pleasure and pain don't motivate you, you cannot survive. However, when they become dominant, their superficial aims also become dominant, and we lose depth, range, and contemplation. Notice how the man and the monster are opposite to each other but also dependent on one another.

Recall the brief exchange between Socrates and the shopper from the previous chapter in their discussion about happiness. Socrates did not have a particular theory; he had a practice. In Plato's dialogues, Socrates shows his interlocutors that what they find salient is taking priority over what they find truthful. One part is overwhelming the other, and sometimes we confuse their identities.

The monster makes things salient to you, and motivates you with urgency. It is constantly racing ahead of what you understand. We are vulnerable to this because salience often exceeds understanding. The man is the part that understands, but the monster is constantly outflanking him, cowing him, drowning him out.

The third part of the soul is the most difficult to explain. In the city allegory, it takes the form of the military. This requires some qualification, so let us return to our earlier examples. What could improve my chance to lose weight? Joining a dojo or an aerobics class. How do students avoid procrastination? They join study groups. As I argued over the last few chapters, we are not just biological creatures but also cultural creatures. Our recent cognitive evolutions are the psychotechnologies that use distributed cognition to resource the individual's agency and competence to codify certain values, amplify certain traits, and use ritual to reinforce more adaptive behavior.

Plato compared the third center of the human psyche to a lion. They are social animals, often depicted as symbols of honor. Consider the military allegory; like many social systems, it works in terms of honor and shame. Honor is to be respected—*lionized*—by your peers. Shame is the feeling of having failed to gain that respect.

We should not confuse shame and guilt; they are not synonyms. Shame occurs when you have lost respect from your peers. Guilt is having failed to meet your own ideal. In the latter case, this personal ideal is certainly informed by internalized social norms but also by your own reflection and contemplation. In Plato, and in much of the theology his work would inform, this ideal corresponds to an ontology and normativity that is far more ultimate than the measure of your peers. It corresponds to the Good itself.

Owing to its social nature, the lion part of the soul can pursue interests of intermediate scope. It sits somewhere between instant appetite and theoretical abstraction. It can pursue midterm goals that are countenanced by cultural forms—meanings that are shared between us. Notice how instinctively you want to bring other people into your experience; you'll share a song that moves you or implore your friend to watch your favorite show. You will push your drink across the table and say: "This is awful. Try it!"

Whatever your immediate response, you want to multiply it with a meeting of minds—not necessarily to gain consensus but to achieve something more primordial: relevance. Something about sharing the experience makes it more meaningful and makes it feel more real. As I have argued, your participation in distributed cognition is one of the most powerful ways you increase your cognitive power and agency in the world.

Plato associates the lion part of the psyche with the chest; this is where we sense many of our social emotions and motivations, like pride, honor and shame. It is difficult to name this part because its Greek word does not have a direct English equivalent. Sometimes people translate it as "emotion," but this does not capture it sufficiently. "Spiritedness" is another translation and seems closer to the mark. I prefer to leave it in the original language: *thymos*.

Plato observes a great deal of conflict in the "city," this family of psychic parts. In *Phaedrus*, he famously analogizes the parts to horses tethered together in a chariot. In order for the soul to have agency and fulfill its Axial project—that is, for the chariot to be self-moving, and meet its mark—it must first be properly ordered. When salience, understanding, and participation fall out of sync, we are more subject to bullshit. Inner conflict makes us vulnerable to self-deception. When we are beset by the double-mindedness of man and monster, we are overcome with anxiety. We must devote cognitive resources to managing the civil conflict. We are constantly contending with threat signals, the dreadful knowledge that something in our city is rotten.

Egocentrism becomes an adaptive response, but it also makes us more oblivious and unobservant. We become alienated from the outside world because it seems less relevant than the conflict within. Our social participation is therefore less reflective. We become wanton, or withdrawn. We lose our sense of agency and become despairing. All of this exacerbates the conflict.

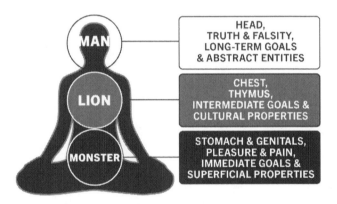

Figure 5.1: Plato's tripart segmentation of the psyche to explain the origin of inner conflict.

As social creatures, thymos seems to have a motivational function for us; we can understand its function from a cognitive scientific lens. One of our greatest adaptations is our ability to link and cooperate. If you drop me into the Amazon or the African savanna alone, my chance of survival is grim. I do not have claws or sharp teeth. I cannot run quickly or camouflage. I am a tall biped that towers above the grass, and my throat and my vital organs are conveniently exposed to predators. My physical attributes give me very few advantages. However, if I can gather in a group of other human beings, with a few sharp sticks and dogs, we can kill almost anything on the planet. Our ability to work together has always been adaptive, and this gives us a compelling evolutionary argument for the lion part of the psyche.

Finding the Optimal Relation: The Training of the Psyche

While we are exploring evolutionary arguments, we should include other parts of the psyche. For instance, why does the monster have more power than the man? Why do immediate gratifications impel us more than distant, abstract goals? We have some very plausible ideas about this, courtesy of the work of psychologist George Ainslie and others[3] on the concept of *hyperbolic discounting* (or temporal discounting).

They found that the patterns of behavior we associate with the monster are not just human but exist reliably across species. Like flow, they are part of an adaptive, universal kind of mechanism. The idea of hyperbolic discounting says the farther away in time a stimulus happens to be—for example, a threat or reward—the less it grabs your attention. The less salient it is for your attention, the more you discount it, and the less it factors into your actions and decisions. This discounting can be graphed on a curve across time:

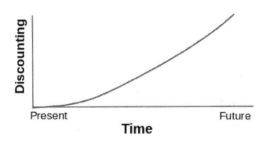

Figure 5.2: Hyperbolic discounting, the reduction of salience, occurs over time in relation to a stimulus. The graph indicates that a stimulus loses its salience over time exponentially.

---

3. See George Ainslie and Nick Haslam, "Hyperbolic Discounting," In *Choice over Time* (Russell Sage Foundation, 1992): 57–92.

A stimulus in the present has a high degree of salience. Something in the future, especially in the far future, is much less salient. It feels much less real. That is why the monster can override the man. This might seem foolish, but it is actually very adaptive. For example, I am about to smoke a cigarette. For simplicity's sake, we might say that there are two possible immediate outcomes. In one outcome, I have a coughing fit. In the other, I feel pleasantly relaxed. We can represent present action and the two future outcomes like this:

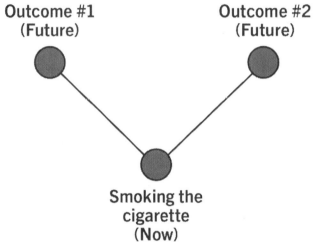

Figure 5.3: A simplified representation of the potential outcomes stemming from a given action. In this example, the action occurring in the present is smoking a cigarette.

Tied to this action are two possible outcomes. For example, the first outcome could be coughing and the second outcome could be not coughing.

The probability of smoking the cigarette is 100 percent but the probability of either outcome occurring is 50 percent.

In this scenario, the probability that I smoke in the present is 100 percent. The probability of either of the two future outcomes occurring is 50 percent. However, with each future outcome, two additional future outcomes become possible. This results in a branching out of the potential outcomes, with the statistical probability of each reducing as the tree progresses.

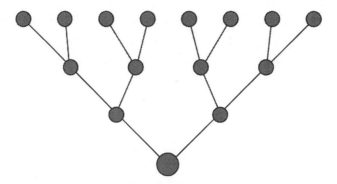

Figure 5.4: Depiction of how all of the possible future outcomes are related to each event. The probability of each subsequent outcome happening lowers as the map continues to branch.

Do you notice what is happening? As you move into the future, the probability of any one of these events occurring decreases very quickly. You pay less attention to them, and for good reason. You *should* pay less attention to things that are less probable. Otherwise, you could be overwhelmed by the possibilities. Imagine: If I get out of bed too quickly, I might twist my ankle. I might be late for class. I might fail the exam. I might underperform in my course. It might affect my degree. It might affect my career. The long road of mishaps may lead to an embittered life alone, in Buffalo, married to a lamp. This outcome is possible but the probability is very low, and therefore worth discounting.

I have hypothesized that some people who experience generalized anxiety disorder have difficulty with hyperbolic discounting. They cannot adequately screen out low probability events and find them to be disproportionately salient. Hyperbolic discounting is indispensable and very adaptive.

The problem with any adaptive machine is that it is subject to maladaptive patterns. Let us return to the cigarette smoking example. In one future scenario, a long causal chain of events leads to me dying in Hamilton from cancer in my left lung. An alternative future has me dying in Hamilton from cancer in my right lung. Another branch leads me to Vancouver, where I die from lung cancer. A fourth leads me to Rome, where the outcome is the same. Each one of these specific deaths has a low probability of occurring because each is well into the future. Yet I do not want to just avoid death in Hamilton, or Rome, or Vancouver. I want to avoid death altogether. I want to avoid death in the *abstract.*

The chance of each of these deaths is low, but if you pool them together, the chance that my cigarette smoking will lead to a premature death is actually very high. The hyperbolic discounting blinds me to each outcome because each is improbable as an independent event. However, in doing so it also blinds me to their common feature: premature death from lung cancer. This adaptive machinery accidentally discounts relevant information and encourages a habit that could make me sick in the years to come.

The project of wisdom has to contend with this unavoidable reality: that the very machinery that makes you adaptive also makes you vulnerable to self-deceptive and self-destructive behavior. We cannot throw this machinery away. Without it, you would be overwhelmed with crippling anxiety, unable to even get out of bed. However, if it's left untutored, you become unable to pursue any good outside of a moment's gratification. You smoke the cigarette, eat the cake, and go to the party. Each time, you reach instinctively for the appetitive good.

To counteract the effect of hyperbolic discounting and overrule the appetites of the monster, human beings must turn to that psychotechnology that began all the way back in the Upper Paleolithic transition, and that the Axial Revolution refined into practice—symbolic thought. This capacity, which developed within the frontal lobe of the brain, enables us to abstract the common feature in these many distant possibilities and represent it to ourselves. It is the man's advantage over the monster; he can grasp the abstract goal of avoiding a premature death. He cannot shut off the hyperbolic discounting, but he can hold it in tension with a countervailing force of suggestion.

Plato's insight about a tripart psychic division has been reproduced in many different forms, even in modernity. Freud famously divided the psyche into the id, the ego, and the superego. There was also a movement in neuroscience in the 1990s that trisected the human brain into three different brains: reptilian, paleomammalian, and neomammalian. We keep rediscovering the Platonic division. However, his insight was not just about structure. It was also about function and transformation.

The "man" part of the psyche is distinguished by its ability to learn, grasp theory, and conceptualize. The lion is not capable of theory. However, the lion can be trained with the reason of man. This is where Socrates and his tradition become so relevant. Plato's dialogues took reason into the marketplace. He wed social interaction to rational reflection. A Socratic method can help the man to train the lion, and the man and lion together can work to tame the monster. This is a vision of wisdom, the justice of the psyche, the ordering of the soul, and the resolution of inner conflict and freedom of self-deception: the teaching of the man, the training of the lion, and the taming of the monster.

This vision of inner dialogue and harmony is also known as an *optimization strategy.* If I let the monster rule, man and lion are disempowered. Instead, I pursue an optimal relation, carefully coordinating the parts of the psyche so each can live more fully without endangering the other two. For Plato, this mutuality—the most existence of each part—is to experience a fullness of being, to be as alive as one can possibly be, and to know the kind of peace that avails itself when the sufferings of inner conflict subside. This peace and fullness of being is one of our most powerful "meta drives," and a goal of many Axial religions and spiritual traditions. Take note of the Socratic effects: as I relieve my inner conflict, I reduce self-deception. I become less egocentric. I have a clearer, less obfuscated vision of reality.

As I have alluded to in previous chapters, the longing to be in contact with reality is very powerful, and closely related to the drive for peace and freedom from inner conflict. Plato is an originator of this insight. Philosophers have used various thought experiments over time to explore this longing. I use the following one with many of my students. Imagine you arrive home from class one day. Your parents are waiting for you. They say they want to show you something. They take you down a hallway that you have walked a thousand times before. They press on part of the wall, and a hidden door opens into a secret room. Inside the room are TV screens, videotapes, and pictures of you at all stages of your life. Then they disclose the following:

For your entire life, you have been participating in a social experiment. Nine months before you were born, we were hired by the government to raise you. They gave us scripts to memorize, they paid us for our trouble, and they instructed us to maintain the appearance of loving and attentive parents. We do not actually love you or care about you, but we carried out the agreement diligently. Now that you have turned a certain age, we are obligated to tell you the truth. But we are still required to be your parents. When we leave the room, you can forget about this. You can pretend this conversation never happened. We'll still tell you that we love you and make sure your needs are met. The only difference will be that now you'll know the truth.

Now ask people, "How would you feel?" Consider that nothing would appear to change. Your parents would say the same words to you and treat you exactly the same way. This time, though, you would know the love is not real. Nearly all of us would be devastated beyond expression. This response is replicated in similar thought experiments. I'll ask how many people are in satisfying personal relationships, and quite a few people will raise their hands. Then I'll ask, "How many of you would want to know that your partner was cheating on you even if that meant the destruction of your relationship?" Almost everyone keeps their hand up. They are willing to destroy the relationship even if it is meaningful and satisfying. For most of us, a ruined relationship is preferable to a fake relationship.

Plato's insight is as relevant now as the year he made it: the meta-drive for realness prevails over most other drives. We hunger for reality more than we hunger for pleasure. Two of your most important meta-drives are being met in the Platonic model: you are reducing inner conflict and becoming more in touch with reality. This harmony begets itself and creates a virtuous circle; I get better at picking up on real patterns in the world, and this skill is improved the clearer my vision becomes.

As I cultivate more inner peace, I am able to pick up on more real patterns. I acquire more acute vision, and skill, and I can apply these to myself to pick patterns in my own thoughts and behavior. I can use them Socratically to cultivate self-knowledge. The better I know myself, the better I teach the man. The better I teach the man, the better I train the lion and tame the monster. The more you know your student, the more effective a teacher you become. As you sharpen your ability to detect real patterns, you can progressively deepen the project of self-knowledge. This equips you to train and acquaint the psychic parts, to reduce your inner conflict, and to appreciate your perception and contact with reality.

The Myth of the Cave: The Hunger for Reality and Self-Transformation

Notice the role of participatory knowing in the "virtuous circle" above. Contact with reality is dependent on my self-transformation. I am not a passive observer forming true beliefs. I am implicated in my observations. The appearance of the world is a consequence of my framing, and I have to change myself to see the world more clearly. When I do, the world itself seems to change, and it places a demand on me to change myself. As I transform, the world discloses more of itself. This is the dynamic of participatory knowing. It is a *reciprocal opening* between me and my environment. I am not just changing my mind or knowing with my mind. I am knowing with my whole self, my whole identity, and all the machinery of my cognition.

The related quests for reality, inner harmony, self-knowledge, and transformation are explored deeply in Plato's *Republic*. The quest is dramatized in the *Myth of the Cave*, perhaps the most famous passage in the history of Western philosophy. It has been interpreted so extensively that a person could spend an entire career examining only the interpretations. I will certainly not presume to offer an exhaustive account here, but it is sufficient for our discussion to note that the myth animates the relationship I have discussed through the chapter—the deep connection between our perception of reality and the process of self-transformation.

The myth begins in a cave. Within the cave, there is a fire. People are sitting on the floor of the cave, chained, with their backs facing the fire and their eyes facing the wall. As other people walk in front of the fire, their forms cast shadows onto the wall of the cave. These shadows are the only things the prisoners can see, and the only thing they hear are the echoes of sound bouncing off the walls. The prisoners take the shadows and echoes to be real objects of perception.

Then one day, one of the prisoners comes free of the chains. He turns to see the fire. He realizes that his perceptions are not the real things but merely shadows and echoes. Something has changed. The prisoner is now able to notice real patterns as opposed to the merely correlational patterns. He starts to notice what these real patterns feel like, and how it feels to know them. He begins to develop a taste for reality. He begins to look around and explore. He sees a shaft of light coming into the cave. He realizes there is a way out.

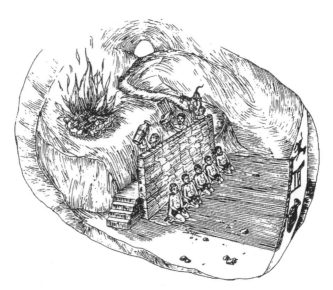

Figure 5.5: An illustration of Plato's Myth of the Cave. Image obtained from Wikimedia Commons, entitled An Illustration of "The Allegory of the Cave," from Plato's Republic by 4edges.

The cave is underground. As the freed prisoner follows the path illuminated by the shaft of light, the path begins to slope upward. His journey is slow and painstaking. Each time he takes a step, he is blinded by the light's intensity. He must stop and wait for his eyes to adjust. His vision and perception—his entire self and cognition—must transform with each step before he can take the next one. At first, the light darkens his vision, and his vision must adapt itself to this new degree of brightness. This is the process of participatory transformation. It is gradual and filled with discomfort.

Eventually the prisoner steps out of the cave and into the real world, bathed in sunlight. He looks around. He wants to see the source of this light, this power that allows him to pick up on the new patterns, to participate in this new reality. It is still more powerful; not only is the light *showing* the reality of things, but this light is also the *source* of this reality and the life of all things visible to him. Where is this source of life and understanding? The prisoner looks around and looks up. He glimpses it, but he cannot stare at it directly. It is the Sun. It is overwhelming. It is beyond his comprehension. It fills him with awe.

The lion is not content to keep a powerful experience private. The prisoner must share the revelation. He scrambles back down into the cave to tell his fellow prisoners what he saw, but the way back is perilous. As he returns to the darkness, his eyes do not work anymore. He stumbles. He says things that do not make any sense to the people in chains. They mistrust him and ridicule them. If they could, they might even kill him, just as they killed Socrates.

This myth reflects an ancient and archetypal motif. It is a myth of *enlightenment*, of coming into the light. It is a parable of attaining greater contact with reality, undertaking the cycle of self-transcendence and self-transformation. You perceive real patterns, and they blind you. You transform yourself and your vision to bring them into resolution. Then you can continue to graduate your perception and relationship to reality.

There is a Greek word for this ascent—*anagoge.* Plato is mapping the Axial movement between the illusory world and the real world, and he is turning it into an account of how you can

115

rationally make your life more meaningful. You can become at once more fully alive and more at peace, just as you come more and more in contact with the real patterns that make sense of reality. You can satisfy, in a mutually supporting fashion, your desire, your meta drive for inner peace, and your meta drive to be in contact with reality. This is what Plato calls wisdom, a fullness of being. We become more and more real ourselves as we become more at peace. We conform ourselves more and more to reality, and in doing so we are made more real.

Plato's *Myth of the Cave* has been reproduced countless times throughout the centuries, in epic poems and stories, novels and paintings. Both the structure and image of the anagogic ascent have been used prolifically as cinematic motifs. *The Matrix* (1999) is one of the most frequently cited examples. Remember: these myths remain popular because they are not stories from the past. They are dramatic recreations of the perennial patterns we face as human beings, like the disharmony we experience in the parts of our psyche, the problem of being trapped in illusion and being out of touch with reality. Plato's myth presents a vision of wisdom—freedom from inner conflict, a path of self-transcendence, a fullness of being and enhanced meaning in life.

In this vision, reason and spirituality are not opposed. They are inseparably bound together. Plato paired the Socratic project (ordering the psyche to overcome self-deception) with the Pythagorean one (the soulflight of self-transcendence and transformation of consciousness). From this marriage, he discovered a way to depict this radical transformation. His depiction is so entrancing that it became a constant refrain throughout the West. We return to it again and again, seeking its wisdom, walking its path through our imagination, trying to gain access to these real patterns of reality.

The Pythagorean side of Plato is important for how we understand these "real patterns." They do not refer to definitions, objects, or figures but the manifesting wholeness of things that unfolds as our perception unfolds, giving reality its depth and inexhaustibleness. Plato uses the term *eidos*, which is usually translated as "form" (easily mistaken for shape) or as "idea" (usually mistaken for concept).

Neither of these translations adequately capture its meaning. When Plato uses the term, it is more like a "paradigm," the pathway we have for understanding something and accessing its reality. The eidos is not just the affordance of our knowing. It is the force of realization itself, the power by which something can be the particular something that it is.

The idea of "real patterns" also helps to provide us with a *psychology of concepts*. If you ask someone to tell you what a bird is, they will likely respond with a feature list. For example, they will describe a creature with talons, wings, feathers and a beak, a creature that flies and roosts. This would suggest that the way we understand something is by enumerating the correct list of features. However, there is a problem with this; I could satisfy this definition of "bird" by pasting together these features—wings, feathers, and a beak—and launching them into the air. This does not give me a bird. It gives me a grotesque mess. What is missing from this definition is a *structural-functional organization*, the way in which all these features hang together, the way they are structured together, belong together, such that the bird functions as a whole, greater than the sum of its parts.

The Germans have an excellent word for this structural-functional organization: *gestalt*. For our purposes, however, we will focus on the Greek word: *logos*. As I mentioned in previous chapters, this word is among the most translated—and mistranslated—words in all of philosophy. It has to do with the order and arrangement of these real patterns, the concentering formula that fits everything together, integrates it with mind, and makes it intelligible to our comprehension. The research shows that our grasp of logos is intuitive, but not something we can define or express. We know it by *conforming* to it, by becoming like it, by matching the pattern of our cognition to the pattern of its disclosure, and entering into that *reciprocal realization* with it. This Platonic idea of knowing by conformity is a critical one for the development of meaning and wisdom, and it was taken up by Plato's greatest disciple and, perhaps, the second most influential philosopher of all antiquity—Aristotle.

6

ARISTOTLE, KANT, AND EVOLUTION

In the previous chapter, we discussed the foundational work of Plato. I explained how his notion of wisdom involved harmonizing the various forces and functions of the psyche. As the psychic parts—the man, the monster, and the lion—become more aligned and integrated, we reduce the obfuscating influences of inner conflict and self-deception. This makes it possible to achieve two significant meta drives: the desire for inner peace and the desire to attain a clearer vision of the world to conform our ways of knowing to the deeper patterns of reality.

Plato provided us with the paradigm-changing insight that a connection exists between our conformity to reality and the necessity of self-transformation. As we track patterns in the world, we can reflectively internalize these patterns to better understand and harmonize ourselves. The inward transformation allows us to refine our grasp on reality, to awaken from illusion, and draw ourselves closer to what is most real.

We discussed how this process of anagoge is mythologized in Plato's Cave. He dramatizes the seminal Socratic insight that revolutionized the Axial period: the knowing of reality cannot be separated from the knowing of oneself.

Aristotle's Theory of Growth: Potential, Causation, and Information

Just as Socrates had a great disciple in Plato, so Plato was fortunate to have a great disciple of his own. Aristotle studied with Plato for about twenty years before he broke from his teacher's thinking. He famously claimed: "While I love Plato, I love the truth more." Aristotle remained a Platonist in some important ways,[1] but he thought an aspect of Plato's work was lacking.

He was deeply influenced by Plato's account of what made something real for the human psyche, but he thought this account did not adequately consider the role of change. Aristotle was influenced greatly by his father, who was a physician. As a proto-scientist, he was more biologist than mathematician, and his analogies reflected the difference. The word that Aristotle used for change is better translated as "development" or "growth." He introduced a more rigorously scientific approach to refine the relationship between meaning and wisdom.

In the previous chapter, we talked about *structural-functional organization,* the idea that an entity, like a bird, is much more than a set of its parts and features but the way that parts and features function together as a whole. This pattern of wholeness—whether we call it gestalt, or logos, or eidos—is difficult to define in language, but it does two important things for us. It *makes* the entity and gives it its paradigmatic nature (i.e., its "birdness"). It is also the pattern by which we come to know the entity. When we can grasp the structural-functional organization, that eidos, we can understand what a bird is —not such that we can define it but such that we can relate to it and act upon it. Aristotle was impressed by this dual function of the eidos, but he wanted to give it a more dynamical approach. He suspected it played a decisive role in how things grew and developed.

Aristotle began with a material analogy. If I have a block of wood, I can fashion the wood into a chair or a table. If it is big enough, I can even use it to build a ship. Aristotle asked: What makes the block of

---

1. Lloyd Gerson, *From Plato to Platonism* (Cornell University Press, 2014).

wood behave like a chair as opposed to a table or ship? What makes a chair act like a chair? What makes the ship act like a ship? If they are crafted from the same material, why do they have such dramatically different natures when converted into these respective forms?

Aristotle proposed that the wood's transition into one of these structures is an important analogy for development. My crafting of the chair is somehow analogous to the growth of the organism. Eidos is the difference between the wood and the chair. When imbued with the eidos of "chair," the wood is structurally functionally organized in such a way that it will act like a chair. The same is true for the table or ship. For Aristotle, the wood is mere *potential*. Eidos imbues it with *actuality*.

We use the terms "potential" and "actual" all the time, usually referring to different degrees of realness. They seem like part of our natural grammar, but they are *actually* an Aristotelian invention. The idea of wood is *potentially* a chair, or a table, or a ship. When one of these forms is given to it, the wood begins to act as a chair, or a table, or a ship. This is where we get the notion of *in-formation*. When you instill the form—the eidos—into the wood, you actualize its potential. You grow and transform it by endowing it with a specific structural-functional organization, and you make it knowable as a specific thing.

What does this analogy mean for biological beings? Aristotle argued that what the craftsman does for the wood, living things do for themselves. Imagine if a chair could somehow impose its own structural-functional organization on its material potential to turn itself into a chair. This is what a living thing does. For example, food is potential within you. When you consume it, it conforms to you and becomes part of you. A code in your DNA informs this raw potential with your structural-functional organization. This does not happen instantly, of course. It unfolds across time. We understand it as a process of gradual change and development, just the transformation of psychic life and cognitive agency.

Explaining this model of cognitive development requires me to delve more deeply into current cognitive science, especially the work of philosopher Alicia Juarrero,[2] who was directly inspired by Aristotle's framework. When we talk about how things change, we usually invoke a model we inherited from the Scientific Revolution, specifically from Isaac Newton. In this model, change occurs by causal impact: I push on an object, and it moves. The model is obvious and noncontroversial. All change or development consists of an event (A) that somehow causes another event (B), which causes another event (C). A precedes B and makes B happen. B precedes C and makes C happen, and so on.

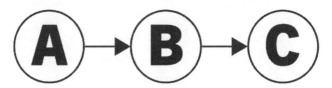

Figure 6.1: Depiction of the standard model from Newton during the Scientific Revolution. It focuses on causal impact as the source of change. Event A precedes and causes event B, which precedes and causes event C.

This vision of causation was prominent during the Scientific Revolution and for everyone who would take up the Newtonian worldview. There was good reason for this; Newton's model (figure 6.1) seemed to solve a lot of problems. This much was observed by Immanuel Kant, a famous philosopher of the Enlightenment (also referenced by Juarrero). Kant was interested in knowing why this Newtonian version of causality was becoming so successful.

The Aristotelian model had been around for thousands of years. Why was Newton's overtaking it so rapidly? Kant speculated that the success of the model was the simplicity of its explanation. We account for one event (C) with a preceding event (B), and we account for that event with a preceding event (A). This version of events is linear and clean, and despite its apparent obviousness, it is deceptively insightful. The linearity of this account prevents circular explanations, which occur when a causal account assumes the very

2. Alicia Juarrero, *Dynamics in Action: Intentional Behavior as a Complex System* (MIT Press, 2002).

thing it is trying to explain. One popular version of a circular explanation is called a *homuncular fallacy*, where we explain a complex cognitive function (how does my brain see a triangle?) by isolating the function to a specific location, like a homunculus, or "little man" inside the brain, and using it to explain the event. If our answer is: "The little man identifies the triangle," the same question could be asked of the homunculus inside the brain. (How does *he* do it?) We may have displaced the question, but we have not answered it.

The homuncular fallacy poses an infinite regress; we are using vision to try and explain vision. We have to propose more homunculi to explain the ability of each homunculus that precedes it. We fall into this kind of circular explanation often, and it thwarts scientific inquiry. Kant lauded the Newtonian scheme for avoiding this problem. If you stick to its grammar and its rules, each cause has to be an independent event that precedes the effect. You may encounter some difficulty when tracing the origin of the causal sequence (what caused event A?) but at least the sequence is linear. It is little surprise that the Newtonian model became such a predominant mode of explanation during the Scientific Revolution.

The Dynamical System: Cause, Constraint, and Self-Organization

Despite its strengths, Kant also encountered a significant problem with this Newtonian model. He observed a tree, and he noticed that it did not follow this linear sequence. What is making the tree? The sunlight. How does the sunlight get in? Through the leaves. What is making the leaves? The tree. So the tree makes the leaves, and the leaves make the tree. Does this mean that the tree is making the tree? Kant coined a new term to describe this process. The tree is *self-organizing*. However, this brought him back to the earlier problem. Living things make use of *feedback cycles*. In a feedback cycle, the output from a system feeds back into the system. The tree makes the leaves, and the leaves gather the energy that feeds back into the processes that make the leaves. When I try to explain a feedback cycle, I fall into a circular explanation.

To account for this, Kant came to a startling conclusion. There could not be a science of living things, he said. Biology was impossible. Kant was a philosophical genius, so a statement like this cannot be dismissed out of hand. If there is biology, and if living things use feedback cycles—which they necessarily do—then they are necessarily self-organizing. When I try to trace out the causation, I fall into a circular explanation, which is vacuous and empty as a scientific account. How do we solve for this problem? Without an answer, we cannot fundamentally understand who or what we are or what we refer to when discussing the nature of growth and development. Physics would remain separate from biology, and that language would forever be separate from scientific understanding.

Where is Kant going wrong? Living things are feedback cycles, which are self-organizing. They grow, they develop, and they make themselves. Something about the linear, Newtonian causal model is inadequate to explain this (figure 6.1). We already know that Newton does not account for relativity. It does not work at the quantum level. So Juarrero made use of an important idea from Aristotle to solve this problem, invoking a new and powerful way of talking about growth, development, and self-organizing processes. This is known as *Dynamical Systems Theory.*

Juarrero first makes a distinction between *causes* and *constraints.* I have an object and I push it. Why did it move? In Newtonian grammar, we explain that it moved because I pushed it. Why else did it move? Think about what has to also be true in order for this to move. There has to be relatively empty space in front of the object. The empty space has to have a particular shape. The object has to have a particular shape. Those are not events. Those are conditions. Causes are events that make things happen. Constraints are conditions that make the events possible. The Newtonian way of thinking has us so fixated on causes that we do not sufficiently account for the role of constraints in causal events.

	Causes	Constraints

Events   **Conditions**
What happens   **What is possible**
Actuality   **Potentiality**

Figure 6.2: The components that make up causes versus constraints. Causes deal with events, what actually *happens. Constraints reflect conditions surrounding the events, which reflect what can* possibly *happen and therefore deal with potentiality.*

Aristotle, because of his Platonic view, actually considers constraints to be more important than causes. When I talk about eidos, the structural-functional organization, I refer to a pattern of constraints. Conditions and constraints are where we find form, or what Aristotle called the *formal cause*. They are structurally functionally organized such that motion for the object is possible. If we follow Juarrero back to our Aristotelian terminology, we might say that causes are actuality while constraints refer to potentiality. Possibility has been shaped by constraints so that some events are more possible than other events. Let us stop here and see if this helps us to solve Kant's problem of the tree and its self-organization.

In a tree, a series of biochemical events occur, and these events produce a particular form for that tree, a particular structural-functional organization. For example, why do trees grow the way they do? Why do they grow outward, spreading their branches and leaves? They are trying to increase the possibility of photons hitting a chlorophyll molecule. The tree's structure is shaping the possibility of these events. The events cause the branching structure, but the branching structure also constrains the events.

I have a series of events occurring inside of me that create a structural-functional organization. That organization creates an internal environment in which the probability of events is dramatically altered. Events that have a low probability happening in the outside environment have a high probability of happening inside my body, and events that have a high probability of happening in the outside environment have a low probability of happening inside my body. That is what it is to be a living being. The events cause a structural-functional organization, an eidos, a form that then constrains the events that shape me.

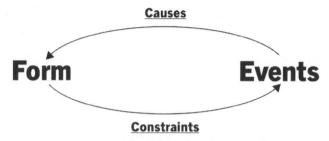

Figure 6.3: The structural-functional organization relationship between the form and events. The adoption of a given form, which is caused by events, constrains future events, making specific events more possible than others. The events that become more possible by the change proceed to further change the form, which further constrains the possible events.

This account (figure 6.3) is not a circular explanation. I am talking about two very different kinds of things—actuality, represented by the events, and potentiality, reflected in the constraints imposed on the events by the form. The discussion of possibility, abstract as it may be, is integral to science, which depends on real potential.

For example, if I lift an object, that object acquires kinetic energy. When I stop moving the object and hold it at a given height, what happens to this kinetic energy? It cannot be destroyed. It becomes *potential* energy. If the principle of the conservation of mass and energy is real, then potentiality is real. Consider this Newtonian equation: F=ma (force is equal to mass multiplied by acceleration). Is this an event? Does it happen every Tuesday at four o'clock? No—this is how things are shaped. It puts a limit on what is possible in the world. Real potentiality is not a fiction or abstraction. It is a reality that is integral to our current science.

Juarrero refines this account even further. She points out that there are two kinds of constraints. The first kind makes a form of event more possible; she calls these *enabling constraints*. The second kind of constraint reduces the possibilities and options for a system. These are *selective constraints*.

This gives us a powerful model for development and change, and we can use it to understand one of the most foundational theories in the science of biology: Darwin's *Theory of Natural Selection*. The theory of Darwinian evolution is perhaps the first dynamical systems theory in science, designed precisely to account for growth and development—not within an individual, of course, but across speciation.

Evolution and the Virtual Engine

Let us examine Darwin's theory more closely. First of all, there has to be a feedback cycle for any dynamical system theory because we are talking about a self-organizing process. What is the feedback cycle in Darwinian evolution? It is reproduction (i.e., goats come from other goats). The animal is produced, and the product feeds back into the system and becomes the producer (the goat makes more goats, which in turn make more goats). That is why we call it *re*-production.

Darwin realized that selective constraints were operating on the feedback cycle of reproduction; conditions in the environment reduced the options for organisms. One of these conditions was the scarcity of resources. Scarcity generates competition; when not everything can live, this reduces the options for the system. Several biologists have argued that there was initially no evolution for about one hundred thousand years because there was an abundance of resources.

This is not the whole story, of course. If it were, everything would die and evolution would end. The selective constraints described above were also paired with enabling constraints that opened up options within the system. Look around at people next time you walk outside; there is considerable variation in the system, which increases the number of options. Throughout the feedback cycle, the selective conditions reduce the available options, and variation increases them. You might imagine the cycle moving in an accordion fashion; variation opens it up and the selective constraints push it down. This pattern continues and refines, constantly changing in a way that fits it better to its environment. Evolution is circular. "Evolve" relates to "revolve." It is a revolution with change. Notice how much this

Darwinian theory, which rests at the foundation of biology, is beholden to Aristotle and Aristotelian ideas.

Juarrero talks about selection as a *virtual governor*. A governor is any device that limits what you can do in a system. For example, a governor for a steam engine limits the range at which it can cycle. Juarrero calls selection a virtual governor because it is not an actual machine. It is the shaping of possibility. Juarrero's account leaves off here, but together with my collaborators—Leo Ferraro, Anderson Todd, and Richard Wu in an unpublished manuscript—I have attempted to finish the metaphor. We proposed that variation would be a *virtual generator* because it is a set of conditions that generate options for a self-organizing system.

When you put a virtual governor systematically together with a virtual generator such that you are systematically regulating a feedback cycle, the whole system is a *virtual engine*. This is a dynamical system theory—a theory that lays out the virtual engine, shows you a feedback cycle and explains why it is not just random and chaotic. It also shows why the engine produces growth and development. A systematic relationship exists between a set of enabling and selective constraints.

Selection
Reducing options
Virtual Governor

Selective
Constraints

Variation
Opens options
Virtual Governor

Enabling
Constraints

Figure 6.4: A diagram demonstrating the dynamical systems nature of Darwin's Natural Selection Theory of evolution. Reproduction creates the feedback cycle. Constraints are placed on this cycle that are either selective (they reduce the options available) or enabling (they increase the options available). Selection arises from scarcity of resources, generates the selective constraints, and limits the system. Alicia Juarrero calls this the virtual governor. Meanwhile, variation generates the enabling constraints. My colleagues and I refer to variation as the virtual generator, continuing Juarrero's metaphor.

All of this is very Aristotelian. He does not use the "dynamical systems" language, of course, but his ideas of causation are their inspiration.

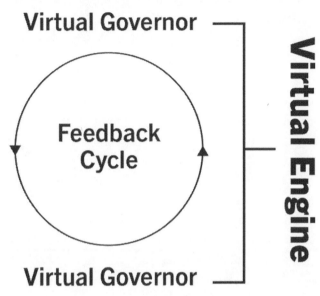

Figure 6.5: Diagram of the virtual engine, a further continuation of Juarrero's metaphor by my colleagues and me. The virtual engine consists of a feedback cycle systematically regulated by a virtual governor that executes the selective constraints along with the virtual generator that executes the enabling constraints.

Aristotle added something that was missing from the Socratic notion of wisdom—an account of growth and development. Remember that Socrates was trying to overcome self-deception. Plato advanced this project with a structural theory of the psyche, showing how we could harmonize ourselves to deepen our contact with reality. Aristotle understood that developing this capacity for wisdom had something to do with maturing your sense of self, the "who" and "what" you are. Aristotle gave us the notion of *character*.

The Golden Mean: Character, Rationality, and Human Purpose

The term "character" is used quite liberally, so like most ancient ideas, it requires stricter definition. Character is not personality; you are born with your personality. It is given to you by biology and the environment you never chose. Your character, however, is the aspect of you that you can refine with cultivation. That cultivation might be conscious or unconscious, direct or indirect, but it is a consequence of your experiences and how you have applied yourself in action and decision. When we say that someone is "acting out of character," we are usually making an existential or moral criticism and referring to virtue (or a lack thereof).

Notice the connection here between virtue and *virtual* engine. When we speak of virtue, we are not speaking of an event but a set of conditions that have been cultivated systematically. This gives us a clue for thinking about character. What is the virtual engine for a person's development? What system of constraints condition your identity and behavior, and what system of constraints have you internalized that regulate your growth and development? If character is the virtual engine for this process, Socrates would say that most of us spend relatively little time on it.

Aristotle proposed a famous method for cultivating the conditions of character, cultivating virtue. He called it *The Golden Mean.* For example, what would it mean to become more courageous? We must pay attention to both kinds of constraints that condition the virtue. Where do you lack the enabling constraints? Where do you lack the selective constraints?

If you lack the enabling constraints, you do not have enough options or generation, and you will tend to behave more cowardly. When you identify too many options as courageous and lack selective constraints, you become foolhardy. You have to train yourself to steer between these, engaging in practices that will create a virtual engine over time.

You are a self-organizing process. Your actions modify the environment. These modifications feed back into you and change you. So here is the Aristotelian question. Are you letting this process run unchecked?

One of the most trenchant criticisms we can make of ourselves is that we are not living up to our potential. This has a significant effect on our estimation of life's meaning. Pay attention to this language.

You have created a virtual engine that controls your development, a system in which self-organization is regulated and shaped into self-improvement. This system regulates your growth as a person, and for Aristotle, the refinement of this system is necessary to a meaningful life.

Wisdom is the ability to cultivate character, to intervene in this self-organizing process so it develops in an optimal fashion to structure your virtual engine and cultivate a set of virtues. Wisdom means taking a direct and conscious hand in your own growth so you actualize your potential.

Aristotle defined a particular form of foolishness that comes from lack of character. He called it *akrasia*. We often translate it now as weakness of the will, but this translation has fingerprints of Protestant influence, which is anachronistic.[3] Akrasia refers to a behavior we all recognize in ourselves. You know the right thing to do, but you fail to do it (recall the chocolate cake from the previous chapter).

Here, we can put Aristotle and Plato together. Plato proposed a structure for the psyche, but Aristotle gave us a much more penetrating analysis of its structural-functional organization. For him, ignorance is when you do the wrong thing because you do not know better, but foolishness is when you do know better and still take the wrong actions or decisions. Although you may have the right beliefs, you do not have *sufficient character*. You have not trained the skills and sensitivities. You have not created a virtual engine that is regulating your development and growth. You are not living up to your potential.

It is difficult to talk about meaning without addressing its developmental aspect. What does it mean to live up to your potential, and why does it matter so much? Once again, it helps to use an Aristotelian analogy. How do we know when a knife is well-made? We might say that a good knife has a structural-functional

---

3. There is increasing scientific evidence to debunk our commonsense idea of will or willpower. The famous ego-depletion model of willpower, led by psychologist Roy Baumeister, has been subsequently challenged, and the associated experimental results have proven difficult to replicate.

organization that allows it to fulfill its purpose. If I actualize the potential in the base metal, organizing and structuring it in the right way, it will function well.

Notice that the idea of purpose is deeply associated with our sense of meaning. But how does a knife relate to human meaning? Human beings are not made the same way knives are made. We are self-organizing, but more than this, we are *self-making*. Philosophers Francisco Varela and Evan Thompson provide a useful term for this: *autopoiesis*.[4] A tornado is self-organizing, but it is not self-making. It cannot regulate the conditions that will create or destroy it. Your nature is different. Your structural-functional organization allows you to seek out the conditions of your development, conditions that will protect and promote your own self-organization. This makes you self-making.

Philosopher Eric Perl introduces this idea in his book entitled *Thinking Being*.[5] Remember that, for Aristotle, the "formal cause" or purpose of the living thing is its structural-functional organization. Autopoiesis is an integral part of the structural-functional organization of human beings, which gives us our Socratic capacity for self-transcendence and transformation. So you might say that the purpose of the living being—*your* purpose, if I may—is autopoiesis: to enhance your self-organizing capacity to be more of yourself, to develop your character and become the kind of being you have the potential to be.

For Aristotle, fulfilling your potential relates to your particularly human capacity. You are a rational, reflective creature. He stratified the potential of living (and nonliving) beings according to their degree of *in-formation*, their kind of structural-functional organization. For example, a plant is self-making, but all it really actualizes is the ability to digest. If you begin with inorganic matter and the inorganic matter becomes in-formed, it becomes a living

---

4. See Evan Thompson, "Life and Mind: From Autopoiesis to Neurophenomenology. A Tribute to Francisco Varela," *Phenomenology and the Cognitive Sciences* 3(2004), 381–398.
5. Eric Perl, *Thinking Being: Introduction to Metaphysics in the Classical Tradition* (Brill, 2014).

thing. At this level of complexity, we have plants. From here, Aristotle's stratum of living things graduates to more complex structures of in-formation. When they become self-moving, we have animals.

Aristotle accords human beings with a particular distinction in this hierarchy. We are self-moving beings that can actualize our self-movement and cultivate it rationally and deliberately with the development of character. Remember the word psyche—the origin of "mind" and "psychology"—originally referred to this elevated capacity for self-movement.

Socrates, Plato, and Aristotle have all contributed this teleology, this vision of human purpose, to optimize our mental capacity and take charge of it while cultivating a character that takes you as high up the hierarchy as you have potential to reach. Someone who lived only as a plant would be a failed and debauched human being, as would someone who lived only as an animal, the unreflective and impulsive monster, incapable of a single reflective decision.

For Aristotle, this hierarchy of in-formation continues past the obvious progression from animal to human being. Being a mere human being is not the highest attainment. You must become a good human being, a rational human being. You must inform your being with a virtual engine that actualizes those attributes—that structural-functional organization—that is most distinctive of humanity, that distinguishes us from plants, animals, and inanimate matter. This means to overcome self-deception, to cultivate your character, to realize wisdom, and to enhance the structure of your psyche and your contact with reality. Attaining your purpose as a human being means *becoming more of a human being*, fulfilling the potential of humanness itself, the very thing that separates you from the other forms of self-moving life.

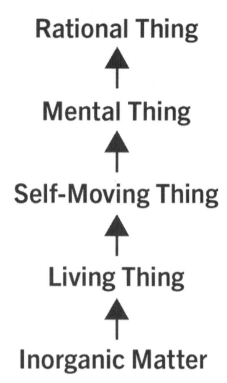

Rational Thing

↑

Mental Thing

↑

Self-Moving Thing

↑

Living Thing

↑

Inorganic Matter

Figure 6.6: The hierarchy reflects a more complex in-formation process occurring at each level, which produces the next evolved being. Inorganic matter is in-formed into living things, like plants. Living things are further in-formed into more complex, self-moving things, like animals. Self-moving things are in-formed into mental things, like human beings. Mental things, following the ideas of Socrates, Plato and Aristotle, can in-form themselves to become rational beings.

With his theory of wisdom and character, purpose and potential, and growth and development, Aristotle joined Pythagoras, Socrates, and Plato as a herald of the Axial Revolution. Though we still use his terms, we have lost the gravity of their significance. They have become tired and superficial. If we are to retrace and rejuvenate them, we need a fuller account of Aristotle's contribution to the historical development of human meaning. In the next chapter, we will explore an Aristotelian concept that is central to this development and, eventually, to the unraveling of this ancient vision of reality—the concept of worldview.

7

ARISTOTLE'S WORLDVIEW AND ERICH FROMM

In the previous chapter, we began to explore Aristotle's contributions to meaning and wisdom. He refined Plato's idea of eidos, structural-functional organization, by giving an account of change as a central element of human meaning. Aristotle understood change in terms of *in-formation*, the actualization of potential. This helped us to explore a cognitive scientific account of growth and development based on Dynamical Systems Theory, the idea of a virtual engine.

We discussed how crafting a virtual engine is related to cultivating virtue and Aristotle's idea of wisdom as the cultivation of character. This means regulating your self-development and self-making nature so you can actualize your potential for rational self-reflection, moving upward through that hierarchy of beings from the inanimate plant to the rational human and living up to the potential that inheres you.

Ataraxia, or foolishness, is the failure to live up to this potential, even when you have the correct set of beliefs. This raises the question for all of us: how much time do we spend on our character, especially when compared to our myriad of other projects?

Rediscovering Rationality: The Conformity Theory of Knowing

Aristotle proposed that rationality defined human beings. Here we must overcome yet another modern misframing. "Rationality" is often reduced to dispassionate logic, but Axial rationality has much more to do with second-order thinking, reflection, and self-correction, realizing potential through the cultivation of character.

Aristotle refined Plato's project of aligning psychic parts and reducing self-deception, but his idea of rationality also contributed to Plato's other meta drive—the need to be in contact with reality. Aristotle took up one of Plato's most persistent questions. What does it mean to truly *know* something? We often take knowledge to be justified true belief (i.e., I know what a chair is if I can describe it accurately), but who knows the chair better, one who can describe it or one who can craft it? Most of us would say the latter; if you can make a chair, if you can cause it to be, you have grasped something about its nature.

Aristotle then asked, "What does the chair maker have that the describer does not?" Remember that a description (like the wings, feathers, a beak, etc., of a bird) lacks the structural-functional organization. This is what the chair maker has that the describer does not. He has the eidos in mind. He can use it to actualize the potential in the wood, much like an architect who holds the blueprint of a building even before it is erected. This blueprint will in-form the material, and the pattern of the building will assume the pattern in the architect's mind. There will be *con-formity* between these entities. They will have the same structural-functional organization.

The architect "knows" in an Aristotelian sense. She could take the eidos in her mind and actualize it within some new potential, bring new material into conformity with the shape of the blueprint. Remember that "shape" is only an analogy for the Platonic/Aristotelian form, but it is a useful one for understanding conformity. I can try to know a cup by describing its shape, or I can conform to its shape by picking it up. When I grasp the cup, and my fingers wrap around it, my hand assumes its form. This empowers me to interact with the cup in a more causally efficacious manner. The interaction is more intimate, complex, and sophisticated.

For Aristotle, knowing is precisely this kind of con-formity. This is an ancient account rather than a modern one because it removes the distinction between knowing and being. Knowing requires that I *become* the cup, that I assume its form. I cannot remain apart from it. When I interact with the cup, I am adapting myself to its structure. I am not simply having beliefs about it. I am being changed by it. *Conformity* does not just change your beliefs; it changes the very structure and functioning of your being. You may begin to see how Aristotle's idea of knowing adds a powerful developmental dimension to Plato's relationship between self-transformation and our contact with reality.

Aristotle's *conformity theory* has been undergoing a meaningful revival within philosophy. Philosophers Charles Taylor and Hubert Dreyfus describe it as a "contact epistemology."[1] This should evoke the idea of *participatory knowing* introduced in chapter 1. To know something is to participate in its form, as opposed to descriptive knowing, where I stand apart from an object and generate propositions about it.

Conformity entails an intimate connection between mind and reality, and this connection is useful for understanding our mental processes. We are coming to see that this kind of contact participatory knowing is more central to cognition than previously thought. This theory of knowing is also a theory of being, and it satisfies the desire to be in contact with reality, to be connected to the world in an intimate way. This connection is so essential to our experience of meaning, and the revival of Aristotelian conformity may be responding to the alienation inherent to modern epistemology, the existential frustration we feel when our personal experience is irrelevant to our knowledge. This separation draws a curtain between us and the world and prevents us from participating in it. It makes us feel irrelevant to reality itself.

---

1. Hubert Dreyfus and Charles Taylor, *Retrieving Realism* (Harvard University Press, 2015).

When I am in conformity with the world, my patterns of sense making (i.e., my patterns of intelligibility)[2] are the same patterns by which the world is organized. However, conformity requires cultivation: second-order thinking, Socratic argument, and rational reflection. We cannot assume the pattern in our mind is the same as the pattern in the world unless we have subjected our thinking to a certain rigor, a rational authentication. For example, imagine for a moment that you have a romantic interest in someone you know ("Jesse"), and you confide the interest in your friend ("Tom").

All three of you were at a party the previous night, and Tom heard Jesse requite the interest. This is encouraging, but the last time Tom said something like this, he was wrong, and you acted impulsively. You want to be sure this time, so you challenge Tom's perception: Was he already drunk? Did he mishear over the music? Can anyone corroborate his story? Tom responds to all three doubts: He says he heard Jesse say this before he got drunk. He was in the kitchen away from the noise. Two of your mutual friends were in the kitchen with him and heard the exact same thing.

These three tests all help to convince you of Tom's information. You ensure that his cognitive organ was functioning normally (i.e., confirm his sobriety). You ensure that the environment did not distort his perception (i.e., confirm he could hear). Finally, you seek intersubjective agreement from other people to add plausibility to the story. Each of these measures help give you confidence that the pattern in Tom's mind matches the pattern of reality.

The Nomological Order and the Concept of Worldview Attunement

These criteria for authenticating conformity are all powerful philosophical techniques. Though they may seem obvious now, they are Aristotle's Axial invention: get your mind into an optimal state, make sure the medium is clear, and use intersubjective agreement to verify conformity. Aristotle's criteria may not be adequate, but they

---

2. Eric Perl, *Thinking Being: Introduction to Metaphysics in the Classical Tradition* (Brill, 2014).

were plausible and practical, and we use them to this day. Aristotle built on the work of the pre-Socratic natural philosophers, and for many centuries, Aristotelian thinking was identical to science itself. He speculated about nature's processes, the laws of motion, and the forces that organized the cosmos.

Like his contemporaries, Aristotle held a geocentric view of the world, and some of his ideas resemble those of Thales discussed in chapter 3. Aristotle proposed that inanimate things moved for the same reasons that animate things moved. When I lift a table, it seems to push against me, and the resistance feels no different than when a person pushes against me. Set aside your modern knowledge and consider how much sense this makes. When I lift an object away from the earth and let it go, it seems to move itself back into place, as though returning to where it belongs.

Aristotle imagined that everything was made up of the basic elements: earth, water, air and fire. Earth was at the center. Things that have a lot of earth in them, like rocks, are drawn back to it. As you move things away from the earth, things fall back toward it. Water rests on the surface, fire moves upward, and air is above. Consider how much sense this makes. When I burn wood, the fire comes up, the water that evaporates spreads out as condensation. The ash, the earthen part, falls down. For Aristotle, these elements are drawn to their natural resting places. Each has an internal drive. Everything moves with purpose, trying to be where it belongs.

This is a meaningful view of cosmic motion. It represents the fulfillment of your goals. It is important that we resist the temptation to scoff at Aristotle's geocentrism. The idea that the earth is not at the center but actually rotating was known in the ancient world.[3] However, there were astute counterarguments to this view; if the earth is rotating and I drop an object, would I not move forward with the rotation as the object falls behind me? Would I not feel the constant breeze on my face?

Until we understand universal gravitation, inertial motion, and other ideas in modern physics, the idea of earth rotating does not

3. Aristarchus of Samos was among the astronomers who challenged geocentrism.

make good sense of these observable phenomena. Aristotle's observations are still plausible and intuitive. Even though we are post-Descartes, post-Newton and post-Copernicus, we still move around the earth as if it is at the center, as if it is not moving. Aristotle's ideas fit together elegantly; we have a geocentric cosmos with the earth at its center, and everything moves by natural motion. The geocentric theory and conformity theory mutually support each other.[4] If I undertake Aristotle's three-part test, geocentrism becomes the intelligible pattern that prevails. It is plausible, it makes sense of what I see, it lends evidence that I am in conformity with reality. Notice these two things are now mutually supporting each other: *an account of the world and an account of how you know the world*. Together, they create a bond of plausibility. They create a *worldview*.

A worldview involves a bond between your understanding of the world and your understanding of your own understanding. The geocentric view is a view that makes sense of your actions. It is a world organized according to purpose, and the structure of the world is similar to the structure of your experience. In this view, the external world becomes an *arena*, a place that is organized in such a way that you know how to act within it.[5]

It makes sense to you, you know where things belong, what actions are appropriate, and how to calibrate your performance. If a football player steps onto a football field, he knows intimately how to interact with it and involve himself in it. It presents itself coherently to him, so he assumes the identity of "football player." Conformity provides *agency*. To be an agent is to be capable of pursuing your goals, to organize your cognition and behavior so that your actions fit the situation and the environment. A worldview is a coupling, a co-identification between agent and arena. The identity of the arena is determined by the identity of the agent and vice versa.

Aristotle's cosmos provided an exceptionally coherent agent-arena worldview. His idea of character explained how one became an

---

4. These terms are hyphenated because they are not separated in this theory the way that they are in our everyday language.

5. See John Vervaeke, Christopher Mastropietro, and Filip Miscevic, *Zombies in Western Culture: A Twenty-First Century Crisis* (Open Book Publishers, 2017).

agent, how you could know and structure yourself to conform to your environment. By providing the geocentric worldview, he also provided an arena—how the cosmos was organized so we could meaningfully interact with it. However, for our purposes it is important to understand that this agent-arena co-identification is not reserved for conformity at the cosmic scale. It is something we do all the time.

We are always assuming an identity. I am doing it now in this arena; I am assuming the identity of someone writing a book and assigning a relative identity to everything around me, including you, "the reader." This arena and my agency are co-defining one another. This is called an *existential mode*—the process by which agency and arena are co-identified to produce a coherent and functioning worldview.

This dynamic notion of worldview comes from anthropologist Clifford Geertz[6] and the idea of existential modes was proposed by philosopher Martin Buber and psychologist Erich Fromm respectively.[7] These ideas have all contributed significantly to our understanding of religion, which I will discuss in forthcoming chapters.

For now, it is sufficient to appreciate the following: if you do not have the agent-arena relationship, none of your particular actions have meaning. If I put the tennis player onto the football field, the relationship is absurd. The arena does not make sense, and the player's actions feel futile. Unless the coupling works, individual projects (recall the analogy to "projectiles") of meaning do not function. Geertz proposed that a worldview is a *meta-meaning relation or meta-meaning system*. The existential mode makes possible an entire system of meanings, like social rituals, rules of conduct, and measures of success and failure. Actions of throwing the ball, kicking the ball, catching the ball, and running to the endzone all have

6. Clifford Geertz, *The Interpretation of Cultures: Selected Essays* (Basic Books, 1973).
7. See Martin Buber, *I and thou*, trans. W. A. Kaufmann (Simon & Schuster, 1970) and Erich Fromm, *To Have or to Be?* Rev. ed. (New York: Continuum, 2005).

meaning for the football player, but their meaning depends on the fittedness and coherence of the agent-arena relationship.

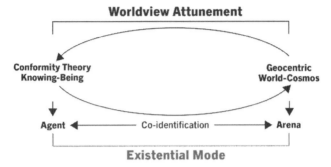

Figure 7.1: A diagram demonstrating the mutually supportive relationship between the geocentric world-cosmos (an account of the world) and the conformity theory (an account of how you know the world). The geocentric worldview is represented as the arena. The conformity theory represents how you become an agent. A worldview involves a coupling and co-identification of the agent and arena. The process of co-identification, which affords a coherent and functioning worldview, is called an existential mode. This whole process is referred to by Geertz as worldview attunement.

Consider that all of this is occurring right now as you read. You have assumed a particular identity, you have assigned one to me, and within this existential mode everything you do takes on a certain purpose and definition. This meta-meaning relationship is a particular instance, or enactment, of worldview. This Aristotelian process is not a static paradigm but a dynamic interplay of mutual fitting and intelligibility. This is why we call it a relationship. Geertz provides us with an appropriately dynamic term: *worldview attunement* (figure 7.1).

Your existential mode is the way you create co-identifications of agent and arena. In order to function, the mode must fit into a process of worldview attunement. Without it, the existential mode will not gain agency. You will be trying to play tennis on the football field. Your existence will feel absurd, and the world will not make sense to you. This is one of the most recurring expressions of the Meaning Crisis. Without a meta-meaningful existential mode, a functioning worldview attunement, we lose the agent-arena relationship, and with it, our sense of contact with reality.

Aristotle provided the ancient world with something both beautiful and powerful—a coherent relationship to the cosmos. He articulated a connection between our intellectual project of trying to understand the world and our existential project of belonging to the world. Many of us no longer find consonance between these dimensions. We have a scientific worldview, a view of how things are, but this worldview gives us no existential guidance or relevance. Our subjective experience vanishes before its objectivity.[8] It does not tell us how to make our lives meaningful.

Aristotle gave us a cosmos that was elegant and intelligible. When we have a worldview that provides reliable worldview attunement, existential modes wherein agent-arena relationships are blossoming naturally, we experience a deep connectedness between our intellectual projects (scientifically making sense of the world) and existential projects (finding meaning, belonging and fittedness in the world).

I call this sense of cosmic coherence the *nomological order.* Nomological order comes from "nomos," which means "law." This interconnected lattice of principles govern the structure and function of the world and all living beings within it. Though the Axial world was not without considerable suffering and privation, the nomological order made the world legible and meaningful. It was part of the symbolic scaffolding that turned the cosmos into a home. When a nomological order breaks down, we are afflicted by absurdity. We start to lose a sense of how we fit in, how we belong.

The Modes of Having and Being

To continue exploring existential modes, we must temporarily shift the focus of our discussion onto a different center of the Axial

---

8. This observation was acutely made by the Danish philosopher Søren Kierkegaard in his book, *Concluding Unscientific Postscript to Philosophical Fragments,* among other works.

Revolution—away from ancient Greece and Israel, and over to ancient India. I mentioned in chapter I that we are in the midst of a Mindfulness Revolution. People are responding to the Meaning Crisis through an intense scientific and existential interest in the phenomena of mindfulness and the philosophy of Buddhism. This Western movement is full of misapprehensions; we cannot understand the practices of meditation and contemplation, or the project of enlightenment, without properly understanding their origins.

If Socrates was the embodiment of the Axial Revolution in ancient Greece, Siddhartha Gautama was its embodiment in ancient India. Like its Western counterpart, the transformation in the East was driven by coinage and alphabetic literacy, but other psychotechnologies also came to the fore.[9] It is very important that we mind our ignorance when retracing these steps. Attempting to separate the Axial figures—Socrates, Siddhartha, and (as we will discuss later) Jesus—from their legacies is a quixotic impulse and misses the point of the project. We cannot presume too much knowledge about the historical Siddhartha or the other Axial figures. The alloy of history and myth generates their cultural impact and allows us to measure their symbolic influence.

The story, or myth, goes as follows. When Siddhartha was born, his father the king invited all of the sages and wise men to his birth. It was prophesized that the boy had one of two possible futures: he would be a great king or a significant religious figure. The king chose the former for his son. To encourage this path, he tried to remove any influence that might provoke Siddhartha into pursuing a religious life devoted to the ideals of the Axial Revolution. He lavished Siddhartha with the benefits of the preAxial world: power and prosperity, a life free from distress, beautiful women, and abundant food, all within the comfort and safety of a beautiful palace.

The palace is an important symbol in the Axial Revolution, not

---

9. The reasons for this are complex. I recommend Karen Armstrong's book *The Great Transformation: The Beginning of Our Religious Traditions*; she tries to explain how psychotechnologies of mindfulness became so prominent in ancient India and gives a coherent explanation about the historical and cultural factors that generated it.

unlike the cave in Plato's myth. It mythologizes a particular existential mode, evoking a certain mood and sensory experience. Its lavish comforts draw comparison to the firelight shadows of the cave, the world of illusion, a state of disconnection from reality that must be overcome for wisdom to be possible. Marcus Aurelius, the Roman emperor and Stoic philosopher, reflected extensively on this irony: that the comforts of health and power are not goals to pursue but obstacles to be overcome: *"It is possible to be happy even in a palace,"* he famously wrote. This is not likely something that a Bronze Age ruler would have written.

What kind of existential mode does the palace symbolize? This brings us to the work of Erich Fromm, a twentieth-century psychologist and philosopher. Fromm defined two different forms of co-identification with reality, two existential modes that determine how we craft the agent-arena relation and how we frame our relationship with ourselves, one another, and the world at large. These two forms, which Fromm calls the *having mode* and the *being mode*, are organized around two different kinds of needs, and they conduct two different forms of agency.

"Having" needs are met by controlling and categorizing an identity, knowing how to manipulate it. For example, to use a cup, I must categorize it as a cup. I invoke my Aristotelian knowledge of its structural-functional organization. I know how it functions as a cup and bears resemblance to all other cups. This allows me to grip it and replace or rebuild it when it breaks.

This kind of agent-arena relation provides power, efficiency, and control while allowing me to meet important homeostatic needs. If I do not have a "having" relationship with food and water, I would find myself unable to consume them. Fromm's "having mode" is very similar to what philosopher Martin Buber called an *I-it* relation. "I" takes the identity of controller or problem-solver, and "it" (my charge) takes the identity of an object or problem. This mode makes effective use of my intelligence and resourcefulness and serves an essential cognitive function. You need to have water. You need to have food. Nothing is immoral about the "having mode"—provided it applies to the right kind of agent-arena relationship.

In the being mode, I am not trying to solve problems, I am trying to make meaning by cultivating "reason" in its original Axial meaning. Being needs are not met by having something but by *becoming* something. Developing virtue or maturity, building character in Aristotle's sense, is not attained by acquisition but by effecting a change in your relationship with being and with the felt meaning of your existence. You are not relating to things categorically but *expressively*.[10]

Having Mode	Being Mode
Having needs	Being needs
Think categorically	Think expressively
Control & manipulation	Reciprocal realization
I-it	I-thou
Intelligence & problem solving	Reason & meaning making

Figure 7.2: The differences between the having and being modes.

For example, when you are in love with someone, you are engaged in a being need; your encounter with the person changes your identity and posture in the world. It changes the way you relate to your life, the way you pay attention, not just to the beloved but also to everything else. The world looks and feels different. You find yourself changing and desiring to change, regathering yourself around this new possibility. You desire to become more, to grow into the love and to follow it in an open-ended way. The change brings meaning, maturity, and growth. It is a relationship of mutual development and realization. This is one way to think about love and its power in the being mode. It is a process, or *anagoge,* of reciprocal realization. Martin Buber referred to this as an *I-thou* relationship.

These existential categories are very useful because they help us to distinguish between relational modes—for example, between love and lust. Notice how we talk about *making* love and *having* sex. When you love, the person you love is singular and irreplaceable. They are not one of many in a category but a category unto themselves. You cannot exhaust them or plunder their uses. There is always more of

---

10. See R. G. Collingwood. *The Principles of Art* (Oxford University Press, 2010).

them to discover, and your love is a willing journey for this discovery. Lust, when it is empty of love, is an appetite that belongs to the having mode. It is a relationship of categorical needs. You desire to consume the person as you would consume food or water. They are replaceable with others in the same category; a beautiful body is just another beautiful body, like the cup that reminds me of all the other cups.

Both modes have their place and proper functions, but Fromm observed that we often confuse them. We assume existential modes that do not adapt us properly to the corresponding need of an encounter. If I treat an Ikea cabinet as a source of wonder and intimacy, I will ignore the instructions and never build the cabinet. Assuming a being mode in response to having needs of life will make it impossible for me to function in the world. Conversely, if I treat a friend or lover as a resource for consumption—to use, control, or replace—I foreclose the possibility of a reciprocal relationship, and any consequent growth for myself or the other person. I may harm both of us in the process. As Aristotle might say, I would be shortchanging our human potential and not living up to myself. If I told my partner that she reminds me of every other woman I have been with, the relationship would end instantly.

Fromm calls this existential misframing a *modal confusion*: using the having mode to respond to the deepest needs of being. Modal confusion can easily be exacerbated by sophistry and bullshit. The whole premise of marketing is to invoke these "being needs"—like the want for intimacy and the striving for a meaningful life—within a having mode. I desire maturity so I buy a car; I long for intimacy so I download a hookup app.

These accessories do not satisfy the needs, of course. Instead, they lead to a *reciprocal narrowing*.[11] They shrink the world, and us, rather than expand them. They deplete our sense of possibility. They generate addictions and perseverating behaviors, vicious circles that deepen the modal confusion, disperse our attention, and cast us

---

11. A term introduced by Marc Lewis. https://memoirsofanaddictedbrain.com/connect/addiction-narrowing-opportunities-in-brain-and-environment/.

further from reason and transformation, away from our meaning-making potential.

Life in Siddhartha's palace is a myth for modal confusion, a vision of life lived entirely in the having mode. Yet the myth continues. Siddhartha's path of wisdom leads beyond the palace walls, just as Plato's leads beyond the cave. As we will discover in the next chapter, mindfulness will become Siddhartha's response to modal confusion and a revolutionary development in the Axial project of wisdom and enlightenment.

8

THE BUDDHA AND MINDFULNESS

The project of the Axial Revolution, along with its ideas of meaning and wisdom, consistently revolves around the notion of *realization*— how we participate in the structure of reality and thereby become more real. Aristotle's conformity theory was precisely this: a contact epistemology, an intimate bond of knowing and being. Our idea of the world and how we knew the world were mutually connected.

This worldview attunement meant a co-identified relationship between agent and arena. It was a meta-meaning system, a relational framework that made all individual acts, events, situations and places intelligible to one another. It gathered the world together and gathered us to the world. Aristotle's worldview married intellectual coherence with existential import; it provided a model of what the world was and how to interact with it. His cosmos was based in a geocentric idea of natural motion, but it was so plausible and well-attuned that it lasted for a millennium.

Worldview attunement provides us with existential modes—ways of framing our relationships as well as our interactions with people, problems, and situations. In the previous chapter, we explored these existential modes through the work of Erich Fromm and Martin

Buber.[1] The *having mode* perceives the world categorically as a problem to solve and control. The *being mode* perceives the world as an affordance for development and transformation.[2]

Modal confusion occurs when we assume an existential mode that misframes the corresponding existential need and fails to respond wisely to it—for example, pursuing belonging by acquiring social media followers or pursuing intimacy with sexual conquest. Modal confusion is a self-perpetuating condition, and it creates vicious cycles of missed projects and frustrated needs. You consume and consume but cannot transform.[3] This creates a narrowing of self and society, a sense of scarcity and futility. The world before you is desacralized, and you are more vulnerable to depression and despair.

This symptom of the Meaning Crisis is both historical and perennial; the dangers of modal confusion are always present in our cognition, but the loss of contact epistemology and other features of the Axial worldview make us particularly susceptible to it. Our modern economy and social rituals are conditioned to reflexively respond to being needs from within a having mode, whether this means acquiring fame, possessions, or other ephemeral gratifications. When we are modally confused, we are particularly susceptible to the blandishments of bullshit and other sophistic devices. Consider this in Aristotelian terms: the more your identity wraps itself around the having mode, the more it constricts your humanness. Our identity and agent-arena relationships are all creating one another, so our actions are existentially reflexive. If all your projects become "somethings" to have, you too become a something to have, rather than a *someone* to become.

---

1. See also the works of Stephen Batchelor, *Buddhism without Beliefs: A Contemporary Guide to Awakening* and *The Awakening of the West: The Encounter of Buddhism and Western Culture.*

2. James Carse makes a similar argument in his well-known book, *Finite and Infinite Games.*

3. In *Zombies in Western Culture: A Twenty-First Century Crisis*, my coauthors and I argue that the zombie's appetite of mindless devouring is a symptom of this modal confusion.

The Palace, the Four Sights, and the Awakened One

In the previous chapter, I proposed that life in the palace is a myth of modal confusion, a symbolic representation of an existence suspended in the having mode of relating. This tableau is where the story of Siddhartha Gautama begins.[4]

As Siddhartha's curiosity grows, he decides to leave the palace. He ventures out with Channa, his charioteer. As they travel, Siddhartha sees a sick person, and he becomes distressed. He wonders what is wrong.

Channa explains, "My lord, he is sick."

Siddhartha asks, "What did he do to cause this?"

"Nothing," Channa replies. "This happens to everyone. It is just the way of things."

This encounter is a turning point in the Axial Revolution. It is the beginning of some new inkling, an awakening, a revelation of the nature of suffering in the world.

"Could I get sick too?" Siddhartha asks Channa.

"Well, of course!" Channa replies.

Siddhartha asks Channa to drive him away. He does not want to see the sick person anymore.

They continue on their journey, and they meet an old person on the road. Siddhartha tells Channa to stop.

"Is that person also sick?" he asks.

"No, my lord," Channa replies. "He is not sick. He is old."

Siddhartha is confused. "Old? What do you mean?"

"This happens to everyone through the passage of time," Channa says.

"You mean he did not do anything to cause it?"

"No," Channa replies. "It was not his fault. He just became old."

After the encounter with the old person, Siddhartha decides to

---

4. There are, of course, many variations on this sacred story. My account of it is focused on a specific purpose, so it is impressionistic rather than canonical. Readers looking for a more precise account should look elsewhere.

return to the palace. On his way, he meets a funeral procession and catches a glimpse of the corpse.

"Is that person sick?" Siddhartha asks Channa. "Is he old?"

Channa replies: "No, my lord. The person is dead. He is not alive anymore."

"But why?" Siddhartha asks.

"Well, my lord, it happens to everyone ..."

Notice what is occurring here. Siddhartha's relationship with the world is undergoing a sudden, radical change. The comforts of the palace, where the conditions of life are gently controlled, is disappearing. It has not prepared him for life's inexorable suffering, the pain of illness, the loneliness of aging, or the absurdity of death. The revelations are overwhelming.

Siddhartha is experiencing a powerful existential crisis. He orders Channa to return him to the palace. He wants to forget these encounters and submerge himself back into the safety of home. But as they hurry back, Siddhartha meets one more person, a beggar. Siddhartha senses a deep peace in this beggar's eyes, a great contrast to his own distress.

"Who is this?" Siddhartha asks Channa.

"He is a mendicant, my lord, a wandering person."

The mendicant is an ascetic who has renounced the having mode and all of life's luxury. His example confronts Siddhartha with an alternative to the palace life he knew. The man has nothing, but his countenance is tranquil. He does not frame life's meaning by what he possesses or controls. Siddhartha feels the contrast poignantly and painfully. The prince's entire worldview has been thrown into confusion. He returns to the palace with these encounters, these four sights, burning in him—illness, old age, death, and this mysterious emissary from another way of being.

The man's example was so unknown to him that it was like an *aporia*, a gaping hole in Siddhartha's plush carpet of predictable quantities. After this encounter, Siddhartha would not be able to find home again. He could not return to the palace, even if he stayed there for the rest of his life.

The physical palace remained, of course, but the mythic

container of the palace, the paradigm and worldview it symbolized, was lost in the wake of these encounters. The four sights seared Siddhartha's vision and caused him profound *disillusionment*. The motif of "disillusionment" is prominent in all Axial myths—coming into consciousness, moving into despair, and experiencing the loss of illusion. It is the passage from childhood to adulthood, the awareness of suffering, the responsibility of existence, and the sense of loneliness we all feel when confronting our finitude and mortality.

The having mode of the palace is illusory because it draws a veil of distraction over these conditions of existence and inflates our despair with the anxiety of avoidance. Once awake, there is no returning to the oblivion of the palace except with the irony of knowing its illusion, much like the prisoner returning to Plato's Cave.

Disillusionment is a one-way journey. As we discussed in previous chapters, we have a powerful meta-drive to be in contact with reality, and this drive prevails over comforts and sybaritic pleasures. After his four sights, Siddhartha realizes he has only one choice left. He must change his life.

However necessary, leaving the palace is not an easy choice for Siddhartha. He has a wife and child, and we might criticize him ethically for his abandonment of his family. However, this myth, and Siddhartha's moral life, rests on something deeper. His responsibility to family is important, but moral responsibility can feel weightless when a person loses his broader sense of meta-meaning.

Morality, however we define it, seems to depend on our worldview attunement, on a prevailing sense of virtue and wisdom that sustains its perspective. We will discuss this connection more in subsequent chapters.

So Siddhartha cuts his hair, leaves the palace, and goes into the forest. He decides to follow the path of the renouncers, searching for a solution to the fear and turmoil that reverberate in him. He encounters various teachers and practices, but the ascetic path does not free him from the having mode. The palace had been rife with self-indulgence, so Siddhartha compensates with self-denial.

Representations of him from this period resemble an anemic specter. He subjects his body to trial and pain to force it into submission. He starves himself until he's gaunt, until his belly withdraws and presses into his spine. He embarks on a path of self-annihilation. He tries to dispel the illusion of the palace, to purge his foolishness by purging himself altogether.

In the wake of his disillusionment, his self has become an unbearable burden, and he wants to be rid of it. You will notice that his efforts are still modally confused. Self-denial is an aspect of the same existential mode as self-indulgence. It is the *negation* not the *transcendence*. It frames his relationship to the world in the same way. Siddhartha's self is still a thing to have or not to have, and he cannot stand to have it any longer.

One day, Siddhartha is sitting on the banks of a river, fatigued. He hears a barge coming down the river. A musician is playing a lyre, teaching his apprentice.

"No, no, no, listen to me," the musician says. "The lyre strings cannot be too tight or too loose. Too tight is just as bad as too loose."

This simple instruction begins to herald a profound change in Siddhartha's perspective, a new relation to life that will begin to unfold. The insight is also catalyzed by a dramatic event. Siddhartha tumbles into the river, begins to drown, and is saved by a little girl. In the culture of the time, it was very demeaning for a man, especially a prince, to be rescued by such a modest figure. Something radical in this occurrence symbolizes the change taking place within Siddhartha. He begins to discover *the middle path*.

You may recall Aristotle's golden mean; the middle path is not a compromise between two undesirable options. It is a transcendence of the having mode of life, a rejection of both extremes: the self-indulgence of the palace and the negating self-denial of the ascetic life. The middle path seeks the right kind of connection with reality, an optimal conformity to the conditions of existence that reduces the unnecessary suffering caused by human foolishness.

Siddhartha remembers the peace he glimpsed in the eyes of the mendicant. His remembrance is not a memory of the encounter itself but a modal memory, the recollection of a way of being, even one he has never experienced. This kind of modal memory does not simply look backward or forward but rather inward. It is the memory of a human identity, of who you are, who you were, who you could be.

It is similar to the sensation of returning to a place you lived but have not visited for some time. You remember the events that transpired there, but when you return, you remember what it meant to be there. You remember what it was like to be yourself in that place and at that time. This modal memory brings you back to a presence of mind. It invokes the perspectival and participatory knowing we were talking about in earlier chapters. The original word for this form of memory is *sati*, but the word we commonly use now is "mindfulness."

Mindfulness evokes a multitude of meanings now, especially in the West where it is undergoing a cultural revolution. The "being mode" is not usually the meaning that comes to mind although some astute authors have made the connection.[5] Many mindfulness practices preceded Siddhartha, psychotechnologies that helped the mendicants gain reflective distance and perspective on the world.

However, although Siddhartha learned from his teachers, he found these psychotechnologies inadequate. He did not just want intellectual insight. He wanted a new way of being in the world, an existential posture that could bear the weight of pain, aging, death, and all the sufferings of existence. His was a quest for realization, to awaken from the somnolent vacuum of his life in the palace and the despair that afflicted him since the day of his four sights. He wanted to find himself in a new relationship with being. The name Siddhartha would eventually take—the name we all know him by— is not a name at all but rather a title. The Buddha means "the Awakened One."

Mindfulness, Memory, and the Meaning Crisis

Enthusiasts of contemporary mindfulness movements have the tendency to romanticize enlightenment, but the project is painful,

---

5. See Stephen Batchelor, *Alone with Others: An Existential Approach to Buddhism* (Grove Press, 1983).

just as it is painful to abandon childhood. Waking up from a halcyon dream brings distress and disorientation. There is precious little triumph in being evicted from a familiar worldview, having to step into a cold and unsolicitous reality. If awakening is enlightenment, it must attain more than the absence of illusion.

The distress that beset Siddhartha in the wake of his four sights is the despair that awaits us in the nowhere land between disillusionment and awakening. This despair is also reflected in Christian and other Axial myths. The loss of the palace (or the garden) is a loss of cosmic home. It induces a consciousness of suffering (or sin) and the lonely responsibility of confronting existence nakedly, without the container of the protective dream. Our Platonic longing for reality is powerful, and it bars us from returning to the palace. It leaves us stranded between one place and another. We outgrow one life without a fuller one to adopt, and we forget what it was like to be the self we knew. This forgetfulness is a kind of existential homelessness, or *domicide*, the sensation of being cut loose from the cosmic order and drifting into an empty vacuum of arbitrary pains and decisions.

The crisis of domicide scales from the individual to the collective. What each person might experience as a feature of her life and growth, we seem to be experiencing as a culture and society. The modern succession of Scientific Revolutions, including those of Copernicus, Newton, and Darwin, have decentered both the earth and humanity from their cosmic priority. They have deprived us from the elegant coherence of Aristotle's nomological order.

The geocentric and anthropocentric cosmos has become less plausible, and we have become less relevant to its motions and designs. The disillusionment comes with a kind of forgetfulness. We have lost the concentering sense of identity, the core humanness that Aristotle valued so deeply. We cannot ignore these Scientific Revolutions and submerge ourselves nostalgically in an outmoded worldview, but neither can we remain in this place of irrelevance and disenchantment, this indefinite existential amnesia. This experience of awakening must include *sati*. We must awaken not just *from* something but *into* something, like the prisoner in Plato's Cave.

His revelation is also a recollection. He wakes up and recovers his world and identity. He beholds everything as if for the first time, a fullness that was ever-present but just out of sight. We can play with the term "re-member" to remind ourselves of the kind of memory that makes us a member to reality again, to rejoin the cosmic order, to relieve the domicide of the Meaning Crisis and belong again to oneself and to the world. This remembrance was the aim of Siddhartha's mindfulness project. It is also, of course, the project of this book.

The modern Mindfulness Revolution has attempted to recover parts of Siddhartha's project, and there has been an explosion of scientific interest in this topic over the last couple of decades. There is much to be appreciated in this movement; it has afforded a more precise empirical account of what occurs in mindfulness practice. However, as any responsible scientist must be, I am also critical of this work. It has created certain misapprehensions about the nature of mindfulness and its aims.

Siddhartha did not seek a single antidote to life's suffering, but cultivated a series of psychotechnologies to help sustain *sati* and recover the being mode of existence. Together with my colleague Leo Ferraro, I have worked to develop an account of the cognitive process at work in these psychotechnologies.[6] A cognitive scientific account of the mindfulness project can help us to understand this project more clearly, but it requires us to place a foot in both academic and practical domains.

I study mindfulness scientifically—that is, I conduct experiments and publish theoretical work—and practically; I also teach meditative and contemplative practices and extracurricular Tai Chi Chuan, a form of moving mindfulness. If we are to understand this project in all its dimensions, we must avoid the modal confusion between "having" a theoretical grasp and "being" a participant in the

6. John Vervaeke and Leonardo Ferraro, "Reformulating the Mindfulness Construct," in *Hypnosis and Meditation: Towards an Integrative Science of Conscious Planes* (Oxford University Press, 2016).

practice. This means minding the distinction between the *language of explaining* and *language of training*.

The language of explaining corresponds to propositional knowing. It allows us to study and scientifically analyze the phenomenon. The language of training corresponds to the procedural, perspectival and participatory forms of knowing. It invites imitation and involvement and helps people acquire the skills to practice. The pragmatics of a situation determine the appropriate mode—for example, am I trying to teach a student how to meditate, or explain what happens in her brain as she meditates? The different languages can inform one another in ways that advance both projects. However, if we mistake their identities, we can confuse both projects and distort their meaning and application.

The "language of training" often involves an imaginal form of relating that conduces a certain phenomenological encounter and agent-arena dynamic. For example, the ancient Greeks and Romans cultivated powerful mnemonics, practices for training the facility of working memory. This psychotechnology evolved and was refined throughout antiquity and the Middle Ages.[7] One of the most effective mnemonic techniques is called the *method of location* or *the method of loci*. You use your imagination to visualize a structure—a "memory palace"—and furnish that structure with images that evoke specific memories or fragments of information.

For example, if I want to retain certain knowledge of Socrates, I might store a figure of Socrates in one room of the imaginal palace and position various items in that room—pieces of furniture, or articles of clothing—to stand for different aspects of his ideas and biography. When I need to remember him, I remember the mind palace. I call up the structure, enter his room, and access the images. I might store Pythagoras in another room and Aristotle in another. The method of loci is a powerful tool. The orators of the ancient world could use it to memorize and recite speeches that would last up to six hours.

---

7. These techniques are depicted in many ancient, medieval, and Renaissance writers, including Cicero's *De Oratore* and Giordano Bruno's *Ars Memoriae*.

Technology has made these memory methods less prolific, of course, but they remain highly effective and powerful. However, these mnemonics can mislead us when they are translated into scientific explanation; we might be tempted to infer that memory is organized like a mind palace in the brain. This is called the *spatial metaphor of memory*: the notion that my memories, like my image of Socrates, are static entities stored in a cognitive library, a chamber of records grouped by topic and association. When I need to recall a memory, I imagine that a homunculus is dispatched to rifle through rooms and files. He pulls the relevant file and passes it up to consciousness. This metaphor is implicit in our everyday parlance. We often use words like search and storage when referring to the workings of memory.

We know now that the spatial metaphor of memory is just that—a metaphor. Your memory does not function this way.[8] A few quick exercises debunk this model. For example, if I ask you to quickly name a color associated with blue, you might say red or green. If I ask you to name a word that rhymes with "blue," you might say "new" or "shoe." "Red" relates to "blue" and "blue" relates to "shoe." But does "red" relate to "shoe"? The association does not carry.

The spatial memory also fails to account for self-aware ignorance. You generally know when you do not know something. What is Meryl Streep's phone number? Have you ever been to Mars? When I ask you these questions, do you embark on a systemic search of your memory banks? No, you instantly know you have never been on Mars. The homunculus does not search the space. In fact, it seems like he does not search at all.

Memory is much more mysterious than it seems. It does not operate in the manner suggested by spatial metaphors. The mind palace is powerful for training your memory, but it is too simplistic as a way of explaining memory. For the same reasons, the language by which we train mindfulness should not be uncritically adopted in our scientific investigations.

Mindfulness practice involves training attention. It is often

---

8. Michael W. Eysenck & Mark T. Keane. *Cognitive Psychology: A Student's Handbook* (Psychology Press, 2010).

described, metaphorically, as shining a spotlight on the present moment, on the "here and now." But what does it mean to be "here and now"? To live in this second? This minute? The last five minutes? The room you sit in? The city you live in? The entire solar system? The "here and now" does not have a singular or scientific meaning. It is called an *indexical*. It is relative to the context we share and establish, used to augment our perception and reweave a relationship with reality.

The language of training is symbolic, but that does not mean it is impotent or unreal. Its reality is phenomenological rather than scientific. Both modes of understanding mindfulness are key to its reformulation, and the recovery of Siddhartha's project of awakening.

Plato can be a powerful ally in this recovery. Remember his concept of the *eidos*. Knowledge is not captured by a list of features. The bird is not just the wings, the feathers, or the beak but the structural-functional organization. Definitions of mindfulness tend to turn into feature lists. To be mindful is to be present, to not judge, to seek insight, to reduce reactivity. These are important characteristics, but they do not amount to an eidos.

We must turn this feature list into a feature *schema* that can reinterpret and explain the structural-functional organization. We can do this by connecting the four core features of mindfulness to independent theoretical claims within psychology and carefully distinguishing between them. For example, being present and not judging are states I can step into, things that I can do or not do, activities I can start or stop. Conversely, insightfulness and reduced reactivity are not states I slip into but rather traits of character that I can develop. These traits are the outcomes, the results of my activities. I want to become more insightful to become less reactive.

By making this distinction, certain questions arise. How does being present or withholding judgment lead to insight or reduce reactivity? How do we understand the causal relation between states and traits of mindfulness? The feature list that lacks an eidos has limited explanatory power. It does not address these constitutive questions about part-whole relationships. Are the traits a part of the states or vice versa? Are they all part of a greater whole? What is the structural relationship between them?

When we begin to answer these questions with the language of explaining rather than the language of training, we will begin to turn a feature list into a feature schema. We will start to access the structural-functional organization of mindfulness and gain a deeper understanding of its works. That will help us to see how mindfulness can bring about the kind of radical transformations that were promised by Siddhartha's realization.

Let us focus on one of these causal relationships. The state of *being present* causes the trait of *insightfulness*. How do we begin to unpack this? The trait of insightfulness is not the event of a single insight. It is a modal transformation that affords the event of insight. Meanwhile, the language of "being present" is relatively nondescript. People often refer to "concentration," but the term is too equivocal. When Siddhartha explains the state, he invokes *right* concentration. This implies that there is also *wrong* concentration. What does that mean? If we explain the difference in terms of attention, we run into the same problem; we default to a particular model of attention that may not apply.

Let us consider this question of concentration more closely and phenomenologically. We will use the work of Ellen Langer, a Harvard psychology professor who wrote one of the first influential books on mindfulness in the West, well before the current revolution was underway.[9] Hold your finger in front of your face. For fifteen seconds, tell yourself persistently to concentrate on your finger so you do not lose focus.

Most of you would find the exercise quite unpleasant. Notice the meaning of the word "concentrate" and the metaphor it paints. You turn your mind into a tunnel and fasten it onto something. You try to hold it there and not let it move. The only training we are typically given in the art of concentration is some version of this command: Yell at yourself, admonish yourself, hold your own attention by force.

Now try it another way. Look at your finger and notice its features.

---

9. Ellen Langer, *Mindfulness* (Addison-Wesley, 1992).

Notice that it is not perfectly straight. Notice it is bent. Notice it is thicker at the bottom than at the top. Notice it is lined and creased. This experience of concentration is quite different. Is it not? Ellen Langer calls this *soft vigilance*; you are not hardening your mind and sticking it to an object. Instead, you constantly try to renew your interest in order to achieve the conformity Aristotle described. You are opening the object to exploration, becoming involved with it, and developing a more intimate and discerning contact with it.

Remember the lesson Siddhartha learned from the musician on the riverbank. Paying attention too hard by forcing or flagellating yourself—tuning the strings too tightly on your instrument—will be laborious and ineffective. However, if you let your attention wander freely without focus or intent—if you tune the strings too loosely—it will be equally ineffective. Attention is an instrument, and there is a musicality to the intelligibility that it can access when it is attuned.[10]

It is not a spotlight, but a very complex optimization process. When you find its golden mean, it conforms you more intimately to the world and allows you to become more involved, more interested, more connected to your own experience. The spotlight metaphor of attention is popular in psychology because it captures the effect of salience. Attention makes things brighter. It makes things stand out, and the brightness determines what seems real and relevant. But while the spotlight metaphor is useful for capturing salience, it misses the mark for explaining optimization, and how essential it is for insight.

Philosopher and cognitive scientist Christopher Mole provides a complex argument for this optimization that I will briefly attempt to summarize.[11] Think about the words "walk" and "practice." If I ask you to walk, the instruction is clear. You know what action to take. If I ask you to practice, you might ask, practice what? The idea of practice always relates to another activity. If I am practicing chess, I am also

10. See also: John Russon, *Bearing Witness to Epiphany: Persons, Things, and the Nature of Erotic Life* (SUNY Press, 2009).
11. See Christopher Mole, *Attention Is Cognitive Unison: An Essay in Philosophical Psychology* (Oxford University Press, 2010).

playing chess. If I practice tennis, it means I am playing tennis. More specifically, I am trying to optimize *how* I play tennis.

One of Mole's insights is this. We pay attention through optimization. The instruction to "pay attention" can mean many different things. It can mean to optimize your seeing so it becomes looking and watching. It can mean optimizing your hearing so it becomes listening. If I ask you to pay attention in the abstract, without working to improve or optimize an activity, you would struggle. Your attention would wander. You would not know what to do. Attention without optimization is adrift.

When we optimize different processes together, such as seeing-looking and hearing-listening, we create what Mole calls *cognitive unison*, coordinating various processes so they harmonize, work together, and share the same goal, just like Plato's tripartite psyche. This unison is one of the goals of mindfulness practice and the cultivation of attention. It equips the capacity for insight—not insight related to a specific problem but a state of awakening that motivates and empowers people to radically transform themselves, giving them a chance to escape from modal confusion and other existential dilemmas.

9

INSIGHT AND MINDFULNESS

In the previous chapter, we discussed the mythic journey of Siddhartha Gautama, and the four sights that exiled him from his luxurious life in the palace. We explored his disillusionment and ascetic self-deprivation, his quest to find a mode of being, and a remembrance of reality (sati) that could ameliorate his existential anxiety. This led us into a discussion of mindfulness, a set of psychotechnologies for cultivating this remembrance, a way of rediscovering a *being mode* of existence that can alleviate domicide—a sense of homelessness in the world that is a perennial feature of life but also a modern historical predicament.

I discussed the revival of mindfulness traditions in the West, noting that modern practitioners often regard mindfulness as a list of states and traits without understanding how they fit together, confusing the language of training (the exercise of practice) with the language of explaining (the scientific account). This mistaken identity also affects our understanding of mindful attention, which is not a spotlight of screwed-up concentration but an absorbing interest that practices and improves some other activity.[1] This insight brought us

---

1. Ellen Langer, *Mindfulness* (Addison-Wesley, 1992).

to the work of Christopher Mole and the idea of attention as a process of optimization.

Attentional Scaling: Transparency and Opacity

You may recall Mole's idea of cognitive unison, coordinating multiple processes of attention around a shared, developmental goal. This concept is critical for explaining how mindfulness trains attention and can make an individual more disposed to experiences of insight. Mole's concept relates to the work of another important philosopher and cognitive scientist, Michael Polanyi, who proposed that attention had a certain operational structure.[2]

Try running the following experiment. Take a pen in your hand and close your eyes. Use the pen to tap another nearby object, like a coffee mug or the book in your hands. Focus your awareness on the object and, as you tap it, form an image of the object in your mind. You are using the pen like a probe to explore the object, to determine its shape, structure, weight, and density. Then, still tapping, try shifting your awareness into the probe. Feel how the pen is moving and shifting. Then, shift your awareness into your fingers. Feel how your fingers are moving. Note the sensations that occur. Now, go backward; feel how your fingers are moving and then feel how the probe is moving. Then allow the tapping to reveal the object once again.

Most people find this experiment relatively easy, but it shows something profound about the way our attention can migrate. When you are initially tapping, you are aware of your object, but less aware of your fingers and pen. When your awareness moves into your pen and fingers, you are less aware of the cup. When your awareness settles into the object, you don't completely lose your awareness of the probe. If you did, you would not be able to manipulate it. You were not aware *of* the probe as much as aware *through* the probe. In a manner of speaking, your probe was "transparent" to you while the object was "opaque."

---

2. Michael Polanyi, *The Tacit Dimension* (Anchor Books, 1967).

People like me who wear glasses have this experience all the time. When my glasses are on, they are transparent to me; I am looking through them, beyond them, and by means of them. However, I can redirect my awareness by taking off my glasses. I can look *at* my glasses rather than look *through* them. When I remove my glasses, they become opaque to me, and I perform what the psychologist Michael Apter calls a *transparency to opacity shift*.[3] When I am aware of the object through my probe, I have what Polanyi calls a *subsidiary or an implicit awareness* of the probe and a *focal or an explicit awareness* of the object.

Polanyi's insight is profound: attention seems to be a structuring phenomenon. It functions through subsidiary awareness (of a probe) and into focal awareness (of an object). In the experiment, you were able to shift the subsidiary awareness into focal awareness—focusing on the object, back into the probe, back into your fingers, and then into the feelings of your fingers. The whole time you were focusing on the object, you were implicitly aware of each link in this sequence.

The spotlight metaphor of attention is missing this layered, recursive, dynamic kind of structuring. Our awareness is dexterous, and the transparency-opacity shift can move in both directions; your focus can move from your fingers to the probe and then back into your fingers. Your attention is doing this all the time—shifting back and forth, flowing in and out, turning objects transparent, turning them opaque, and then turning them transparent again.

As Christopher Mole observed, attention involves many different processes being coordinated and integrated together. When this coordination happens, it optimizes and prioritizes a particular object, scene or situation.[4] Though attention does not always involve vision in the literal sense, we often use spatial metaphors that correspond to the way vision is oriented in our bodies—for example, metaphors such as "stepping back," "looking at," or "looking through."

When you were exploring the object through the probe, you were

3. Michael J. Apter, "Metaphor as Synergy," *Metaphor: Problems and perspectives* (1982): 55–70.
4. See also: Sebastian Watzl, *Structuring Mind: The Nature of Attention and How It Shapes Consciousness* (Oxford University Press, 2017).

somehow dwelling inside the probe. Your perspective was inside its experience, and you participated in its encounter with the object. You were not knowing the pen, but knowing through the pen.

The interest that guides your attention is something closer to Aristotle's conformity. Interest derives from *interesse*—"to be between"—and it connotes a deeper kind of concern. My interest conforms my attention to the probe, and through the probe into the object. This model of attention is not only true of technology, like the glasses or the pen, but also of psychotechnologies. This is how we attain the second-order thinking discussed in previous chapters. We have integrated literacy into our cognition so thoroughly that we do not merely look at it. We look through it. We think by means of it.

Attentional Scaling: Feature and Gestalt

Polanyi's transparency-opacity shift crosses axes with another important kind of attentional scaling. We often imagine attention, in the metaphoric language of training, as something that moves "in" and "out" or "up" and "down"—whether it is directed out in the world, or inside, toward the center of the mind. Our attention searches for the right level of focus. For example, consider the following famous image:

TAE CAT

Figure 9.1: The feature-gestalt axis of attention. Although the second letter in each word is identical, you perceive it as an "H" in the first word and an "A" in the second word. Your attention simultaneously moves up from the features (the letters) to the gestalt (the word) and back down from the gestalt to the features. This allows you to read the ambiguous words clearly as "the cat."

In all likelihood, you read this image as "the cat." Then you noticed that you read the same undefined letter in two different ways —as H in "the" and A in "cat." Why did you do this so automatically? It just fits, you might say. But how did you arrive at it so quickly?

Let us use the language we developed in a previous chapter. In the above image, the letters are the features, and the phrase is the gestalt, the overall structure. Reading poses a problem—an almost Zen-like problem—if we think of our attention in a linear, sequential manner. In order to read the words, I must read each individual letter. But to disambiguate each letter, I must read the whole word. The spotlight metaphor of attention cannot address this catch-22 between feature and gestalt. If this model is true, reading must be impossible.

Reading is not impossible, of course, so our model of attention must change. In chapter 7, we discussed the concept of self-organizing, dynamical systems, and selective and enabling constraints. Our attention must be understood with this machinery in mind. When we read, our focus is moving up and down simultaneously—from the features (the individual letters) to the gestalt or eidos (the words or phrases) and back to the features. Meanwhile, we are in a constant flow of transparency-opacity shifting. We read through the words on a page until we come upon a word we do not know. Then we look at the word, learn it, and begin to see through it. Your attention does this continuously. It is doing it right now, as you read this page.

Mindfulness has to do with making use of this complex, dynamical processing: the "up-down" scaling of feature/gestalt, the "forward-back" movement of transparency/opacity. These dynamic, self-organizing processes can be optimized by mindfulness practices.

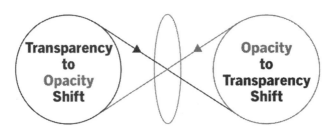

Figure 9.2: Directionality of the transparency-opacity shifting nature of attention.

It is important to understand that there is no absolute marker for transparency-opacity, no given position that is always more transparent or opaque. These are always relative positions, and the direction matters. For example, when I move to the left, following the diagram (figure 9.2), I am shifting from transparency to opacity (stepping back and looking at). When I move to the right, I shift from opacity to transparency (stepping in and looking out). We can also improve this diagram by adding the up-down nature of attention:

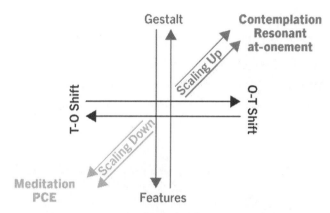

Figure 9.3: Depiction of the right-left (or in-out) nature of attention through transparency-opacity shifts with the up-down nature of attention as it moves up from the features to the gestalt or vice versa. This is not a cartesian plane because the relationships between these components are relative and not absolute. No point is inherently a gestalt or inherently a transparent state.

Much like transparency-opacity, the positions of feature and gestalt are always relative. Nothing is inherently or absolutely a feature. Letters are features in a word, but a word is a feature in a sentence, and this sentence is a feature in this book. This is why the diagram is depicted with double arrows. It is not a Cartesian graph but a schema.

Although I can describe these two axes independently, they are almost always operating in a highly integrated fashion. As I am moving toward a gestalt—grabbing a "bigger picture"—I am using the pattern to look more deeply into the world. I am stepping into the picture as it grows. Moving from feature to gestalt synchronizes with my shift from opacity to transparency. This is what we do in science:

features constellate into a pattern, and we perceive through that pattern to peer in the world.

Consider Newton's *F=ma*; he integrated the variables of force, mass, and acceleration, allowing us to speculate more deeply about the physical nature of reality. Conversely, when we step back and look at our minds and awareness processes, we are often breaking up the gestalt view into features. In the previous chapter's experiment, you divided the perception of your finger into specific details in your finger. In the probe experiment, you divided the whole of the object into individual moments of contact with your probe, breaking up the entire sensation to individual sensations. The two axes of movement synchronize to scale our attention and create our experience of the world. We can summarize this scaling in the following diagram:

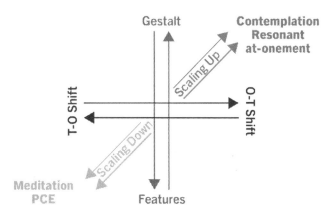

Figure 9.4: The scaling of attention. The different directions of attention come together to produce a dynamical, highly integrated system. We move from feature to gestalt to gain a "bigger picture" or more comprehensive understanding. This involves a shift from opacity to transparency and is a scaling up of attention. When I move from gestalt to the feature—for example, when I am trying to understand the details of my awareness processes—I shift from transparency to opacity. I scale down my attention.

Mindfulness Practice: Meditation and Contemplation

Now that we have explored the attentional machinery, we can begin to map the mindfulness practices. I teach vipassana, a very traditional form of meditation. Metaphors for meditation often refer to a movement toward the center. It is closely related to this idea of scaling. In vipassana, we typically train people by telling them to pay attention to their breath and track the feelings and sensations in their abdomen as they inhale and exhale.

The meditator is trying to cultivate that soft vigilance we practiced in the finger experiment. It is an exercise of optimization. The practitioner is trying to maintain and renew their interest in their breath to keep it salient to themselves. For beginners, it is very challenging to maintain this interest; we don't normally pay attention to our embodied sensations. Meditation requires more deliberate transparency-opacity shifting. We usually pay attention to the world through our feelings and sensations.

Vipassana requires us to step back to look *at* our feelings and sensations. The shift from transparency to opacity is paired with a scaling from gestalt to feature. We often experience our affective states as a morass, a tangle of different, even contradictory feelings that form an amorphous mass within us.

Meditation allows us to scale down our attention so we can break apart this gestalt mass and observe individual feelings and sensations —the different parts of our experience. You can imagine why these practices would be attractive to one who seeks wisdom, whether Socratic self-knowledge or Siddhartha's *sati*. Our tangled feelings often leave us anxious or confused. There is obvious value in a practice that can help to distinguish and examine those affective forces that motivate our actions and decisions.

Meditation and vipassana—moving toward the center—involve a scaling-down process of attention. It is, therefore, advisable to pair these practices with a complementary technique that can move in the opposite direction. Consequently, I also teach my students a contemplative practice that scales attention up. The West often treats meditation and contemplation as synonyms, but this reflects a profound misunderstanding.

The Latin etymology of contemplation features the word "temple" at its center. This word originally referred to the part of the sky where we looked to receive signs from the gods. To contemplate is to look up, to gaze toward the divine. The Latin *contemplatio* is translated from the Greek word *theoria*. This is the origin of "theory," of course, but theoria did not mean simply generating a propositional theory.

Theoria was an embodied state of being. It referred to the process of seeing and participating more deeply in reality. While meditation is a movement inward (scaling down), contemplation is a movement outward (scaling up). When I first learned these practices, I was taught three techniques in an integrated fashion: vipassana meditation, a scaling down strategy; *metta contemplation*, a scaling up strategy; and *Tai Chi Chuan*, a movement strategy to integrate these attentional scales while cultivating a flow in these inner and outer movements in a dynamic and optimizing fashion. It is important to remember that mindfulness, properly understood, is not a single practice but a system of psychotechnologies that optimize your cognition for insight.

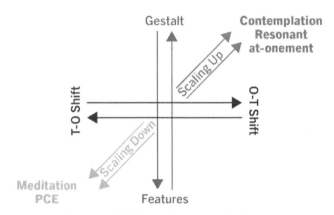

Figure 9.5: The difference between meditation and contemplation. Meditation is associated with scaling down, and contemplation is associated with scaling up.

Let us return to the nine-dot problem from chapter 1. Why do we find it so difficult to join nine dots with four straight lines? We automatically project a square onto the grid and presume to understand the kind of problem we are solving—in other words, a connect-the-dot problem whose lines must turn only within the square. But as I already showed you, the solution requires us to break this square and not treat this problem as a typical connect-the-dot schema.

This is difficult because it requires a change in the way we pay attention to the problem. I must break the inappropriate frame. To do this, I must break up the gestalt so I don't frame the problem so unconsciously or categorically. Psychologist Günther Knoblich[5] and others have shown that our ability to solve insight problems can improve with processes called *chunk decomposition* and *constraint relaxation*. Chunk decomposition means breaking up gestalt (i.e., into featural chunks) by scaling down attention while constraint relaxation means de-automatizing your cognition to become more conscious of your thinking and cognitive processing, which necessitates a shift from transparency to opacity.

Even when all of this is functioning, it is still not enough for insight. Not only do I have to break up the inappropriate frame to solve the nine-dot problem, but I have to project an alternative frame, a more adaptive one. The shift from transparency to opacity can alert me to an insufficient perspective—the fact that I am finding the wrong details relevant to solve the problem—but I also have to find the right details, the features that were formerly in the background. I need new relevance to look through, new things to turn transparent. I must find deeper, broader patterns I had not considered before.

To fashion a new frame, I have to scale my attention back up, like putting a blurry photo back in focus to see the entire scene of the picture and zero in on new relevant features. We have independent evidence that a strong connection exists between insight and the ability to scale attention, whether this ability is trained or naturally disposed.[6]

However, attentional scaling can also inhibit your insight. If I just

5. Günther Knoblich, Stellan Ohlsson, Hilde Haider, and Detlef Rhenius, "Constraint Relaxation and Chunk Decomposition in Insight Problem-Solving," *Journal of Experimental Psychology: Learning, Memory, and Cognition* 25 no. 6 (1999): 1534–1555.
6. Jacquelyn Baker-Sennett and Stephen J. Ceci, "Clue-Efficiency and Insight: Unveiling the Mystery of Inductive Leaps," *Journal of Creative Behavior* 30(1996): 153–172.

scale up and maximize (like tightening the string) I'll immediately project the square on the nine-dot problem. I'll become locked. If I only scale down and keep breaking up gestalts (like loosening the string), I'll never make the solution. I'll choke myself.

If you are sparring with a partner, one way to catch him off guard is to pay him a compliment. In all likelihood, he will automatically begin to scale down and analyze the features of his technique. This will break up the gestalt and disrupt his flow of attention. Scaling down attention can improve the chances of insight by breaking up a bad frame, but it can also disrupt your problem-solving by causing you to choke. Scaling up attention can improve your ability for insight by creating a better frame, but it can sweep you into an inappropriate frame and lock you in fixation.

Mindfulness Mystical Experiences: The Pure Consciousness Event and Resonant At-Onement

How should we avoid these problems? As Siddhartha learned, you want the strings of attention neither too tight nor too loose. Mindfulness, when taught effectively, trains both skills. It teaches us to scale attention up and down and to develop a flow and proper tension between them. This flow is called *opponent processing*. You force the two skills to pull and push on each other. They are forced to coordinate and strike the right degree of attentional engagement, the scale that is most dynamically fitted to the world. This is why you should not equate mindfulness just with meditation. Mindfulness that follows the Buddhist Eightfold Path includes an ecology of meditative practices, contemplative practices, and activities that teach a person to flow between the attentional opposites until she learns, as in a martial art, to cultivate her fittedness to the world in such a way as to constantly evolve it.

It is well-known that mindfulness practices can produce *mystical experiences*. To account for this carefully, we need to review what we know about mindfulness. It teaches us to appropriate and train our flexibility of attentional scaling. This allows us to intervene effectively in how we frame our problems and increase the chances of insight when insight is needed. When I scale down, I make my mind less representational and less inferential. In doing so, I gain awareness and mastery over my processes of *problem framing* and thereby train the skills that will make me more insightful.

If we solely practice scaling down, and persist in the practice for a long period, we can attain a kind of mystical experience known as a *pure consciousness event (PCE)*.[7] This is a well-attested phenomenon among researchers and some practitioners who have extensive mindfulness experience, including me. The PCE is a difficult experience to come by. When you practice meditation, you step back to observe the lens of your mind, but the observation is hard to maintain; we have all developed involuntary habits that spur our thoughts and feelings, and we are seized by the myriad of distractions these habits provoke.

In meditation, these distractions scale our attention back up and turn our feelings transparent. For instance, a fleeting thought about your spouse might suddenly put all your other thoughts and feelings in the mood of your spousal relationship. The meditator has to retain a soft vigilance toward these distractions. She returns her attention again to the scaling down project by renewing her interest—the *optimizing* interest that Mole discussed—in her breath and its sensations. She continually recenters, steps back, and looks at her mind again, even as stray thoughts pull her forward. The process is arduous, and most novice meditators find it tedious and discouraging. But dealing with distraction is a necessary part of training attention. Each time you refocus, it is like doing reps in weight training.

The skill of meditation is developed over time, and those who develop it find they can shift their attention more dexterously between probe and object as well as between feature and gestalt, all the while exercising more patience, precision, and control over their own cognitive processes. A PCE is a direct consequence of this careful cultivation, when a meditator scales her attention down to the finest

---

7. Robert K. C. Forman, *The Problem of Pure Consciousness: Mysticism and Philosophy* (Oxford University Press, 1990).

features of her cognitive processes and deepens the space between each thought, feeling or sensation. She finds deeper layers of mind from which to observe the shallower ones.

Eventually, she "steps back" so far that she seems to observe her consciousness itself. She is not looking through anything. She is not conscious of any feeling or sensation. She is not even conscious of herself. She is just conscious.

Scaling attention up with the same steady practice (for example, in metta-contemplation) often creates a different kind of awareness, a counterpart experience to complement the PCE. The phenomenology of this state will sound familiar to anyone versed in the Buddhist tradition. It creates a sense of flow, a felt impression of interconnectedness and impermanence. When we attain a view of overarching gestalt, it seems to include and encompass the practitioner. We experience the *resonant at-onement* we discussed in earlier chapters, a super flow state that gives us a deeper sense of participatory knowing and makes us feel coextensive with the world.

This model of mindfulness explains why people seek these kinds of mystical experiences. If they practice meditation diligently, they may induce a PCE. If they master a contemplative practice, they will develop this participatory sense of belonging to the world and experience this resonant at-onement.

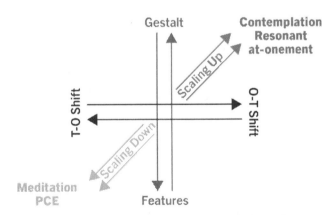

Figure 9.6: The relationship between different forms of attentional shifting: scaling down (meditation, which affords the pure consciousness event) and scaling up (contemplation, which affords resonant at-onement).

"I am Awake": Prajna, Nonduality and Altered States of Consciousness

Remember that effective mindfulness ultimately involves an opponent process, scaling down and scaling up together. Following breath is a powerful way of cycling both opponents. As you inhale, you scale up to contemplation, catching the outward flow of your attention and the sense of resonance with the world beyond you. As you exhale, you scale down into the features of your attention and try to step back as close as you can to the pure consciousness event.

You will often have to practice this oscillating pattern for years before it produces a mystical experience. When the experience occurs, it may occur not as pure consciousness or resonant at-onement but as something that includes and transcends both. The opponent process can produce a third state, a kind of mystical experience called *prajna*.

Prajna is another term for wisdom, and it creates a state of *nonduality* that many practitioners pursue. This state gives us insight into our existential modes of being and affects the guts and grammar of the agent-arena relationship, the way we interact with the world. It pushes us to the ground of our agency and to the circumference of our arena.

One of Siddhartha's great innovations was to join vipassana meditation and metta-contemplation practices together, and prajna was the attainment of his mindfulness project. It is what most people mean when they talk about Buddhist enlightenment, the very excellence that turned Siddhartha into the figure we recognize and follow.

After Siddhartha's transformation, many people noticed that his visage had changed. You might imagine this change if you recall observing someone in the flow state, like a prodigious musician or athlete. You might recall their grace, their energy, the musicality of their movements and gestures. You perceive it to be beautiful, powerful, and charismatic. In each moment of daily life, Siddhartha seemed filled with this kind of countenance.

His presence was so awe-inspiring that men of his day asked

Siddhartha if he was a god. He answered them clearly: he was not. They asked him if he was an angelic messenger or prophet. He replied clearly: he was not. Then they asked him if he was a man, and he responded clearly: he was not.

Frustrated, the men asked him, "Then what are you?"

Siddhartha replied, "I am awake."

The profoundness of Siddhartha's transformation is reflected in the language he uses. He moves from talking about his identity as something to have—whether ascetic or aristocratic—to an act of being, a fundamental way of existing ("I am awake"). He remembered himself in the way of sati. He recollected what it meant to be a human being and lived this recollection forward in every waking moment.

As a cognitive scientist, especially one who studies the connections between Buddhism and cognitive science, I am fascinated in these experiences that people have in mindfulness practices. I am fascinated that we can train ourselves to cultivate a systematic set of insights that optimizes our entire being and that triggers and empowers a fundamentally transformative experience. Many of my colleagues and collaborators are also interested in these phenomena, especially now that they have resurfaced so pervasively. Why do we pursue ACSs? Why is the Mindfulness Revolution so powerful? Why are we going through this psychedelic revolution?

Unlike other therapeutic pharmaceuticals, psychedelics work by inducing an ACS. The pursuit of this state may not be exclusive to our species. Some research suggests that the more intelligent a creature is, the more it will pursue these altered states. Caledonian crows, as I mentioned earlier, will risk their lives tumbling down rooftops in order to make themselves dizzy. Some of these psychedelically altered states and mystical experiences, used in a therapeutic context, can afford powerful transformations of character and perspective, recapitulating their functions in the Axial Revolution.

Siddhartha's metaphor of awakening is helpful for understanding the phenomenology of the experiences. When you are in a dream state, you think that world is real and interact with it as if it is real.

When you wake up, you realize it was just a dream, and your waking world becomes more real.[9]

When we emerge from a certain ASC, like a marijuana high, we often dismiss the phenomenology as something less real than the experience of waking life. But in other ASCs, the opposite occurs. The person who emerges from a mystical experience often declares that the state was more real, really real, and that normal waking life seems less real by comparison.

She gains access to a *higher state of consciousness*, like the real world of the Axial Age, and returning from this state feels like returning to Plato's Cave after bathing in sunlight. She realizes that the everyday world, her surroundings as she knew them, were only echoes and shadows, and this new contact with reality effects a desire for sati—to remember and recapture what that state was like and to change herself in order to re-attain it. This is true for a great many people who, after a profound mystical experience, embark on a journey to transform their whole lives and selves.

This incitement to transcendence is known as *Quantum Change Theory*[8]. It helps us understand what happened to people like Siddhartha. Most of the world religions that emerged at the Axial Revolution are predicated on the idea that certain higher states of consciousness should empower, challenge, and encourage us to undertake transformation. It is at the core of Buddhism (experiencing *satori* and realizing *sunyata*), Vedanta (in moksha and release) and Taoism. It also plays a significant role in Islamic Sufism, the Christian Mystic tradition and Kabbalah. These mystical experiences seem to carry sacred authority and significance in all of the world's religious traditions, where they have become central catalysts for radical cognitive development and modal transformation.

Surveys indicate that 30–40 percent of the human population has experienced these events.[9] Much like flow, mystical experiences occur across cultures, genders, language groups, and socioeconomic

---

8. William R. Miller and Janet C'de Baca, *Quantum Change: When Epiphanies and Sudden Insights Transform Ordinary Lives* (New York: Guilford Press, 2001).
9. Steve Taylor, *The Leap: The Psychology of Spiritual Awakening* (New World Library, 2017).

statuses. They are universal in the sense that they are not relegated to any one class or order of human beings, and they seem deeply correlated with how a person appraises her life. Both scientifically and historically, this kind of universality is an important phenomenon. Many people who undergo higher states of consciousness consider them to be among the most significant experiences in their lives, and much of the significance relates to subsequent quantum changes. Deep connections exist between awakening and recovering meaning, just as between awakening and insight.

My lab at the University of Toronto is among those that have explored this relationship between mystical experiences and meaning in life. We completed a fine-grained analysis, which proved consonant with the conclusions of Samantha Heintzelman, and other experimental work.[10] Evidence suggests that mystical experiences are conducive to something like a capacity for insight or sense-making, which is often called "coherence" in the relevant literature.

The significance we feel in these states seems related to this coherence, which is usually described as "ineffable" by those who experience it. Research indicates that the meaningfulness of a mystical experience seems not to coincide with its content as much as the sense-making itself, the feeling of connectedness to reality. To use our previous language, the mystical experience optimizes and integrates our attention in powerful ways and affords an anagoge of perspective that bootstraps our insight.

---

10. This work was presented at the following conferences:

Thalia Vrantsidis, Philip Rajewicz, Juensung Kim, and John Vervaeke, "An Integrative Account of the Experience of Meaning in Life," Paper presented to the August 2019 meeting of the *American Psychological Association,* Chicago, USA.

Juensung Kim, and John Vervaeke, "Making Sense: Coherency and Religiosity Predict Meaning in Life Following Mystical Experience," Poster presented to the August, 2019 meeting of the *American Psychological Association,* Chicago, USA.

John Vervaeke and Anderson Todd, "Mystical Experience Predicts Enhanced Meaning in Life via Coherence" to *Mapping the Mind with Mushrooms 4,* September 22, 2018, University of Toronto.

John Vervaeke and Anderson Todd, "Mystical Experience Predicts Enhanced Meaning in Life" to *4th Canadian Conference on Positive Psychology,* May 24, 2018, University of Toronto.

While an individual's mystical experience can take on the language or symbolism of her religious belief, the non-propositional dimension of her experience—the participatory knowing—that is universal. I am not claiming that the religious content is generally irrelevant, or that these traditions are all identical, but there seem to be common truths and properties about the nature of attention, mindfulness, and higher states of consciousness that transcend the differences between the traditions that name them.[11] They alleviate existential anxiety, create a systematic kind of insight, and induce transformation of the agent-arena relationship that forges transformation. When we thread the needle through these projects, as the Buddha did, we find his inexpressible remembrance of being. Is this not the awakening sati for which Siddhartha yearned and suffered? Is this not the relief we seek when we long for wisdom and meaning?

---

11. I do not share the view of *perennialism*—made famous by Aldous Huxley—that all religious traditions share a single truth, a common identity of belief which is obscured only by superficial differences.

10

CONSCIOUSNESS

After the previous chapter, you will appreciate that the reasons for practicing mindfulness are not trivial. Mindfulness is a way of cultivating insight, but the insight we cultivate is not a party trick. It is not a luxury or accessory. It is a necessity. If we do not change ourselves to respond more adaptively to problems, if we do not develop character in the Aristotelian fashion and resolve modal confusions, we lapse into very foolish and destructive behavior. We estrange ourselves from our own potential and fall into existential distress.

Learning to harness attention through transparency-opacity shifting (in meditation) and feature-gestalt scaling (in contemplation) as well as finding flow and opponency between the two increases your cognitive fluency. If we can take these practices to the depths of our self (as in the pure consciousness event) and the depths of reality (in the resonant at-onement) and integrate these depths, we can bring about *prajna*. The mystical experience of non-duality can transform our worldview and its agent-arena relationships, bring us closer to reality, and change the way we find meaning in life.

The Nature and Functions of Consciousness: Relevance and Salience

Recent cognitive science—including some of my own theoretical and experimental work—seems to support the claim that these higher states of consciousness can bring about quantum changes of character.[1,2] But trying to understand these states lands us squarely into one of the most difficult problems in science. David Chalmers famously called it the "hard problem of consciousness."[3] Arthur Schopenhauer called it the "world knot."[4]

Trying to comprehensively explain consciousness is like trying to explain God; I am not going to attempt it. However, we need to spend some time with the problem of consciousness to appreciate the function of altering it.[5] We can ask questions about both the *nature* of consciousness (i.e., what is it, and how does it emerge from the properties of the brain?) and the *function* of consciousness (i.e., what does consciousness *do*?). When we examine the issue closely, these turn out to be very different questions.

You may be surprised to learn that there is no scientific consensus on the function of consciousness. Most people know that consciousness is a mystery, but what consciousness does is also a mystery. You love your consciousness. You identify with it. You cannot step outside of it, and it is somehow synonymous with all of life's meaning. You would not give it up for any power or wealth because the significance of power or wealth depends on being conscious of them. However, many features of your cognition can function

---

1. William R. Miller and Janet C'de Baca, *Quantum Change: When Epiphanies and Sudden Insights Transform Ordinary Lives* (New York: Guilford Press, 2001).
2. David B. Yaden, Khoa D. Le Nguyen, Margaret L. Kern, Nancy A. Wintering, Johannes C. Eichstaedt, H. Andrew Schwartz, Anneke E. K. Buffone, et al, "The Noetic Quality: A Multimethod Exploratory Study," *Psychology of Consciousness: Theory, Research, and Practice* 4 no. 1 (2017): 54–62.
3. David Chalmers, "Facing Up to the Problem of Consciousness," *Journal of Consciousness Studies* 2 no. 3 (1995): 200–219.
4. Arthur Schopenhauer, *On the Fourfold Root of the Principle of Sufficient Reason.* Open Court Publishing Company, 1997.
5. John Vervaeke, Richard Wu, Anderson Todd, *Scale Invariant Mutual Modelling Theory of Consciousness.* Unpublished manuscript.

perfectly well without consciousness. How does something this mysterious arise out of matter, and what function does it serve? I will not dare to answer these questions in any final way but rather show how some of the best work on this topic can teach us about the value of ASCs.

One of the best accounts for the function of consciousness is called the *Global Workspace Theory*. In this model, your consciousness functions like the desktop of your computer. When your attention activates a file and brings the information onto the desktop, it can interact with other pieces of information. You can then broadcast the interaction, and anything you learn or change, back to any other file. In this analogy, the files stand for all of your brain's unconscious processing.

Your consciousness retrieves the file and brings it into a space of working memory (i.e., your desktop). You then activate the unconscious processing (i.e., your files) so the pieces of information can interact with each other, and then you broadcast the interaction back to all of the existing unconscious processing (i.e., your other files). There is an economy to this model.

You do not want all of your files activated at the same time because this would be disastrous and overwhelming. Instead, you want to be able to observe your own unconscious processing and select the pieces of information that are relevant. The Global Workspace Theory proposes that consciousness performs this function. The theory was originally proposed by Bernard Baars[6] and further developed with Murray Shanahan.[7] Baars continues to address these questions in *The Cambridge Handbook of Consciousness*.

According to the theory, the architecture of the Global Workspace helps us to solve the frame problem; it allows us to zero our attention on relevant information to respond effectively to a given problem or situation. Mathematically, the amount of information available to

6. Bernard J. Baars, "In the Theatre of Consciousness: Global Workspace Theory, a Rigorous Scientific Theory of Consciousness," *Journal of Consciousness Studies* 4, no. 4(1997): 292–309.
7. Murray Shanahan and Bernard Baars, "Applying Global Workspace Theory to the Frame Problem," *Cognition* 98, no. 2 (2005): 157–176.

you in your surroundings is astronomically vast, and the same is true for your memory. Trying to use or account for all of the information at any given time would overwhelm you.

To navigate this problem, you must select from that vast repository only those pieces of information that are useful for the moment's purpose. Then, you must put those pieces of information together. This next task incurs the same overwhelming problem; there are incalculable possible configurations.

Consciousness is helping you zero in on the relevant information from your memory and surroundings to put those pieces of information together in the way it is most needed. This is just like what you do with your computer. You search your memory, select what is relevant, and bring it onto the desktop. You put it together in a relevant manner, and then you use it in a relevant way.

Once again, we cannot use a homuncular explanation to account for this process. There is no little man pushing paper inside our brains. Consciousness seems to be performing these functions in a self-organizing manner. This helps explain why consciousness is so tightly associated with working memory and why working memory correlates with intelligence.[8,9] According to this model, it seems that the core function of consciousness is to help you notice and attend to the relevant information that is key to working memory and general intelligence.

A more neuroscientific and psychological account of consciousness was proposed by Daniel Bor and Anil Seth called the *Prefrontal Parietal Network (PPN)*.[10] When we measure conscious brain activity, we observe a process of chunking or restructuring information, much like the process of insight. Bor and Seth argue

8. Andrew R. A. Conway, Michael J. Kane, and Randall W. Engle, "Working Memory Capacity and Its Relation to General Intelligence," *Trends in Cognitive Sciences* 7 no. 12(2003): 547–552.

9. James M. Broadway and Randall W. Engle, "Validating Running Memory Span: Measurement of Working Memory Capacity and Links with Fluid Intelligence," *Behavior Research Methods* 42, no. 2(2010): 563–570.

10. Daniel Bor and Anil K. Seth, "Consciousness and the Prefrontal Parietal Network: Insights from Attention, Working Memory, and Chunking," *Frontiers in Psychology* 3(2012): 63.

that one of the key functions of consciousness is just this: the ability to manipulate attention to afford insight. It seems essential to your capacity to zero in on relevant information.

One of the most prominent theories about the nature of consciousness right now is Giulio Tononi's *Integrated Information Theory.*[11] Tononi's theory relates to integration: one piece of information in your brain is causally dependent on affecting and interacting with other pieces of information in your brain. The more tightly integrated the information becomes, the more powerful and complex the cognitive processing, and the more likely that this complexity—or *complexification*—will afford consciousness.

To explain the function of this complexification, Tononi proposes something like a Turing test for consciousness. He says you can test to see how conscious a system is by giving it anomalous pictures and asking it to determine whether or not the pictures make sense. I propose that Tononi's test is relying on this integrative process; the way our brain is complexifying information is tracking the complexity of patterns in the world and working to make sense of them. So perhaps a main function of this integrated information processing is this: allowing you to determine if pieces of information are relevant to each other and relevant to you.

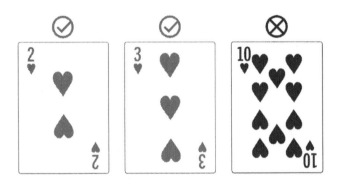

Figure 10.1: An example of an anomalous picture. A conscious system would be able to identify that the third card does not fit in with the first two cards, as the hearts in the third card are not red.

11. Giulio Tononi, "Integrated Information Theory," Scholarpedia 10, no. 1(2015): 4164.

I am not proposing, of course, that every instance of relevance realization is consciousness. I am instead arguing that consciousness is a way of coordinating attention and other abilities of awareness to optimize how insightfully you can make sense of your world. It is particularly adaptive to complex situations that require insight and problems that pose a high degree of novelty or challenge. For instance, you can weaken the intensity of your conscious attention when a problem has become very well-defined; when you become an experienced cook, or driver, you can manage these activities without the same degree of conscious rigor.

I do not claim that this is a complete account of the function of consciousness. You may notice, however, how this functional theory interacts with our discussion in the previous chapter. When you have a moment of insight, it often feels like a sudden brightening of consciousness. It is not difficult to understand why people may want to alter their state of consciousness to gain access to new insights, new ways of integrating the significance of the information we already have available.

Consciousness creates a *salience landscape*. It picks out certain features from among these vast and incalculable surroundings and commends them to your attention. These details become the foreground of the landscape, and the remaining information is backgrounded as irrelevant. Recall the attentional scaling we discussed in the last chapter; the foregrounded features become the basis for a gestalt view. I use them to create a figure. We use this language all the time when we refer to "figuring out" a problem— putting details in the right arrangement to signify them and determine their most optimal relevance.

As I scale my attention "up" and "down," the gestalt figure makes the chosen details even more salient to me, and I configure them together to create a frame of action, reference, and perspective. This is a dynamic, complex system at work, and your consciousness plays a decisive role in creating and managing the salience landscape. It sees the world dissolve and resolve continually as new details are foregrounded and backgrounded and new insights and perspectives rise out of the unintelligible mass. All of this is happening right now as I try to integrate these concepts into theory, and as you read and digest these ideas.

The Nature and Functions of Consciousness: Salience, Presence, and Depth

Consciousness and the salience landscape have important roles to play in our cognitive agency. For example, imagine a cup of coffee sitting in front of you. Your salience landscape makes the cup stand out, and a problem arises. You want to pick it up. But in order to pick it up, you must move around the cup to get into an optimal position.

If you move too close, you see the details but lose the gestalt. If you move too far away, you may see the whole but lose the details. You must achieve something that the phenomenologist Merleau-Ponty called an *optimal grip*[12]. In this case, of course, the grip is literal, but Merleau-Ponty uses grip as a metaphor for interactional contact. The optimal grip refers to an optimized tension between the gestalt and featural as well as between transparency (looking through) and opacity (looking at).

When I find myself in a salience landscape, and I adjust into an optimal grip, an *affordance* becomes available to me, a window for action in the world. In other words, the salience landscape lights up an arena, and I become an agent within that arena.[13] The cup becomes "graspable" to me. The graspability is not a property of the cup per se (it is not graspable by a praying mantis) nor a property of just my hand (my hand alone cannot make the cup). An affordance is a relationship of coordination between the constraints in the cup and the constraints in my hand. They shape one another, and seem to share the same identity.

This happens at the level of participatory knowing. Many affordances involve this co-shaping of oneself and one's world. Most of them are unconscious, unnoticed until needed. The salience

---

12. Maurice Merleau-Ponty, *Phenomenology of Perception*, trans. Colin Smith (London: Routledge, 2005)
13. See James Gibson, *The Ecological Approach to Visual Perception* (Houghton Mifflin, 1979).

landscaping bootstraps perspectival knowing, our capacity to notice those affordances automatically. Psychologist James Gibson observed this about our relationship with our environment: You do not really see colors and shapes. You see affordances. I see that this path is walkable, or this table is movable. The salience landscape places you in contact, and the optimal gripping shifts you into a realization of affordances, an agent-arena relationship. I present myself to the cup and it presents itself to me. I am the grasper, and the cup is graspable.

This arrangement of structure and function should remind us of the Aristotelian relationship between conformity and causation. We discussed this in previous chapters. A worldview is emerging from this conformity. Consciousness is setting up a salience landscape, and the optimal gripping discloses a *presence landscape,* an entire network of affordances. These are not enough, however. Your brain must be able to differentiate correlational patterns from causal patterns. This binocular perception produces a *depth landscape.*

If we observe them closely, we can see children forming these landscapes all the time: two-year-olds pick up spoons and drop them over and over again. They use their salience landscape to realize affordances and causal patterns around the spoon—is it graspable, or throwable, or droppable? The repetitive motions help them to figure out the causal patterns around the spoon, transforming their salience landscape into a presence landscape and then into a depth landscape. They are developing a deep kind of understanding—not a knowledge that could be expressed in words, but one that is expressed playfully and interactionally. Consciousness is helping to facilitate this. Attention to the relevant information, the (re)configuration of the world, and your capacity to meaningfully interact with it.

Transforming consciousness means transforming this entire dynamic process: my salience landscape, my presence landscape, my depth landscape. The patterns I can track, the kind of agent I can be, the kind of arena I can find—each of these is going to change. I will not simply have a flash of insight, like in the nine-dot problem. An ASC changes the mood and tone of the world. The same spaces become different places entirely. We wake up inside our consciousness as though breaking the surface of some oceanic dream —a dream we live in, without knowing it, for so much of our everyday lives.

When this happens, it's not just our perceptions that are augmented but our values, interests, and attitudes. Different things call out to us. Different decisions become available. Things that consumed us may recede or clarify, and things we neglected come forward to reveal new importance.

The analogy to waking from childhood appears over and over in accounts of these altered states, and for good reason. The analogy is given credence by Jean Piaget's pivotal work in childhood psychological development[14]. Consider the following experiment. You place five wrapped candies in a row in front of a four-year-old. Then, you lay out a second row of five candies directly beneath the first. The only difference between them is that the candies in the second row are more spaced apart. The four-year-old knows that each row has the same number of candies, but if you ask her to choose one, she will confidently pick the second.

Figure 10.2: A schematic demonstrating the layout of the two rows of candies. Despite the fact that both rows contain the same number of candies, four-year-old children will reliably select the second row of candies. The child is making a systematic error.

In this experiment, the child is making an important kind of error. Before Piaget, most IQ testing discounted errors and focused only on correct results. Piaget had the insight to consider whether there was a meaningful pattern in these errors. If they were systematic and not random, they may betray constraints in the child's

14. See Jean Piaget, *The Child's Conception of Number* (Routledge, 1997)

cognition, and we perhaps could better understand child development by understanding how these constraints shaped a child's sensorimotor interaction.

Piaget found that the errors were indeed systematic. The child selected the second row precisely because it took up more space. The space that the candy occupies is very salient to a child, and she is more attentive to this space than to each individual candy. As an adult, you do not fall prey to this error because you have a different salience landscape. For you, the extra space is "non-candy space" and therefore not relevant.

The child does not pick up on that; her salience landscape is not sizing this up, so she does not have the same affordance. You see through this illusion because your salience landscape has been trained to notice and integrate multiple variables at the same time while discounting irrelevant information. This is one of the reasons you are wiser than the child and can therefore avoid certain self-deceptive illusions.

It is important to remember that these developmental errors are systematic. Even if you correct the child about the candy space, she will still be impeded by other problems of the same kind. She remains locked into a particular stage of development. However, what if you have an insight that is not just a single insight but a systemic insight that changes the whole system? It would not be relegated to one feature of your conscious experience but a gestalt insight about your consciousness as a whole.[15]

This is what the child does when she develops and changes her salience landscaping. The whole system of errors falls away, and she starts to see through an illusion and into reality. It is important to see the child's error as analogous to your own. You may not make the mistakes of a four-year-old, but you fall prey to many systematic illusions without realizing it. Our salience, presence and depth become significantly more sophisticated as we grow, but they always remain in need of systemic insight.

---

15. This is an idea I am currently exploring with Juensung Kim.

Onto-Normativity and Higher States of Consciousness

When we have salience that systematically tracks presence in depth, we have what I shall call a *significance landscape*. If this functions properly, it can afford a more comprehensive, flowing relationship with our environment. ASCs have the potential to create insights of great significance, but they can also do the opposite. They can distort your salience landscaping and make you more prone to bullshit and self-deception. That is why most ASCs are rejected as illusory and delusory.

Yet as I explained in the previous chapter, some of these altered states yield experiences that are so wakeful and transformative, so really real, that we feel as though they usher us into a new state of life. We feel we have become adults to our former selves. The newfound realness becomes a property of both agent and arena.

"This is the way the world really is!" we say. "And this is also who I really am." As we discussed in the previous chapter, many people are moved to make seismic changes in their lives on the basis of experiencing these higher states of consciousness. The experience challenges people. It demands change and calls us back to ourselves.

I call this the problem of *onto-normativity*. The higher state of consciousness seems to reveal something about the structure of reality (ontology), and the revelation demands an improvement in our character and action (normativity). Innumerable first-person accounts now support this generalization, and we have to take these experiences seriously.[16] Work from the Griffiths lab in Johns Hopkins Center for Psychedelic and Consciousness Research has shown that a

---

16. As I mentioned, these states are historically important and pervasive across cultures. For example, Steve Taylor's book *Waking from Sleep: Why Awakening Experiences Occur and How to Make Them Permanent* contains 150 interviews with people who have had these experiences. Andrew Newberg's book *How Enlightenment Changes Your Brain: The New Science of Transformation* presents an online survey of fifteen hundred people in 2016. Larger general surveys focus on how often people have these kinds of experiences and they range in intensity, but it is around 30 to 40 percent of the population.

subset of mystical psychedelic experiences has triggered the kind of quantum change discussed in the previous chapter[17].

These radical transformations seem driven—and thereafter justified—by these experiences, and the desire to maintain faithful contact with them and the sense of realness they leave glowing in their wake. They often frame events and conditions in our lives in ways that never occurred to us. In doing so, they make our own behavior more intelligible and coherent to us and give us a new configuration for our beliefs, memories, and experiences. Higher states of consciousness are world-breaking.

When you have a singular, powerful experience that does not cohere with the rest of your life, it challenges the rest of your life. Remember Plato's insight: we are attracted to what feels real. In order for our attractions and behavior to change, our vision of reality must change. Not the belief we hold in mind but the relationship we carry in our body, the entire worldview that holds our experience together.

When these visions of reality do not cohere, the encounter foists us with a decision, an either/or. We must embrace one vision and reject the other. Higher states of consciousness do not provide us with any new intelligible content. They are generally ineffable and transrational. They are temporary and fleeting. They do not provide us with any argument, explanation, or justification. Should these so-called higher states not be the ones we reject?

The power of onto-normativity was the core of the Axial Revolution, and for good reason. Some higher states of consciousness are real enough for us to reject the model of reality that accords with our everyday experience. The everyday becomes the dream. The higher state becomes the reality. We also have good evidence now to suggest the possibility that these higher states can bring about certain developmental improvements.[18] Many people's lives get better

---

17. Katherine A. MacLean, Matthew W. Johnson, and Roland R. Griffiths, "Mystical Experiences Occasioned by the Hallucinogen Psilocybin Lead to Increases in the Personality Domain of Openness," *Journal of Psychopharmacology* 25, no. 11 (2011): 1453–1461, https://doi.org/10.1177/0269881111420188.
18. David B. Yaden, Khoa D. Le Nguyen, Margaret L. Kern, Nicole A. Wintering, Johannes C. Eichstaedt, H. Andrew Schwartz, Anneke E. K. Buffone, et al. "The

after encountering the "real," by measures of meaning, problems, and relationships.[19] But we need to make sense of this development.

First, we need a descriptive explanation, an account of the underlying cognitive brain processes that explains the experiential nature of these states. Why do they feel it as more real, and why does this feeling justify and motivate a transformative experience? Then we need a prescriptive account. Are these states legitimate? Is there any rational basis for the transformations people attribute to them? Is their claim to onto-normativity just an illusion, or philosophically justifiable?

Having these accounts is not sufficient. They must be integrated to yield a coherent explanation. Good cognitive science undertakes this integration. It can account for the cognitive processes at work in the mind with recourse to psychology. It can account for the information processes at work with recourse to artificial intelligence and machine learning. It can draw on neuroscientific accounts of what is happening in the brain.

A plausible, descriptive account of higher states of consciousness must simultaneously elucidate each of these: the cognitive mechanisms, the machine learning mechanisms, and the neurological mechanisms. I will endeavor to show how these processes, if integrated together, can provide a rational justification for the transformation that people undertake. It may not be the kind of justification you expect; these higher states do not seem to provide any new evidence or special knowledge. We should not use them to buttress or challenge our scientific claims. But that does not mean these states are irrational.

As I have taken great pains to explain, rationality means so much more than acquiring beliefs. When the child no longer falls prey to an illusion, it is not because any new facts have been discovered. The child in the experiment already knows there are five candies in each

---

Noetic Quality: A Multimethod Exploratory Study," *Psychology of Consciousness: Theory, Research, and Practice* 4, no. 1 (2017): 54–62. https://doi.org/10.1037/cns0000098.
19. Measures of meaning, relationships, and problems are qualitatively assessed through validated scaled questionnaires. Statistical analysis is used to establish significant changes in the participants' responses.

row. So what changed? The change was not knowledge; the change was wisdom. The child saw the same information in an entirely new way. She had a moment of systemic insight. She learned to see through illusion and into reality.

Higher states of consciousness are rational not because they provide us with new knowledge but because they provide us with wisdom. People can emerge from these states with very difficult conclusions and metaphysical claims.

Some may say: "I knew God!"

Others say, "I knew there was no God!"

A person's expressed belief may or may not change, but the propositional content is less relevant. The true change is inexpressible. Your participatory knowing is the seat of this transformation. It is your cognitive functioning and your sense of connectedness to what is real, the skills, sensibilities, and sensitivities of your significance landscaping that transform your existential mode and worldview.

The Buddha famously refused to answer metaphysical questions about nirvana or enlightenment. These questions were not the point. He was not trying to access supra-scientific knowledge. He was seeking wisdom and transformation. He was trying to get an optimal grip on the world.

11

HIGHER STATES OF CONSCIOUSNESS (PART 1)

When we closely examine higher states of consciousness, we begin to discover—or indeed, rediscover—something very significant about the nature of meaning and wisdom. We moderns consistently correlate wisdom with knowledge, as though being wise meant having certain beliefs about reality. However, wisdom is not a belief unless we are to understand "belief" in a more nuanced way, as a relationship we embody rather than an opinion we hold.

This deeper kind of belief may be indicated by our propositions, but it is lived out in the other dimensions of knowing—in our procedural activity, our perspectival sense of presence and place, our participatory engagement with the world. Higher states of consciousness seem to affect us so profoundly precisely because they activate these deeper, non-propositional dimensions. They change the way we participate, which changes our sense of presence and place, which affords different skills and ways of interacting with our environment. Experiences in these higher states move people to radically transform their lives, their sense of self, and their interpersonal relationships in order to maintain a connectedness to this deepened vision of reality.

In the previous chapter, we discussed some of the cognitive scientific theories and experiments that have explored the nature and function of consciousness. Since the higher states of consciousness seem to impact our significance landscape at various levels of knowing, we must pay particular attention to the first-person experiences. Any account of these higher states must account for the phenomenology, what it *feels like* to be in these states. We will explore three components of the phenomenology: (1) How is the world being experienced? (2) How is the self being experienced? And (3) How is the relationship between the world and the self being experienced?

Higher States of Consciousness: The World

People who emerge from the higher states of consciousness often report a tremendous sense of clarity about reality. This clarity is both cognitive and perceptual. Cognitively, the world seems coherent in a way that it has not seemed before (think of the gestalt). Meanwhile, the perceptual aspect of clarity is often experienced as *brightness*. The details in the world seem to shine forth and display a vividness and intensity that eclipses that of waking life (think of the featural).

This shining, interestingly, is the original meaning of *glory*,[1] which in the Bible is given most frequently to describe the presence of God. Glory is not a moral descriptor but a term that captures an ineffable, divine quality of presentation. This shining quality is also something people reliably report in the flow experience.

Accounts of higher states of consciousness describe the clarity as a comprehensive expansion of vision. This reminisces of mindfulness and attentional scaling. People become aware of the whole of the world but remain attentive to finite things. They feel a deep interpenetration between the whole of everything and the parts found in the finest of details. This paradox of perception somehow makes better sense of the world and was famously captured by William Blake: *To see a World in a Grain of Sand, And a Heaven in a Wild Flower, Hold Infinity in the palm of your hand, And Eternity in an hour.*

---

1.   We get the word phenomenon from the Greek word "phainein," meaning coming to view, bringing to light, or shining forth. There are deep connections between intelligibility and the presence-ing of things—"the shining."

People almost universally describe this sense of wholeness and clarity with expressions of awe. "The world is beautiful," they say. It seems alive, pregnant with energy and significance. Each feature of the world carries illimitable depth and complexity but also simpleness and singleness. The experience collapses into a sense of oneness, a deep and profound integration, as though we make contact with the eidos of the world.

Higher States of Consciousness: The Self

This feeling of connectedness—or anagoge, as you may remember—means a fundamental change in our sense of self. Many people report a profound sense of peace in this experience. Peace does not simply mean satisfaction or freedom from conflict. It means the harmonized psyche that Plato depicted in *Republic*, that state wherein the various components of personality and cognition work in concert rather than undermining one another. This sense of inner harmony creates a connectedness within a person and, therefore, to her environment.

People often report that the self-conscious, egocentric voice disappears into the radiance of the experience, just as it does within the flow state. This connectedness induces a feeling of joy—not merely pleasure but the surge of affect we feel when we make contact with the good, when we are overcome with a memory that reminds us that we, and life, are *real*. This sati ameliorates many of our anxious fixations and inhibitions.

People say: "I remember my true self. I remember who I really am!"[2] Remembering oneself by forgetting one's ego might seem like a Buddhist paradox, but it tells us something important about our nature: that we become "true selves" when that nattering voice falls silent and our attention becomes continuous with the disclosure of the world. With this internal coherence, we make a profound shift

---

2. This also lines up with Plato's notion of *anamnesis*, which is where *amnesia* comes from. Plato's sense of a deep remembering, deep recovery of the deepest levels of the psyche.

from opacity to transparency. We are relieved of the inner conflict and skirmishes that force us to pour over our pains, and our selves become the affordances of connection.

By disappearing to itself, the self becomes a vessel, a host of this at-onement, the way of participating in the world and connecting to that intelligible pattern that gives shape to consciousness and experience. This shared identity with reality should remind us of Aristotle's *Conformity Theory of Knowing*.

The participatory knowing experienced in higher states of consciousness is so superlative that it is deemed ineffable. This makes it difficult to account for with any descriptive theory. How can experiences that have no articulable content bear the signature of ultimate realness? A deep continuity exists between these higher states and flow experiences, just as between flow and insight. They share a similar ineffable quality. However, it would be a mistake to equate them.

Higher states of consciousness are more powerful and more elusive. They are often preceded by disruptive strategies designed to interrupt your normal cognitive functioning. Siddhartha's mindfulness practices of meditation and contemplation were long-term versions of these strategies; their disruptive effects were incremental but, nevertheless, profound. Shamans, in order to interfere with their normal level of cognition and induce the shamanic state, pursued shorter-term disruptive strategies like fasting, sexual and sleep deprivation, drumming and chanting, and psychedelics.

We have some initial evidence that combinations of these strategies have a synergistic effect on cognition. A recent experiment in the Griffith's lab[3] showed that people who were practicing mindfulness before taking psychedelics generally had a richer

---

3. Roland R. Griffiths, Matthew W. Johnson, William A. Richards, Brian D. Richards, Robert Jesse, Katherine A. MacLean, Frederick S. Barrett, Mary P. Cosimano, and Maggie A. Klinedinst, "Psilocybin-Occasioned Mystical-Type experience in Combination with Meditation and Other Spiritual Practices Produces Enduring Positive Changes in Psychological Functioning and in Trait Measures of Prosocial Attitudes and Behaviors," *Journal of Psychopharmacology* 32, 1(2018): 49–69.

experience than people who were just taking psychedelics. Evidence also suggests that disruptive strategies are key to cultivating insight; they break the frame of perspective and allow it to regather.

An experiment by Yaden et al[4] featured 701 participants who experienced a higher state of consciousness, 69 percent of whom reported an experience of onto-normativity, and a sense of enhanced realness. This experience predicted a significant improvement across many dimensions of their life, including family ties, health, sense of purpose and spirituality, and relief from the anxiety and fear of death. More empirical evidence now says these states guide progressive transformation.

Yaden's study also makes an important observation that was not clear in Newberg and Taylor's work on onto-normative experiences in higher states of consciousness. These disruptive strategies lead to an experience of *decentering*, a phenomenological shift of experience from an *egocentric* state (a first-person orientation) to what we call an *allocentric* state (a third-person orientation). An egocentric orientation describes things and motions relative to my position: in front of me, behind me, to the left or right of me. An allocentric description places my ego in relation to external features.

While individuals are describing the higher state of consciousness, they are less egocentrically oriented and more allocentrically oriented, as though the salience of reality, for the period of their experience, eclipsed the narcissistic glow of their ego and released them from its preoccupations. It is worth noting that the term *nirvana* originally meant to blow out or extinguish, and the Vedanta term *moksha* also means release. Higher states of consciousness appear to release us from imprisonment by our egocentric perspectives as well as the self-deception and bullshit that so often accompany the ego's need for preservation.

---

4. David B. Yaden, Khoa D. Le Nguyen, Margaret L. Kern, Nancy A. Wintering, Johannes C. Eichstaedt, H. Andrew Schwartz, Anneke E. K. Buffone, et al, "The Noetic Quality: A Multimethod Exploratory Study," *Psychology of Consciousness: Theory, Research, and Practice* 4, no. 1 (2017): 54.

Insight, Fluency, and the Continuity Hypothesis

As I have suggested, these higher states of consciousness seem to scale our experience of insight and make it more comprehensive and transforming. The feeling of making contact with an underlying pattern of unity and coherence, one that you could not perceive before, changes what feels real and important. Samantha Heintzelman has produced experimental evidence that finding these underlying patterns significantly improves our estimation of life's meaningfulness,[5,6,7,8] even if we are simply detecting the pattern in a series of basic pictures. The act of making sense, rather than the particular sense made, dramatically deepens our intelligible connection to reality, giving us an inarticulable understanding of self and world along with the incalculable subtleties of their interaction.

These cascading experiences of insight, understanding, and meaning in life significantly buoy a person's confidence to cultivate a path of wisdom. This was certainly true for Siddhartha. Psychologists Sascha Topolinski and Rolf Reber talk about insight as a *fluency* spike.[9] Fluency is not just flow but a general property of all of your cognitive processing. Initially, fluency was correlated with the ease of

---

5. Samantha J. Heintzelman, Jason Trent, and Laura A. King, "Encounters with Objective Coherence and the Experience of Meaning in Life," *Psychological Science* 24, no. 6(2013): 991–998.

6. Samantha J. Heintzelman and Laura A. King, "Life Is Pretty Meaningful," *American Psychologist* 69, no. 6(2014): 561.

7. Samantha J. Heintzelman and Laura A. King, "(The Feeling of) Meaning-as-Information," *Personality and Social Psychology Review* 18, no. 2(2014): 153–167.

8. Since the production of the video series, some of Heintzelman's experiments have failed to replicate (Ratner et al., 2016). A plausible explanation that I am exploring in my lab is that Heintzelman has conflated the passive recognition of standard meaning with the insightful act of making new meaning. We already know that insight and flow tend to increase people's sense of well-being and a sense of connectedness to their environment. It is perhaps not so much the coherence itself that Heintzelman emphasizes as it is the act of transforming ill-defined incoherent information into coherent useful information, which provides the enhanced sense of meaning. Plausibly, translation of ill-defined incoherent information into useful coherent information results in an increase in fluency. Topolinski and Reber (2010) have argued that the a-ha! experience is a fluency spike.

9. Sascha Topolinski and Rolf Reber, "Gaining Insight into the 'Aha' Experience," *Current Directions in Psychological Science* 19, 6(2010): 402–405.

processing information. On a white background, for instance, the same text will seem truer in black font than it will in orange, lending the words confidence and credibility regardless of their semantic content.[10]

Now, however, it seems that fluency has less to do with ease than it does with accessibility and application. I would argue that fluency depends on how the formatting of a stimulus allows your attention to zero in on the relevant information. Remember our discussion of psychotechnologies. Alphabetic literacy made your cognitive processing more fluent. That fluency improved your ability and cognitive power, giving realness and importance to the information.

According to Topolinski and Reber, sudden spikes in cognitive fluency occur during insight experiences.[11] When you are cognitively fluent, you process information very efficiently, and you tend to judge the information you process therein as more real. This is not a perfect strategy, but it is domain-general and seems to be part of our evolutionary heritage. Therefore strong, independent logical arguments indicate that this *fluency heuristic* is actually a very good strategy for your brain.

Generally, though not always, if you are processing real-world situations fluently, you are likely picking up on real patterns. Insight is zeroing in on relevant information, and flow produces an insight cascade. These states are conducive for implicit learning, wherein you pick up on complex causal patterns that you cannot consciously declare. Mystical experience, meaning in life, the loss of self-consciousness, your sense of connectedness to realness... all of this is evoked in the higher state of consciousness. It feels effortless, graceful, and intrinsically rewarding.

If we are to attain a scientifically legitimate, scientifically plausible explanation of what is going on when somebody claims enlightenment (like Siddhartha) or radical self-transcendence (like Plato), we want a good explanation for what is actually happening as

---

10. Daniel M. Oppenheimer, "The Secret Life of Fluency," *Trends in Cognitive Sciences* 12, no. 6(2008): 237–241.

11. We propose that fluency is measuring how well information is formatted to help you avoid ill-defined problems.

well as justification for why someone should seek the transformative experiences. This pursuit of scientific plausibility has led me to a hypothesis, the *Continuity Hypothesis*.[12]

The Continuity Hypothesis is the idea that fluency is enhanced in insight, and insight is enhanced in flow. Flow states can be elevated into mystical experiences, which can bring about transformative experiences. The higher states of consciousness evinces this continuity. The hypothesis proposes that the same cognitive machinery is used in each of these experiences but scaled in the process of exaptation. Newberg argues that if you have many such "little enlightenments," they will eventually prime and produce transformative experiences. Mindfulness practices are predictive of insight and flow, which in turn prepare us for mystical states and transformation. The more you practice mindfulness, the more you can prime this pump.

This idea of the Continuity Hypothesis may begin to explain what occurs in the higher states of consciousness. It can connect the phenomenal and functional features to the cognitive machinery we already trust and understand. We know, for instance, that flow requires a certain relevant expertise, when your skills and competence can meet the demands of a situation. If you do not have the relevant skills, you cannot attain the flow state. I can acquire this state as a martial artist because I have cultivated the expertise. I can acquire it while lecturing because I have been teaching for three decades. If we are to follow the continuity, we might well ask: What is flowing in higher states of consciousness? What expertise are you using?

Optimal Grip and Categorization

I might propose a more fundamental kind of expertise, one that is central to your everyday sense-making. This is inspired by the work

---

12. A version of this hypothesis has also been proposed, independently, by Newberg. For further reading, see Andrew Newberg and Mark Robert Waldman, *How Enlightenment Changes Your Brain: The New Science of Transformation* (New York: Avery, 2016).

of Hubert Dreyfus, who is famous for bringing Merleau-Ponty into cognitive science, and Charles Taylor, who reintroduced many people to the idea of contact epistemology.[13] As I explained in the previous chapter, the felicitous term *optimal grip* harkens back to the conformity theory of cognition.

When I am trying to perceive an object, especially if I do not know what it is, I do not remain static. I move around the object until I find the right place for my perception and until I see as many details of the object as possible without losing my view of its overall structure. I perch myself to balance between feature and gestalt.

When you draw a face, you try and capture the perspective of that optimal grip, both the parts and the whole, without zooming in too closely on an eye or lingering too far in the distance. This effort is usually not conscious. You learned to do this as a young child, and the same principle applies to other activities.

When you are learning to track a sparring partner in martial arts, you seek an optimal grip on your opponent. This is known as "tiger eyes" in Tai Chi; we do not want to focus hard on the person's face, or any specific feature. This petrifies our grip and prevents us from tracking significant movements.

Psychological research has shown that individuals who have been held at gunpoint can give an accurate description of the gun but usually not the individual holding it. They lose their soft vigilance in the midst of their fear. You want your wandering attention to flow over an opponent, but not blurrily. You want to see a body but not to lose its features.

Eleanor Rosch pointed this out in our use of categories.[14] When you see a dog on the street, you don't call it a mammal. We default to "dog" as the basic level of address because it best describes our relationship with the addressee, and frames the relevant interaction.

---

13. Especially in Merleau-Ponty's *Phenomenology of Perception* and Dreyfus and Taylor's 2015 book *Retrieving Realism*.
14. Eleanor Rosch, Carolyn B. Mervis, Wayne D. Gray, David M. Johnson, and Penny Boyes-Braem, "Basic Objects in Natural Categories," *Cognitive Psychology* 8, no. 3 (1976): 382–439.

The category of "dog" affords our most optimal grip; it equips us to train, bond with, and care for the animal we perceive.

Categorizing for optimal grip involves a careful trade-off. I want as much similarity as possible within a category and as much difference as possible *between* two categories. As a category scales up and generalizes, it becomes more abstract and loses relevant differences. As I focus on the details, the category becomes too specific and loses its generality.

"Cats" and "dogs" give us an optimal cognitive grip on the world, a simultaneous shift up to the gestalt and down to the featural. We are constantly trying to toggle our names and interactions to achieve this balance. The same principle is especially true on dates or in interviews. If we set our attention to the right level of detail, we have a better chance of naming and knowing other people, acquiring an impression of the whole, with attention to those features that are most pertinent to the situation.

Every activity and interaction involves this optimal gripping. You have practiced the skill so thoroughly that your proficiency is unconscious. For example, Dreyfus observes that most of us know how close we should stand to someone, depending on the nature and intimacy of the relationship as well as the context of the interaction. There is no algorithm for this, but most of us do it without thinking. The expertise that is flowing in the higher state of consciousness is this optimal gripping.

You will recall that I used this example of how close to stand to someone in a previous chapter to account for the invisible patterns of ritual. Significant continuity exists between the skill of optimal gripping, the state of flow, the ASCs, and the efficacy of ritual. All of these involve scaling our attention dynamically in order to refine our existential mode and conform ourselves more precisely to the world.

Higher states of consciousness combine and intensify these insight processes. The disruptive strategies break and dissolve maladaptive framing. Mind wandering is a good example of a disruptive strategy. It distracts you from how you have framed the situation and can, in moderation, help to refresh your perspective and improve your cognitive flexibility.[15,16,17] This is why we have developed extensive mythologies around incubation and artful distraction.

When faced with difficult dilemmas, we advise to "sleep on it," or "go for a walk," or "take a shower." We code the disruptive strategy of distraction deliberately into our decision-making. We know experimentally that if you pose a problem to a person and then introduce entropy, or noise in a moderate amount, it will help him to provoke an insight.[18,19,20] When your brain is engaging in insight there is good reason to believe that a significant shift occurs between the left and the right hemispheres, an internal disruptive strategy.[21]

Finding Good Invariance

Psychotechnologies can, of course, augment these cognitive processes. Disruptive strategies can de-automatize the process of insight by increasing variation in what you pay attention to and break apart a frame that has been hastily, unconsciously composed, like the

15. Zachary Irving and Evan Thompson, "The Philosophy of Mind-Wandering," In *The Oxford Handbook of Spontaneous Thought: Mind-Wandering, Creativity, and Dreaming* (Oxford University Press, 2018).

16. Eric Williamson, "Finally, the Real Answer Why Your Best Ideas Come While Showering," UVA Today, October 5, 2022, https://news.virginia.edu/content/finally-real-answer-why-your-best-ideas-come-while-showering.

17. Eliaz Segal, "Incubation in insight problem solving," *Creativity Research Journal* 16, no. 1(2004): 141–148.

18. Damian G. Stephen, Rebecca A. Boncoddo, James S. Magnuson, and James A. Dixon, "The Dynamics of Insight: Mathematical Discovery as a Phase Transition." *Memory & Cognition* 37, no. 8 (2009): 1132–1149.

19. Damian G. Stephen and James A. Dixon, "The Self-Organization of Insight: Entropy and Power Laws in Problem Solving." *Journal of Problem Solving* 2, no. 1 (2009): 72–102.

20. Damian G. Stephen, James A. Dixon, and Robert W. Isenhower, "Dynamics of Representational Change: Entropy, Action, and Cognition." *Journal of Experimental Psychology: Human Perception and Performance* 35, no. 6(2009): 1811–1832.

21. Mark Jung-Beeman, Edward M. Bowden, Jason Haberman, Jennifer L. Frymiare, Stella Arambel-Liu, Richard Greenblatt, Paul J. Reber, and John Kounios. "Neural Activity When People Solve Verbal Problems with Insight." *PLoS Biology* 2, no. 4(2004): e97.

square in the nine-dot problem. Increasing variation is crucial because it gives us more awareness of what is invariant.

The more I change my attention, the more I become aware of what is not changing. Variation alerts us to constancy. As I move around an object to see different features, I develop a model of what is unchanging about the structure, the form that presides over the details. This invariance gives me contact with the reality of the object and allows for a more consistent optimal grip. However, there is *good invariance* and *bad invariance*. Good invariance alerts me to real, unchanging patterns in the world, but bad invariance is a repetitious encounter with a poorly framed problem, something I try again and again to solve but will not yield or open to my understanding. The bad invariance refuses to open because I need to change something in my attention. My attentional scaling is barring me from access, so the problem seems petrified and insoluble.

To track good invariance and avoid bad invariance, psychologists Kaplan and Simon[22] propose that we use a heuristic, a strategy we call a *Notice Invariance Heuristic*. When you increase variation across your different problem formulations in an attempt to solve a problem, you can notice what is not changing in each formulation and, therefore, notice what you are not changing in the way you pay attention. Oftentimes, the thing you neglect to change is precisely what you need to change in order to disassemble the inadequate frame. Applying this heuristic involves a certain humility because it requires a steadfast attention to your failures.

Kaplan and Simon observe how the Notice Invariance Heuristic intervenes in a single problem. However, what if I have not just one error but a whole system of errors? The child in the previous chapter who privileged the space between candies will apply this error systematically in many different domains. Children undergo a profound developmental change only when they find a systematic pattern of errors, and they apply that insight systematically to all of those interrelated problems. When they have that systematically

---

22. Craig A. Kaplan and Herbert A. Simon, "In Search of Insight," *Cognitive Psychology* 22, no. 3 (1990): 374–419.

penetrative insight, they can acquire new agency and problem-solving capacities. This ushers in a meaningful cognitive maturation.

A version of this maturation happens in the enlightenment experience. By opening up variation, you not only connect more efficaciously to the world, but you can discover and solve for the ways you are being held back in your own development. You can identify the systematic errors in your attention and afford radical developmental change. One of the hallmarks of wisdom is what McKee and Barber called "seeing through illusion."[23]

Childhood is the prototype for such transformations, but their importance extends across the span of a human life. As the child is to the adult, the adult is to the sage. The legacy of the Axial Revolution was focused on this developmental journey, and higher states of consciousness were erstwhile ways of catalyzing these changes in our adult lives.

Though many Axial structures, like the two-world mythology, are no longer accessible to us, we must consider the consequences of abandoning these powerful psychotechnologies of self-transcendence. If we can undertake such practices wisely, they may retain a great power to transform our lives and to train our attention for value and reality, precisely when we struggle to find the good invariance in our world.

---

23. Patrick McKee and Clifton Barber, "On Defining Wisdom." *The International Journal of Aging and Human Development* 49, no. 2(1999): 149–164.

12

HIGHER STATES OF
CONSCIOUSNESS (PART 2)

When we apply the machinery of cognitive science to the phenomenology of higher states of consciousness, we begin to see how the Axial project of self-transcendence, enhanced inner peace, and connectedness to reality could remain available to modern people. However, many unanswered questions remain that bar the way. How do we find a place to vouchsafe the precious value that these states can confer when we no longer believe, or even understand, the two-worlds mythology?

The world in these higher states of consciousness is comprehensive and detailed, intricate and interesting. It is highly intelligible, beautiful, and carries an ineffable sense of oneness and sati, just like Plato's anagoge. According to the Continuity Hypothesis, these states function on the same cognitive machinery that guides our everyday experience—the optimal grip, the fluency of reading, the cascades of insight that are exapted into more mystical experiences, and quantum changes of character.

As I explained in the previous chapter, this cognitive continuity explains how disruptive strategies can be used to cultivate higher states, increasing variation in your attention to reveal meaningful invariance in the world. The "good" invariance allows you to see patterns that remain unchanged; implicit processing and learning are enhanced to track causal patterns. Competent science does this more explicitly through experimentation. The "bad" invariance, conversely, is a consequence of persistent misframing, which must be broken by a developmental insight that causes a systemic—and systematic—change to an entire nexus of problems.[1]

Egoic Decentering and the Solomon Effect

The process of egoic decentering seems central to these experiences. Cognitive Scientist Igor Grossmann has produced strong experimental evidence that decentering strategies are highly relevant to wisdom cultivation.[2] He has called this the *Solomon Effect*.[3,4,5] Take a moment to recall a messy, interpersonal problem that had you stuck and frustrated. Both our deepest dilemmas and salvations are found in relationships with other persons. They are generally predictive of how meaningful our lives are, but they are also our most complex sources of anxiety.

When people describe an interpersonal problem, they are first mesmerized by the mirage of their egocentric perspective. Something happens, however, when you ask someone to redescribe the same problem from a third-person perspective. They decenter. They have an insight and often break the frame that enclosed and frustrated them. They realize the ways in which they have been obtuse, systematically blocked, unable to solve their problem or access the

---

1. Juensung Kim and I have, together in conversation, explored the idea of development being a systemic and systematic insight. Systemic meaning it is occurring throughout the cognitive system and systematic meaning that it is happening in an ordered and coordinated fashion. It is a system of insights not just a single insight.

2. This was also prefigured in earlier work by the Berlin Paradigm.

3. Ethan Kross and Igor Grossmann, "Boosting Wisdom: Distance from the Self Enhances Wise Reasoning, Attitudes, and Behavior," *Journal of Experimental Psychology: General* 141, no. 1(2012): 43–48.

4. Igor Grossmann and Ethan Kross, "Exploring Solomon's Paradox: Self-Distancing Eliminates the Self-Other Asymmetry in Wise Reasoning about Close Relationships in Younger and Older Adults," *Psychological Science* 25, no. 8 (2014): 1571–1580.

5. Paul B. Baltes and Ursula M. Staudinger, "Wisdom: A Metaheuristic (Pragmatic) to Orchestrate Mind and Virtue toward Excellence." *The American Psychologist* 55, no. 1(2000): 122.

other perspective. This phenomenon is called the *Solomon Effect* because it provokes a wiser, more balanced ingress to a problem. It addresses the systematic errors of egocentrism that fog our perception and cause us to treat our relationships too hastily and foolishly.

Higher states of consciousness, when they produce moments of awakening and decentering, are interventions in systematic human error. We should not romanticize these experiences; they can be jarring, terrifying, and even traumatic. Pursuing them alone in an autodidactic fashion is a dangerous undertaking. Autodidacts tend to fall into their own echo chambers, vicious circles of egocentric entombment.

The Buddha gave us a useful parable about this risk. To catch a monkey, you spread pitch on a piece of wood until it looks shiny and tasty. When the monkey grabs the wood with its hand, it gets stuck. Then the monkey uses its other hand to free itself, and that hand gets stuck. Then it uses its right foot, and its left, and then its head and mouth. Then it is completely trapped. The hunter comes and kills it.

Decentering can alleviate foolishness and ill-framed invariance. But if it occurs in isolation, untutored by tradition and ritual, it can be severely damaging. Personal transformation comes with great risk, and it is dangerous for people to take psychedelics without having placed them properly within ritual, a wisdom tradition, or a community that can guide them sagely through consequent upheavals.

Many people now pursue psychedelics wantonly without the support of this guidance or tradition. This wisdom vacuum is among the defining symptoms of our time; we have sources of information and institutions of knowledge, sciences with specialists and respected experts. We do not have this for wisdom. Individuals like Siddhartha deserve our admiration for attaining this wisdom as individuals (though the Buddha himself had mentors along the way). However, we should not overestimate the necessity of community and formal teaching. The Buddha made it very clear that the sangha of the community was necessary for the cultivation of these transformative states.

This radical decentering is a participatory change, a newfound conformity with the world outside oneself. It does not just involve the machinery of cognition or consciousness but alters their structure and functions, therefore precipitating a fundamental transformation of character. The world seems to reveal itself more deeply to you, and you too seem more revealed. This mutually accelerating disclosure creates a powerful coupling and conformity between self and world. We experience this mutual disclosure when we fall in love. We might say, therefore, that the participatory knowing we attain in the higher state of consciousness gives us the experience of falling in love with being.

Some recent cognitive science research may give us some understanding about the function of this egoic decentering. For example, the work of Sui and Humphreys suggests that one of the functions of your self is to act as *glue*.[6] Your self pieces the world together. By making things relevant to yourself, you make them relevant to one another, sticking them together and causing them to belong as a whole. Remember that the meaning of *logos* refers to this dynamic, the gathering together into optimal arrangement. I simultaneously glue things together as I glue myself together.

The self, however else we might conceive of it, is a powerful set of functions for integrating and complexifying the way we process information. When we have a transformative and decentering experience, these functions can exapt and rescale their attention, and we can turn this machinery of integration—normally reflexive and self-focused—to reveal deeper underlying patterns in the world.[7,8] That is why the world seems to come alive in these experiences and reveal such infinite depths.

Imagine the intimacy of your self-knowledge, all the resources

6. Jie Sui and Glyn W. Humphreys, "The Integrative Self: How Self-Reference Integrates Perception and Memory," *Trends in Cognitive Sciences* 19, no. 12(2015): 719–728.

7. Philip Novak, "Buddhist Meditation and the Consciousness of Time," *Journal of Consciousness Studies* 3, 3(1996): 267–277.

8. Guy Claxton, "Neurotheology: Buddhism, Cognitive Science and Mystical Experience," *The Psychology of Awakening: Buddhism, Science, and Our Day-to-Day Lives* (2000): 90–111.

and energy spent on arranging and cohering yourself, being turned upon the world. This occurs in radical decentering; all of the time, effort, processing, skill, memory and structures we have built into our ego can be exapted to disclose the world beyond us. This turn effects an existential shift into the being mode, a flowing optimal grip, and an enhanced awareness of invariance and systematic error.

The Importance of Disruption: Neural Networks and Metastability

The information processing functions of the self machinery and our understanding of mystical experiences are increasingly being informed by machine learning and artificial intelligence. Researchers use disruptive strategies to provoke machines into being better learners. For example, Alexander Woodward[9] introduced randomization into a neural network, a powerful and cutting-edge form of artificial intelligence that mimics some aspects of brain function. When training these neural networks to learn for themselves, researchers introduce noise, entropy, and randomness.

Woodward argues that such randomness is an essential aspect of the self-optimization process.[10] Researchers are trying to make neural networks that learn better as well as self-optimize, and disruption seems essential to this project. Powerful machines sample from the world, but these patterns need authentication if they are to be generalized and relied on. We invented statistics to deal with this question. How do I know if the patterns in my sample match the patterns in the world?

9. Alexander Woodward, Tom Froese, and Takashi Ikegami, "Neural Coordination Can Be Enhanced by Occasional Interruption of Normal Firing Patterns: A Self-Optimizing Spiking Neural Network Model," *Neural Networks* 62 (2015): 39–46.
10. Ibid.

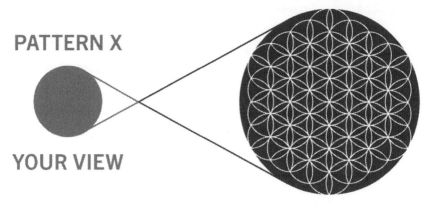

Figure 12.1: This figure depicts the difference between your view and the world. You are always sampling from the world, so your view is much smaller, and what you see represents a portion of what happens in the world. From what you see, you may pick up on a pattern. This "pattern X" is represented as a blue circle in this figure. You are trying to determine whether or not this "pattern X" in your view is also a pattern of the world. The question marks represent this uncertainty.

Very often, these neural networks will overfit to the data. They will pick up on the pattern in the sample too tightly, even when it does not generalize to the rest of the world. Think of a line of best fit in a scatterplot. We try to find the function that generalizes to many different contexts, but sometimes the neural networks track a function that perfectly describes the sample but does not generalize to the population.

How does one address this problem? You introduce some noise into the system. You turn off half of the nodes. You disrupt the processing to compress the data and prevent you from overfitting to it. The compression allows you to find the real invariance, the real patterns that will generalize across all the varying contexts.

Just as it is important not to overfit the data, it is equally important not to underfit it. In the latter case, you will not pick up on any real patterns at all. Disruptive strategies have to be set within powerful pattern detection. Once again, these systems must toggle. They must disrupt and break frame, reorder the information, and remake the frame to better fit the information. They are seeking an optimal grip between disruptive variation and compression, detecting real patterns that allow us to become good learners.

This is exactly what we are seeing in these higher states of consciousness and why it is essential to have the experiences couched in traditions and rituals that can afford powerful pattern detection and introduce the required disruption when needed. This helps a person toggle between disruption and compression. Jamming without skill gives you junk. It does not give you jazz.

Just like these machines, the brain is constantly engaging in this kind of pattern compression, the toggling of attention we observe in higher states of consciousness. Dr. Andrew Newberg has conducted extensive brain scanning during these kinds of experiences.[11] His studies show increased activity in the frontal area and the parietal area of the brain. These two areas, according to the *Parieto-Frontal Integration Theory*,[12] are most associated with your general intelligence and your ability to attain an optimal grip on the world.

Initially these areas become hyperactive in the experience. Then, the opposite occurs. They become hypoactive (inactive). Throughout this process, we observe enhanced activity in the thalamus, the area of the brain that tries to integrate different kinds of information together.

The greater the disruptive shift, the more powerful the insight. You bring all this cognitive machinery to bear to frame the pattern. Then you have to dramatically disrupt it. Then the system reorganizes itself. I would suggest that this cyclical process of dissolution and resolution is precisely what occurs in these awakening experiences.

We can see this kind of shift occurring in the brain during psychedelic experiences. According to recent work by Carhart-Harris,

---

11. Andrew Newburg, and Mark Robert Waldman, *How Enlightenment Changes Your Brain: The New Science of Transformation* (Avery, 2016).
12. Rex E. Jung and Richard J. Haier, "The Parieto-Frontal Integration Theory (P-FIT) of Intelligence: Converging Neuroimaging Evidence." *Behavioral and Brain Sciences* 30, no. 2 (2007): 135–154.

et al.,[13] psilocybin increases your *metastability*.[14,15] Normally your brain is either integrating or segregating. With psilocybin, your brain is doing both. Therefore, it is also complexifying.

Complexification occurs when your brain is simultaneously integrating and differentiating information, and it gives rise to new abilities and emergent functions. The way you grow and self-transcend as a system is precisely by complexifying. Psilocybin, by putting you into metastability, helps your brain facilitate this process and accelerates it. It allows you to see the world, so to speak, in a grain of sand.

Plausibility: Elegance and Trustworthiness

These scientific accounts—psychological, neurological, and machine processing levels—must be placed within the proper sapiential context. We need traditions and institutions, a committed community of cultivating wisdom. This leads us back into the prescriptive argument. Why should we listen to people who have been in this state, and why should it justify some transformation in your life?

In order to answer this, I must introduce the notion of *plausibility*. Plausibility is central to your perception of reality. The word has two meanings. One is usually a synonym for "highly probable," but this is not my use. I use "plausibility" to mean an argument made sensibly that stands to reason and should be taken seriously.[16]

Most of the time you cannot base your actions on certainty. You must rely on plausibility. This involves something Rescher calls

---

13. Robin L. Carhart-Harris, Robert Leech, Peter J. Hellyer, Murray Shanahan, Amanda Feilding, Enzo Tagliazucchi, Dante R. Chialvo, and David Nutt, "The Entropic Brain: A Theory of Conscious States Informed by Neuroimaging Research with Psychedelic Drugs," *Frontiers in Human Neuroscience* 8 (2014): 20.

14. Emmanuelle Tognoli and J. A. Scott Kelso, "Brain Coordination Dynamics: True and False Faces of Phase Synchrony and Metastability," *Progress in Neurobiology* 87, no. 1(2009): 31–40.

15. J. A. Scott Kelso, "Multistability and Metastability: Understanding Dynamic Coordination in the Brain," *Philosophical Transactions of the Royal Society B: Biological Sciences* 367, no. 1591(2012): 906–918.

16. This use of plausibility was made famous by Rescher (1976) and others.

trustworthiness. We regard a proposal or theory as trustworthy if it has been produced by many independent but converging lines of evidence. Remember Aristotle's criteria from an earlier chapter. You will regard information as more real if it comes through multiple senses.

If I rely only on my sight, it may be illusory. But if I can see, touch, taste, hear, and smell the same phenomenon, it is far less likely to be illusory. Science is preoccupied with numbers for this reason. They allow us to converge the senses. The convergent senses do not give me certainty, but do they give trustworthiness. They reduce the likelihood that I am deceived.

Convergent senses and accounts are important for examining how we come by information. But these are not sufficient for plausibility. We must also look forward to determine what we can do with the information. We want a model that we can apply to many new domains, which will open up the world for us and give access to new possibilities. When I can use the same model or theory in many different places, it becomes *elegant*. We need convergence for trustworthiness, but we need elegance for power and multi-apt application.

This balance must be highly fluent in your cognition. It must be something you can internalize and use readily. If I have convergence without much elegance, it amounts to triviality. Trivial statements might be true, but they are not powerful. We consider many truisms to be trite precisely because they lack any causal efficacy or instruction.

The opposite, of course, is also problematic. Some models or theories have precious little convergence yet much promise of power. This is when they become farfetched. Conspiracy theories often have this feature. If they were true, they would explain so much. The Meaning Crisis would be far more soluble if we could attribute it to water fluoridation. However powerful this explanation is, we have little trustworthy evidence for it.

As Elijah Millgram claimed, we want our *backward commitments* and *forward commitments* to match one another.[17] We only commit forward when we have trust in the model we produced. When all of this falls into place, we find not only fluency but also plausibility. When we have deep convergence, deep elegance, and efficient fluency, we find the theory or proposal to be profound.

In a higher state of consciousness, the brain is constantly disrupting itself and evaluating the plausibility of its processing: decentering, de-automatizing, identifying systematic error. This complexification yields emergent new functions and the exaptation of the insight and self machinery into new abilities.

Plausibility is not certainty, but it is what we rely on for our actions and decisions as individuals, and collectively for our scientific worldview. Almost all of the theories proposed in the history of science have turned out to be false in some significant way. Science is not believed because it gives certainty. It is believed in because it gives us self-correcting plausibility. Before we conduct any experimental work, we use plausibility to determine which hypotheses to test. When I run my experiment, I have to control for alternative explanations, but I don't control for all possible alternative explanations, only the plausible ones.

Good science involves inference to the best explanation.[18] I identify the questionable phenomena, and then I produce candidate explanations for what causes the phenomena. Then I put these explanations into competition with each other. The hypothesis that best explains the phenomena becomes "real" and is given scientific validity. But this is still only a matter of plausibility.

Certainty would involve searching an infinite number of possible explanations. This would be combinatorially explosive and therefore impossible for a human being. Science cannot be certain because the "winning" explanation is only as good as the competing hypotheses it defeats.

Science relies on plausibility judgments—when we choose our hypothesis, when we choose the variables we control for, and when

---

17. Elijah Millgram, *Practical Induction* (Harvard University Press, 1997).
18. Peter Lipton, *Inference to the Best Explanation* (Routledge, 1991).

we interpret the data. The number of interpretations I can give for any data set is also infinite. Plausibility is therefore indispensable.

Plausibility in Higher States of Consciousness

This higher state of consciousness is an optimization of your cognitive processing and plausibility machinery. You need an optimal grip before you can appraise a situation. You must zero in on the relevant information before you can use it. You must formulate a problem before you can resolve it.

These higher states seem to exapt and enhance all of these fundamental processes. The higher state gives us systematic insight. It flows very fluently into many domains of our life, converges many reliably powerful processes to foster trustworthiness, and provides a wide and deep application to foster their elegance. In doing so, the higher states cultivate an optimal grip, toggle between trade-offs, and find the best relation between generalization and discrimination. This is why these states are such good guides for transformation and ways of relieving self-deception, provided they are set within a set of sapiential practices and a sapiential tradition.

Sometimes people return from these higher states and make pronouncements about reality. Despite their extraordinary effects on our plausibility machinery, these states can produce pronouncements that seem spurious or implausible. As I noted in the last chapter, two people with similar experiences can present vastly different beliefs or conclusions.

We must remember that the wisdom provided by these states is not found at the propositional level of knowing. Higher states of consciousness do not provide secret metaphysical knowledge, at least not the kind that is neatly expressed. Wisdom and character are the fruits of these higher states. If we prioritize these fruits, their value can reorient the meaning of rationality and the role it plays in our philosophical discourse and scientific inquiries.

13

BUDDHISM AND PARASITIC PROCESSING

In the previous two chapters, I attempted to explore a cognitive scientific, psychologically sound approach to mystical experiences and higher states of consciousness. The purpose of this discussion was to examine their prolificity and their claim to rationality. In chapter 12, this claim focused on plausibility and how these states coopt existing processes in the brain: the flow state, optimal gripping, implicit learning and problem-solving.

Even without giving us confirmable theories or metaphysical claims, these states heighten our cognitive fluency, granting us life-altering insights that allow us to connect more meaningfully with ourselves and other people. With this framework, we may begin to understand the awakening experiences of the Buddha, the *sati* of the being mode, and the project of overcoming systematic illusion that is so analogous to the development from child to adult. We need to have these tenets in place if we are to understand the project of Buddhism.

The Interpretation Crisis of Buddhism

Historically, Western attempts to understand Buddhism have been misleading. Author Stephen Batchelor[1] is one of the most astute chroniclers of these interactions and argues that the West faces an *interpretation crisis* in relation to Buddhism. We tend to take one of two approaches. The first claims that you can only interpret Buddhism from within a Buddhist tradition. A good argument can be made for this; as I keep arguing, wisdom and self-transcendence are less about altering your belief and more about transforming your perspectival and participatory knowing. If you are not engaged in transformative practice, you do not understand Buddhism. It has to be practiced *emically*, one might argue, known and lived from within its native cultural context.

This approach is sensible but somewhat myopic. Buddhism has so many traditions, and each is relative to a time and place. To claim that one particular interpretation, sect, or tradition is the sole pathway to understanding Buddhism would seem narrow-minded and even parochial. The alternative to traditional practice is typified by an academic approach—the scholarly study of Buddhism, for example. This approach counters bias with intellectual rigor.

However, it introduces another problem. Most students who study religion do not engage in any religious practices. They often presume that if they became too involved, they would lapse into subjectivity, losing comparison and critical reflection. The academic approach attempts objectivity, but it loses participation.

This crisis is very reminiscent of the problem that Socrates faced between the sophists and natural philosophers. Practicing Buddhism through tradition provides transformative relevance, but the academic study of Buddhism supports an attempt to access the truth. Much like the Socratic project, Buddhism must include both aims, and Batchelor argues that we have to transcend the biases in the academic and tradition-based approaches.

---

1. Batchelor has written a series of books that inform this discussion: *The Awakening of the West: The Encounter of Buddhism and Western Culture, Alone with Others: An Existential Approach to Buddhism,* and *Buddhism without Beliefs: A Contemporary Guide to Awakening.* These are followed by an even more radical book entitled, *After Buddhism: Rethinking the Dharma for a Secular Age,* in which he takes the position of somebody who is post-religious, which is very germane to many of us.

We might say that the interpretation crisis of Buddhism symptomatizes one of the general dilemmas of the Meaning Crisis—the tension between truth and relevance, between scientifically minded plausibility, and the felt significance of personal participation. Our own cultural context often seems to put these at variance and leaves us stranded somewhere between two dangerous fixations: apathy and disaffection, or an unquestioning adherence to certain cultural beliefs.

According to Batchelor, our access to Buddhism is impeded by both kinds of fixation, modes of engagement that are fixed and calcified, misframed like the nine-dot problem. Both positions share a misapprehension of Buddhism as a set of beliefs. This creedal approach to spiritual tradition, a dubious inheritance from post-Christian enlightenment, has somewhat distorted the Axial legacy and reduced the project of wisdom and transcendence to a singular preoccupation with our convictions. We often equate belief with religious practice and use it as a synonym for faith. We have become so oriented by this reduction of spirituality that we appraise religious practice solely on the basis of whether the propositions seem scientifically plausible.

Breaking out of this reduction will be crucial for addressing the Meaning Crisis. Belief systems and ideologies are attempts to create meaning. They often fail, however, because as we know, meaning-making machinery is not occurring primarily at the level of propositional knowledge. Wisdom and religious tradition are not synonymous with belief in any modern sense of the term. Instead, Batchelor proposes that we need to look at Buddhism existentially.

In *Alone with Others,* he invokes Fromm's distinction between existential modes and proposes that Buddhism is a remembrance (*sati*) of the being mode. Traditionally, the Buddha's four noble truths are taken as propositions, and Buddhism is understood as the belief in these propositions. This may not be wrong, but it is simplistic and incomplete; Buddhism is not merely a set of beliefs but a series of transformational processes taking place in our perspectival and participatory knowing. Their functions and effects augment machinery of the self in the ways we discussed in the previous chapter: provoking higher states of consciousness, improving insight and cognitive fluency, and affording a more optimal grip in the agent-arena relationship.

The four noble truths are affordances for the transformations we are discussing. The point is not to believe them, but to believe *in* them, to use them as forms of *sati,* enacted mnemonics that recreate the conditions for Siddhartha's enlightenment. Batchelor proposes, therefore, that we should not call them the *four noble truths* but rather the four *ennobling* truths. I propose that we can take this clarification even further. "Truth" is a property of propositions, so we might instead call these the four ennobling *provocations.* They are trying to provoke people into change.

Let us examine each of the four "noble truths," as ennobling, enabling provocations. By doing that, we will attempt to access the Buddha's teachings and nuance our understanding of his tradition. I will present the standard way of representing each truth and a reformulation to address Batchelor's criticism, interconnected with the argument we have been developing.

The Meaning of Suffering: Traditional Noble Truths to Ennobling Provocations

The first traditional noble truth of Buddhism is famous even to non-Buddhists: *All is suffering.* If this statement were believed straightforwardly, it would be evidently false. Suffering is a comparative term, and comparative terms cannot be extended to everything. It would be like saying: "everything is tall." Tall is relative to short. Suffering is relative to peace or equanimity. However, the precept is conveying something about the nature of existence that penetrates all of our experience.

What is the "all"? Does it mean all existence? We should be careful here; the Buddha was famously reticent to give metaphysical interpretations to awakening experiences, and as we discussed, a propositional conclusion will not capture the significance of an insight, especially when we mistake the semantics of the utterance. Like many such terms, the meaning of "suffering" has been trivialized over time. When people hear suffering, they usually hear pain or distress. But this is not the original meaning.

To suffer means to be beset, to lose agency in the world. Pain is a powerful way to lose agency, of course; it is disruptive and often damaging. But positive experiences compromise our agency just as readily. You can suffer joy, for example; you can experience so much of it that you lose control of yourself. Understood this way, it is not oxymoronic to say I am suffering pleasure.

Pain or pleasure are relative terms, but suffering is a loss of agency. In the previous chapter, I introduced the parable of the monkey that grabs the pitch, becomes stuck, tries to free itself, and is captured and killed. This is a parable for suffering. Most of the Buddha's metaphors are not pain metaphors but entrapment metaphors. They involve being fettered and losing your agency.

The Buddha did not describe enlightenment in terms of relief but in terms of freedom. Wherever you dip into the ocean, he said, it has one taste, the taste of salt. So it was with his teaching; wherever you dip into his teaching it has one taste, the taste of freedom.

So let us convert the truth of "all is suffering" to the following provocation: *realize that all of your life is threatened with a loss of freedom, a loss of agency.* There is a word for this kind of loss, so often translated as suffering: *dukkha.* The etymology of the term is provocative: imagine a wheel off center on its axis. The axle is not resting properly through the center of the wheel, and as the wheel turns, it grinds against itself.

The same thing occurs when your arm is out of joint; as you move your arm, the movement itself is injuring it. Dukkha refers to an empty gap filled with dirt and grit. As things move within it, they are damaging themselves. The Buddhist idea of suffering is a loss of agency with self-destructive movements. The idea that "all is suffering" reminds us that all of life is existentially threatened by a capacity for self-destructive, self-deceptive behavior.

You can see how this provocation sits so firmly within the Axial tradition. As I have suggested, the very cognitive processes that make you adaptively intelligent also make you vulnerable to foolishness.[2] For example, when you encounter an event and interpret it as "bad," your brain immediately tries to predict and anticipate other events like it. Encountering something painful or distressing sensitizes you to anticipating it in the future, and your brain works to assess its probability.

As we know, however, you cannot process all of the information available to you; the variables are indefinitely vast and combinatorially explosive. We therefore use our *heuristics*, shortcuts that try to bypass this vastness and zero in on relevant information. We use a representativeness heuristic, which judges how probable an event is by how prototypical and salient it is, with an availability heuristic, which judges how probable an event is by how easily you can remember or imagine a similar event occurring.

These heuristics are astute and well-adapted. However, they also create certain biases. When you are in a bad state because something bad has occurred, it triggers something called *encoding specificity*. When you are sad, it is easy to remember sad events and much more difficult to remember happy ones. Memory is not mere historical fact but moods, sensations, and states of mind—our perspectival and participatory knowing.

If you lose your keys when drunk, getting drunk again is a reliable way to reinvoke the memory and locate the keys. Classic experiments demonstrate this. In one case, a group of people are placed into a room to learn a set of words. They are then separated into two groups, A and B.[3] Group A is tested on the words in the same room, and group B is tested in a different room. Group A remembers more words than B simply because they remained in the same room.

This is very adaptive; your brain is trying to always fit you to the environment. It does not merely store information. It stores the context of the agent-arena relation. One state can therefore recall

---

2. John Vervaeke and Leonardo Ferraro, "Relevance, Meaning and the Cognitive Science of Wisdom," In *The Scientific Study of Personal Wisdom: From Contemplative Traditions to Neuroscience* (Dordrecht: Springer Netherlands, 2013) 21–51.
3. Steven M. Smith, Arthur Glenberg, and Robert A. Bjork, "Environmental Context and Human Memory," *Memory & Cognition* 6, no. 4(1978): 342–353.

another of the same salience. When in a bad state, it is easy to recall bad things and predict higher probability for their occurrence. The two adaptive processes reinforce each other.

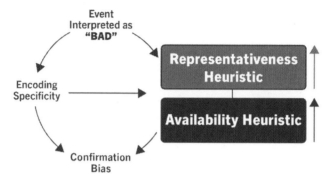

Figure 13.1: When you interpret an event as "bad," your use of the representative heuristic goes up, and you judge the probability of bad things happening to be increasing. This provokes your use of the availability heuristic. You feel it more probable that similar bad things will happen. Both of these processes reinforce each other, represented by the double arrow. This leads to a confirmation bias, an adaptive strategy that causes you to look only for information that supports your current belief. Interpreting an event as "bad" activates your encoding specificity, causing you to more readily remember previous events that were "bad." This reaffirms your confirmation bias.

This is called the *confirmation bias*. I look only for information that supports my current belief because it is often difficult and complex to find disconfirmation. As I search my memory and imagination, I look for things that confirm my judgment that an event is highly probable. While adaptive, all of these heuristics can mislead us.

Fears of air travel, for example, are embellished by the availability heuristic. It is quite easy to imagine a plane falling from the sky, and when plane crashes do happen, the tragedy makes them feel disproportionately salient. We therefore judge airplane crashes to be highly probable even though they are low in occurrence. Meanwhile, most of us take automobiles to get to the airport without thinking twice about the probability of fatal collision, which is significantly higher than a plane crash. We misjudge probabilities all the time because of these heuristics.

Dukkha: Parasitic Processing and Reciprocal Narrowing

These mechanisms, just like reading or hyperbolic discounting (discussed in chapter 5), operate automatically in a self-organizing fashion, both bottom-up and top-down. We cannot live without them, but they easily lead us astray. The judgments of heuristics are not emotionally neutral. When your brain projects a high probability for negative events, you get anxiety. You lose cognitive flexibility. Your framing becomes very narrow, rigid and limited, and reduces your ability to solve problems. You become more prone to error and failure, which redoubles your anxiety and gives a dreadful presentiment of bad events.

All of this gathers into a pattern in your mind: "I am doomed." The world feels fatalistic. You start interpreting more events, even neutral events, as inauspicious. The pattern feeds and fulfills itself. That is what it means to say that all of your life is threatened by dukkha.

Every time you exercise intelligent agency, the very processes that make you so intelligently adaptive also make you vulnerable to self-deception and self-destruction. Leo Ferraro and I call this *parasitic processing*,[4] depicted in the following figure:

4. John Vervaeke and Leonardo Ferraro, "Relevance, Meaning and the Cognitive Science of Wisdom," In *The Scientific Study of Personal Wisdom: From Contemplative Traditions to Neuroscience* (Dordrecht: Springer Netherlands, 2013) 21–51.

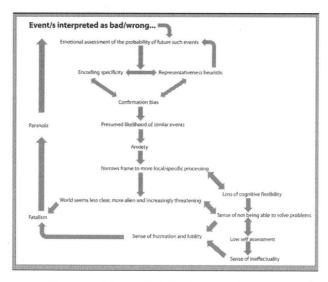

Figure 13.2: A diagram depicting the nature of parasitic processing.

This concept of parasitic processing is very similar to a prevailing model of depression, which is schematized by some MIT researchers in the figure below:

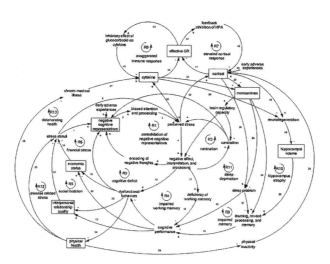

Figure 13.3: A schema for depression put forth by MIT researchers (Wittenborn et al., 2016).

This schema for depression (Figure 13.3) demonstrates how the brain gets into many different kinds of spirals.[5]

We call this parasitic processing because the pattern resembles a parasite that takes up life within you and takes your life away. It causes you to lose your agency. Your cognitive capacity to be self-organizing, heuristic using, complexifying, systematic—all of this can be hijacked when possessed by a pernicious pattern. When you are in one of these spirals, it runs off of the same machinery, and your beliefs and propositional knowledge are impotent to restrain it. This is a complex, self-organizing adaptive system. If you try to intervene in one point, the rest of the system reorganizes itself around your attempted intervention. It can adapt and preserve itself even as you try to destroy it.

No matter where you are or what you are doing, parasitic processing is a perennial threat. I have joined my colleague Mark Lewis in identifying a significant connection between addiction and the loss of agency.[6] Addiction is distressing and painful, but we usually diagnose it by how dysfunctional a person becomes, how much he loses his freedom of will. You are a video game addict if your gaming prevents you from pursuing the desired goals in your life or the personal relationships that are most meaningful. If video gaming robs you of those agentic processes and developments of character, it has become addictive.

Dr. Lewis challenges the standard model of addiction, which he believes to be incorrect. The standard model presumes a biophysical, chemical dependency; when the chemical is removed, we get an overwhelming compulsion to seek it. If the chemical is withheld, our suffering is similar to hunger or thirst. This account is commonsensical, and the media likes it. However, it is almost

---

5. A. K. Wittenborn, H. Rahmandad, J. Rick, and N. Hosseinichimeh, "Depression as a Systemic Syndrome: Mapping the Feedback Loops of Major Depressive Disorder," *Psychological Medicine* 46, 3(2016): 551–562.

6. Dr. Lewis is one of the foremost neuroscientists studying addiction and a former addict himself. I strongly recommend reading his book *Memoirs of an Addicted Brain* (previously referenced) and "Brain Change in Addiction as Learning, Not Disease," *New England Journal of Medicine* 379, no. 16 (2018): 1551–1560, https://doi.org/10.1056/NEJMra1602872.

completely false.[7] You can be addicted to processes, like gambling, that have no biochemical basis.[8]

Second, if the compulsion model was correct, you would have great difficulty explaining certain facts. For example, most people spontaneously give up addictions in their thirties.[9] Many American soldiers were addicted to opioids during the Vietnam War, but when they returned to the United States, the vast majority of them spontaneously stopped using the drug. How was this possible? Was there not a biochemical compulsion?

We must think about this in existential terms. When in Vietnam, the soldiers had a particular agency (soldiering) in relation to a particular arena (war). They lived out a certain existential mode and took on a certain identity. When they returned to the United States, they became citizens in a peaceful country. A different agent-arena relationship changed their identity. It broke the frame and dissolved the pattern that inculcated the addictive behavior.

Addiction is conditioned, or disarmed, by our agent-arena relationship, and Dr. Lewis proposes a model for addiction that he calls *reciprocal narrowing*. We introduced this term in chapter 7 to describe Fromm's modal confusion. In the throes of drug addiction, for example, drug use is connected with a particular agent-arena relationship. When you first take the drug, you start to lose some of your cognitive flexibility, and your number of options in the world begins to decline.

---

7. I am not denying that there are biochemical aspects of addiction, but it does not adequately explain much of the important data surrounding the use of addictive substances – for example, people spontaneously discontinuing use of these substances under certain non-chemical conditions.

8. By this, I mean no chemical stimulation. I am not excluding endogenous biochemical changes.

9. This data was presented at the Society for Philosophy and Psychology conference in 2018 with the theme of "Addiction and Problems of Agency." The presentations included: Melissa Koenig and Marc Lewis (Psychology, Radboud University): "Addiction as Entrainment: A Perspective from Embodied Cognition." Peg O'Connor (Philosophy, Gustavus Adolphus): Shame and Addiction: Feeling as if You Must Use." Hanna Pickard (Philosophy, Princeton): "The Puzzle of Addiction." Kent Berridge (Psychology, Michigan): "Is Addiction Compulsive? An Incentive-Sensitization Perspective."

As the options decline, you lose the variability in your cognitive agency. It gets tighter, narrower, less flexible, and the environment seems to deplete. The world feels less accessible and scarcer. The agent and arena reciprocally narrow to the point where you cannot perceive any remaining pathways for action. Your agency is left to flounder. You are stuck inside of yourself, trapped somewhere you cannot stand to be. But you don't know who else you could be or how the world could be otherwise.

The heuristics work against you, and the state begets itself. As C.S. Lewis famously wrote, "The doors of hell are locked on the inside." You are locked into a relationship with reality that seems more fatalistic, more despairing, more diminished. It is a zombified form of participation, a sluggish dream from which you cannot seem to wake.

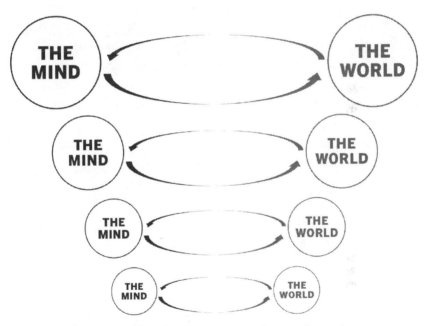

Figure 13.4: A diagram depicting the nature of reciprocal narrowing.

Dukkha is the carrefour of both phenomena: parasitic processing within, reciprocal narrowing without. The two processes reinforce each other. The Buddha tried self-denial as a means of escape, but this is like trying to hop over your shadow. You cannot escape dukkha because it is endemic; the agent-arena relationship, with all of its self-organizing, complexifying and relevance realizing, is indispensable to your cognitive agency. This, perhaps, is what the Buddha meant in his first ennobling provocation. All of your life is threatened by this dukkha, and you must be cognizant of this threat before you undertake any moves toward enlightenment.

Reciprocal Opening and The Eightfold Path

The second noble truth is traditionally presented as follows: *Suffering is caused by desire.*

That presentation raises a few problems. If desire is the cause of dukkha, would the desire to be free of dukkha not entrap you more in dukkha? You may find it more useful to interpret desire as attachment—the addictive dependency we have just described, the pattern of need that leads to the narrowing of self and world, the loss of options and agency. The addict is attached to their drug, but calling this compulsion "desire" implies a base definition of desire as opposed to the rational, human desire for reality that Plato and Aristotle prioritized.

The third truth is traditionally presented as: *The cessation of suffering is attainable.* I propose to reformulate as follows: *Realize that you can recover your agency.* I propose that the downward spiral of reciprocal narrowing has a counterpoint, a reverse movement of *reciprocal opening* that scales the same cognitive machinery. What would it mean to spiral upward? What about an agent-arena relationship where agent and world are mutually expanding, strengthening our insight, and appreciating our optimal grip on reality?

We have been talking about this at length already, of course: this is *anagoge*, that Platonic move to enlightenment depicted in the ascent from the cave and enacted in the Buddha's mindfulness practices. You deal with a pernicious dynamical system by cultivating a counteractive dynamical system, one that does not intervene at one point in the *dukkha* but coordinates to all points simultaneously.

What if I created a counteractive dynamical system? This system would not just tutor my beliefs but could also provoke me into ASCs and allow me to develop skills and traits of character that I had scarcely yet discovered.

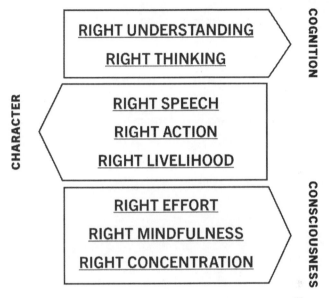

Figure 13.5: A diagram depicting the Eightfold Path. The eight elements can be separated into three categories: those that pertain to cognition, character, and consciousness.

This is what the Buddha offered in the *Eightfold Path,* a dynamical system that counteracts parasitic processing and reciprocal narrowing. That is why it is represented by an eight-spoked wheel, a counter to the grinding wheel of *dukkha*. This self-organizing system turns itself. Each part is interdependent on the others, but each must be cultivated in its own virtue: right understanding, right thinking, right speech, right action, right livelihood, right effort, right mindfulness, and right concentration.

It is important to note that "right" does not mean moral righteousness, but right-handedness. It refers to the expertise of optimal grip. The Eightfold Path can be split into three sections, dealing with your cognition (right understanding and thinking), character (right speech, action, and livelihood) and consciousness (right mindfulness, effort, and concentration). It deals with ethical aspects, existential aspects, and sapiential aspects of existence. It means to turn you beyond the prison of the ego and its everyday world and realize the deeper memories of being.

This is what the Buddha was offering. His four noble truths are ennobling provocations designed to simulate Siddhartha's first sights outside the palace, to unsettle you in the complacency of a dream, that blithe, modally confused life beset by agentless influence. Yet even as he threatens us, he also encourages us. He reminds us that a life beyond is possible. Just as in the Socratic tradition, threat and courage both are required to induce this metanoetic turn. One awakens us to the presence of illusion and our dissatisfaction. The other orients our aspiration, reignites our eros for reality, and gives us the drive to undertake transformation.

14

EPICUREANS, CYNICS, AND STOICS

The interpretation crisis of Buddhism, so elegantly presented by Stephen Batchelor, is a general affliction of our relationship with sacredness. If we hope to recover the import of philosophical and religious traditions, we must find an existential way to conjugate them back into our lives. That way, they might be augmented by our scientific worldview rather than compete with it. This is why I have attempted to reinterpret the Buddha's pronouncements.

We moderns place significant faith in propositional belief, and consequently, the ideas of faith and belief have been reciprocally narrowed by their diminishing relevance and plausibility. Language is limited in its capacity to capture experience, so the idea that all truth and reality should be linguistically communicable or comprehensible should seem naive. Therefore, it is an exercise of optimal gripping to interpret sacred creed not as proposition but provocation, a way to access non-linguistic patterns of knowing, enact new ways of being, and counter the various existential threats like anxiety, addiction, and parasitic processing.

The Eightfold Path is exemplary for this dynamical, systematic intervention, but having concluded our brief review of the Axial Revolution in India, we shall return our attention to the aftermath of the Axial Revolution in the West and the evolution of the Socratic tradition.

The Death of Alexander and the Domicide of the Hellenistic World

Socrates was fortunate. He had an exemplary disciple in Plato, just as Plato had in Aristotle. However, the Axial tradition in ancient Greece suffered a great aporia in the rise of Aristotle's disciple. Alexander the Great created an empire that hellenized most of the known world, but Alexander himself resembled a Bronze Age conqueror. He was a glorious figure. His mythology seemed to alloy humanity and godhood like the pharaohs of ancient Egypt.

Yet the glory of his reign was matched by brevity and cataclysm. Despite its titanic influence, his life was brief. He died in Babylon at the age of thirty-three, and his child (and presumed successor) was killed soon after. His major-generals fought among themselves. They carved his vast empire into four smaller empires that were locked in perpetual war for the next three hundred years.

This chaotic period of history is known as the Hellenistic era. The life and death of Alexander marked a great disruption in the turn of the ancient world—a disruption of language, commerce, politics, religion...all meaningful features of Axial civilization.

The world of Alexander was different from the world of Aristotle. If you lived in Greek culture at the time of Aristotle, you likely lived in a *polis,* a city-state like Athens or Sparta.[1] You knew many of your fellow citizens, and (if you were an adult male) you participated in the city's proto-democratic process. You lived close to the seat of governance and knew its executors.

Everyone spoke your language. Everyone had ancestors, like you did, that tied you to the land, whose names reached back beyond memory. Everyone practiced the same religion and professed the same allegiances. Your polis was not just a place to live. It was the site of a coherent worldview, an intimate agent-arena relationship. Each person was deeply embedded in the environment and knew how to

---

1. This is the word from which cosmopolitan is derived.

interact with it. The polis was home, and one of the severest punishments a person could suffer in this ancient world was exile from the polis—severance from all identity and belonging, all culture and history, all orders of sacredness. For many citizens, death or imprisonment were preferable.

Alexander's life brought an end to the polis, and so doing, forced this exile upon an entire civilization. By his conquest, Greek culture was distributed into Africa and the Levant, into Asia Minor and Proper, right up to the borders of India. Various Greek kingdoms, like Bactria (modern-day Afghanistan), integrated Greek culture with Buddhist philosophy and religion. In this new Hellenistic era, populations were shuffled and displaced. They belonged now to far-flung empires, thousands of miles removed from the seats of power and governance.

The social moorings and civic participation of the old polis were dissolute. The people around you were strangers now; no one lived in one place for very long, and few retained a sense of history and ancestry. Your neighbors spoke different languages and worshiped different gods.

The loss of the polis induced *domicide* in the Hellenistic world.[2,3,4] Domicide is the destruction of home. It can mean the physical destruction of your house, or—in this case—refer to a cultural exile, a kind of cosmic declension that takes away all affinity, all identity, all sense of belonging to your environment. Domicide is a useful term because it captures the Meaning Crisis in gestalt, the prevailing mood of aimlessness, the vacuous feeling of having lost our place in the universe.

We talked extensively about disruption in previous chapters and its effects on an individual's cognitive complexion. Imagine, as Plato did, the affinity between the psyche and the polis. Think of ordinary

2. Douglas Porteous and Sandra E. Smith, *Domicide: The Global Destruction of Home* (McGill-Queen's Press, 2001).

3. Brian J. Walsh, "From Housing to Homemaking: Worldviews and the Shaping of Home." *Christian Scholar's Review* 35, no. 2 (2006): 237.

4. John Vervaeke, Christopher Mastropietro, and Filip Miscevic, *Zombies in Western Culture: A Twenty-First Century Crisis* (Open Book Publishers, 2017).

culture shock and imagine its effects on a civilization. In this domicide, you are no longer being reflected or instructed. The world no longer knows you or speaks to you. Events around you seem unorganized and unpredictable.

The more it goes unseen and unaddressed, the more you lose your connection to yourself. You fade into obscurity and insignificance. This is much the same domicide that Siddhartha suffered after he left the palace and met his four sights. Domicide introduces absurdity, anxiety, and the threat of meaninglessness. This is what happened to the Hellenistic world. The worldview by which human beings homed the world was irreparably broken. There was no going back.

The anxiety of the Hellenistic period found reflection in different facets of the culture. The art became more frenetic, tragic, and extreme. The confidence enjoyed during the periods of Socrates, Plato and Aristotle was gone. Greece had suffered titanic civil conflict —the Peloponnesian War—and was in crisis even before it was overwhelmed by Macedonia.

When Alexander spread Greek culture throughout the world, the culture began to thin. It lost its depth and changed its form, perforated by so many foreign influences. Alexander's conquest of hellenization produced a profound syncretism across his fragile empire. Cultural deities came into contact with one another and new religions emerged from their encounters. Greek and Egyptian deities were integrated together (into Serapis, for example) and mother goddesses (like Isis) were elevated to pancultural importance, perhaps to nurture the anxious soul with a presence of divine maternity.

Epicurus, and the Anxiety of Mortality

In the face of this Hellenistic Meaning crisis, philosophy found new significance. The project that began in Socrates, Plato and Aristotle did not come to an end, but adapted itself for new purposes. Until now, the practices of wisdom tried to address the persistence of human foolishness, to lead you out of the cave of illusion. This goal was not abandoned, but now it seemed insufficient.

Epicurus, one of the great philosophers of the Hellenistic period, famously said: "Call no man a philosopher who has not alleviated the suffering of others." The pursuit of wisdom now took on therapeutic aims, and a new metaphor emerged. The philosopher was the physician of the soul, and his aim was to relieve you of the existential suffering caused by your domicide.

This aim translated into new philosophical schools. Two of the most influential of these schools were the Epicureans—based on Epicurus—and the Stoics. Both movements took Socrates as an exemplar, and developed his legacy in different ways. The Epicureans were novel in the ancient religious world because of their secularity, and they offered a diagnosis of the condition that afflicted their contemporaries. They proposed that fear was our source of suffering. This was a compelling idea for many reasons, but just like our previous reinterpretation of the Four Noble Truths, I propose an adjustment of terminology may allow us to access the deeper meaning of Epicurus's diagnosis.

For this reinterpretation, let us consider the distinction between *fear* and *anxiety*. These terms are often used interchangeably, but they have different meanings. Fear involves a direct and observable threat, such as scaling a great height or confronting an attacker. Fear can be paralytic, but the prescription for action is usually clear; you know what you need to do, even if you lack the courage or skill to do it.

Anxiety, however, has a different mood. We often confuse it with eagerness or excitement ("I am anxious to see you tonight!") but this is an error in terms. Anxiety implies distress, suffering the loss of agency, or the gravity of agency, and living with a dreadful, nebulous threat. You are not quite sure what the threat is, and you are not sure what to do about it. This is why anxiety is the preferred term used by

Kierkegaard and Heidegger as well as the theologian Paul Tillich, who makes the contrast with fear more explicit.[5,6]

Anxiety is associated with the existential dimension of human existence, the particular combination of being ignorant and mortal while having an aspirational relationship to character and meaning-making. Living a meaningful life is necessary, but how does one measure it? How do I determine which actions are right? How do I know when I fail? What do I do when I fail? How do I deal with being culpable for my faults and foolishness? These paradoxical conditions place an uncanny kind of stress on every human being—a stress of the spirit.

The Epicurean diagnosis proposes that we suffer because we cannot manage fear. However, the fears they discuss are not fears that have clear solutions. I propose that they are better defined as anxieties. According to the Epicureans, we do not control our imagination or our thinking, and therefore suffer from anxieties that cripple our agency and grip on the world. For example, many people are anxious about death, and we often invoke the existence of death as a sign that life's meaningless. ("I am going to die anyways, so what does it matter?")

If you expose people to triggers about their own mortality, they become cognitively rigid and lapse into a form of parasitic processing.[7,8] How does one contend with the problem of death? One response, of course, is to pursue immortality. Religions of the ancient world offer this although the Axial accounts of eternal life are often

5. Søren Kierkegaard, *The Concept of Anxiety: A Simple Psychologically Oriented Deliberation in View of the Dogmatic Problem of Hereditary Sin* (WW Norton & Company, 2014).

6. Paul Tillich, *The Courage to Be* (Yale University Press, 1952).

7. Jeff Greenberg, Tom Pyszczynski, Sheldon Solomon, Linda Simon, and Michael Breus, "Role of Consciousness and Accessibility of Death-Related Thoughts in Mortality Salience Effects," *Journal of Personality and Social Psychology* 67, no. 4(1994): 627.

8. John Vervaeke and Leonardo Ferraro, "Relevance, Meaning and the Cognitive Science of Wisdom," In *The Scientific Study of Personal Wisdom: From Contemplative Traditions to Neuroscience* (Dordrecht: Springer Netherlands, 2013): 21–51.

simplified and misunderstood. Modern religious movements, like transhumanism, also strive for this goal.

As a cognitive scientist, I think this is a doomed strategy; overwhelming evidence says mind and consciousness are emergent from your brain and dependent on it. The phenomenological mystery of death—the fact it is unimaginable and outside of conscious experience—does not annul this fact. When your brain dies, it is likely that your consciousness, character, and sense of self die with it. Death is the purest, most unavoidable fatalism for human beings.

Epicureans have a different strategy for contending with death anxiety. Instead of pursuing immortality, what would it mean to accept mortality, to realize it without anxiety? Philosophers offer some provocative arguments to acquaint this possibility. First of all, if death means your nonexistence, consider the world before you were born. You have not existed for most of cosmic history. You cannot experience your prior nonexistence, but it does not terrify you. You have no trouble conceiving of it, and finding value in the histories and lineages that precede your birth.

You might find this argument dissatisfying, though; the *loss* of existence, you might say, poses the terrifying prospect. It cannot compare to that blissful "before" when nothing existed to lose. The Epicureans, however, would argue that you can never experience a total loss of life. They famously said: "Where I am, death is not. Where death is, I am not."

If you are aware of the loss, you are still alive and have not lost. If you have lost everything, you have also lost awareness and cannot be aware of having lost. The anxiety of experiencing death is an ill-founded fear, the Epicureans say, and the fears of life's decline—the onset of pain, or the reduction in your human agency—are easily caused by other states. So if you are not afraid of experiencing death, or the attendant decline, what are actually afraid of?

The Epicureans propose this. You are afraid to lose that which is good. However, the Epicurean meaning of "good" requires some nuance. It is often understood as pleasure, and Epicureans are frequently mislabeled as hedonists by casual readers. Consider our common use of the word, for example, which refers to gourmet tastes and sensibilities. The original Epicureans do not measure pleasure by bodily sensation but by those quantities of life that provide the most sustained meaning and equanimity.

We equate many things with pleasure that tend to recede as we age, such as wealth, sex, ableness, or notoriety. However pleasurable these might be, their eventual loss brings proportionate pain and distress. They are therefore not the most meaningful quantities. Instead, the Epicureans propose an alternative good, directly inspired by Socrates. Friendship, they say, grants the greatest meaning.

The Epicurean meaning of friendship is specific, and uniquely for the time, it included both men and women. It did not refer to sexual relations but those meaningful relationships that became arenas for philosophia, the social pursuit of wisdom and self-transcendence. As long as you remained in friendship, these higher pursuits were always available, and the pains of loss were manageable.

Whether or not you agree with the Epicureans, it is important to understand their project. They question the desire for immortality, and once properly diagnosed, they refuse to accept the fear of death. The real fear is the loss of agency, they say, so often confused for transitory fortunes. But ultimate happiness lies elsewhere, among those pleasures that are not dislodged so easily by changing winds. As long as you have cognitive agency, you can cultivate philosophical friendships. Epicurus himself lived these words to his very last moment, even as he suffered from illness.

Epicurus was one of the first philosophers to break from traditional theism. He was not anxious about the gods and famously crafted some of the first arguments that are used by modern day atheists. I would not, however, characterize Epicurious as an atheist. He is perhaps better described as a nontheist; he does not argue against the gods' existence, but he challenges their relevance to the philosophical agent. He considers their threat to be nebulous and irrational, just like the fear of death.

In the traditional frame of mind, meaning is ceded by the afterlife, and threats to the afterlife are threats to meaning itself. Instead the Epicureans propose that we deal directly with our death anxiety, without spurious appeals to immortality—which is, by many accounts, a prospect that becomes more undesirable the more closely we examine it.

Epicurus's contributions to philosophy, whether persuasive or not, are exemplary of its sagacious potential. Any wisdom tradition must give us a way of responding to our mortality and those other perennial conditions of our existence that predispose us with anxieties. Epicurus took up the Socratic legacy of philia and mentorship, and his disciples modeled his example. They wrote his sentences on their household walls and utensils. They formed communities to adopt his practices, and they used one another to retain the memory of philosophical perspective, and rigorously disarm the forces of anxiety that were overwhelming their contemporaries.

The Stoics and the Cynics: Internalizing the Sage

However progressive, I do not find the Epicurean diagnosis sufficient. I cannot agree that the Meaning Crisis of the Hellenistic period—nor of our time—was driven solely, or even primarily, by the anxiety of mortality. This anxiety has always been with us and always will be. Periods of chaos and domicide exacerbate our anxieties[9,10,11] but do not create them. We need a deeper explanation, and for this we turn to our second school of Hellenistic philosophy.

In my estimation, *Stoicism* provided a more refined diagnosis to this Meaning Crisis as well as a more refined response. This tradition

---

9. We know this from mortality salience research. Things that make us feel more vulnerable tend to make our mortality and our terror around it more salient to us.

10. Abram Rosenblatt, Jeff Greenberg, Sheldon Solomon, Tom Pyszczynski, and Deborah Lyon, "Evidence for Terror Management Theory: I. The Effects of Mortality Salience on Reactions to Those who Violate or Uphold Cultural Values," *Journal of Personality and Social Psychology* 57, no. 4(1989): 681–690.

11. Jeff Greenberg, Tom Pyszczynski, Sheldon Solomon, Abram Rosenblatt, Mitchell Veeder, Shari Kirkland, and Deborah Lyon, "Evidence for Terror Management Theory II: The Effects of Mortality Salience on Reactions to Those Who Threaten or Bolster the Cultural Worldview," *Journal of personality and social psychology* 58, no. 2 (1990): 308.

is a direct ancestor to some of our most effective forms of modern psychotherapy, like cognitive behavioral therapy and rational emotive therapy.[12] Stoics also believed that human beings suffer from a chronic kind of anxiety and loss of agency, consistent with the domicide of their day. However, they ventured a different interpretation. Understanding it properly requires us to take a few steps back and track the development of the Socratic legacy.

Socrates had two prominent disciples, Plato and Antisthenes, who carried the lion's share of his legacy after death. Plato's dialogues are, among other things, formal attempts to emulate and eventually internalize the Socratic elenchus, that process of inquiry that Socrates made famous. Meanwhile, when Antisthenes was asked what he had learned from Socrates, he replied: "I learned how to converse with myself."

We converse with ourselves constantly, of course. Our lives are filled with inward dialogues and ruminations, where we relive memories, fantasize desires, admonish or motivate ourselves. Therapy often centers on the idea that these ruminations can be hijacked by parasitic processes discussed in the previous chapters. This often characterizes anxiety and depression, an inner voice or pattern that sabotages you, inculcates destructive habits, and prevents you from acting in your best interests.

Antisthenes learned to do with himself what Socrates did with him. He internalized the dialogical pattern that Socrates conducted, and by doing this, he found that he could access Socratic insights and states of mind. This internalization became the foundation of Stoic practice. Socrates was turned into a systematic set of psychotechnologies that internalized into a person's metacognition.

While Plato's dialogues prioritized Socrates's argumentation, Antisthenes's idea of transformation required a confrontation with Socrates himself. We can find merit in both perspectives because Socratic elenchus is an alloy of both practices: careful argument couched in provocative confrontation.

---

12. For example, Aaron Beck's book entitled, *Cognitive Therapy and the Emotional Disorders*, argues for this, citing Epictetus and Marcus Aurelius, among others.

Antisthenes had a follower, Diogenes, who epitomized this confrontation and brought dramatic texture to the original insight. Diogenes did something akin to provocative performance art. He would roam the streets of Corinth like a vagabond, lurching and leering, attempting to jar his contemporaries from their somnolent states. Diogenes tried to induce aporia, that Socratic encounter with ignorance and absurdity that stupefies and challenges you, awakening the need for transformation.

Instead of using discussion or argumentation, like the Socrates of Plato's dialogues, Diogenes used his mien for provocation. His loud antics and disheveled appearance famously resembled *The Hermit* card in tarot (see figure 14.1); he would wander into the marketplace carrying a lamp, searching to and fro. When everyone asked what he searched for, he would reply, "I am looking for one honest man." The answer galled his fellow citizens, but they were hard pressed to deny the truth of it. In the marketplace, after all, everyone was lying.

Figure 14.1: An image depicting the tarot card of the hermit with the lamp. This image is actually a representation of Diogenes. This image was obtained from Wikimedia Commons, scanned by Holly Voley for public domain, originally retrieved from http://www. sacred-texts.com/tarot

From the safety of your reading, it is tempting to look admiringly at Diogenes's modest figure and to laud him for being so cool and courageous. But this is the distance of history. You would not find him more attractive closer to home. We do not take any kindlier to Diogeneses now than did our ancient counterparts. Diogenes famously masturbated in the center of the marketplace and lived outside the city in a barrel.

He simulated the behavior of a dog, which he considered a more authentic manner of existence. He barked at people to shock them. He bit his friends to wake them from facile concerns. One famous story (in many versions) perhaps best summarizes Diogenes's aporetic character. Alexander the Great, busy in his ascent to glory and godhood, came to see him in his barrel, flanked by his extensive entourage.

The emperor stopped before Diogenes and said, "I can give you half the world. What do you want?"

Diogenes replied, "Could you move a little to the left? You're blocking my sunlight."

Antisthenes and Diogenes were the beginning of a new tradition in philosophy. Their followers called themselves the *Cynics,* which derives from the term "dog-man." We must not confuse this word with its modern use. The game of the ancient Cynics was far more complex than suspicion or mistrust. They too had a diagnosis of the Hellenistic domicide, and their antics were proffered as a wakeful, more natural alternative.

Like the Epicureans, the Cynics believed our condition was caused by foolish and transitory loves, attachment to things—like wealth or emperorship—that were unreal and impermanent. We set our hearts on the wrong things, and those things inevitably failed us and caused us to suffer. You may note some similarity between the Cynic way of life and the harsh asceticism that the Buddha practiced when he initially left the palace.

The Cynics concluded that the Hellenistic period had shaken people loose from certain artificial moorings. It showed that people took many things for granted as part of the structure of reality, but these were not as essential or fundamental as believed. Our status and worldly identity, our institutions and social structures—these did not have natural permanence. They were fabricated, man-made, historically and culturally dependent, and therefore temporary.

The natural currents of the world would easily wash them away, and if we fixed ourselves to them, we would be left bereft, homeless, and heartbroken. Domicide was caused by these frail attachments. The only sensible response was to set our hearts and lives on something that was not so contingent.

Diogenes did not just profess this; he lived out the belief. He took on the life of an animal, not to surrender to base instincts but to relinquish his membership to man-made institutions, politics and value systems—which would inevitably perish—and conform himself instead to the patterns and conditions of natural law.

The Cynics did not just believe in natural law but also in moral law. There was a right way to be a human being. Cynics made a distinction between *moral principles*, which they believed to be natural, and *purity codes,* which were culturally dependent. These two categories were easily confused.

A useful way of understanding this distinction is to draw it with modern language: *guilt* in contrast to *shame*. Guilt is the distress of having broken a moral principle. Shame is the distress of having violated a purity code. If my pants fell down while teaching a class, I would be embarrassed and experience shame. This would violate a cultural code, which dictates I must be clothed in public. But my gaff is not a moral transgression; I would feel shame but not guilt.

These two codes are sometimes pitted against one another. You may be made to feel shame for actions you believe are moral. Many people who supported Black Americans during the Civil Rights Movement were subjected to shaming, even though their actions were guiltless. Purity codes run on that powerful machine of ritual. They are designed to maintain the consensus and categorical boundaries of a culture. They are usually bound to established power structures, invested in a status quo.

Just like most systems, purity codes can be highly adaptive and maladaptive. They succeed in tracking meaningful patterns and guard important boundaries, but they also get locked into outmoded frames. For example, no one would be distressed by me drinking water from a cup, but if I spit into the glass and drank it, it would disgust you.

An important purity code is at work here; my body is a boundary, and things inside it should not be issued. John should not spit, puke, burp, or pass gas in front of people. Even leaving a bed unmade can violate a purity code; it exposes an impression that belongs out of sight, even though each of us is implicated in private.

It is all too easy to confuse these categories. We often mistake our disgust reactions, which relate to these purity codes, with moral judgments, which should be based on reasoning. For example, most of us do not want to see our parents having sex. This, in all likelihood, produces a disgust reaction. However, your disgust is not a moral judgment; your existence depended on their sexuality, after all.

Many people's sexual activity would produce this reaction from you, but that does not entail any moral objection to their character or sexuality. Homosexuality has often been persecuted, for instance, because people confused their purity code and disgust reactions for legitimate moral objections.

We moderns still struggle with these distinctions; many spurious moral accusations are levied from unreflective moments of disgust. Diogenes and the Cynics, in their artful provocations, worked to separate moral codes from purity codes. Diogenes did nothing immoral when he masturbated in public, even though it disgusted people. Conversely, most commerce in the marketplace was rife with mendacity, but these behaviors were culturally acceptable.

Just like Socrates before them, Cynics did not confuse cultural consensus with moral rectitude. They saw the inherent fragility of our man-made structures, a fragility that had been laid bare by the chaos of the Hellenistic period. They saw how volatile our offices and identities were, how they could obfuscate the patterns of nature and be made to tyrannize other human beings.

The Cynics tended to be hostile to Plato because of his emphasis on argumentation, but this attitude eventually changed. Diogenes had a disciple named Krates, who had his own disciple, Zeno of

Citium.[13] Zeno was deeply influenced by the Cynics, but he was sympathetic to Plato's form. He saw value in argumentation as well as in performance, and he crafted a way of life that could integrate Cynic provocation and Platonic reasoning. Zeno would walk up and down the *stoa*, a covered colonnade in Athens, teaching this new integration. Zeno valued the Cynic way, but he believed that the Cynics concentrated too much on the objects of our attachment rather than the manner of it. They cared too much about the what and not enough about the how.

His insight would become the basis for *Stoicism*. The Stoics agreed that culture and institution varied across history. However, human sociability was not variable. It was a part of our nature. Diogenes and Socrates had to enter the polis to practice their philosophy. Zeno believed that philia sophia was not about what you set your heart on but rather how you set your heart. This was a hallmark of rationality: do not just focus just on the products of your cognition; find value and attention in the processes.[14,15,16]

This act of setting your heart is a kind of co-identification, that process by which this relation of agent-arena is established and identities are assumed. As we know from previous chapters, this co-identification process is occurring constantly, and our agency and identity emerge from it. Most of the time it is unconscious though. This is the Stoic point. If you co-identify mindlessly with the world, if you allow this process to be automatic and reactive, you will—if you'll allow me the acronym—*mar* the relationship. It will be open to all manner of distortion, self-deception, and parasitic processes.

You will notice that the Axial ideals and Socratic project remain steadfastly present in this new formulation: to understand how we relate and identify with the world and apply a conscious rigor to

---

13. This is not the Zeno of Zeno's paradoxes. This is a different Zeno.
14. This relates to recent work on rationality done by Keith Stanovich.
15. Keith Stanovich, *What Intelligence Tests Miss: The Psychology of Rational Thought* (Yale University Press, 2009).
16. Keith E. Stanovich and Richard F. West, "Individual Differences in Reasoning: Implications for the Rationality Debate?" *Behavioral and Brain Sciences* 23, no. 5 (2000): 645–65.

these processes of attachment so we can strengthen our agency and face the threat of domicide. In the next chapter, we will examine the Stoic practice more closely and explore how these practices are being taken up in our own psychotherapeutic endeavors to deal with our modern equivalent.

15

MARCUS AURELIUS AND JESUS OF NAZARETH

Good philosophy strives to reveal problems we do not see and disarm problems that arise of our own making. The Stoics thrived in this aim. They worked to dissociate feelings and realities that were unduly conflated in our experience and whose conflation caused us unnecessary error and suffering. They resembled the Buddhists in several ways. They practiced *prosoche*, paying attention to how they paid attention and how they passed judgment.

Just as the Cynics helped us to separate morality from purity codes, the Stoics pulled apart two things that blend seamlessly in our unconscious experience. They learned to differentiate an inward mood from an outward occurrence between the existential mode and meaning of an event, and the event itself.

This Stoic separation is key to most cognitive psychotherapies: distinguishing between the event and the meaning we grant it. When we become trapped inside the frame problem, meaning and event unconsciously fuse together. We lock into transparency and gestalt but cannot shift back to opacity or featural self-reflection and, therefore, cannot disrupt our scope of attention.

All of the cognitive systems we discussed in previous chapters— the worldview attunement and agent-arena relationship, the significance landscaping that gives the world its shine—become vulnerable to parasitic processing. Events are events, but the meaning of events, and our response to them, is shaped by these co-identifying processes and identities. An event and its given meaning can be mismatched when we are not well-conformed to the situation, and our reactions can create beliefs that are not essential and become like self-fulfilling dreams.

If meaning and the event are fused, the only way we can alter the meaning is by altering the event. But it is not always possible to alter an event, and our attempts to do so often lead us into misadventure. The Stoics gazed soberly into the fatalism and domicide of their time, and they reasoned it very carefully. We often do not have control over the events of our lives, the actions of other people, or the movements of the world. We must find a wiser way to live with this predicament.

Marcus Aurelias and the Stoic Exercises

Epictetus was one of the great Stoic philosophers, and his manual for Stoic life began with the following insight. Wisdom is knowing what is in your control and what is not in your control. This existential confusion is a chronic human problem. We have already learned this in Erich Fromm and his existential modes. Fromm was directly influenced by the Stoics. His distinction between the having mode and being mode was inspired by their teachings.

The having mode, you may recall, corresponds to quantities in the world we can control, such as water, food, and shelter. But most of our most pertinent needs are not met by exercising control. They are met by enhancing meaning. The being mode is met with a path of maturity, developing the agent-arena relationship. When I become more mature, I come to inhabit a different arena.

My agency is more courageous, more discerning. This is why we do not let small children get married, drive cars, or own guns. They are not yet prepared to move in certain arenas. If you cannot separate the meaning from events, you are liable to serious modal confusions as an agent, and you might pursue sacred values (like love or significance) with transitory worldly acquisitions (fame, for example, or empty sexual conquest).

These strategies tend not to work. They do not exercise any real control over the world, and as the Stoics and Cynics both agree, they lead to disillusion and disappointment. The Stoics reminded people that the meaning of an event had a nature that was distinct from the event. Very often, only the former was vulnerable to our influence, and by minding the difference, we could train our attention and recalibrate our sense of control. This practice was called *procheiron*, which means ready to hand, remembrance in the sense of Buddha's *sati*. Just like mindfulness, the Stoic practice evokes something about our nature that calls our worldview into question. It disrupts our framing with different attentional scaling, and allows us to gain insight and perspective.

A famous book exemplifies the procheiron: *The Meditations* by Marcus Aurelius. This book is often misread. It is not filled with propositions to persuade the reader. The book is a series of reminders, written to Aurelius himself. The philosopher Pierre Hadot called these *spiritual exercises*.[1] They attempted to make conscious that process by which the author related to his world. These artful reminders renewed his attention to the unchanging, to the unavoidable conditions of existence, and to pursue a sense of equanimity in them.

This was a particularly difficult task, given his station. Marcus Aurelias was among the greatest emperors of Rome, ruling at a time when the Roman Empire was near the peak of its expanse. His power, wealth, and fame were incalculable, and it would have been easy for him to succumb to an illusion of permanence, to identify his own name with the eternal city and emblazon his existence with godly purpose.

Instead, Aurelius stood in contrast to Alexander. He did not style himself as a glorious god-man. He gave his attention to his ineluctable humanness, his mortality, and his fallibility. He famously said: "It is possible to be happy even in a palace."

Marcus Aurelius, unlike Siddhartha and the Cynics, did not leave

---

1. Pierre Hadot, *Philosophy as a Way of Life: Spiritual Exercises from Socrates to Foucault* (Wiley, 1995).

the palace, though he came to similar conclusions about its nature. He learned to live with his sumptuous surroundings because leaving would have shirked the moral responsibilities that came with his position.

One of Aurelius's spiritual exercises was a practice that Pierre Hadot called *objective seeing*.[2] This practice involved the kind of mindful attentional scaling we discussed in previous chapters—between feature-gestalt and transparency-opacity—to change our view of everyday experience. For instance, Marcus Aurelius contemplated sex as merely "the friction of a piece of gut and, following a sort of convulsion, the expulsion of some mucus."

It sounds crass and reductive, rather like Diogenes in the marketplace. But Marcus Aurelius was not a prude. He was married, and he loved his wife deeply. He simply reminded himself that the basic nature of sex was distinct from the romance we find in it. The biology is perfunctory, even disgusting. But we perceive it within a halo of desire and aspiration. This meaning is not false, but it is not a necessary or essential part of nature.

If we hope to protect ourselves from sudden domicide, *the thousand natural shocks that flesh is heir to*, we must develop a mindfulness of this difference and learn to see ourselves—our love, our goals, our experiences—from the impersonal eye of the cosmos, a perspective outside our perspective that is unfettered by our narrative frames.

Another Stoic exercise focused on the reality of impermanence: find a cup that you like and use it every morning. Find in it a sense of home and familiarity, a gradual, growing attachment. Then smash the cup. The act, if undertaken purposefully, will ritualize the Stoic reminder and become a mindful symbol of this distinction between objects and their meanings.

The same reminder can be given to far more significant attachments. One such practice, which many people find morbid, is called *premeditatio*. When kissing your child goodnight, say to

---

2. I am not quite happy with that term because of some of the associations with the word objective.

yourself, "I may lose her to death tonight." It is a painful act of imagination, a small excerpt of the devastation one might feel if the worst should happen. But the excerpt equips a confrontation with this domicidal experience. You have tremendous agency in your child's rearing, but you have very little agency in the physics of her mortality. You can take actions to protect her, but you cannot move the universe. Her fate is beyond your control.

Fatality: The Stoic Diagnosis

We still have many customs that fuse meaning and events. They give us a distorted view of our agency and encode foolish expectations. When these expectations shatter, we often shatter alongside them. Many of us are devastated to find that romantic love, though profoundly meaningful, is different from romantic comedies, where it is insured by a cosmic narrative that conspires to bring two people together.

The realities of love disappoint us; the beloved suddenly dies, or falls out of love, or succumbs to social expectations. The world does not cradle or nurture our happiness. The cold, impersonal tides of circumstance tear us loose from these attachments, dispossess us of our narratives, and ruin the best laid plans. We have tragedies, of course, to remind us of this; they fulfill important Stoic functions in our cultures.

Nevertheless, we spend much of our time trying to bury the unromantic reality. The sublimated anxiety becomes a silent partner in life, an ominous shadow on the face of our relationships. When the worst happens, it is all the more devastating; in addition to the grief of loss, I also suffer a dreadful existential disillusionment. I have not only lost a relationship. I have lost all the promise and possibility that came with its symbolic significance. I have lost an entire worldview. I am left alone in absurdity, and my grief turns into despair.

This leads to the Stoic diagnosis. It is not our mortality that makes us anxious, but rather life's *fatality*. Here again, we have lost the meaning of an important word. We confuse it with mortality. But death is not the root of "fatality." The root is *fate.*[3] This does not mean predestination by some magical force. I am talking about the oceanic force of circumstance that overpowers our agency. Events occur, unintelligibly, from their own causal necessity, concealed from human comprehension and ungoverned by our intent or design. When we forget the Stoic distinction and fuse meaning to events, we suffer this fatality.

Death has become so synonymous with fatality because it is the most powerful instance thereof and, therefore, its most primordial symbol. It is that infinite aporia, the unimaginable place where all of your meaning, narrative, and identity depart from the events of the universe. It stands for the final loss of agency and the absurd clash between two estranged perspectives: the sense of purpose in human meaning and the indifference of a universe that washes us all away.

Stoic exercises ritualize the remembrance of cosmic fatality. If you read through *The Meditations*, you will encounter *the view from above*. This practice makes use of the Solomon Effect we discussed in chapter 12. When you confront a vexing problem or situation, your anxiety is couched in a certain mood, a perspective constrained by your instincts and interests. The Stoic elevates his perspective to free himself from its undue influence as well as the anxiety that clouds his reactions and decisions.

He lifts himself through space and time. He imagines himself, and the entire situation, as if from a higher vantage—from high above the city, or high above the earth, somewhere in the distant future, or from the end of time. As he imagines this change of view, the arena around his problem changes, as does his agency. He becomes freer, more flexible, able to pursue a longer-term response. He becomes more capable of careful reflection.

These benefits have been evidenced now in *Construal Level Theory;* a body of psychological research suggests that when people alter their temporal or spatial scope of attention, it has significant

3. Margaret Visser, *Beyond Fate* (House of Anansi Press, 2002).

effects on their cognitive processing.[4] Most Stoic-based therapy is perspectival. It provokes people to temporarily step back from the identity that gives a problem its existential stakes. This whole process is known as *cognitive reframing.*

These exercises, practiced by Stoics like Marcus Aurelius and Epictetus, enact Antisthenes's goal of internalizing Socrates. The modern cognitive behavioral practices that Stoicism inspired use a form of Socratic inquiry to separate meaning from event, reality from rumination. For example, a client may come in and say: "Everything I do is a failure. Everyone hates me!"

A competent therapist does not simply console the client but asks questions to provoke a change in perspective: "Is *everything* you do really a failure? Did that include your morning drive or the breakfast you made? What do you *mean* by everything?"

The ennui or anxiety of a perspective can disguise itself as a worldly belief. The Stoic-Socratic inquiry helps to prevent an affective state from deceiving us and claiming reality for itself. When I feel that "everybody hates me," I should press the belief with a Stoic inquiry. The smoke conceals the size of the fire.

It may transpire that this global feeling is coming from a single relationship, and its salience is slipping into all of my other relationships, causing me to bullshit myself. Meanwhile, perhaps the term "hate" is used in place of something more accurate. Perhaps it is an expression of my insecurity rather than a keen perception of someone's attitude. If I can discern the difference between my affect and the world, I can improve my self-control, diagnose a problem properly, and triage my own impressions and reactions.

By separating affect from argument, a view from above can clarify the objects of our anxiety. Therefore, it can help relieve our modal confusion, disabusing us of whims that are expressions of anxiety rather than desires in themselves. For example, let us briefly return to the question of immortality, which we raised with Epicurus in the

---

4. Yaacov Trope and Nira Liberman, "Construal-Level Theory of Psychological Distance," *Psychological Review* 117, no. 2(2010): 440–463.

previous chapter. If I gave you immortality, what would you do with it?

You might start with a few sybaritic indulgences, like eating lots of chocolate or having lots of sex. These would quickly bore you, though, and you might pursue more complex challenges: take up chess, or archery, or learn to code, or study a new language. But then what? You could continue pursuing new skills until you ran out or until the acquisitions lost their novelty.

There is an excellent parable, written by Julian Barnes in his book, *A History of the World in 10 1/2 Chapters*. In the parable, the deceased ascend to heaven, and they are given immortality. One man practices golf until he gets a score of eighteen. Then he wonders what he should do. He goes to Saint Peter and expresses his restlessness.

"What is wrong?" Saint Peter asks. "Are you not doing everything you want?"

The man answers: "I am. I've gotten good at everything, and now I'm finished."

Then St. Peter says, "Now you understand the point of heaven. The point of heaven is not to live out immortality. It is to make you accept death."[5]

This is not classic Christian doctrine by any means, but it epitomizes the Stoic ideal. As long as we formulate identity horizontally, as a narrative of unending duration, it will fail. Even if human beings somehow attained immortality, would it satisfy us? Take the view from above; unending life would exhaust us in ways we can scarcely imagine. It would amplify absurdity and despair rather than alleviate them.

When I take a Stoic perspective, this becomes clear in my own life. I instinctively avoid death like most other human beings; I enjoy living, and I don't step into traffic. But I don't want to live forever. I don't think that John Vervaeke should exist for all time. Life wears on me, as it does for most of us as we age.

I tire of the ways I have been foolish, ways I have been immoral,

---

5. Julian Barnes, *A History of the World in 10 1/2 Chapters*, 1st Vintage International ed. (New York: Vintage Books, 1990).

ways I have failed and let myself and other people down. I sense the inevitability of these failures, so endemic to a being of finite knowledge. These would not be ameliorated by longevity but infinitely multiplied by them. Extending that through all of time seems to me an ontological mistake, a misguided evil to inflict on reality, one I could not stand to bear.

It reminds me of a passage of *Moby Dick*, in the sermon of the ship's priest, as he prays to his Father over the infinite sea: *"I leave eternity to Thee; for what is man that he should live out the lifetime of his God?"*

The Stoics do not crave length of life. They crave fullness of life and depth of meaning. This depth, represented vertically in the diagram below, is our rightful connection to eternity. Perhaps it should remind us again of Blake's poetic condensation: *the world in a grain of sand, heaven in a wildflower, infinity in the palm of your hand...* Unending time is a symbol of our craving, an artful expression of a spiritual want. But as with most objects of reverence, it is perilous to literalize a symbol. It misdirects our hearts, and gives us a quivering life.

Since Tibullus and Virgil, Rome has been known as *the eternal city*. But it too will be lost to time. Its eternal nature has less to do with its permanence than with symbolic depth, the way it catalyzed both myth and technology, conversion and transformation.[6] Its greatest emperor already knew this when he wrote *The Meditations*. "Everybody dies," Marucs Aurelius wrote. "But not everybody has lived."

---

6. Jonathan Pageau, "Introduction to Iconography" (lecture, Consciousness and Conscience Conference, Thunder Bay, ON, September 18, 2022). Lecture is available on Jonathan Pageau's YouTube Channel.

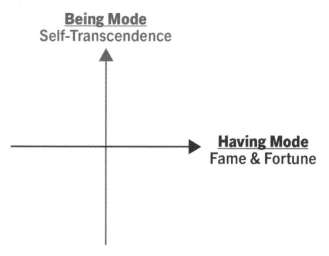

Figure 15.1: A diagram depicting the axes of the being and having mode. On the horizontal axis is fame and fortune, the having mode. The vertical axis represents the self-transcendence, the being mode.

The Stoic exercises train us to identify with this vertical axis, the axis of the being mode. If we have this experience of eternity, even for a moment, we lose our need for immortality. The fullness is not based on duration but on quality. Even watered down in modern therapies, Stoic practices are still powerfully effective, and the modern Meaning Crisis has revived the relevance of their original traditions. They are further enriched by being placed into meaningful dialogue with our current cognitive science.

We need some wisdom to afford us a life among the depths, an ontological identity rather than a merely historical one. If we can couple our attention to this fullness of being, we may find a way to respond to our predicament—not only our mental health crisis but our existential distress about fatality. You will have noticed that certain tenets of the Stoic and Epicurean philosophies bear striking resemblance to those of Buddhism. This is not an identity claim, of course (there remain many important differences) but it is important to remember that Western children need not look so far east to find viable psychotechnologies of self-transcendence or relief from existential anxiety.[7]

Jesus of Nazareth: Christianity, Kairos, and Agape

The Hellenistic period came to an end with a return to world empire. The ascent of Rome was yet another combination of pre-Axial glory (e.g., in the godhood of Caesar) imbued with Axial sapience (e.g., the writings of Cicero, Seneca, and Aurelius). Rome was another place of syncretism, but its central governance and integration of foreign lands, though checkered and coercive, made Roman identity more coherent than the scattered remnants of Alexander. Power and prosperity integrated many different cultures into a cosmopolis of diverse influences. In the midst of Roman ascendancy, a world-altering event occurred elsewhere in the Mediterranean. This returns us, of course, to ancient Israel.

You will recall from chapter 2 that the two-worlds mythology in Israel was a movement in time, out of bondage and into a promised land. The real world was the future, and God was the open creator. The faithful endeavored to participate in his creation, to follow the patterns of his will and participate in the unfolding of history. But human beings, in our fallibility, also distorted these patterns. We trespassed, and fell off course. We had to be redeemed, returned to the rightful path by the words of teachers and prophets, who helped to translate God's voice and give moral import to human action.

One of these individuals was a young Jewish man, raised in the Hebrew tradition, whose birth and death would change the historical calendar for much of the ancient, medieval, and modern worlds. This, of course, was Jesus of Nazareth. I am going to address Jesus very specifically in this book: as Jesus of Nazareth rather than Jesus Christ, a figure of singular historical influence. I shall remain agnostic as to his metaphysical nature, neither arguing for, nor against, his status as son of God. His significance in this argument

---

7. I would strongly recommend to you Pierre Hadot's books, *Philosophy as a Way of Life: Spiritual Exercises from Socrates to Foucault* and *What Is Ancient Philosophy?*

resembles that of Socrates before him, a pivotal pedagogue and symbol in the history of humanity as well as a sage of incalculable wisdom.

For early Christians in the first and second centuries, Jesus signified a turning point in the Israelite Axial legacy. In chapter 3, we introduced a Greek term from the New Testament: *kairos*. In kairos, the fullness of time is realized in a single occurrence, an intervening act that shifts the course of events and brings futurity and eternity into present tense.

Imagine, for example, you have a close and intimate friend. You share romantic feelings for one another, but you are not yet in a romantic relationship. There is deep potential here and compatibility but also great risk. Revealing these feelings may rupture the friendship. One day, the time feels right, and you decide to kiss her.

If you get the kairos right, the course of your relationship deepens. Its potential is realized, and both of your identities are changed. Kairos is the idea that there is a right time for such an action, or conversation, a right time to realize everything that is not yet said or spoken, to bring the invisible pattern into proper visibility.

The Israelite conception of kairos related to the whole nation. God would intervene at decisive moments in history, often in the words of prophets. These words were the logos of God, the same logos by which He spoke creation into existence. God's logos then became the kairos of history. The advent of Christianity introduced a new idea about God's creative logos, informed by the Hebrew tradition, but also by the Greek. Logos did not just mean the spoken words but their intelligibility, the formative principle and underlying structure of reality.

The Gospel of John begins: "*In the beginning was the Logos, and the Logos was with God, and the Logos was God* (1:1)." Then it continues, "*And the Logos became flesh, and dwelt among us...(1:14)*" In the Christian Synoptic Gospels, God's logos was incarnated in a particular individual. Jesus of Nazareth was now the ultimate kairos; all the other kairoses led into him, were summated by him. He represented the final turning point, the *metanoia* of humanity, not only historically but also personally.

Metanoia is often translated as "conversion," but its meaning is much closer to "awakening." *Noia* means noticing (your perspectival awareness), and *meta* means beyond. As a person, you can identify with Jesus, develop a relationship with Him, seek yourself in His works and deeds, and find Him within your own humanity. The kairos He embodied can take place within you. Just as Socrates personalized the Axial Revolution and brought it into confrontation, the encounter with Jesus signified the turning point of your personhood.

Jesus spoke of this using a metaphor of rebirth. It meant a radical shifting of your salience landscape, a perspectival and participatory transformation. Jesus incarnated the principle by which the kairotic intervention could occur, and it occurred as profoundly in your personal history as it did in cosmic history. In Jesus, the two histories were now connected. In Him, you restored your relationship to God and, therefore, to all of creation.

How did this kairos take place? What did it look like? And what could possibly cause this kind of transformation? The Christian answer will make you laugh because it sounds so quaint. The word *love* has all but emptied of meaning. We use it to describe so many different things. I love peanut butter cookies. I love Saturday mornings. I love my girlfriend. I love my son. I love a good game of tennis. Each of these uses varies in intensity. Is love a reaction? An affection? A decision? We think of love as a feeling or emotion, but this collapses quickly under scrutiny.

Loving someone produces a wide variety of emotions: joy in their presence, sadness in their absence, anger in their neglect. Love is not a feeling. It is a modal way of being, a certain kind of agent-arena relationship. Jesus incarnated a new kind of love that was unexampled in the ancient world. His love became a kairos that changed the course of history, forever altering our moral orientation as human beings. This love was called *agape*.

To understand agape, we must contrast it from two other kinds of love: *eros* and *philia*. Eros is the love that seeks union. This union can be spiritual, sexual, or appetitive. We can feel oneness with nature, with the food we eat, or with a person we bed. When Socrates said he knew the ta erotika, he did not just refer to sex. He simply knew what to care about. Eros is the love that is satisfied through consummation.

Philia, meanwhile, is a love that seeks cooperation. We love our friends because we share in reciprocity. We grow together, learn together, and solve problems together.

Agape is distinct from these two loves. This, Jesus said, was the love God had for human beings, analogous to the love that a parent has for her child. When you bring an infant home from the hospital, he is not yet a cognitive person (though he still has moral status). He does not gratify any needs. He does not give friendship or reciprocity. He has nothing to offer in return for your love.

However, you love him nonetheless, and by loving him, you gradually turn him into a person, a discerning moral agent capable of a meaningful life. If we examine this with fresh eyes, it almost seems miraculous. In some early, indistinct phase of your existence, you were loved. Even if this love was imperfect, it begot you and shaped you. It made you into a self. Agape, simply put, is the love of creation.

Jesus did for adults as adults do for their children. He loved them into personhood. As early Christianity spread, agape was exapted from its parental context and made available to all persons of the ancient world, a world rife with harshness and fatality. With this love, Christianity would eventually take over Rome. With agape, Christianity could declare to all nonpersons of the Empire—the women, children, the sick, the poor, the widowed—that now, in Jesus's name, they could become persons. Now, they too could belong to the kingdom of God.

16

CHRISTIANITY AND AGAPE

Even for non-Christians, the idea of agapic love is somewhere at the foundation of Western culture. It often jars us to see depictions of pre-Christian civilization, which did not provide for the sanctity of each individual. Western values encode the idea that each person has a share in the eternal, some higher value beyond her station or worldly status. Secular customs and laws, ironically, are founded on these religious convictions; theists and atheists share them together, often without realizing their origins.

We access agape without invoking Jesus, just as we access self-inquiry without invoking Socrates. Nevertheless, the concept of Christian love became an essential filament in our normative worldview, and it continues to attune our moral sensibility while we profess to live in a post-Christian world.[1]

It is difficult to place ourselves into the footsteps of Jesus, however we conceive of His nature. Like Socrates, His figure is mythic and atopic. The Jesus of scripture is impossible to predict, and it disorients us to imagine His perspective. Most of us think of His

---

1. Tom Holland, *Dominion: How the Christian Revolution Remade the World* (Basic Books, 2019).

benevolence, but we are quick to forget His moments of ire and judgment. His actions were unintelligible for the customs of his time.

He was untempted by status or wealth and gave care to those, like prostitutes, who were most denigrated by society. So the Christian strove to live in Jesus's example, his mysterious countenance, his uncanny kind of solicitude. In Him, the Christian found a home of unending aspiration that she could strive to become, unite with, and commute into other relationships. It is difficult to qualify this kind of faith; as with Socrates, it was not just carried in teachings or propositions, but the aporia of its shamanic character. Jesus was a figure of numinous confrontation that shattered the frame of human perspective. Like Socrates before him, he disrupted worldly categories and embodied a new way of participatory knowing.

Agape and Forgiveness

The kairos of Jesus provided a way for Christians to participate in God, to sensitize to His agapic love, to know themselves by it, and to become a part of time's unfolding. In him, they fulfilled the Platonic appetite for a greater reality. For many of us, this is a very difficult experience to understand, but it may help to turn fresh eyes toward a like phenomenon.

Each of us human beings is born of a love that precedes us. Other human beings—parents, guardians, friends, family members—have devoted themselves to us, and from their devotion, we gradually grew from instinct-driven infants to minded moral persons. Where such love is withheld, human growth is often marred by trauma and disorder.

The child's relation is therefore erotic: they consume the love of the parent. They depend on it. They internalize the parental attention, become one with it, and their concept of self becomes identical to what the loving parent provides. The parent knows the child better than the child knows himself, so the child grows by participating in his parent's knowing.

Freud famously noticed this erotic union of child to parent, but reduced it—erroneously, in my view—to sexuality. As long as we define eros more Socratically, we can avoid this simplistic reduction, and better understand the profundity of this process.

From the parent's perspective, the relation is agapic. Nothing challenges egocentrism more forcibly than having a child. Even a self-centered person, when faced with parenthood, may experience this metanoia. You are no longer the center of your own salience landscape. Your child becomes the center, and your life becomes a process of creation—not through ego, but through sacrifice.

Parental love is a symbol for Jesus's kairos. For Christians, His agape became the transitive connection between God and humanity. A parent sacrifices herself to participate in the creation of her child. Through this sacrifice, she participates in the same love that created her. Her loving act binds her to her origin, to the source of her creation, and she becomes part of that source, an extension of its power and vitality.

Jesus embodied and exapted this sacrificial binding. He lifted the love of parenthood from something instinctive to something purposeful, something that could behold each person as a child, as God might see them, and to love that about them which was most real and eternal. People could imitate His comprehension and find in themselves a capacity for His creative love. They became vessels through which agape created other persons, so their deeds became works of God.

Agape was not just an act; it was a source of reality. By giving it, we realize *we* were given it, so our sacrifice for others becomes a gratitude for being, a kind of Platonic anamnesis (or sati) that returns us to the source of our creation and redeems us with a memory of our true identity—who we are, originally, standing before God.

The advent of agapic love, in its power to redeem and recreate identity, had a revelatory effect on the ancient world. Phenomenologically, it fulfilled both dimensions of the realization we discussed at the outset of this book. It turned people into themselves, and it made them more real. The transformation was also a recollection, and it gave powerful plausibility to insights that emerged from it. It was therefore a new way of knowing oneself and knowing others as selves. There was a propulsive, apotheosizing force in the early Christian community even while it was oppressed by Roman law.

The early Christians felt they were conduits of this divine creative process that turned nonpersons into persons. They felt they were participating in God's works, knowing Him in the very act of their participation. The First Letter of John famously captured this change of identity and sounded the call for Christian love: *Beloved, let us love one another, for love is from God; and everyone who loves is born of God and knows God. The one who does not love does not know God, for God is love* (I John 1:4–7).

Like many famous passages, "God is love" has grown trite from misinterpretation, but imagine it in these terms: God is the process of agape itself, the kairos of reciprocal opening. Each person who loves in this way takes on the identity of this process. Their agency grows, and so does their arena, their significance landscaping, and their capacity to track depth in the world around them.

The act of agape was both transitive and reflexive. By loving, you remembered being loved, realized you were loved, and were transformed by both memory and realization. The love preceded you, flowed through you, and you made it real by passing on to others. In doing so, you also made yourself more real.

Agape was the psychotechnology of Christianity, a new form of perspectival and participatory knowing. It would allow this new faith, in a few short centuries, to conquer the culture of the Roman Empire. In Jesus's name, anyone could enter a community of Christians and find fellowship within a community of persons, bonded together in agapic love.

As with Socrates, many different movements and communities formed around Jesus, and most involved the sacrificial element of agape. It was especially embodied in the practice of forgiveness. It is difficult to understand how revolutionary and counter intuitive this concept was. We are accustomed to thinking of forgiveness as a resolution of conflict, a peace bond between quarreling opponents. But this mistakes its nature. It is not eros, seeking to consume. It is not philia, requiring reciprocity.

When I forgive, I make myself an affordance for someone to

become what he is: a person before God. Let's play with the word as *fore-give* which means giving before a person earns—because the person, as known by God, is significantly more than his earnings. This is why forgiveness was so central to Jesus's teachings; it reached for the divine perspective, and made the forgiver more receptive to God's beholding presence, which saw the whole of the person that was hidden from human eyes.

My capacity to receive God's forgiveness and agape—and therein, my gratitude for being itself—was found in my willingness to forgive others. This idea became central to the core Christian commandment, the golden rule of *doing unto others*... Before God, your actions are reflexive. What you do is done to you; your brother is therefore you. Giving love sensitizes a person to receive it.

The Most Excellent Way: Paul the Apostle and the Road to Damascus

Many who followed Jesus only cared about His teachings, but in the fullness of time, His death would become the defining focus of Christian theology. It was an embodiment of that sacrificial forgiveness and redemption, fulfilling the identity between God and agape. Jesus's death inspired His followers to internalize this sacrificial love and carry it forth to transform other human beings.

This was not true of everyone, of course; there was much enmity and resistance to Jesus during His life. Just like Socrates, His presence was disruptive and unsettling, and the animosity He faced in life was passed on to his followers after his death. Before Christianity emerged in name, Jesus's adherents were simply known as followers of *The Way*, a term referring to this new agapic orientation, the path provided by the metanoia. The early days of The Way were marked by violence and persecution.

One of these early persecutors was a young man named Saul. His story is among the most formative in the Christian faith. It is recorded throughout the New Testament, most notably in *Acts of the Apostles*. Saul's story has the quality of myth, and precisely this quality makes it so efficacious. Saul was both a Jew and a Roman citizen, at a time when the two factions were mutually hostile to one another, locked into war and revolt.

Their dissonance reflected Saul's personality. He was committed to law. He valued organized rules of behavior and conduct. The movements of Jesus and his followers affronted both Saul's Jewish heritage and his sense of Roman order. Saul's story coincided with the first uses of the term "Christianity." The term Christ meant "the anointed one." It was bestowed by Jesus's followers who believed him to be the subject of Judaic messianic prophecies.[2] However, when the term was used by Romans like Saul, it was levied as an epithet.

Saul's first appearance in the New Testament seems ignominious. He is present as the first Christian—Stephen—is martyred. While Stephen preaches Jesus's message of agape, the witnesses lay their robes at Saul's feet before stoning Stephen to death. Saul is zealously involved in Christian persecutions, and he requests cooperation from synagogues in Damascus to round up followers of The Way. But while on the road to Damascus, Saul has a shocking experience. He is blinded by a bright light and struck to the ground.

A voice speaks to him: "Saul, Saul, why are you persecuting me?"

Saul says, "Who are you, lord?"[3]

The voice responds, "I am Jesus, whom you are persecuting, but get up and enter the city, and it will be told you what you must do." (Acts 9:4–6)

This is among the more famous passages in the New Testament. The flash of light reenacts the motif of enlightenment and carries a powerful surge of onto-normativity (discussed in chapter 10). Saul has the sense that he is confronting something significantly more real than himself. The philosopher L.A. Paul describes these events as *transformative experiences.*[4]

Just like in Plato's Cave, the experience is disorienting. When the individual emerges from the cave, he is blinded by the vision of

---

2. Judaism does not recognize Jesus as Christ. This remains a significant difference between Jewish and Christian faiths.
3. In this context, lord is not a title for God. It refers to anyone with a higher or more important status.
4. L. A. Paul, *Transformative Experience* (Oxford University Press, 2014).

reality. The same is true on the road to Damascus: "Saul got up from the ground, and though his eyes were open, he could see nothing." (Acts 9:8)

When Saul arrives in Antioch, he is taken in by the very people he planned to persecute. This is his first contact with forgiveness. Under their care, Saul's sight is restored. This experience, and the vision before it, awaken a deep inner conflict in him, reminiscent of Plato's psychic parts. The very thing Saul persecutes has induced an experience of awakening. How can he reconcile this?

His hatred for agape embodies a persistent pattern in Christianity and a central teaching of Jesus and the apostles. We are loath to acknowledge the reality of being loved, being created. Our personal fables style us as *causa sui*—self-made, self-directed, self-secure. Agape challenges these egoic ideas in a very profound way. It forces us to consider the idea that something comes before us, that it could know us better than we know ourselves. When we peer closely at these novel Christian insights, it is not difficult to see the influence of the Socratic tradition somewhere in their roots.

Whereas Plato addressed this conflict with reason and dialogue, Saul must resolve it with a personal confrontation. After he recovers, he withdraws into the desert. This too is a biblical, mythological paradigm for kairos and self-reflection. When Saul returns, he has reached a higher state of consciousness and undergone a radical, transformative experience. He is a new person, with a new identity: he changes his name from Saul to Paul.

When Paul returns from the desert, he bears a radical message. His hymn to agape, appearing in his first letter to the Corinthians, is among the most famous passages in the Bible. Even if you are not Christian, you have certainly heard it read at weddings. It is often misread as an encomium to romantic love, but Paul is talking about an agapic, spiritual kind of love. While agape certainly has a presence in romantic relationships, its meaning is dulled by the association. Paul begins by saying: "And now I will show you a still more excellent way." (I Corinthians 12:31). He does not make an argument, like Plato. Instead, in this well-known passage of I Corinthians 13, he presents this agapic love in a frame of participatory knowing:

If I speak in the tongues of men or of angels, but do not have love, I am only a resounding gong or a clanging cymbal. If I have the gift of prophecy and can fathom all mysteries and all knowledge, and if I have a faith that can move mountains, but do not have love, I am nothing. If I give all I possess to the poor and give over my body to hardship that I may boast, but do not have love, I gain nothing.

Paul describes agape not as a feeling or belief but a path, a process of conformity, anagoge, and reciprocal opening. He knows this love by identifying with this love, becoming this love. He takes on the identity of the path itself, as though love were not something to have, but someone to become.

Love is patient, love is kind. It does not envy, it does not boast, it is not proud. It does not dishonor others, it is not self-seeking, it is not easily angered, it keeps no record of wrongs. Love does not delight in evil but rejoices with the truth. It always protects, always trusts, always hopes, always perseveres. Love never fails.

It is strange to think of love as unfailing. But we are not talking about the romantic context, which is rife with envy, jealousy, and recorded wrongs. We are born from romantic love, but we are born *again* from agape. By definition, this love is constant and unconditional, therefore creating the conditions for personhood. It allows a movement toward that ineffable wholeness of an individual that cannot be captured in propositions, but only by participation.

But where there are prophecies, they will cease; where there are tongues, they will be stilled; where there is knowledge, it will pass away. For we know in part and we prophesy in part, but

when completeness comes, what is in part
disappears.

Paul then proceeds to give a familiar metaphor, that archetypal analogy for development, maturity, and transformation that we have already discussed in previous chapters:

> *When I was a child, I talked like a child, I thought*
> *like a child, I reasoned like a child. When I*
> *became a man, I put the ways of childhood*
> *behind me.*

When you are a child, you have a particular identity and salience landscape. Things matter to you in a certain way. The accession to wisdom is symbolized by the transition from childhood to adulthood. As an adult, the world takes on an entirely different salience, away from toys and play and toward relationships and responsibilities. Agape precipitates this kind of metanoia, this fundamental reorientation of the person.

> *For now we see only a reflection as in a mirror; then*
> *we shall see face to face. Now I know in part;*
> *then I shall know fully, even as I am fully*
> *known. And now these three remain: faith,*
> *hope, and love. But the greatest of these is love.*

Paul's letter, just like his vision on the road to Damascus, reminisces of Plato's Cave. The illusions of egocentrism are marked by shadows and echoes. As long as we look out at the world and see only our reflection, we remain childlike and confined. Our concerns remain egoic, and we withhold ourselves from meaningful contact with reality.

In agape, our participatory love creates the reciprocal opening. We grow in another's understanding. They grow in ours. Each of us grows more into ourselves. Our perspectives must deepen to fit this ongoing disclosure—our disclosure, and the disclosure of the world itself. Agape grants us an unfolding access to reality. We associate it with parenthood, but Paul writes of a love that can be given to any relationship.

Romantic love can become agapic when it creates an ongoing commitment to the mystery of a person, when you give up the arrayed pursuit of many erotic partners in order to deeply know and be known by someone else. This commitment is analogous to the process of growing up. Paul refers to a way of knowing—*gnosis*—that can only be accessed in this way of loving.

Justice and Love: The Inner Conflict of Christianity

As I noted above, these core tenets of Christianity—God as agape, forgiveness, the creation of persons—are now fundamental to our Western moral worldview. They hold us up without us knowing. In saying this, I am not advocating for Christianity. I want to show how profoundly this expression of meaning, transcendence, and wisdom has taken root in the human psyche. However, as with all virtues, there is also a danger in agape.

This conforming gnosis, the oneness of knowing and becoming, means that my knowing of myself and my knowing the other are intimately intertwined. Jesus says this of his relation to God: that he and the Father are one. Paul will say, "It is not I who lives, but Christ who lives in me." Agape involves a deep bonding of identity, a transformation around the other person as they are realized, created, and disclosed.

However, this bonding does not necessarily involve rational self-reflection. Therefore, there is a danger to this bonding process; any aspect of yourself you do not properly understand can be unconsciously projected onto the person you love. This often occurs between parents and their children. It is wise to pair agape with Socratic self-inquiry, especially in a romantic context; the degree to which you are self-ignorant is also the degree to which your participatory knowing can be twisted and darkened, and unrecognized aspects of yourself can become confused for the person standing opposite you.

For all of his astonishing spiritual brilliance, I believe this projection was occurring in Paul. His inner conflict was profound, and he languished over Aristotle's *akrasia,* a weakness of will—knowing what he should do but being impelled to do the opposite. Paul used the language of civil war to describe this conflict, someone who stands at the center of their citadel while the outlying provinces are in revolt.

He found himself suspended between two identities. Saul wanted to follow the law, but he felt guilty, angry, and rejected by God while Paul was a man of love, who felt deeply connected to God. This is another idea that has now become endemic to our culture—the conflict between the "old me" and the "new me." Paul tried to midwife himself from his predecessor. He personalized the God of history, and he understood his own inner conflict as reflecting an inner conflict in God.

This, I think, is the source of projection. In Paul's shadow, God becomes conflicted within himself. Now, He has two aspects. One part represents law, justice, and order. Insofar as God represents that, we stand in judgment. We are measured by a sword of appraisal, and we invariably fall short of it. We cannot attain the unfaltering virtue that moral perfection demands of us. Our agency has diverted us—and continues to divert us—from His path.

We are therefore, by definition, condemnable by His law. But God is not just a judge. He is also love, the agapic parent of unconditional compassion. Paul takes up the notion that Jesus's death embodied the sacrifice of God's agapic love and that his sacrifice satisfied God's demand for justice and fulfilled the goodness of his creation.

The kairos of Jesus unites these two aspects of God's nature, realigns the cosmic narrative, and redeems human sin and our relationship to God. Many iconic representations of Jesus use his left and right hands to symbolize the paradox of these interrelated aspects—the agapic love and lawful judgment. These are also sometimes depicted as feminine and masculine aspects respectively.[5]

There are many theological disputes about Jesus as a redeemer,

5. Jonathan Pageau, "Introduction to Iconography" (lecture, Consciousness and

but these are not relevant to our discussion. However, it is important to note that within this revelatory idea of gnosis and agape there is also an involuntary projection of one man's internal conflict. Paul's tension helped to naturalize the idea that the course of reality was enmeshed in a conflict between justice and agape. His human tension was also a cosmic tension, and it produced significant historical consequences.

Christianity was drawn together from both aspects. Whether we understand the aporetic tension to be an internal contradiction or a paradox with mysterious symbolic symmetry, people who experienced deep inner conflict found a welcoming home within the auspices of Christianity, especially those riven by a sense of personal failure and frustrated aspiration, who anguished over their imperfection, and desired more than anything to come into a completeness of their own personhood. We still swim in these Christian waters, even though most of us do not profess to be Christians. We experience personal failure in the face of judgment, and we long for the creative power of gnosis. However, without the Christian metaphysics of cosmic redemption, these longings induce powerful experiences of despair. Camus famously said: "Can one be a saint without God? That is the problem, in fact the only problem I am up against today."[6]

Camus, of course, famously came to the conclusion that reality was radically absurd. This is a price we have latterly paid for the gifts and grace that Christianity gave us: expectations of love, transformation, growth into personhood, relief from inner conflict. These expectations are not well met in our post-Christian worldview. We still carry the grammar of God, but much of it is now unconscious, discontinuous with those scientifically minded propositional beliefs that narrowed the field of plausibility and erased its presence from the cosmic worldview. We are left with nowhere to place it and therefore nowhere to place ourselves. Our

---

Conscience Conference, Thunder Bay, Ontario, September 18, 2022). Lecture is available on Jonathan Pageau's YouTube channel.
6. Albert Camus, *The Plague*, trans. Stuart Gilbert (London: Penguin Books, 2001).

aspirations for gnosis and wholeness are left to founder in some back alley of our experience, and we suffer the absurdity of disproportion —their deep significance to us, and their apparent irrelevance to the universe.

In chapter 7, we explored the *nomological order* of Aristotle's conformity theory and the way it arranged the agent-arena relation for the Axial worldview. In the following chapters, I will discuss two other complementary orders that were composed in the confrontation between Christianity, emerging from the Israelite Jewish heritage and the Axial spirituality of Greece, especially Neoplatonism and Stoicism. These confrontations created both conflict and confluence, but their syncretic posterity would ultimately become the new foundation of meaning of the Western world.

17

GNOSIS AND EXISTENTIAL INERTIA

With the dawning of Christianity, the concept of gnosis took on new valances. It provoked the longing to be recreated, to shed the skins of former selves and be born again into a wider world. For many spiritual schools of the day, transformation of the self became the religious imperative, the realization of one's true nature emerging from the husk of a former person, like Paul the apostle emerging from Saul the persecutor. Yet just like Paul, the desire for metanoia was marked by existential frustration.

The transformation that people sought so desperately was fettered by inhibitions. There were many locked doors inside the psyche, barricades that impeded us from within, put us at variance with ourselves, and caused us to suffer inexplicably. Our own inner lives were such effective inhibitors that they seemed under the influence of some cosmic force, a soporific spell that weakened our will, bound our agency, kept us asleep, and restrained our attempts to realize our potential.

The Gnosis of Plato

The term *gnosis* had already been used by Plato in the fourth century BCE. It signified that knowledge we acquire by direct apprehension, the participatory knowing wherein the knower becomes the known, sharing in its nature, shaping itself around its identity. "Knowing demands the organ fitted to the object," as Plotinus would later write. In the Greek nomological order, gnosis was possible because of a metaphysical affinity, the resonance between an individual's soul (*psuche*) or spirit, and the transcendent cosmos whose nature it shared. The knowing soul could, by the recollection and perception of his mind (the Greek *nous*), realize his own likeness to the good and partake more fully of its nature.

In the Platonic and Neoplatonic traditions, gnosis was mediated by philosophical practice. It strengthened the soul's functional disposition for this contact epistemology, training it to fly upward and conform itself to the highest value. This anagoge is depicted in the myth of Plato's *Phaedrus:* the well-disposing soul is depicted as a charioteer, questing to the rim of heaven.

The place beyond heaven—none of our earthly poets has ever sung or will ever sing its praises enough! Still, this is the way it is—risky as it may be, you see, I must attempt to speak the truth, especially since the truth is my subject. What is in this place is without color and without shape and without solidity, a being that is really what it is, the subject of all true knowledge, visible only to intelligence (nous), the soul's steersman. Now a god's mind is nourished by intelligence and pure knowledge, as is the mind of any soul that is concerned to take in what is appropriate to it, and so it is delighted at last to be seeing what is real and watching what is true..."[1]

In this myth, the horses tethered in the chariot are the conflicting parts of the psyche we explored in previous chapters. They must be marshaled by the steersman so they pull in a single direction, bearing us to conformity with this higher state of realness. This moment of contact and conformity—*gnosis*—requires harmony between the psychic parts, like instruments of an orchestra playing in concert to catch the cosmic melody. When harmonized, our intellect tuned itself to the good, as though the shape of mind were cast from a mold

---

1. Plato's *Phaedrus*, 247c–247d.

of the truth it beheld. The soul's capacity for conformity was inborn but cultivated through philosophical rigor, just like musculature can be conditioned, through exercise, to reach its optimal state of fitness.

The Gnosis of Sensibility Transcendence

The idea of gnosis can seem very mystical and esoteric, but we can explore its phenomenology by using some of our cognitive scientific vocabulary. We have already explored the concept of worldview attunement: a deeply integrated and dynamically coupled way of understanding agency. The world is an arena, and your relationship to it frames your perspectival and participatory modeling. A worldview is simultaneously modeling the world to you and modeling you to shape the world. It is a mutual conformity, a reciprocal revelation.

I have a peculiar experience sometimes when I am reading, lecturing, or taking a walk. It happens especially when I read the works of Spinoza, the seventeenth-century philosopher. Spinoza is a profound and complex thinker, and I have spent many hours trying to understand his arguments. Over time, my understanding has grown. His ideas have become more choate, and I relate them together more systematically. But then, on occasion, something else occurs.

Usually, I read what Spinoza is *saying*. But sometimes, I see what Spinoza is *seeing*. First, he is an object for study. Then, I imagine stepping into his subjectivity and glimpsing the world as he glimpses it. I begin to see the world *Spinozistically*. This sudden moment of conformity induces a shift from opacity to transparency; Spinoza is now the lens by which I am seeing the world and seeing myself. I am living the world through his worldview and experience, participating in his particular knowing. I perceive the livability of his worldview, and I take on his agent-arena relationship.

My experience in these moments is similar to something that

cognitive scientist John Wright calls *sensibility transcendence*.[2] His idea is originally based on the work of Iris Murdoch, who wrote a seminal masterpiece called *The Sovereignty of Good*. In this careful study, Murdoch set out to contemplate the idea of morality beyond the rules and reasons that so often reduce it. She wanted to understand the viability of a moral posture and the way our attention determines our relationship to the good. In our language, we might say that she explored how our salience landscape and agent-arena relationship create our normative worldview.

Murdoch provides a moving example of a moral metanoia. Imagine a terse relationship between a mother and her daughter-in-law. The mother finds her daughter-in-law to be coarse, loud, and uncouth. She wishes her son had married someone different. She tries to be polite, but she carries reproach into all of their interactions. But one day, something unexpected happens. The mother glances at her daughter-in-law and sees something different, like a hidden image in a reversible figure.

The mother no longer sees the daughter-in-law as coarse but as honest. She is not uncouth but rather sincere. She doesn't lack elegance; she possesses authenticity. Her brusqueness is not unkind. It just conceals a different kind of affection. In a single moment, the mother's entire perception of her daughter-in-law changes. The daughter-in-law becomes a new person before her eyes—yet also perhaps the same as she had always been. More of her person is suddenly revealed, recollected by the mother's insight. She has, in some manner of speaking, become more real.

This revelation is profound for the mother, and it is the beginning of a more significant change. Her sudden insight reframes her perspective of her daughter-in-law, as though freeing her from an interpersonal nine-dot problem. But the insight is not just a local insight, solving for a specific problem. The new glimpse of her daughter-in-law—like my glimpse of Spinoza—causes a global insight. In order to reframe how she sees the daughter-in-law, she

2. John R. Wright, "Transcendence without Reality," *Philosophy* 80, no. 3(2005): 361–384.

must also reframe how she sees herself. As her own reflection changes (as an agent), so must her corresponding perception of the world (as an arena).

These changes are all coordinated and mutually entailing; both agent and arena sides of the relationship are reshaped together. This is a moment of *transframing*, a transformation of the whole framing process. The mother-in-law realizes that the way that she has habitually framed other people has been narrow and myopic, projected from many categorical assumptions, misapprehensions about the world that were tied to past experiences and patterns of thinking. Her worldview had become rigid and unyielding, so her insight about her daughter-in-law becomes a systematic insight about her worldview itself and about how her attention is directed.

The attentional shifts we described in previous chapters—from feature to gestalt, transparency to opacity—are occurring now in both directions. She experiences the kind of development we explored in chapter 10, when the child no longer finds salience in the space between the candies and refocuses on the candies themselves. The mother now perceives an entire system of errors she has been making and is now capable of correcting for them. This sudden change begins with participatory and perspectival knowing, but it also changes the procedure of how she relates to her daughter-in-law and the propositions she might use to describe her to family and friends.

Wright calls this insight an example of *sensibility transcendence*, but after the previous chapter, we might just as readily call it an example of agape. The mother forgives her daughter-in-law and seeks forgiveness for her mistaken perception. Remember that forgiveness in this case does not mean excusing a particular transgression. It means perceiving—and being perceived—beyond the relevance of those transgressions. Being so forgiven, the daughter-in-law can now be something that she could not be before while the mother-in-law is becoming someone she could not become before.

Where before she saw her own reflection, now she stands face to face. Each grows in the other's growth. Both beholding subject and bolden object undergo this sensibility transcendence, an aspect shift that reveals their mutual possibility for transformation. This makes them more vulnerable to the disclosure of one another's attention. It is not just the insight itself that is meaningful. It is the fact that the insight was possible.

The event of this sensibility transcendence, this experience of knowing by loving, becomes a newfound part of reality. It brings a new sense of possibility. The contrast between the two perspectives of the daughter-in-law—and the distance traveled between them—provides an opponent process, a stereoscopic vision that gives a new sense of depth to the world and indicates the presence of still more undiscovered perspectives.

The mother becomes more sensitive to the limits of her knowledge. She begins to develop something like what Nicholas of Cusa called *learned ignorance*.[3] The insight of sensibility transcendence is something like what occurs in a higher state of consciousness. It begins a process of reciprocal opening that can continue beyond this first revelation.

As I explained in the previous chapter, Christianity was revolutionary for offering this kind of sensibility transcendence, the possibility of becoming a different kind of person. But new ways of being are not always so accessible. In his book entitled *The Reasons of Love,* Harry Frankfurt talks about how much our reasoning depends on what we love. Our loves create our agent-arena relationship and form the heuristics that guide our attention. Love makes certain things available to our worldview and certain things unavailable. For better or worse, certain realities become *unthinkable.*

We can run inferences and imagine scenarios, but we cannot make certain possibilities viable, and we cannot inhabit certain worldviews. For instance, I can imagine disinheriting my children. The scenario has some advantages. My home would be cleaner, and I would enjoy more disposable income. But I could not bring myself to inhabit a world where this was a live option. My love for my sons forecloses the possibility.

---

3. Jasper Hopkins, *Nicholas of Cusa on Learned Ignorance: A Translation and an Appraisal of De Docta Ignorantia* (A.J. Benning Press, 1981).

My agape makes the moral choice clear because my sons are infinitely more real than anything I could gain in their place. They are ends unto themselves, worlds of immeasurable meaning. The prospect that anything could prevail over them is unthinkable and unlivable. I can understand the proposition, imagine the procedure, and take on the perspective. But I cannot participate in this world.

I'm grateful for my particular unthinkable, but limits on participatory knowing can become suffocating when they trap us inside an ingrown worldview. We can become stuck inside modes of participation that feel inadequate but find that we cannot outgrow them. We feel locked from the inside, unable to find the sensibility transcendence that would open us to a new mode of being. We imagine a change but cannot make it. We become trapped in a version of ourselves we cannot escape and experience a deep *existential inertia*.

As Carl Jung observed, people often enter therapy for exactly this reason—not to cure an ailment but to gain a fuller access to oneself, to escape a form of life that distorts our view of reality. Consider someone who has a series of failed romantic relationships. He craves a connection that is deep and profound. He imagines it but cannot find it, and after years of repeated failures, he senses that something about his own worldview inhibits him. Something in his mode of participation thwarts his own goals.

His efforts are circular, and he cannot break the inertia. His agency suffers; depression occurs. He feels he cannot live with himself unless he can change himself entirely. But how does he get from here to there? How can he access a fuller version of himself? Where does he look to find agapic revelation? The therapist's office can be helpful, but it is not sufficient on its own to guarantee this transformation.

This existential inertia is a significant theme in L. A. Paul's book, *Transformative Experience*. However much we crave transformation, the possibility of it also stupefies us. It represents a threshold between two different persons, and in this threshold is an epistemic gap, a kind of existential ignorance for our perspectival and participatory knowing. L. A. Paul shows this first with a trivial example. Imagine someone offers you a fruit you have never tasted. Your reaction will be bimodal: you will either like it or dislike it. But you do not know which reaction you will have until you bite the fruit.

Should you try it? In this case, perhaps it does not matter; there is nothing significantly at risk. Nevertheless, the example shows that your perspectival knowing is entirely dependent on your state of being. You do not know what your salience landscape will be like when you eat this fruit until after you have eaten it. There is no way of knowing in advance. You have to go through the experience to know what it is like to have the experience. L. A. Paul calls this an *epistemic transformation.*

While the fruit example is trivial, some of these transformations are profoundly personal, the same epistemic gap combined with a significant existential consequence. Now more is at stake: not just having a particular perspective but being a particular person. Some of these experiences—like serving in war, getting married, having a child, becoming a priest—carry a new worldview on the other side of them, a new agent-arena relationship.

You shall become a new person through the experience, but you cannot know what it is like to be that new person until the change has already occurred. For L. A. Paul, a transformative experience is one that involves a radical change in perspectival knowing and participatory knowing. She uses a provocative thought experiment to make this point.

Imagine the following fantastical scenario: your friends approach you and reveal a secret. They give you indubitable evidence that they can turn you into a vampire. This prospect is not without appeal as it offers power and longevity. But should you do it?

The experience is inaccessible because it lies on the far side of an epistemic gap. You cannot make any inferences about what it is like to be a vampire. You do not know who you are going to be when you become a vampire. Your preferences, appetites, behavior and general character are all sure to change. Your salience landscape will radically change. You do not know what the world will feel like, and you cannot predict who you will be inside of it.

Once you go through this change, you may have lost a way of

being. Your old life may become unthinkable, and you will not be able to return to it. You cannot know what you will lose until you go through this transformation—but if you do not do it, you do not know what you will miss.

Vampirism could be a new way of being that is profound and wonderful. You are caught in the epistemic gap, and you cannot reason your way through it. Are your current values the right set of values? Or would your vampiric values be a better set of values? There is no higher common ground that you can use to triangulate the two perspectives and appraise the two states of being. Nothing is certain. Everything is at risk.

The Gnosis of Play

The vampire example may seem silly, but as with any thought experiment, the point is to acknowledge the logic of the problem. L. A. Paul reminds us that we face these kinds of dilemmas at very important junctures in our lives. One of the examples above is particularly relevant to our discussion of agape: should you have a child? If you remain childless, you will never experience the salience landscape of a parent. You will never know what you are missing. But if you decide to have a child, the change is irreversible, and you stand to lose many features of your life, including some that define its ambition and possibility.

Accounts of other people's experiences are helpful when you consider these decisions, but they can't substitute for your firsthand experience. You face a radical existential ignorance. Should you stay where you are, or should you make the leap? Both options are fraught with existential danger.

Paul uses a familiar example of the transition from childhood to adulthood. The child cannot imagine what she is going to lose by becoming an adult. She does not understand that the phenomenology of her childhood—all of those unnamable states and sensations, the unfettered sense of novelty, the heightened wonder that comes with childhood innocence—will no longer be available to her. But she also cannot imagine the meaningfulness of adult experience, the gifts of learning, the depth of relationships, the power of agency.

Though we all age, many of us struggle to accede from the open-ended possibilities of childhood, and we eschew irreversible commitments that threaten to break this spell. The Peter Pan syndrome, or *Puer Aeternus*, is the motif for this condition. If you choose a career, or a course of study, or a person to marry, you sacrifice many potential realities, perhaps some wonderful ones. But should you instead avoid these commitments and keep all possibilities open? This does not seem like an optimal solution. You remain a finite being. You will not be able to realize each possibility, even if you knew what they were. If you never choose, what are you missing? We can be stupefied as we face the need for radical transformation. It is not merely that we can bring ourselves to do it, we are not even certain that we should do it.

People lapse into a certain *aspect disguise* when stuck and stupefied. Consider the following situation. While sitting with a therapist, you explain that you feel stuck. She asks you to elaborate, and you say: "I am so stubborn. I need to be more flexible." Then later in the session, she asks what you like most about yourself and you reply, "Well I am persistent. I don't give up." We step into these contradictions frequently. The very thing we are trying to change is the very thing we are loath to relinquish, the thing we identify with mostly closely.

We discuss the same characteristic under two different aspects— one positive and adaptive, one negative and maladaptive. We are stuck and stupefied by this *aspectualization*, and we stall in inertia and indecision. We cannot imagine how to make an alternative worldview significant or viable. We cannot rationally make the choice. This inertia becomes even more paralytic if it is paired with parasitic processing and modal confusion.

How do we get free of this suspended animation? How does someone resolve the dilemma of parenthood, for instance? Some people wait so long that the possibility closes. Others charge forward without thinking. But some people put themselves through a deliberative trial, a process of playful contemplation. When trying to answer the dilemma of parenthood, I have noticed many people get a dog.

Having a dog is not the same as having a child, of course, but it simulates certain features of the experience. A dog requires constant attention and diligent care. It calls forth steadfast responsibility. Training your dog properly requires skill, patience, discipline, and inexhaustible love. If he undertakes the project diligently, a person can step a foot halfway into the worldview of parenthood and imagine more fully what this world feels like from the inside. A similar proxy for marriage is travel or cohabitation: to determine compatibility, many couples try traveling together or move in together for a short amount of time.

Though responsibilities in their own right, these half-measures of transformation are also serious kinds of *play*. When faced with the unthinkable, we use a theater of pretend, rituals of enactment that allow us to trace a foreign experience with an embodied imagination, the way a child puts on a cape to try on virtues of courage and heroism. We do this for fantastical identities and scenarios (including vampires) but we also do this for domestic situations.

Adults undertake these imaginal rituals through different kinds of role-playing games in different arenas: tabletop games, virtual reality games, escape rooms, etc. This kind of imaginal pageantry is becoming more prolific, and taking on more dynamic forms of practice. For example, a Scandinavian style of role-playing called *jeepform* simulates difficult situations by putting them into an improvised, live-action drama.

A player is given a scenario to act out, and the traditional role of the dungeon master is like a movie director, cutting scenes and switching roles. The whole point of jeepform is to stage emotionally difficult scenarios, preparing the players for life's more difficult or aporetic confrontations. This phenomenon is called *bleed*. While I am role playing, the director is trying to provoke a transframing through the role play, artfully blurring the line between the psychodrama and my real life. The game places me in a liminal zone between present and future worlds so I can enact a possible, aspirational future within the safety and knowability of the present.

It is no coincidence that as organisms become more intelligent, more in need of developmental transformations, they also become more playful. Play is not a frivolous thing, and we trivialize it at our peril. It can be fun, certainly, but fun is not the primary objective when people adopt a dog. Play is a confrontation with possibility, a courtship with the process of transformation. It creates an *enactive analogy*—not an analogy of words or thoughts but one of imaginal and embodied perspective. It takes skill and artistry to do this well, a kind of dramaturgical astuteness.

A good director can draw out the player by applying their experience to an undiscovered context, using familiar terms to articulate something they have never lived out. In the same way, a creative therapist sometimes helps a client to realize their own feelings by dramatizing a conversation with a parent or spouse, someone who can analogize part of their perspective and allow them to participate in it.

The enactive analogy must draw a careful tension. Like an archer's bowstring, it has to bend your worldview without snapping it completely, taking aim at the world you aspire to reach. It has to be known enough *and* unknown enough, both accessible and novel. Recall our discussion of virtual engines from chapter 6 and the necessity of both selective and enabling constraints. This play is a delicate opponent process, a symbolic balancing act, the kind that makes for the most sublime narratives.

Play bridges this world into the next, and finds a way to acquaint and compare them together. When I play, I use this world analogously to frame and understand the next world. This is another psychotechnology of exaptation, like a child using a stick to simulate a sword, or exapting gestures into spatial metaphors to capture concepts at higher levels of abstraction.

Ritual is a complex form of play and therefore integral to religious practices. Here too, we live between two worlds—one that is immanent and finite and one that is transcendent and infinite. In these various spiritual traditions, making the second world viable is the process of anagoge, the transformation of attention facilitated by the flow of ritual play, whether it be through mindfulness practice, a

Socratic dialogue, a Stoic view from above, or the agape in Christian liturgy.

The enacted analogy, the imaginal instrument of ritual play, is as indispensable for us as it was for the shaman. Without it, other worlds remain as distant as the stars while this world becomes a place of darkening, diminishing returns, a narrowing arena that slowly suffocates us, freezing us in time while slowly putting us to sleep.

The Christians feared this existential slumber and its despair. Awakening from this state, then and now, is the project of gnosis. A set of psychotechnologies create a ritual context—like jeepform, martial arts or therapy—that shakes us free from existential entrapment. These psychotechnologies can help generate those higher states of consciousness discussed in earlier chapters, sometimes augmented by shamanic disruptions or psychedelic aids that transform our ways of knowing and give us a taste of a greater reality, a new vision of life itself.

18

GNOSTICISM AND NEOPLATONISM

When human beings are beset by existential inertia, we feel like we are trapped in a bad relationship with reality. In a world of enacted analogies, this one might come the closest to simulating the intense, all-consuming distress. Nearly every person, if we live long enough, has such a relationship, whether romantic or familial. These situations make us feel desperate, hopeless, guilty, resentful, and reckless—sometimes all at once. They seem to infect the world from the inside out, and spread to every corner of our experience.

We feel utterly dissatisfied with life but also unable to change anything. We don't know what will happen to us if we leave the relationship or even give voice to the tensions we feel. The things we say cannot be unsaid, and if we call the worldview into question, everything could unravel. We don't know what we might hear, what hurt we might cause, or what guilt we might incur. Will I have ruined something beautiful? Will I discover that I am to blame? Will I have sabotaged my one chance and be unloved for the rest of my life?

These paralytic fears keep many people from risking change, and understandably so. Eventually, though, many come to the realization that if they are to have a chance of a genuine life, they cannot remain unchanged. They use friends or therapists to seek serious play and simulate the confrontations that might break their world apart. In a great many cases, however much they prepare, their world *does* break apart. Transformation is unavoidably painful. If a person is not braced with ritual, with community, with a chance of new perspective, the end of a relationship can leave disastrous consequences in its wake.

Despite the considerable existential dangers, many people doggedly pursue transformative experience. They are driven by a *gnostic* appetite. The craving for gnosis is the felt need for transformative experience. We need relief from a suffocating worldview, and when this need becomes desperate, we begin to feel oxygen starved. Kierkegaard and Nietzsche were among the philosophers who used metaphors of asphyxiation to describe the feelings of nihilism and despair.

In chapter 3, I quoted Paolo Costa's observation about meaning, the atmospheric quality of significance that surrounds us, and encloses both the agent and arena.[1] When the relationship is decadent, it can feel as though this atmosphere is polluted. When transformation seems inaccessible, we begin to feel hopeless. Some become suicidal and self-destructive, or they vent their distress on others. These effects, en masse, have characterized the Meaning Crisis.

Our *vis-à-vis* with the world must now somehow be reopened. As I argued in the last chapter, we need a wise recovery of serious play and the anagoge it affords through new states of being and consciousness. But cultivating these states, and seeking transformation, also brings risks of bullshit and parasitic processing. New age psychedelic movements are good examples of what happens when wanton exploration is not properly paired with philosophic rigor. Changes of consciousness must be nested inside the right rituals. We need pedagogy and the fellowship of those who can help steady us in the empty space between worlds. If we do not have these supports, we may change in ways we do not desire or intend. As Jung famously wrote, we must beware of "unearned wisdom."

---

1. Costa, "A Secular Wonder," 138.

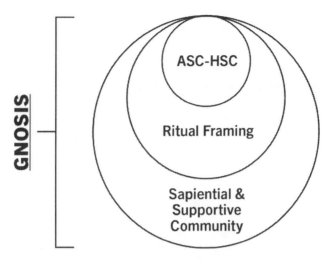

Figure 18.1: Depiction of the definition of gnosis. Gnosis relates to
a deeply transformative perspectival and participatory knowing
that takes place in an altered state of consciousness (ASC) which
has elements of a higher state of consciousness (HSC). This
experience must be ritually framed and embedded within a
sapiential and supportive community.

The Gnosis of Gnosticism

The new age movements of modernity have exploded in number and
prolificity. Whether they involve occult societies of secret knowledge
or conspiratorial world orders, they are the modern rebirth of an
ancient movement that gathered around the hunger for gnosis. This
movement strove for a spiritual emancipation, seeking a "red pill"[2] of
awakening to lift the veil of illusion and malaise that dulled their
senses and their will.

Their myth is familiar enough to all of us: a single individual,
directed by an inner intuition, has a Platonic recollection of some
greater reality. He follows his inner light to realize a divine power
within him to behold the secret code, sees through the illusions of his
lesser world, and defeats the godlike overlords who preside over the
bewitchment of humanity. Every philosophy professor in the last two

---

2. Red pill is also now also used in reference to gender politics, but this is not the
context I am invoking here.

decades has taken pains to point out that *The Matrix* is a depiction of Plato's Cave. But as April DeConick[3] and many others have noticed, the 1999 film that inspired the "red pill" neologism is also one of many contemporary stories descended from the mythology of *Gnosticism.*

As we discussed in the last chapter, the idea of gnosis traces back to Plato's metaphysics: the everyday world is like the shadows and echoes of the cave, temporal and illusory. The images of the material world participate in the forms, the patterns of intelligibility, and the realness that is realized therein. To bind the two worlds together, Plato imagined a mythic intermediary power that connected the unchanging forms, timeless and spaceless, to the sensory world of change.

He crafted a symbolic bridge to relate time and eternity together. This bridge was a figure called the *demiurge,* a godlike craftsman of rational agency who shaped the temporal in the image of eternity. He bound together the sensible and intelligible so that one was continuous with the other. Though images were not to be mistaken for reality, they nevertheless referred to it as the shadows in the cave referred to the light that cast them. Eternity could be known through time, and a coherent continuity remained between perception and reality.

This was a very important epistemic feature in the nomological order that followed and helped to hold the worldview intact. Science generally still holds this Platonic idea. We use experiments of change to infer the law-like principles that govern the universe. We trust that these law-like principles, while subject to human misapprehension, nevertheless have an inherent integrity that makes them knowable and trustworthy.

For Plato, the demiurge craftsmen and the Greek pantheon of gods were generally virtuous powers. However, they were not ultimate ones. The Good itself was supernal to these entities. You may remember that the *Phaedrus* passage referenced in the previous

---

3. April D. DeConick, *The Gnostic New Age: How a Countercultural Spirituality Revolutionized Religion from Antiquity to Today* (Columbia University Press, 2016).

chapter refers to a "place beyond heaven." This was a radical turn in the Axial period.

As the Platonic tradition gave way to early Christianity, these ideas were accentuated, and the significance of the demiurge began to change for some of its followers. The problems of illusion and inhibition—everything that prevented our quest for gnosis—were not solely attributable to our own foolishness, but to a more agentive kind of repression. In Christianity, the prevalence of sin impeded gnosis. It obscured the soul's recollection, blinding it to agape and forgiveness. But other ideas also formed on the periphery of early Christianity and were rejected by its orthodoxy—that the quest for gnosis was a purely personal quest, thwarted by malevolent cosmic forces.

This became a central idea for the *Gnostics*. These groups (so named by their enemies) were not a single, unified collective. They did not have a specific community or school of belief. They were a style of spirituality, a way of thinking like existentialism or fundamentalism. Many Gnostics considered themselves Christians by some definition. They aspired to the gnosis of Jesus, they shared the Christian preoccupation with will and agency, and they anguished over the inner conflict that kept us from fulfilling our divine destiny[4].

The gnosis of the Gnostics was more transgressive than its Platonic forerunner. The Gnostics believed we had a divine spark of spirit, a *pneuma*, that was consubstantial to a primal God, an entity that transcended the deities depicted in pre-Christian traditions. Our divine spark did not relate to God by affinity, but by identity; it was not *like* God, the way a wooden carving is like a tree. It *was* God, the way an inlet of sea is the ocean beyond the land that secludes it.

This metaphysical revision from the Platonic to the Gnostic meant a different goal for spiritual exercises. Instead of building up the strength of the perceiving soul, the Gnostics aimed to tear down

---

4. For further reading, see Hans Jonas, *The Gnostic Religion: The Message of the Alien God and the Beginnings of Christianity*, 2nd ed., rev. (Boston: Beacon Press, 1991).

the material dressings that masked the light of this divine spark—removing the mass of land isolating the inlet from its ocean home.

The Gnostic apotheosis drew allegations of heresy from Christian orthodoxy. It is not important for us to discuss the various disputes, except to say that the Gnostic modes of practice differed significantly from the apostolic Christians. The latter valued sacerdotal authority, and their emphasis on creeds foreran the rise of the universal church. Gnostic rites were more dynamic, malleable, individualized, and committed to the emancipation of the spirit from the captivity of lesser gods and creeds. Many of these captor deities were Bronze Age holdovers, stratified into a cosmology informed by Egyptian, Hebrew, and Roman influences.

For Gnostics, reality did not exhaust in these deities; they represented irons to be cast off in the course of the gnostic quest. In some of these Gnostic mythologies, the Hebrew Old Testament Yahweh was identified with the Platonic demiurge. This time however, the demiurge was considered a tyrannical force, a despot of the materiality that constrained the divine spark and prevented the spirit from ascending.

The Gnostics considered these deities to be agents of suffering; their design of the world was either malevolent or incompetent. The Gnostics endeavored to transcend them, and pursue the agapic God of the New Testament. This *God beyond God* offered transformation and beckoned us back to our divine connection. The Gnostics did not prioritize Jesus's crucifixion but generally focused on His teachings. They did not seek a static dogma but an array of spiritual practices and psychotechnologies. They appropriated the burgeoning Christian literature and mythos but subjected it to their personal convictions and experiences.[5]

Much like its forerunners in the Axial Greek project, Gnosticism strove for emancipation from those confinements that are endemic to

---

5. Even Paul was talking about this in the Bible when he spoke about powers and principalities that keep us imprisoned: "For our struggle is not against flesh and blood, but against the rulers, against the authorities, against the powers of this dark world and against the spiritual forces of evil in the heavenly realms." (Ephesians 6:12, New International Version).

human failure. Their sense of entrapment reacted to the after effects of the Hellenistic domicide. In many ways, the malevolent deities that were the jailors of humanity also stood for the variety of wordly forces—cultural, political and economic—that prevented most people from achieving a satisfying station on earth.

It is important to understand how radical the Gnostic transgression was for its time and even for ours; they desacralized the gods, and they inverted the servant style of spirituality that had made human beings deferential to the gods since the Bronze Age, shifting the ethic from worship into self-cultivation. Though Plato had certainly laid the path for this, the insurgent character of the Gnostics was a very different ethos.

Gnosticism was in many ways a prototypical counterculture, a revolution within the Axial Revolution, attempting to appropriate the quest for wisdom and bring it to culmination. The Gnostics sought secret knowledge and apotheosis. Their texts were mystical and psychedelic. They believed a cosmic identity lay between the pneumatic self and the divine center of the cosmos. If we could remember the connection and remove the oppressive forces, we could awaken from our repressed state and ascend to our rightful nature.

The Gnostics languished over the same existential frustration as their contemporaries: human aspiration being constantly thwarted by embodiment, by mortality, by temporal confinement, by the same fatality that the Stoics and Epicureans tried to resolve with equanimity. The Gnostics longed to be free of these human frailties and believed that the aspiration itself stoked the spark of divinity within us. Their struggle was a significant undercurrent in the evolution of Western spirituality and helped to steer its course. "Ultimately," writes April DeConick, "the gnostic story is about the human self, what it is, and how it became damaged."[6]

Gnostic stories continue to abound because they follow a mythic structure. Like most prevalent myths, Gnosticism recreates perennial

6. April D. DeConick, *The Gnostic New Age: How a Countercultural Spirituality Revolutionized Religion from Antiquity to Today* (Columbia University Press, 2016), 167.

patterns, especially the tension between our infinite aspirations and temporal limitations. The Gnostics combined elements of both Platonism and Christianity, they and facilitated dialogues between them. This movement was a site of syncretism. It was Socratically erotic, poetic, and inspiring for generations to come. However, it also carried a darker side.

The Gnostics are ancient antecedents to modern *conspirituality*, the fusion of spiritual appetites and conspiratorial thinking, the belief that most human beings are chained by invisible forces that obfuscate our knowledge of the truth. There is an intractability to the Gnostic character that reappeared in different guises over the centuries, and scapegoating became commonplace in some of their visions. They tidily attributed all of life's absurdity, chaos, and suffering to a single malevolent force, thereby removing a certain reflective responsibility for individuals while emboldening their ambition.

For instance, when some Gnostics mythologically severed the loving God of light of the New Testament from the wrathful, jealous God of the Hebrew Old Testament, they helped to sow the seeds of bigotry in Western culture, the belief that Jews were part of a conspiracy to keep us from realizing our true heritage. The apostolic church drove many Gnostic Christians underground, but their prejudices periodically reappeared across time, including in the twentieth century.

Nazism was not primarily a political or socioeconomic movement. It was a distorted Gnostic response to the Meaning Crisis, magnified by the conditions in the Weimar Republic of Germany. Gnosticism can quickly lead to utopian ideologies and exclusive societies comprised of cliquish fixations with a chosen race or class. When a privileged few take on a self-appointed quest of emancipation, violence becomes an acceptable recourse against any purportedly evil system.[7]

---

7. I recommend the work of Chris Hedges and his book, *American Fascists: The Christian Right and the War on America*. The book examines fundamentalist Christianity and its pervasive portrayal of a grand conspiracy. He also wrote a book

Gnosticism has a mixed legacy, and it is appropriate to consider it with an ambivalent attitude. The mythology has important motifs of awakening and imagination as well as the necessity of having a personal relation to the sacred. But it can also be a carrier for this cultural scapegoating and magical thinking. The practices and beliefs lack coherence and consistency, but they are also remarkably dynamic and creative. I would not advocate a return to Gnosticism, but we should consider how we might salvage the more edifying aspects of gnosis from the remains of ancient Gnosticism. We can ask the same question of many of our ancient traditions, of course: how we might adopt the virtue of agape without every letter of Christian doctrine or how we can access the Greek dialogical tradition without trying to rebuild the ancient nomological order.

To this end, Gnosticism was very influential for some pivotal modern thinkers, figures who have provided elegant diagnoses and responses to the Meaning Crisis. These thinkers include the theologian Paul Tillich, psychologist Carl Jung and philosopher Henry Corbin. These men were contemporaries in the twentieth century. Given the breadth of their learning and concerns, each of their aforementioned titles could arguably apply to all three of them.

Tillich took up the idea of a *God beyond God* and extracted it from the more pernicious aspects of Gnostic mythos. He proposed it could be a way of renewing our relationship with the mystery of being, the aporetic sense of faith that suffused classical Christianity. He was concerned with addressing our existential suffering and freeing our religious life from misguided literalism and other features of modern theism that had calcified in the post-scientific world.[8]

Jung's analytic psychology is for Gnosticism what cognitive behavioral therapy is to Stoicism. He adapted elements of the Gnostic

---

entitled, *I Do not Believe in Atheists*, which looks at how new atheists also represent a utopic perfectionism that sanctions violence.

8.   One of my friends and colleagues, Jonathan Pageau, thinks that Christianity will, in fact, go through this kind of self-transformation so it can move beyond the Meaning Crisis.

mythology into a psychotherapeutic context, cultivating enacted analogies and rituals of play to develop a conversant relationship with the symbolic structure of the psyche. For Jung, applying a more mythic understanding of the self became a way to midwife our unique characters and facilitate personal growth and transformation.

Corbin was a French philosopher and had many complementary ideas with Jung and Tillich. Informed by the Islamic mystical tradition and other classical influences, Corbin reintroduced the idea of the *imaginal world* into the Western vocabulary. Like Jung, he recovered a creative mysticism that used imagination to augment perception for the sake of understanding. Corbin felt we had lost a way of knowing that was essential to a spiritual life, and he was concerned with how we could draw on ancient wisdom to recover this agency.

Tillich, Jung and Corbin all present a path forward for gnosis, taking the creative parts of the gnostic quest and putting them back into dialogue with other ideas, disciplines and traditions. When we pair their efforts with the cognitive scientific project we have been unfolding, we may be able to access a more nuanced account of mysticism and sacredness, one that does not rely on the Gnostic's supernaturalistic mythologies or conspiratorial tendencies.

The Gnosis of Neoplatonism

As I have explained, Gnosticism played a significant historical role in the syncretism that followed the advent of Christianity. It facilitated dialogues between Christianity and classical Platonism, but it also helped to influence the emergence of a third form of spirituality, a colossal movement in philosophy that began in the second century and became an immeasurably influential force in its own right.

Neoplatonism was influenced by both Gnosticism and Christianity, but it would prove equally as formative for each of those movements in turn. Over time, Neoplatonism would wreathe together the final orders in the grammar of meaning in the West—the overarching cosmos that provided the sacred canopy and a system of thought, practice, and vocabulary for bridging together many schools of wisdom for the centuries to come.

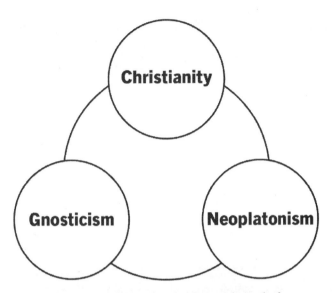

Figure 18.2: A diagram depicting the crucial triangle of Christianity, Gnosticism, and Neoplatonism as well as their interaction. We could perhaps also include Hermeticism, but that is beyond the scope of my argument right now.

Take the following analogy for Neoplatonism: right now, scientists are trying to integrate the two great theories of theoretical physics, quantum mechanics and relativity. If they succeed, they will have a grand unified theory, a structure that will provide a holistic means of interpreting the laws and physical phenomena of the universe. Einstein tried and failed to reach this unified theory, and many, many other theorists have approached an answer only to find that it collapses under scrutiny and experimentation.

In the third century, Plotinus did philosophically what Einstein attempted scientifically. The Hellenistic philosopher composed a unified field theory of ancient spirituality. He adopted Plato's spirituality and the idea of anagoge. He adopted the Aristotelian theory of knowing and nomological worldview. He adopted the Stoic's therapeutic project for overcoming modal confusion. Plotinus then integrated these elements together in a powerful, synergistic way. His composition would become the foundation of Neoplatonism.

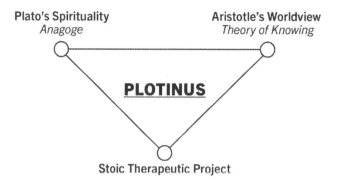

Figure 18.3: A diagram depicting the three central elements that Plotinus integrates from the previous work of Plato, Aristotle, and the Stoics.

Few systems of thought in history have been as beautifully integrated, as comprehensive, or as plausible as Plotinus's system. Through his writing, you can enter through any one of these three points of influences and find yourself suddenly steeped in the other two, as though they were natural elements in an ecology that had always been evolving together. When reading Plotinus, you are not just reading an argument. You are also undergoing a spiritual exercise that is trying to transform your state of consciousness and cognition.

Let us return to Aristotle and the conformity theory we discussed in chapter 7. In this structure, we know something by conforming to it, by sharing its same structural-functional organization. Aristotle proposed levels of being based on this organization. The lowest was pure potentiality, and the highest was pure actuality. Plotinus too proposed that there were different levels of reality, levels of realness, and we knew these levels of reality in a deeply participatory fashion —a gnostic fashion—that made them livable.

We conformed to them, *became* them, and we changed through this conformity. As we conformed to each level of reality and shaped ourselves to it, we were also moving to a higher level of the self.[9] Each level of realness had a corresponding level of self, and we *realized* this level of self upon conformity with the corresponding level of reality.

This ascent, of course, is Plato's anagoge: as we alter the level of self, we are more capable of living in that higher level of reality. The process of anagoge is also a process of anamnesis (Plato's recollection). As we ascend, we gain the memory of ourselves, and the memory of reality. We become more of ourselves the more of reality we become, the more we behold in memory, and the more we are beheld by the conformity.

These beholdings share the same ontology and identity—*as above, so below.* By threading this needle, Plotinus mapped Aristotelian conformity onto Plato's anagogic ascent. The escalating realness and authenticity of oneself was like a gnostic quest without the mythological accoutrement. This version of gnosis also engaged the Stoic therapeutic project. As we became more ourselves, and more real, we graduated from the having mode into the being mode.

Socrates and Plato taught us about our ontological drives. We care about whether things are real. We are driven by a pursuit of realness, but when we cannot identify it, we become more susceptible to bullshit. So what makes something real? For Plotinus, realness relates as much to our process of sensibility as it does to the objects we sense.[10] In other words, the same property of realness that organizes something structurally functionally is also the means by which we sense its organization.

What makes something sensible to us as real? The answer seems simple, but it is actually quite profound. Remember the concept of logos from previous chapters; what makes something real is how *one* it is, how unified and integrated it is, or how coherently it is structurally functionally organized. For example, we treat a concrete object as more real than a shadow because it is more structurally functionally integrated.

---

9. This is Eric Perl's brilliant idea, which he outlines in his translation and commentary of Plotinus's *Ennead V.1: On the Three Primary Levels of Reality.*
10. Eric Perl discusses this in his book, entitled *Thinking Being: Introduction to Metaphysics in the Classical Tradition*, which I would highly recommend to you.

When I understand something, my understanding involves linking together a series of separate entities. I understand the entities as separate precisely when I find how they are all one, how they can be made to belong together. Understanding an object means to understand how its parts are integrated together. (Remember the logos of *bird* from chapter 6?) Once I integrate many different things together and understand them, I can integrate one group of entities —like objects or ideas—with a second group of entities and better understand them both.

For Plotinus, things become more real to us as we integrate them together, and they also become more real in themselves. As we try to find the deeper underlying principles that gather things together, *we* become more gathered together. We become more real.

This process of *realization*, of course, also relates to Plato's anagoge. As I become more integrated, my inner conflict diminishes. My inner integrality allows me to conform myself to these deeper, more integrated levels of reality, to realize them and make them viable. This ongoing integration maps to the Aristotelian process of growing in-formation that we discussed in chapter 6. It is the graduation from potentially into actuality.

This is not just a theory. It is also a change in my existential mode. Remember that this ontological growth is also developmental; as I integrate and harmonize as a person, I am becoming more real, and more aware of what is real. This change in realness is also a change in character.

Plotinus proposes a basis for all of this realness and understanding, a principle that makes everything else real, that gathers everything together. Because it is the source and draw of all integration, it cannot in any way be multiple. Plotinus calls this *The One*. By this he does not mean "the single." He means that by which reality is realized, by which our mind realizes reality.

Plotinus invokes Plato's metaphor for the Good: the light itself is invisible and makes everything visible. In this same way, you cannot know the One—it is that by which you know, that by which you are, that by which everything is, and by which everything is known. For Plotinus, the One is therefore unknowable. It is beyond all understanding because understanding breaks things apart. It cannot be broken, so it cannot be thought. It cannot be known even by the most beautiful theory. You cannot *have* it. You can only *be* it. It is only known in gnosis.

At the height of Plotinus's system is a higher state of consciousness, an awakening experience. Notice how the system integrates elegantly with the best science and psychotherapy of its time. There is no deep division in Plotinus between spirituality, science, and therapy. They are all interwoven, mutually supporting, and playing together in concert. Plotinus took all the instruments of his time, composed them into an orchestra, conducted their tones, and listened for the deepest harmony. His Neoplatonism was the culmination of the Greek Axial Age.

19

AUGUSTINE AND AQUINAS

Plotinus died around 270 BCE. His death coincided with the beginning of the end of the Roman Empire, a slow, steady decline that would be complete by 476. This generation would mark the end of the ancient world. Though the period after Plotinus was marked by a sense of dread, it continued the syncretism between the Axial schools of thought.

One of the most significant figures in this syncretism was a Roman citizen, born in the province of Numidia (present day Algeria) in the fourth century, who would evolve the relations between Christianity, Platonism, Neoplatonism, and Gnosticism. He was influenced by all of them, though he would eventually give priority to Christianity and become one of its most formative Church Fathers. This Roman citizen would eventually become the figure we know as Saint Augustine.

Saint Augustine and the Integrating Power of The Confessions

Perhaps in reaction to the senescent state of his empire, Augustine was first attracted to the Gnostic religion of *Manichaeism*, which began with the Parthian prophet Mani. Manichaeism had many of the features that characterized Gnostic mythology: a belief that the world of matter was inherently evil and clouded the light of the spirit and that salvation depended on a special knowledge that could recover the soul's affinity to God.

Augustine was deeply preoccupied with the question of evil and its inherent presence in the world. His preoccupation was not simply intellectual but also profoundly personal. He was riven with inner conflict. He suffered the existential inertia we described in the previous chapters, and its hunger for transformation. This inner conflict and inertia were complex, but they most famously revolved around his compulsive sexual behavior.

"So my soul was in rotten health," he wrote. "In an ulcerous condition it thrust itself to outward things, miserably avid to be scratched by contact with the world of the senses. Yet physical things had no soul. Love lay outside their range."[1]

His desire was impelling, but it was matched by self-awareness, and his revulsion at his own incontinence exacerbated his despair. He languished in self-loathing and struggled to recover his agency and free himself from the repetitious pattern. He despaired of his own weak will, of not being able to bring himself to the threshold of change.

"Grant me chastity and continence," he would famously pray, "but not yet."[2]

We know these inner conflicts so intimately because he chronicled them in one of the most significant books ever written in Western philosophy. Augustine's *Confessions*, as its title suggests, was written as one side of a confessional dialogue, with God as its addressee. The book has much in common with Marcus Aurelias' *Meditations*, a series of memories and contemplations, written in reflective prayer. It is a spiritual exercise that edifies the writer and gathers him together.

If one reads his work with a syncretic perspective, one might see Augustine's form as an integration of the Gnostic, the Stoic, the

---

1. St. Augustine, *Confessions*, trans. Henry Chadwick (Oxford: Oxford University Press, 1991), 35.
2. Ibid, 145.

Christian, and the Neoplatonic. His personal reflection is not an exercise in navel gazing. It seeks to know, and to be known, by divine measures. He reaches for God by the acts of repentance and reminiscence, using stories of his life to access Platonic anamnesis, a deeper recollection of self and reality found in the mystery of God's comprehension.

Augustine's Platonic-Christian anagoge is like a Gnostic quest of self-revelation, but it also traces Plotinus's escalating conformity with reality. By beholding himself in prayer before God, he is made more real by the beholding, and opens himself to a purgative process that can free him from worldly attachments and addictions. Though there are innumerable differences between the Christian and Stoic traditions, this contemplative practice is not unlike a Stoic spiritual exercise designed to abrogate an overextended having mode, and cultivate the being mode of existence.

The innovation and influence of this project cannot be overstated. Augustine uses a dialogical form of contemplation to conform himself to the omniscient knower, to give account of himself to the very divinity upon whom his being rests. Thus he comes to know himself, and realize himself. He binds his relation to this greater power and is gathered to himself. In being gathered together, he can ameliorate his inner conflict, become more real, and release himself from evil's gravitational influence—a lingering Gnostic concern.

The Christian innovation finishes the excellence of this integrative effort. This entire anagogic journey is framed by the confession of sin, a kind of Socratic humiliation that recalls his need for agape and sensitizes his capacity to receive God's forgiveness. This is an artful exercise of reciprocal opening and sensibility transcendence. With *Confessions*, Augustine integrated the theory and practice of the Axial period into a single symbolic exercise and framed it as an essentially Christian project.

He folded the private and personal quest for transformation, favored by the Gnostics, into the public prayer and liturgy that was essential to the apostolic Christians. In doing so, he created a new form of literature, prayer, and philosophy. *Confessions* was the first autobiography ever to be written in the history of the West. Yet unlike most modern autobiographies, Augustine's was not an egoic project. His personal reflections yield to a deeper philosophical aim, one of understanding and revelation.

Confessions recounts some of Augustine's most formative experiences, those that—upon his reflection—had come to symbolize the foundations of his psychic conflict and eventually his faith. Among his various memories is a first encounter with sin. When he was young, Augustine and some of his friends broke into a courtyard, and Augustine stole pears from a tree.

Most of us later in life would dismiss this minor theft as an adolescent misdemeanor, easily excused by the folly of youth. But Augustine saw in this act a kind of mythic structure, a perennial pattern that betrayed something about his nature and about the nature of humanity. Augustine had not stolen the pears because he wanted the fruit nor because he was hungry. He wasn't trying to impress his friends. He didn't have a grudge against the owner. He did not steal the fruit despite it being wrong. He stole the fruit *because* it was wrong.

Augustine was profoundly affected by his recollection of this incident—not for its consequences, but for its deeper revelation. He had been driven by an impulse he did not fully understand, and it held dominion over his agency. Something was forcing his hand, dragging him down into something bestial, almost like the reverse of a higher state of consciousness. He was deeply troubled by this incontinence.

It is little surprise that the Manichean worldview would appeal to him later in life; it carried a Gnostic emphasis on the evil of matter and its impulses as well as the dark side of reality and the anger, desire, and destructiveness that diminished people's spirit. As an adult, Augustine found these pathologies in his own bodily impulses, especially in his sexual addiction.

As an adult, Augustine traveled the world, taught rhetoric, and became highly philosophically literate. He encountered the work of Plato, and he was entranced. Augustine wrote glowingly of the Platonists throughout his life, and when he encountered Plotinus, he felt that "Plato lived again." In the Neoplatonist's writing, he saw a different way forward, a viable alternative to the Manichean worldview.

Augustine read Plotinus in exactly the manner we discussed in the previous chapter—as a spiritual exercise. He felt himself ascend through the experience, rising through the levels of reality and the levels of his self. In Plotinus, Augustine reached a profound mystical experience.

Profound as the experience was, Augustine could not hold on to it. The darkness in him had too much gravity, and it pulled him back to the world, toward lust, and to the *reciprocal narrowing* of his addictions.[3] Augustine was tormented by the existential impasse. Why was the gravity of darkness so hard to resist?

He would later describe it as a hole in being that was sucking the light away from him. He had what some people report having after a mystical experience, a rebound effect of despair. It was as though he found a tropical paradise filled with life and beauty, the kind of place a person yearns for all his life, only to have it vanish. The darkness and squalor seemed all the more punishing by comparison.

Falling into despair, Augustine went to visit his Christian mother, Monica. While sitting in her courtyard, he heard a child's voice: "Take it and read."

In the courtyard lay an early version of the Bible. He picked it up and chanced to read the work of Paul. In Paul, he found a deep affinity, a kindred spirit. He found that same torment, the same inner conflict, and he had a penetrating insight.

Plato and Plotinus wrote that we were driven by two powerful loves—the love of becoming one within and becoming one with what is most real. Our reason is driven by these loves—a love for what is true, for what is good, and for what is beautiful. Love was therefore at the heart of reason.

Augustine realized that his incontinence and sexual addiction were not failures in his capacity to reason, but failures in his capacity to love. He was loving something less real. He needed a way of loving

---

3. Marc Lewis, https://memoirsofanaddictedbrain.com/connect/addiction-narrowing-opportunities-in-brain-and-environment/.

deeper into reality, a way that could draw him out of sin. There was a love within reason that draws beyond reason, reaching for what reason always sought.

This was agape, and by participating in agape, we grew in love. We became more real. Neoplatonism needed Christianity, Augustine realized, and so did his Gnostic drive. The healing and response to evil he sought was to be found in Christ. In Christianity, Augustine could draw himself together.

The Three Orders: Normative, Narrative, and Nomological

Augustine's *Confessions* was more than a treatise, of course. It was an existential manual for transformation. To use our terminology, it was not a propositional theory but a perspectival, participatory exercise of gnosis. Plotinus had already augmented the Aristotelian nomological order, the scientific account of the structure of reality and how reality was known. He gave us an account of how we could move up the levels of reality, up the levels of consciousness, up the levels of the self, and appreciate our relationship to realness.

The bottom levels of reality were less real, less unified, less sensible, and less integrated. When I destroy something, I make it more disordered and fragmented. I take away its structural-functional organization. As we descend the chain of being, entities have less form, less eidos. They are less intelligible, less understandable, and far more chaotic.

Augustine took up this Plotinian idea in the context of goodness and evil. As I descend, I lose truth, goodness, and beauty, everything that makes me sensible and intelligible, everything that makes me what I am. At the lowest level of reality there is a tear in being, a gaping hole that vacuums virtue and intelligibility. The project of gnosis is to move in the opposite direction, to what is more true, more good and more beautiful.

This ascension is driven by a love of what is real, a desire to know it and become it. For Augustine, like Plato before him, the highest level of reality represents the Good. It is the *normative order*. While the nomological order determines the structure of reality, the normative order is a person's movement to the Good, the process of becoming a better being, countervailing the presence of evil, and deepening the realness and meaning in your life.

In Aristotle's nomological order, everything moves where it belongs. In Augustine's normative order, everything must move toward the Good. He believed that Christianity threaded these orders together. Everything moves on purpose, toward purpose, and the purpose is *realization* for both self and world. The purposeful movement is driven by the love of agape, the gnosis of transformation. The movement was eternal, but it also unfolded through time.

This was the *narrative order* of Christianity. The Hebrew concept of the telic history still lay at its foundations; the course of history moved toward a final consummation, a promised land. This was the history of God's agape, His redemption, and His open future. Agape was not just a historical force in the world. It was also a normative force in each person, leading each upward toward the Good. In Christianity, the orders came together: organized according to the nomological, progressing through history according to the narrative and becoming more real according to the normative.

We know from our current cognitive science that three important components contribute to meaning in life: a sense of *coherence, significance and purpose.*[4] The more coherent things are, the more intelligible, the more they fit together for you, the more real they become, and the more meaningful you find your life. Coherence corresponds to the nomological order, how things fit together and make sense. Significance corresponds to the normative order, referring to the value, depth and goodness of your life. A sense of purpose and direction refers to the narrative order.

---

4. Based on work by Samantha Heintzelman and others. More recently, Heintzelman's work has failed to reliably replicate. So her more specific notion of coherence should be held in question. I propose we move to the more encompassing notion of intelligibility that thwarts a feeling of absurdity. Also, more recent work has shown that there is a fourth and probably most important factor, viz., mattering. This is a sense of making a difference to something that has a reality, and value becomes one's egocentric concerns. It is the sense of connectedness to something "bigger."

Augustine agreed that a nomological order was provided by Aristotle's worldview, and he could give a Christian explanation of its functioning. Meanwhile, Christianity addressed the human desire for significance, the anagogic drives for inner peace and contact with reality. It folded together reason and agape, and it offered overarching purpose and cosmic story—a narrative order.

Augustine drew these powerful cosmic orders together just as the societal order was collapsing. The Roman Empire was in its final days. The barbarians were at the gate, laying siege to the city. Meanwhile, though, Augustine's work was relentless. He was a profound thinker and theologian, but his robust sense of service had drawn him to accept a station as the Archbishop of Hippo in Northern Africa. His deeds married intellect and faith, and his works prepared the foundations for the medieval worldview to come.

The three orders of meaning were the culmination of the Axial legacy and all of its historical development. They were like the three dimensions of a geometric figure, a beautiful image of reality itself. The nomological connected us to what was real, the normative to what was good, and the narrative to our own destiny.

These orders were not three separate entities. They were like the three axes, three dimensions of space, harmoniously synthesizing the historic, scientific, spiritual, therapeutic, and existential without any conflict or antagonism between the parts. The vision of meaning was so powerful and enriching that it lasted for a thousand years.

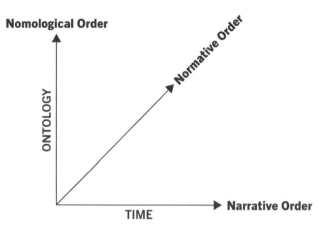

Figure 19.1: A diagram demonstrating how the nomological, normative, and narrative order create the space of meaning. Here all three orders are depicted on the three axes of space (x, y, z) to draw the comparison of how they occupy the three planes in the space of meaning.

Invoking these orders in the present tense brings a surge of grief. We have looked upon this meaningful reality with the tragedy of dramatic irony, beholding the richness of what has been lost. The memory of the past provokes the question of the future. Why did this beautiful cosmos fall from the sky? Is it lost irredeemably?

I remain convinced that all is not lost, and a response is possible. This book, after all, is entitled *Awakening from the Meaning Crisis.* However, we are still working to formulate the problem. Accounting for it historically is necessary before beginning to propose a solution. Through these three cosmic orders, we can better understand now how meaning was woven into our cultural framework, into our cognitive machinery, into the very tissue of our existential modes. But the question remains: why did it all fall apart? Now that we better understand the nature of the meaning lost, we must begin to account for the genealogy of the crisis itself.

The Great Schism, and the Loss of Lectio Divina

The collapse of the Roman empire brought a tremendous sense of chaos. It was not as cataclysmic as the Bronze Age collapse—and only happened in the West—but it brought a traumatic loss of cities, literacy, trade and commerce. The standard of living that was lost in the Roman Empire would not be recovered again until 1750 in London, England.

Nevertheless, the sacred canopy given by Augustine and his influences remained aloft. It sustained a cosmic sense of home for people throughout this turbulence and turmoil. Its foundations remained strong for several more centuries as the Western ancient world slowly transitioned into the medieval period.

By the tenth century, however, the sacred canopy had slowly begun to tear. The Roman Empire only collapsed in the West, but the Greek-speaking Eastern Empire had endured. There were many philosophical, cultural, historical and socioeconomic differences in how Christianity was understood between the East and the West. In 1054, the two worlds split apart.

The *Great Schism* divided Christianity into two traditions —*Eastern Orthodox* in the East and what would become *Catholicism* in the West. This schism weakened the culture of Christianity and slacked the force of tension that held the three orders together as a unified entity. By separating from the East, Christianity in Western Europe lost some of its deeper Neoplatonic roots, especially its mystical theology. This compromised the integration, the *oneness* of the orders and therefore their realness.

The sense of mystery and mysticism, inspired by writers like Pseudo-Dionysius, slowly attenuated, and with it the phenomenology of gnosis and normative ascent, the access to symbolic language and higher states of consciousness. The West slowly became less and less Platonic and more exclusively Aristotelian.

The gradual declension of the orders began with a change in psychotechnology. To examine this more closely, we turn to the works of two significant twentieth-century thinkers: theologian Ivan Illich and historian Edward Cranz, both of whom examined the reorientations of thought and practice that pivoted the course of the

Western mind.[5,6,7] Jung and Corbin, who we briefly visited in the previous chapter, were also keen students of these changes. Illich examined the work of a twelfth-century theologian, Hugh of Saint Victor, who was influenced by Augustine and wrote deeply about the relationship between art and Christian spirituality as well as the ontology of its sacraments and rituals. His mystical theology chronicled a shift in reading after the Great Schism.

Before this sundering event, reading was an oral tradition. Early church fathers like Augustine usually read aloud in a communal setting. Reading was embedded in a cultural context and in a sapiential community. It was recitation. Not a propositional exercise undertaken in private, but a participatory exercise, performed and witnessed in communion.

Think back to Augustine's *Confessions*. The act of reading or praying aloud was not just to be witnessed by onlookers. The publicity of the act also allowed it to be witnessed by oneself. This was an Axial inheritance, one not restricted to Christianity. Plato's dialogues, though written, were meant to provoke oral practice. This was also true of the Islamic tradition; when the angel Gabriel speaks to the prophet Muhammad, he tells him to recite rather than to write.

Think of the difference between reading a poem and saying it aloud. The intonation makes it a far more textured and embodied experience, adding depth, presence, and resonance. This is even more true when paired with music. In Christian liturgy, scripture is sung as well as read. This is not simply for aesthetic effect. Recall that intimate, Socratic relationship that beauty has to truth and goodness, which was taken up by Augustine and the Neoplatonists.

Song draws attention in a participatory way. It attracts you. It inspires a longing for realness, for a depth of feeling and experience.

5. Tom Cheetham, *Imaginal Love: The Meanings of Imagination in Henry Corbin and James Hillman* (Spring, 2015).
6. Tom Cheetham, *The World Turned Inside Out: Henry Corbin and Islamic Mysticism* (Spring Journal Books, 2003).
7. The discussion entitled "Vervaeke Cheetham Dialogue on Corbin and the Meaning Crisis" between John Vervaeke and Tom Cheetham can be found on John Vervaeke's YouTube channel.

It creates a mood and sense of place that engages the senses more vividly and in a more potent perspectival fashion. People take on new identities when listening to music. Their imaginations become more porous. Their vigilance softens. Our cognitive processes become more flexible and elastic.[8]

When spoken, poetry and scripture have similar effects. The way we read them is not the way we read a scientific paper, the back of a cereal box, or even an analytic argument. A poem suspends us halfway between transparency and opacity. We know by means of it, and we inhabit its text as though it were a topography. We cannot truly know a poem, or a scriptural text, without being changed by them, without altering our identity, without conforming to their sights and sounds. We cannot know them without gnosis.

This is how the early Christians read the Bible. They did not look for historical facts or scientific beliefs. They looked for gnosis. When people were reading the Bible, and reciting it communally, they were undertaking a practice of *Lectio Divina*. It was an evocative, mindful way of reading a text wherein the text itself could speak, could be allowed to provoke the readers into meaningful shifts of perspectival and participatory knowing. It was a way of listening in a more vulnerable and open-ended way as you would a stirring piece of music.

The goal was not to come to a conclusion about its beliefs (if indeed there were any to conclude) but to follow its patterns and trace its movements, to open yourself to its unique kind of speech and mood of life. People who are religious will often talk about God's presence in the text. The idea of the "living word" was passed from the Greek into the Christian tradition. The idea is certainly found in the Gospel of John but reaches all the way back to Heraclitus's fragments: *listen not to my words, but to the logos within them.* Ivan Illich described this kind of reading as "ontologically remedial."[9] It

---

8. See Michael Casey, *Sacred Reading: The Ancient Art of Lectio Divina* (Triumph Books, 1996).

9. Ivan Illich, *In the Vineyard of the Text: A Commentary to Hugh's Didascalicon* (University of Chicago Press, 1996).

was designed to heal and transform you, engaging a deeper memory of being.

Over the medieval period, the practice of Lectio Divina began to decline. People began to read differently. The beginnings of this change were reflected in the transition between two significant philosophers of the Islamic Golden Age, who were contemporaneous with the Great Schism. Avicenna (the anglicized Ibn Sina) was a great Persian philosopher and a dominant interpreter of the Augustinian worldview. He gave priority to the Neoplatonic spiritual tradition.

Henry Corbin observed that Persian philosophy often tried to keep the Neoplatonic and Gnostic elements of spirituality alive.[10] In the twelfth century, Avicenna was replaced by Averroes, who was a more Aristotelian thinker and gave exclusive priority to definitions and propositions.[11] Reading became a silent and private exercise. People valued coherence in language rather than transformation within themselves. What mattered now was how the various terms and logical connectives fit together.

In the Axial worldview, our thought conformed us to the world, articulating, developing, and expanding into the process of gnosis. There was an embodied identity between speech and reality, between knowing and becoming, between the structure of self and the structure of the cosmos. In the medieval world, a new model for thought emerged: to know was to have precise propositional language, a coherent set of propositions in your head.

With this shift of reading and knowing, Edward Cranz observed that the human sense of self also underwent a profound change. The Axial world drew together an *extensive self*, a self that was conformed and connected to the world, continuous with the cosmic orders. It was not simply subjective or objective, but *transjective*.

With the medieval change, we shifted to an *intensive self*—a self inside our heads, inside our beliefs, affirmed through propositional language. People begin to prioritize coherence within our inner

---

10. Persia has played a much greater role in world and cultural history than we in the West have presumed.
11. Aristotle was trying to understand the eidos as essence. Essences are definitions. That is very problematic as many things do not have definitions.

language instead of conformity in our outer existential modes. Material conditions contributed to this change; the world was starting to open up again. There was a growing appetite for scientific knowledge, and this gave value to logically coherent, well-organized theories and argumentative skills. This had many adaptive and powerful advantages for innovation. However, the shift in focus meant a gradual loss of the psychotechnology of psycho-spiritual and existential transformation.

There was another significant factor in this shift. The Crusades from the eleventh to thirteenth centuries provoked a rediscovery of the works of Aristotle, which had largely been lost to Western Europe. This posed a problem for Christianity. Here was a figure that could not be ignored. He was one of the primary authors of the cosmos that the medievalists inherited from the ancient world.

However, Aristotle's second rise to prominence brought his orientation toward the external world. He offered explanations for things that were ignored by Christian mythology, and there was a tremendous attraction to the new explanatory power: clear definitions and syllogistic inferences along with a more precise kind of knowledge. Aristotle's eminent authority made him impossible to reject out of hand, but neither could he be easily assimilated into the Christian worldview. As more and more people began to read in this Aristotelian fashion and emulate his scientific manners, a crisis began to emerge within Christianity.

One prominent Italian friar noticed this looming threat; he saw the change in the psychotechnology of reading and the way people were starting to look at the world. He took up the task of solving this problem, integrating Aristotle's scientific modality into Christianity. Thomas Aquinas, like Augustine before him, would become a "Doctor of the Church," a pivotal figure whose philosophical and theological works would influence interpretations of Christian doctrine for centuries to come.

There is some dispute between theologians, philosophers, and mystics about whether Aquinas should be considered Aristotelian or Platonic. I have vacillated on this question myself although I have come to suspect that Aquinas was more of a Neoplatonist than many people believe, and many of the attributions made of him are confused with other pure nature philosophers who succeeded him.[12],[13]

In his project of assimilating Aristotle, Aquinas found a brilliant point of intervention; he returned to the grammar of the two-worlds mythology. As we discussed in chapter 3 (figure 3.2), the everyday world and the real world were often depicted on a continuum of transcendence. Aquinas reimagined the relationship between the worlds but gave more ontological status to this everyday world. This world too was real, and it was possible for us to have real knowledge of it through reason and science. However, the real world was still more real.

Aquinas invented a distinction that has become second nature to modern people, but that was new for his time (though precursors of it existed in Pseudo-Dionysius and Augustine). The idea was this: The everyday world is the *natural world*, studied by reason and by science. The real world is the world above the *natural world*. The word for "above" is *super*. The real world was the *supernatural world*. It could only be accessed by faith.

12. Sebastian Morello, *The World as God's Icon: Creator and Creation in the Platonic Thought of Thomas Aquinas* (Angelico Press, 2020).
13. W. Norris Clarke, *Explorations in Metaphysics: Being-God-Person* (University of Notre Dame Press, 1992).

Aquinas' Transformation of the Two Worlds Mythology

Figure 19.2: A depiction of Thomas Aquinas's augmentation of the Axial two-worlds mythology. The Everyday World, now referred to as the Natural World, can be studied by science and reason, which can produce real knowledge. The Real World, now referred to as the Supernatural World, is a spiritual world, which cannot be studied in this way. The world of faith and love moves the will. These two worlds are no longer on a continuum. This results in the fundamental separation of faith and love from reason and science. Ultimately, the Supernatural World becomes less real.

After Aquinas, the two worlds became completely distinct. Their continuum was sundered. There was no way of moving between them by the vessels of love and reason. This signaled a profound change in the notion of faith. Reason was placed in the everyday, natural world. Love was elevated into the real, supernatural world. The definitions were no longer coextensive. In Plotinus and Augustine, love moved reason. For Aquinas, love moved the will and asserted things it could not know through reason.

Faith became an act of willful assertion, a reasonless act driven by the love of God, asserted in propositions and the profession of creed. The schism between love and reason also meant a schism between science and spirituality. If something was spiritual, it was not scientific. If there was love, there could not be reason. In this great divorce, we see the beginnings of Romanticism and many other movements of art and philosophy that would respond viscerally to the profound estrangement.[14]

Aquinas tried to save the Axial worldview by reformulating its

---

14. For those who want to pursue this in more depth, see Mark C. Taylor, *After God* (Chicago: University of Chicago Press, 2007).

grammar. But there was a danger he did not foresee: the study of the natural world through science and reason would become more successful than he could have imagined and would draw attention and plausibility away from faith. It would make the second, supernatural world seem more distant and less relevant. Without the continuum of worlds, and the bridge of love and reason, one world would begin to grow at the cost of the other. The entire project of self-transcendence, and the normative order that made the project possible, now threatened to fall apart.

20

THE DEATH OF THE UNIVERSE

Aquinas's separation of the natural and supernatural worlds had immediate and lasting consequences in the medieval scholastic tradition as well as in Christian mysticism. These two domains of thought and experience became more distinct from one another. A chasm now existed where before there was continuity. Love could no longer lift reason up into the supernatural world, which meant that faith—that category of spiritual life that pertained to an individual's relationship with God—gradually lost its presence in the everyday. This change led to a variety of different movements and positions within Christianity, philosophers, and mystics who attempted to respond to these changes. Two of these figures are particularly important for our discussion: Meister Eckhart and William of Ockham.

The Primacy of Will and the Rise of Nominalism

Eckhart was an exemplary figure among the *Rhineland Mystics*, a German movement that was intent on bringing about a transformation in human spirituality. Eckhart was influenced by the Neoplatonic undercurrent within Christianity, with its tacit Gnostic history. His writings ushered a new understanding of the normative order. Self-transcendence disappeared from spirituality, as did the wisdom of self-knowledge. Instead of an upward ascent, mystical transformation now involved the condescension of God.

Aquinas had written of love driving the will in faith, but the Rhineland Mystics replaced this ascent spirituality with a descent spirituality—God came down to us now, rather than the reverse. They also changed the relationship between love and faith. Love did not move the will. Instead, it was now the way by which the will moved. In other words, love was the will negating itself.

The Rhineland Mystics picked up on the sacrificial aspect of love that was so key to Christianity. When my will is self-centered and egocentric, it is oriented away from agape. In order to become a conduit for agape, I have to sacrifice and negate my willful self-assertion.

For Eckhart, a person must make space so that God can dwell within him, and the way to make this space is by negating one's own will to remove all resistance to God's will, to His agapic love. A person must negate his own self-assertion the way he expresses himself. He must make a space so that God can flow in.

After Eckhart, self-negation became central to spirituality. It valorized the inner conflict that was so characteristic of the faith of Paul and Augustine. The paradox of turning one's will against itself was a spiritual aporia. Conflict within oneself became a condition for the willful self-emptying (or *kenosis*) that prepared a person to receive God.

This new form of faith overlapped with another emerging worldview in medieval scholasticism. William of Ockham, an English friar and theologian, understood God's will as His primary faculty. Unlike in Augustine and the Neoplatonic tradition, God's reason and intelligibility were no longer the source of God's being.

Aquinas made will the faculty of access to the supernatural. It therefore became the defining attribute of God's divine nature. Understanding the medieval view of God's nature is critical, regardless of our personal beliefs in God. The human relationship to God through history is also the essence of human identity, the human relationship to being itself. Your model of God has a tremendous influence on how you understand yourself and reality.

The change in God's nature was therefore a profound change in humanity's self-concept. God's will became the source of his divine capacity. He spoke the world into existence, and this speech was an act of assertion. God's will superseded His reason. He was not bound by reason or rational principles the way that the Greek pantheon was bound to the Good in Plato. There was nothing, therefore, to power an ascent from the natural to the supernatural world. Any order we found in existence was arbitrarily imposed by God's will.

Just as in the ancient world, God's putative nature was a cosmic reflection of man's nature; any order in us was arbitrary and subject to will. For example, I have many books on different kinds of subjects, but each belongs to the category of "books." In the Axial world, they all participated in this shared identity, this form of structural-functional organization.

After Ockham, this Platonic realism was challenged. He asserted that any order or pattern found between entities was made by will and therefore was arbitrary. This view was called *nominalism*. In this paradigm, nothing in reality groups books together according to that category. Only my mind, by using the term, groups them together. I cannot help but see a book as a book, but this is a product of my creative imagination. There is no universal *bookness*. My thought and speech draw this order together and compose this mental entity. Out in the world, there are only raw individuals and their indiscernible causal relations.

Consider the effects of these paradigmatic changes. I am now reading inside my head rather than aloud. The world is willed rather than reasoned. Entities are gathered by speech rather than by an existing ontological structure. The thing we call knowledge is the coherence of linguistic signs. Their order exists in language and only in my mind. There is nothing out there in the world.

In fact, the world is not inherently intelligible. It is, in a very real sense, absurd. The real world, now the supernatural world, is not a source of rational order, and spirituality is now the negation of our human will. This new paradigm of God and humanity lacked the cosmos and coherence of the Axial era, and it pulled at the seams of the normative and nomological orders.

The Black Death, Commercialism, and New Forms of Life

While this new nomalist paradigm was emerging, something disastrous occurred—the Black Death. The Bubonic plague[1] laid waste to a third of Europe's population. The plague overlapped with Ockham's death and some of the later Rhineland Mystics. In the Bible's *Book of Revelation*, the world's end is heralded by the Four Horsemen of the Apocalypse: death, war, pestilence and famine. Each of these seemed to appear contemporaneously in the fourteenth century.

The Bubonic plague brought massive pestilence. An extended wet period destroyed crops and created food shortages. The Hundred Years' War between England and France created ongoing upheaval in Western Europe, and the Crusades against the Cathars—a Gnostic revival within Christianity—inspired the creation of the Holy Inquisition. Imagine how analogous this period felt to the Hellenistic domicide: rampant death, villages blotted from existence, a mistrusted and mistrustful church, and a radical disruption of social order.

The world seemed at an end. People's confidence in the inherited worldview was undermined. Most institutions and social structures were broken or put under significant strain. Disruption in social order spurred more migration, and the high mortality meant chronic labor shortages. This time reminisced of the Bronze Age collapse or the end of the Roman Empire.

The prolific labor shortage meant that people could sell their skills and attain new status through their own efforts. The rigid feudal structure that existed through the medieval period was beginning to elasticize. The chaotic conditions also reinforced a nominalist worldview; the world was not fundamentally ordered. Our given social and cultural orders could easily be dissolved,

---

1. Most scientists think the Black Death is probably the Bubonic plague.

revealing the true chaos and arbitrariness of reality. Order and identity were attained through will. God was less and less a source of rational order and more a source of arbitrary power.

Many historians argue that the Black Plague opened Europe to new social experimentation. People started selling their labor, becoming more mobile and entrepreneurial. This precipitated a rise in commercialism. A person could now make use of disparity and demand, and they leveraged it to accrue wealth. If a merchant in a given region had a lot of wool, he could sail to another region where there was a high demand for his product and trade. Then he could return to his region, buy more wool, and repeat the process.

He could achieve all of this by his own efforts. It had nothing to do with the church or the aristocracy, or with raising grain or farming the land. This new agency was revolutionary, almost magical. It was certainly not absolute; aristocracy was still a political obstruction to the emerging middle class, and trade brought dangers if your wares or products were spoiled. But these dangers inspired new structures and institutions—banks to lend money and finance commercial expeditions and insurance companies to protect your interests in case your ship sank or your caravan was lost on the Silk Road.

To avoid taking all of the individual risk, groups of people could gather together and undertake them jointly. The church was the body of Christ, a corpus composed of different elements that gathered around a logos of order and purpose. Now, similar bodies were also forming in the natural world, outside the domain of faith. People could incorporate their interests, share the risks and rewards of commerce, and divide the profits and dividends.

The advent of the corporation forced new constraints on the powers of state, competing with church and aristocracy. The creation of contracts enforced rules on these social institutions. This was the beginning of corporate capitalism and the corporate state. People were no longer consigned to a station in life; they could seek power and use their will to change their lives.

Behavioral norms now had nothing to do with the church or aristocracy, and a secular source of power was dawning, a way to wealth and prestige. They gradually secularized the state to safeguard their secular projects, everyday endeavors to which the supernatural world was almost entirely irrelevant.

The Copernican Revolution, and the Epistemic Gap

The various ventures of commercialism and trade required their proponents to develop better proficiency in various psychotechnologies. They needed to process information faster and more efficiently. People began to replace Roman numerals with the Hindu-Arabic numerals, a cultural import that came via trade with the Arab world. It was a more expedient psychotechnology for numeracy and calculation. Algebra was another significant addition to the roster of commercial aids. Using letters rather than numbers to represent variables allowed for new, more precise kinds of calculation —like the concept of zero, and the use of negative integers to represent debts and deficits.

Mathematical psychotechnology also improved celestial navigation. Astronomers could observe the stars more carefully. Merchants could now sail the waters faster and better with less chance of capsizing and losing their profits. The logical, inferential, Aristotelian way of thinking acquitted itself very adaptively in this new commercial world. Meanwhile, however, the orderliness of the heavens had begun to unravel.

They did not behave the way the ancients had presumed. These more careful observational methods, allied to more precise mathematics, revealed how chaotic the heavens actually were. It became more difficult to calculate and predict celestial motion with a geocentric model. This all changed, of course, with Copernicus. The math worked better, he noticed, if you put the sun at the center. He validated Aristarchus's position from a millennium earlier, but this time his contemporaries were receptive to this new way of thinking. There was a general commitment to new mathematical psychotechnologies, and this methodical Aristotelian way of thinking. If a heliocentric world made the math work better, this was good enough.

The *Copernican Revolution* has become a symbol for changing worldviews throughout history. It was not just the worldview that changed, however, but our epistemic capacity as human beings. Remember the Aristotelian criteria for knowledge we discussed in chapter 7, carried over from antiquity. Is the relevant organ functioning? Is the medium not distorting the information? Do other people after rational discussion agree with you?

This was a powerful heuristic, but it failed to foresee this turn of events. This time, it was morning. The sky was clear. We were sober. We all had perfect vision. We watched the sun rise in the east, pass overhead, and sink in the west. We all agreed that this is what we saw, but we were all wrong.

Our rational methods had not immunized us from illusion. So if this was an illusion, what else was illusory? Which other beliefs were next to be dispelled? All of a sudden, everything was now in question. If we could not trust our senses, our logic, our basic social concurrence, how could we know if anything was real? Aristotle's criteria were powerful, but Copernicus disempowered them. Math could now undermine the most coherent of beliefs. The theory of conformity had failed us. We had lost touch with the world, held at bay by the veil of our sensory experience. We held a line to reality by a narrow channel of math, available only to the numerate few.

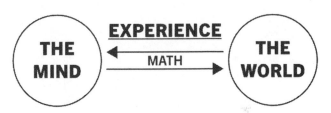

Figure 20.1: A diagram depicting how your sensory experience forms a barrier between your mind and the world. You are no longer in touch with the world, and math is the only thing that can cut through this barrier.

The epistemic gap called everything into question. How could we know, and how could we know that we know? We had lost our perspectival and participatory knowing of the world. We could assert this new proposition that the Earth is not at the center of the universe, but it did not translate existentially into our experience.

Imagine the absurdity of this revelation and the horror of it; we had become radically disconnected from the world. Our reasoning was disconnected from the truth.

Ockham's influence lingered in these dilemmas, but shortly after Copernicus, Galileo emerged and proposed a response to Ockham. He argued that while we could not trust language and sense experience, mathematics was the true, trustworthy language of the universe. This was an old Platonic view, and Galileo updated it with Aristotelian logic and new techniques of observation.

In the ancient world, math was primarily understood via geometry, with Euclid's elements as the quintessential text. The medieval period brought arithmetic and calculation, but Galileo did something else. He used the geometry in a completely abstract fashion. If sense experiences could not be trusted, scientific analysis needed not correspond to them. There did not have to be any sensual or experiential similarity between my thoughts and the world. For example, Galileo used a triangular model to discuss the relationship between distance, time, and speed, even nothing is specifically triangular about speed.

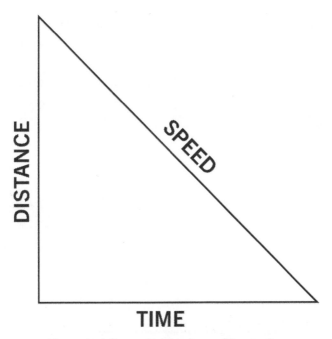

Figure 20.2: A diagram depicting the use of the triangle to abstractly explain the relationship between time, distance, and speed.

Galileo used the geometry of a triangle to represent abstract mathematical relations, but these relations had nothing to do with worldly experience. There was no longer any conformity between the geometrical representation and the sensible contact with our environment. Galileo undertook extensive observations, but he subjected these to careful measurement. He saw a chandelier swinging in a church, and he measured it with his own pulse. He rolled balls down inclined planes.

What came out of all of this? Galileo discovered inertial motion. Things did not move because of an inner drive. They did not move toward a purpose or somewhere they belonged. Things moved because they were hit by a purely random, arbitrary external force, and they would continue moving this way until they were stopped by another random external force. Before Galileo, everything was alive. Everything was driving, trying to get where it belonged, making the universe a more beautiful, ordered place. After Galileo, there was no purposeful narrative way of understanding the world. Everything was dead. There was no inner life to matter. Nothing moved on purpose at all. Galileo had killed the universe.

When Galileo killed the universe, human beings became castaways on a lone island of purpose, surrounded by an ocean of purposelessness. We stood in a world of lifeless objects, and we had no reflection in them, no affinity with them. We were alone, strange, belonging nowhere. The universe was an indifferent machine. *Inert* meant dead, lifeless, and not capable of moving itself.

This forever changed the view of matter. In the old worldview, matter was the potential for information, but now matter was inherently resistant to form. Matter resisted human will, but there was no agency in its resistance. The resistance was scientifically helpful when it served to dispel illusions, but it betrayed no signs of psyche. Human beings found themselves in a lifeless universe, thrown into a battle between isolated, illusion-prone wills, inside the vast, inert, willess, resistant machinery of the universe.

Understanding matter as a material substance rather than the potential for information also had another consequence. It removed any basis for evil in the universe. Before that, there was a cosmological explanation for evil. It was a hole in being, pure potential and chaos. Now, there was no such thing. Matter was just "stuff." We lost the metaphysics and ontology of evil. Many people now, when pressed, are uncertain as to the nature of evil. They think of it simply as excessive immorality, or else deny its existence altogether.

The Scientific Revolution inherited its legacy from the Axial Revolution. It dedicated itself to countervailing the illusions of our senses. Galileo refined this process for the modern world. The mathematical properties of something, like length or mass, were now the real properties of the thing. They were *objective*. The mark of realness was mathematical measurement, and all of the other properties that pertained to subjective experience—like how sweet honey is or how beautiful a sunset is—were properties of mind rather than world, figments in an internal chamber that had no measurable connection to reality.

Meaning was trapped inside you along with value, beauty, and all of those qualities that give experience its texture. The world itself was not purposeful, beautiful, or truthful. These were simply human projections of mind. The world was not even filled with chairs, cups, or tables. Those were not mathematical entities. They were illusions created by your meaning-making mind in an ongoing fit of willful self-deception.

After Galileo, the orders broke down more rapidly. One of the great strengths of the Aristotelian worldview was that your view of knowledge and your view of the world mutually supported each other, and your nature shared in the nature of the cosmos. However, the great weakness of that worldview was now exposed. As one started to unravel, so did the other. As the Aristotelian world broke down, so did the Aristotelian theory of knowing.

They continued to unravel in an accelerating fashion. We were disconnected from the world, trapped inside our heads. We had lost perspectival and participatory knowing along with the project of self-transcendence. There was only purposeless, inert, chaotic absurdity. Our inner conflict remained, but now it languished in a vacuum.

This revelation of the universe's inertial nature and the ensuing feelings of purposelessness left a lasting imprint on humanity. This was the true emergence of the Meaning Crisis, an existential trauma for humanity that persists to the present day. We woke up to a world in which our own existence was arbitrary. Everything we hold to be most meaningful was unreal and illusory. Each of us was just a complex pattern of atoms, and the universe itself was cold and unfeeling, indifferent to our narratives and aspirations. We had no narrative journey anymore, no normative ascent, no nomological connection to the structure of the cosmos because it had no coherent structure itself. The indifferent universe revealed by Galileo became a much greater source of despair than the malevolent universe envisioned by the Gnostics.

21

MARTIN LUTHER AND DESCARTES

As our historical discussion takes us further into the onset of the problem, it is important that it be possessed with the right attitudes and the right humility. We are attempting to trace a pattern that unfolded across time. Each of these historical figures, I propose, had a role to play in the worldview changes that led to the Meaning Crisis. However, the dramatic irony in these depictions does not reflect the intent of their subjects. We are not concerned primarily with what each person—whether philosopher, scientist or theologian—personally professed as much as how their life view or modes of engagement were taken up and performed by the generations that succeeded them.

For instance, when we examine theologians like Paul, or Augustine, or Aquinas, we can either take an *emic* perspective (i.e., experience their beliefs and worldview from the inside), or an *etic* perspective (i.e., look at their beliefs from afar, and explore their psychological implications on subsequent generations). An emic perspective would mean a theological argument, whereas an etic perspective is an argument of historical derivation.

For example, we do not need to subscribe to Stoicism to have been affected by its therapeutic model. Similarly, even if we do not share Augustine's Christian propositions or ideas about original sin, his *Confessions* created a narrative model of personal testimony and aspiring redemption that we are still living out in popular culture.

Our genealogy takes a more etic perspective; we are trying to track the gathering effects of the Meaning Crisis, and these effects are not attributable to the intent or stated beliefs of any of the figures we discuss. It would be both inaccurate and unjust to say that Galileo set out to kill the universe, or that Ockham is solely responsible for supplanting Plato's realism with nominalism.

We are endeavoring to trace the evolution of a situation that could not have been known to any one individual when they first made a proposition or ventured an idea that unwittingly contributed to our modern predicament. This is not an exercise in scapegoating but in understanding. Each figure is a piece of the narrative, but each is bound to the perspective of their time, and each made significant gifts of understanding to humanity.

We must forebear from moral judgment as we gather together more of this genealogy. This spirit of forbearance must be conferred to all our historical subjects and especially the two figures we will discuss in this chapter—the great Protestant reformer, Martin Luther, and the philosopher René Descartes.

Martin Luther and the Protestant Reformation

Martin Luther was deeply influenced by the Rhineland Mystics as well as by Aquinas—including his discreet divisions between natural and supernatural domains. Luther was an Augustinian monk, so he was also distantly influenced by the Neoplatonic tradition. From both Saint Paul and Augustine, he adopted the concerns of inner conflict and self-negation, the depravity of sin, and our human inability to achieve mystical union with God unaided.

Our human condition of inner conflict corresponded to the tension between God's agapic love and His judgment of our sinfulness. Luther was terrified of God's wrath. He experienced the human self as radically reflexive, folded into itself, immorally self-centered and self-obsessed. This self-centeredness severed us from

God and reality and locked us into a self-destructive process. Our pride constituted a rebellion against God.

Luther was prescient in many ways. Like Augustine before him, he noticed that people were unconsciously subject to pernicious patterns that undermined their will—like when someone gets into a relationship, falls into a parasitic process, recognizes it, and then moves into a new relationship only to discover they are living the same pattern. Freud, Jung and the whole psychodynamic tradition would later develop this observation that we fall into these processes automatically despite our conscious efforts to change our behavior.

Augustine had believed that the Neoplatonic, mystical ascent had to be supplemented with the love of God, a love revealed in Christ. Luther took this idea even further. He was convinced that any effort of his own was insufficient for grace. Our personal wretchedness blocked us from being agents of our own salvation. This led Luther to a radical interpretation of Paul, an interpretation that—among other things—put him at odds with the Catholic church. We were saved by faith alone, and faith was a complete acceptance of God's saving grace.

Luther did not entirely dismiss the importance of reason, but he relegated its value to the natural, everyday world. The supernatural world, the domain of faith, was subject only to God's love. Reason had no place in faith, so it did not participate in the eternity of human salvation. This escalating separation of God and reason had significant effects for the role of participatory knowing in Christian doctrine.

The diminishing relevance of reason meant a diminishing role for human agency. Our sense of self was less relevant to the process of salvation. In the longer term, it would therefore seem less real, and more illusory. Though this was not necessarily true of Luther himself, many who followed him would take faith to mean the mere acceptance of a proposition, an acceptance undertaken in spite of oneself without any process of discernment or development.

The self-negation of the Rhineland Mystics seemed to have come to fruition. You could do nothing to ensure your salvation. Luther rejected something that his fellow theologian, Erasmus, called *synergism,* the idea that God and human beings were working together for human salvation. Even in synergism, God's agency was significantly more decisive in this collaboration, but the human being had a role to play in his soul's preparedness, by disposing himself in faith to be receptive to God's love.

Luther rejected the synergism of Erasmus; human participation was no longer a necessary condition for salvation, and no reason, no conceivable human virtue or feat, could merit God's grace and forgiveness. This theological development was similar to Augustine's —for him too, God's agapic love was always more than any human being could merit—but it seemed to remove the necessity of his restless Socratic search, the reason that recognized one's own deficiency and found the "God-shaped hole" inside of one's heart.[1] Reason was no longer involved in our salvation. Even the affirmation of the Christian creeds was something that must be given to you. Since a person could do nothing to causally affect God's behavior, His salvation now seemed completely arbitrary.

There was a certain irony in this theological development, one that played out in the subsequent centuries. Luther tried to rescue us from our idolatry and self-obsession. He reminded us that we were inherently worthless before God. We were all guilty under His law. For many Christians who would follow, this conviction would translate psychologically into a form of self-loathing, and the only solution to this self-loathing would be arbitrary, unearned divine regard.

Though it was certainly not Luther's intent or stated belief, this combination—inescapable self-obsession, with a desire for unearned positive regard—carried a tacit grammar, a cultural training in narcissism. It is conceivable that this religious grammar unwittingly helped to enable the rampant narcissism we find rife in our culture today. Luther himself would not have sanctioned this, of course, any more than he would have sanctioned the appellation of "Lutheranism" or the fragmentation of Christendom that began after

---

1. Blaise Pascal, *Pensées* (Penguin Publishing Group, 1995).

he nailed his famous 95 *Theses* to the door of a church in Wittenberg, Germany, and triggered the Protestant Reformation.

Luther's doctrinal protests and institutional disputes brought him into significant conflict with the Roman Catholic Church, which had a very different doctrine of salvation. In the Catholic church, each human being had a very active, participatory role in their own salvation. Some aspects of this participation had decayed into superficial corruption, like the plenary indulgences that Luther protested. The Catholic church of the time emphasized the show of sacrament, the participation in community.

In this way, it carried forth the Israelite notion of history and tradition. Luther thought this emphasis was misplaced. Though it was not initially his intent to defect from the church, he gave priority to scripture over tradition, and the inward movements of conscience over the outward shows of ritual.

The term *conscience* originally meant knowing yourself. There were many legitimate criticisms in Luther's protestations, and he was not without respect for tradition. However, the Protestant movement that ensued had a number of long-term effects on the grammar of spirituality. One of these was the withdrawal of spiritual authority and meaning into the isolated, individual mind. This became a uniquely Western idea and the basis for our modern obsession with individuality.

There was both virtue and vice in this Lutheran turn. The emphasis on individual responsibility meant that a guilty conscience could not seek expedient absolution in his institutional affiliations. However, it also paved the way for cults of authenticity;[2] the idea of being true to reality was superseded by being true to yourself.

The Monastic Tradition and the University

The university was a medieval creation and very much a part of the wisdom project, a way of acquiring a universal education and

---

2. Theodor W. Adorno, *The Jargon of Authenticity* (Northwestern University Press, 1973).

understanding as much of reality as possible. It was not simply a vessel for knowledge but also for wisdom. Early universities were tied to monasteries. The monastic life, in many ways, was a legacy of the Axial Revolution, a place that conducted the project of self-transcendence. Universities were a response to the emergence of Aristotelian science, and then the new science of people like Bacon, Copernicus, and Galileo. These two institutions, universities and monasteries, represented an important synthesis of human development. They were joint tutors for how to make sense of ourselves and find a meaningful life.

Monasteries placed a huge premium on self-transcendence. But for Luther, the project of self-transcendence carried deep risks of pride and self-delusion. The Axial project was no longer a necessary means to salvation. The diminishing relevance of the monasteries—along with many political and economic factors—led to the suppression and dissolution of many monastic traditions, and their participatory rituals of faith.

Meanwhile, the university was unmoored from its monastic affiliations and the existential import of their projects. The province of education no longer had wisdom as a companion to guide its relevance. The structure and purpose once provided by the monastic traditions would, in many places, eventually be provided by the state. Wisdom would be replaced with politics. This shift to power-oriented knowledge would have many famous commentators in the centuries to come, most notably in figures like Francis Bacon, and more recently, Michel Foucault.

The suppression and closure of monasteries meant a loss of the psychotechnologies of wisdom and of cultural communities that were committed to providing guidance and support to people who pursued this project. We continue to feel this loss today, the *sapiential obsolescence* of our knowledge. We know where to seek information but not wisdom.

Knowledge is inextricably bound to the machinery of the state, market, and politics, and it has become a means for the willful assertion of propositions that must be accepted or rejected. The Protestant Reformation was a meaningful occasion for Christianity to reflect and refine its theological tradition. However, the cultural consequences were titanic, just like those of the Scientific Revolution. Both of these movements had a profound and joint effect of hastening the obsolescence of those wisdom traditions that had defined the Axial legacy.

As part of his shift to personal responsibility, Luther advocated what he called the priesthood of all believers. There was no necessary mediator between you and God. The church and clergy did not have domain over your salvation. You had a direct, personal relationship with God, and everyone had equal spiritual authority. While we have already discussed some of the negative effects of this turn—the diminished importance of learning, growth and self-transformation—it also had positive consequences.

Luther argued for a complete form of democracy within the church and rejected its authorities and hierarchical structure. This democratic sensibility did not extend to the state, however. The *Two Kingdoms Doctrine* held the religious domain—i.e., who we are before God—as distinct from our worldly stations and appearances. This distinction was a precursor to the separation of church and state. Our earthly lives require political authority to wield the sword of power. But within the church, before God's love, these norms did not apply. The normativity was now distinct in each domain. Spiritual life remained interior, private, and secluded, separate from worldly identity. Life was rife with separation where before there was continuity. The sacred was now separate from the state, from science, and from the university.

The Protestant Ethic and Fragmentation of the Church

One of the effects of the Protestant Reformation was a heightened anxiety over salvation. When salvation appears arbitrary, we do not know who is saved. Sociologist Max Weber famously made this observation early in the twentieth century, and though his argument has come under some criticism, the core insight is still valuable.[3] Human beings had no causal role in salvation, which also meant there was no causal evidence. How then do we know if we are saved?

The question provoked ongoing anxiety. There was a dramatic tension in Luther, a double bind. Each person could only rely on their individual conscience, but that inner world was also overwhelmed by self-deception. What, therefore, could a person do? There was nothing official to absolve you, but if you worked hard to improve your life and achieved socioeconomic success, this surely was a sign of God's love and favor.

People began to develop what Weber would famously call the "Protestant work ethic." They worked hard to succeed but did not use their wealth to promote themselves. Any conspicuous consumption would be a sign of pride. Instead, they put acquired wealth back into their businesses. This would be another enabling constraint for the emergence of corporations, and the ascendancy of the commercial class. According to Weber and others, this ethic was a significant factor in the advent of capitalism.[4]

Luther was brilliant in many ways. His emphasis on biblical literacy made scripture and liturgy more accessible for generations to come. His German translations of the Bible made it readable for his German contemporaries and made him a foundational figure in modern German. For Luther, scripture was paramount. He thought that more Biblical literacy would bind Christianity together and rightfully replace the authority of the Pope.

While the latter turned out to be true, the former did not; the shift to individual conscience and the disempowering of tradition and institution led to rapid fragmentation. Protestantism split into denomination after denomination, fractured by minor doctrinal quibbles and liturgical disputes, a *narcissism of small differences.* People wanted to distinguish themselves by their subjective interpretations, their unique forms of prayer, worship, and belief.

---

3. Max Weber, *The Protestant Ethic and the Spirit of Capitalism*, trans. Talcott Parsons (London: Routledge, 2001).
4. Ibid.

Worship became an idiocentric, sometimes egocentric project. The implicit narcissism of these movements and the general fragmentation of Protestantism began to march in lockstep at an accelerating pace.

Meanwhile, God was withdrawing. By the time of Luther, God's presence had become arbitrary will. By the time of Galileo, the world was emptied of purpose, and human meaning became arbitrary too. The absurdity of this new mood was reflected in the writings of Shakespeare, who lived and wrote shortly after Luther's death. Shakespeare plumbed the depths of the human psyche in many profound ways, yet God is largely absent from his works. There is certainly a presence of the supernatural: there are the witches in Macbeth, and ghosts in Hamlet. But God is never present.

The domain of the supernatural is arbitrary and absurd. It is an agent of chaos and fatality that thwarts people in their endeavors. The effects of the Protestant Reformation—the arbitrariness of salvation, the fracturing of the church, the withdrawal of God's presence, the decline of community and the monastic traditions—accelerated secularization in the West and ceded more everyday importance to commercial life and its endeavors. We still carry this grammar in our culture. We work hard to evince our worthiness, desperate to find that mark of uniqueness that distinguishes us from the crowd and has us adored, delivered from the damnation of God's judgment and the general obscurity of life's growing meaninglessness.

Descartes, the Idea of Certainty, and the Concept of Artificial Intelligence

The Scientific Revolution, the beginnings of corporate capitalism, and the Protestant Reformation, were all mutually reinforcing. They were sources of tremendous anxiety. The discoveries of Galileo had orphaned people from the world. The Protestant Reformation had orphaned Christians from their mother church, tradition, and history. The individual was left to spend this exile alone, though he believed himself incapable of bearing the existential burden.

People were cut off from reality and from their wisdom institutions, consigned to a restless battle of wills. It was a time of great existential dread, and the philosophers of the time, like Blaise Pascal, tried to account for the loss of the cosmic orders and the eternal aspect of the person no longer reflected in the heavenly canopy. Pascal was a mathematical genius. He looked out at the cosmos and was terrified by the infinite space. The cosmos was now cold and terrifying; its vastness was inhuman and crippling to the human spirit.[5]

Another French philosopher, a contemporary of Pascal, tried to address the anxiety of this existential vacuum. His name became synonymous with one of the most significant developments in Western philosophy. René Descartes wanted to take the grammar of the Scientific and Protestant Revolutions—the idea of math as the marker of reality, the primacy of the individual subjective experience in salvation—and use it to find a solution to this emerging crisis of realness and meaning.

Descartes was a genius. He invented a new psychotechnology that would become indispensable for future generations to perceive and understand the world. One day, while lying in bed, he noticed a fly buzzing around the room. He noticed that he could plot the fly in the room by coordinating the tiling on the floor and walls. This was the origin of Cartesian graphing, the same XYZ system we use today. It became the canonical scientific strategy for information processing and presentation.

Descartes took the new algebra of Galileo and developed it into analytic geometry. Geometrical shapes could now be converted into algebraic equations capable of capturing reality. Descartes fulfilled Galileo's radical Platonic return to the primacy of mathematical truth. Equations did not need to resemble the entities they represented in order to access them. We could use them to cut through illusion and fasten a grip around reality. This new mathematics carried a promethean kind of power that would accelerate over the next few centuries. It allowed for unprecedented technological innovations

---

5. Blaise Pascal, *Pensées* (Penguin Publishing Group, 1995).

and a new kind of contact with reality—not through conformity or participation but through proposition. By the twentieth century, a formula like E=MC^2 could empower human beings to take a paperclip worth of matter and level a city to the ground.

Descartes thought mathematics was the key to the crisis of modernity, a way to address the anxiety and sense of disconnection. He understood the modern crisis of meaning as an unsatisfied hunger for certainty although he framed the uncertainty in exclusively propositional terms. His was not a question of Aristotelian conformity or Neoplatonic gnosis. For Descartes, math cut through all illusions and empowered us. His answer to the crisis was to transform our minds into machines of logical representation and mathematical certainty. Descartes proposed that each of us must deal with the anxiety of the age by adopting a method that would turn us into *computers*—this term was originally applied to people who were exceptionally proficient in logic and mathematics.

In the Cartesian worldview, reasoning was being reduced to computation. We were beset by an epistemic impasse, a disconnection from what was real, but if we could make our minds into purely computational machines, we could achieve certainty and relieve the anxiety of this impasse. The Cartesian grammar made for a powerful companion to the Lutheran self-doubt and its inward fixation. The culture of the time vacillated between a derived Lutheran paradigm—faith without evidence or reason—and a Cartesian paradigm, which hungered for certainty and only accepted something if it was beyond question.

As cultural dispositions, both proved to be pathological; removing the relevance of agency in faith radically undermined meaning in life. Meanwhile, the pursuit of certainty through mathematical science revealed itself to be a fool's errand. After Descartes, it became clear that science could not provide certainty. Einstein would show that even things that Newton thought were certain—like absolute space and time—were not as certain as we all supposed. Science meant ongoing revelation and discovery, but no one scientific theory or conclusion could be trusted unconditionally. Propositional certainty about the nature of the world could not be sought as an existential solution to the loss of connection to ourselves, the world or to other minds.

Once again, a deep sense of irony in Descartes's efforts revealed itself over time. His attempt to address the burgeoning loss of connections resulted in exactly the opposite—an increased sense of disconnectedness. The scientific and philosophical history that unfolded over the eighteenth, nineteenth and twentieth centuries undermined the idea that human beings could achieve certainty.[6]

A contemporary of Descartes, English philosopher Thomas Hobbes, interpreted Descartes's cognition to mean computation (referring to it as *ratiocination*).[7,8] Hobbes proposed a radical idea based on Galileo's inertia. Matter is a substance that resists our will, but resistance of this kind was good. It helped us resist our own biases. Matter's resistance to our will was all that remained of ancient conformity. If matter is real, Hobbes said, what if I built a material machine that did computation? If cognition is just computation, and I can build a machine that computes, I will have made cognition.[9] I will have made a mind. Here, in the heart of the Scientific Revolution, Hobbes proposed *artificial intelligence*.

Artificial intelligence is not just a modern idea. It is a child of the Scientific Revolution and of the advent of the Meaning Crisis. Galileo killed the universe, and Copernicus killed the reality of our sense experience. Hobbes's idea, however, did something far more personal. Even in a world of dead, inertial matter, with illusory senses and solipsistic experience, humanity still retained something special, a distinction of mind.

We still had something unique and spiritual that defined us. But if I could now build a machine, a purely material mechanism capable of computation, I could make a mind that would not require any soul

---

6. Heisenberg's *uncertainty principle* became one significant theory in twentieth century physics.
7. Thomas Hobbes, *The Elements of Law, Natural and Politic* (Cass, 1969).
8. His exact phrasing is "By ratiocination, I mean computation." Many would disagree with this idea of cognition. Brian Cantwell Smith, a colleague at the University of Toronto, does important work on the metaphysics of computation.
9. Some of the first automatic machines are being built at this time. Calculating machines are an example of this.

or spirit to give it form or life. The concept of artificial intelligence then threatened—as it begins now to fulfill—the possibility of another revolution, one that would decenter humanity even further from its spiritual life and sense of cosmic exceptionalism. This new revolution, if it came to fruition, would eclipse the Copernican Revolution by many orders of magnitude. The effects would be unimaginable. Today, of course, the effects appear imminent. If Galileo killed the universe, Hobbes killed the soul.

22

DESCARTES VERSUS HOBBES: THE PROBLEM OF MIND AND MATTER

The Lutheran and Cartesian paradigms were formative coparents of the modern West. Their impact on our cultural grammar was not only philosophical and theological. They also carved psychological, commercial, and political troughs that would deepen over the next few centuries and become the molds for many other movements and beliefs. The individualism and sense of personal isolation cast a tacit shadow of narcissism.

The sapiential obsolescence in the wake of monastic suppression along with the growing division of church and state accelerated the rise of secularism. The emerging Protestant work ethic helped to pave the conditions for corporate capitalism. Meanwhile, the Cartesian response to the epistemic gap revealed by Copernicus, Galileo, and the Scientific Revolution deepened the existential exile that so aggrieved Pascal.

Descartes's emphasis on mathematical equations was an attempt to bridge the epistemic gap, using computation to achieve certainty and relieve the anxiety so characteristic of the time. These two aspects in the grammar of meaning shared a common mood, and each cast a shadow on the other. Each centered on the paradigm of an isolated, individual mind. Luther placed emphasis on conscience while Descartes placed an emphasis on consciousness.

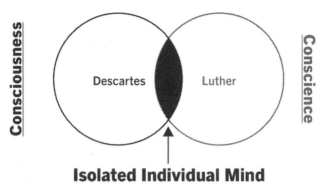

Figure 22.1: The overlap between Luther and Descartes; though their thought differed in many ways, they shared the isolated, individual mind.

Consciousness and conscience turn out to be very related terms. The tradition that Luther initiated came to value propositional belief without question, evidence, or argumentation. The Cartesian view accepted belief only under the condition of absolute certainty. Neither option would be viable in the long term. Descartes, much like Luther, proposed a new paradigm that severed itself from tradition and institution, relying solely on the individual mind as the arbiter of realness and relation. In one sense, the Lutheran and Cartesian worldviews seem so opposed to one another.

Simplistic and reductive versions of these paradigms have become our modern caricatures for faith and science, and their mutual hostility persists in our contemporary culture wars. However, they are alternating aspects of the same grammatical mood, the pained expressions of the existential condition Pascal perceived when he peered into the unsheltered sky and beheld its infinite vacuum.

Luther's Protestant faith refracted into the undiscerning acceptance of creed, and Descartes's famous *cogito ergo sum* ("I think, therefore I am") came to represent the pursuit of logically derived certainty. These two paradigms, despite their enmity and mutual sanctimony, have shaped and influenced one another, tacitly agreeing on the same ill-begotten frame. These paradigms shared a devotion to propositional knowing and a model of the self that was stranded from the world.

Logical versus Psychological Certainty

As we discussed in the last chapter, Thomas Hobbes proposed Descartes's cognition as identical to computation; if matter was real, we could build a material computer, and we could artificially make cognition. Artificial intelligence was a product of the Scientific Revolution and the advent of the Meaning Crisis in modernity. It would threaten an existential obsolescence as totalizing as the sapiential one, a soul-death for humanity and its spiritual life. Without the distinction of soul, what uniqueness or dignity could exist in a human self? The idea of the individual as a source or arbiter of truth would become absurd. We would become as purposeless as the rest of the cosmos and as inert as the most lifeless object in the universe. Our behavior, decisions, character and agency—everything that Aristotle defined as constituting our unique humanness—would become meaningless and incidental.

Descartes took Hobbes's proposal about artificial intelligence very seriously. He recognized the scope of the problem. Here, it is important not to take Descartes himself lightly. It has become philosophically fashionable to blame Descartes for the mistakes of modernity.[1] However, we should all wish to have made Descartes's mistakes. He was incalculably brilliant, and his errors were so profound that they absorbed into the skin of Western culture.

Descartes rejected Hobbes's proposal of artificial intelligence, and the reasons for that rejection are still scientifically and philosophically relevant. His rejection of Hobbes's materialism was not argued on religious grounds, contrary to a common belief. He did not argue from bad faith. Instead, he met Hobbes on shared ground, responding within the paradigm of the Scientific Revolution. His response, though brilliant, would unwittingly prove as problematic as the problem itself.

Let us explore this argument carefully. Hobbes and Descartes shared the following claims: (1) matter was real, (2) reality was

---

1. There is a famous book, which I regard highly, by Antonio Damasio entitled *Descartes' Error.*

mathematically measured, and (3) the meaning and value of things was not in the things themselves. Descartes proposed the following: if Hobbes was making an argument, engaging in reasoning as opposed to just computation, that meant he actually *cared* about the argument.

He had a goal, or he held to a standard of truth. Reasoning meant acting on purpose and toward purpose. It meant working toward the goal of truth, which depended on meaning. A reasoning claim needed to be intelligible. So reasoning acted on purpose, it acted in reference to meaning, and it cared about standards or goals. Therefore, reasoning worked in reference to a normative standard of behavior. Here, we can see the flickers of our old flame, the Axial worldview.

Normativity lies at the heart of rationality. Many claims are laid to rational thinking in our contemporary culture wars, but advocates of rationality invoke very little of this insight. It is not easy to integrate notions of rationality with scientific materialism, and many who advocate a Cartesian model of rationality, who champion logic as a means to truth and certainty, ignore the criticisms of Scientific materialism made by Descartes himself.[2] It is common for fierce debaters to advocate one side of a phenomenon without paying attention to central criticisms made by its progenitor.

By making this argument about rationality, Descartes pointed out to Hobbes something that goes overlooked by modern scientistic thinking: normativity—our sense of meaning and purpose, how things "ought" to be—is central to our reasoning. Their correspondence reflects Descartes's contempt toward materialistic thinking.[3] The Scientific Revolution made matter inert and purposeless. There was no meaning in matter, so how could we have a material reasoner?

Ockham's razor of nominalism, preferring explanations with fewer entities, cut away many of the patterns, laws, and fields that were central to science, considering them to be mere acts of mind and speech. Reasoning acted in terms of "ought." Science, however, did

---

2. Sam Harris, for example, comes to mind.
3. René Descartes, *Descartes: Philosophical Letters* (Clarendon Press, 1970).

not act in terms of ought. It only described how things actually were. It had no values. It taught us that the world was purposeless, and matter was valueless. There was no normative structure in materiality. And as the Scottish philosopher David Hume would famously say in the eighteenth century, "We cannot derive an *ought* from an *is*."

How, then, could one possibly draw purposeful reasoning from matter? Hobbes responded to Descartes with an example. Imagine many little automated abaci, each with little pieces of paper attached to them. Those pieces of paper could be manipulated, much like the letters on a computer screen, to produce a meaningful sentence: "The cat is on the mat."

In his response, Descartes accused Hobbes of making a fundamental mistake. Hobbes was English, and Descartes was French. So Descartes used "chat" rather than "cat." The words presented differently, but each referred to the same object. There was no intrinsic meaning in the material marks of these letters. If ocean waves happened to toss pebbles onto a shoreline, and they scratched the word "cat" into the sand, would we think the ocean is talking to us? The event would be random, Descartes argued, and not intrinsically meaningful. The words "cat" or "chat" only have meaning when possessed of the meanings in our minds.

For Descartes, Hobbes's view of matter making rationality was deeply problematic. It undermined the historical concept of rationality itself. For Descartes, rationality was not just the logical manipulation of propositions. Rationality meant caring about the truth, on purpose, according to normative standards and values. None of these criteria could be found in the scientific model of matter. Descartes's argument was compelling and historically astute. We must pay close attention to its implications. The notion of rationality, so often brandished in discussion and debate, is actually very mysterious and philosophically problematic. Hobbes had raised a problem first faced by Galileo. For Galileo, mathematics was the language of reality. This, of course, was originally a Platonic idea, but in the early modern period after Descartes, it led to the idea that there were two kinds of properties to reality:

1. The properties measurable by math were called the *primary qualities*. These properties were objective; they resided in the object regardless of our perception or involvement.
2. The qualities of experience were not mathematically describable, like the beauty of a sunset or the sweet taste of honey. These were called *secondary qualities*.

Secondary qualities did not exist in the object. They only existed in our minds.[4] They were part of the cosmic veil that Copernicus and Galileo had penetrated, those experiences that came between us and reality, preventing us from touching the world. In the Scientific Revolution, these qualities were merely subjective, and they took on lower ontological status. Matter resists us. The word *object* means "to throw against." *Subject*, on the other hand, means "to throw under" and therefore dominate. Philosophers often use the term *qualia* to refer to these secondary, subjective qualities. They existed only in mind.

There are many unresolved debates on the topic of *qualia*. However, they seem central to consciousness and part of the fabric, content, and nature of experience. One of the paradigms of the Scientific Revolution was that objective reality lay in matter and the world while subjective reality was only in mind. Matter did not possess these qualia, as Descartes reminded Hobbes, and there was therefore no obvious way to manipulate matter to generate consciousness. This would have devastating implications for the project of AI. Not only will the AI not have meaning, purpose, or any normative values. It would also not have any conscious awareness of its cognition.

Another aspect to Descartes's thinking was less explicit but is quickly derived from his followers and contemporaries. By the seventeenth century, everything meaningful was withdrawing from the world and into the mind. The mind was becoming increasingly isolated, trapped inside itself. Descartes worried about this problem.

---

4. Notice how this follows on Copernicus.

He famously took certainty as a goal of his meditations and undertook a search for something he could not doubt. In so doing, he seems to have made—at least in my estimation, and those of other philosophers—a mistake about the notion of certainty.

There are two ways of understanding certainty, one logical notion and the other psychological. The *logical notion of certainty* is something like absolute deductive validity; it is impossible for the premises to be true and the conclusion false. This is different from the *psychological notion of certainty*. Psychological certainty is the inability to doubt. A person can find something certain simply because she is incapable of doubting it.

These two ideas of certainty are by no means identical. Remember Frankfurt's idea of the *unthinkable* from chapter 17. Someone who is fervently ideological, committed to a social prejudice, is perhaps psychologically incapable of doubting her belief because it springs from a certain agent-arena relationship and significance landscape. She is embedded in a specific form of participatory knowing, which cedes a certain perspective. Her worldview may have psychological certainty, but not logical certainty.

There is no direct identity between psychological and logical certainty, but Descartes seemed to think that if he pushed psychological certainty far enough, it would somehow become logical. It never did. Descartes resolved to doubt everything he could. Even his commitment to math could be subject to psychological deception. There could be an evil genius, like in a Gnostic story, who programmed Descartes's brain, making him believe in the axioms of math. Before judging this as a ridiculous thought experiment, consider the Copernican revolution that had just occurred and the cosmic illusions it dispelled. Modern physics had rejected the axioms of Euclidean geometry, even though they were once taken to be absolutely unquestionable. Anything seemed possible.

Descartes famously found a place to connect psychological and logical certainties—the question of his own existence. In order to be subject to illusion, his mind must necessarily exist. Even the most impenetrable illusions guaranteed him the existence of his mind. The famous *cogito ergo sum* was not a logical argument. It was a statement wherein psychological certainty became indistinguishable from logical certainty. In order to be suffering from an illusion, I must exist to suffer it. Notice what is happening here. The mind used to touch the world directly. Then it could only touch the world with math. Now, the mind could only touch itself.

Consciousness is a strange, uncanny phenomenon. If I asked, "How do you know this book is in your hands?"

You would reply, "I can see it, feel it, interact with it."

But how do you know you are conscious? You know you are conscious by being conscious. Unlike Hobbes, Descartes found a place in his thinking for the noncomputational aspect of mind. Self-consciousness was where the mind made contact with itself. Self-consciousness was not possessed by matter. The Scientific Revolution took this epistemic contact out of the world, so for Descartes, the only place it still existed was in the mind's contact with itself. This withdrawal would unfortunately lead to devastating philosophical problems.

Subjective Isolation versus Objective Meaninglessness

When considering AI, we must pay attention to a distinction that was made famous by John Searle—the distinction between "weak AI" and "strong AI." Weak AI refers to machines that can perform tasks that typically intelligent animals or human beings can perform, like computation. Your laptop and smartphone are examples of weak AI. It is ubiquitous in all of our everyday lives and activities (like working, banking, shopping, dating, studying) and in disciplines like medicine, architecture, transportation, and engineering. We have become utterly dependent on weak AI. Though it advances our scientific innovation in many incremental ways, it does not constitute the paradigm shifting revolution that Hobbes and Descartes were debating.[5]

Strong AI is what that average person means when he uses the

---

5. A lot of people now use the term artificial general intelligence to talk about strong AI.

term AI, the kind dramatized in books and film. Strong AI would be an instance of mind. It would mean a fulfillment of Hobbes's project. Defining the success of this project is very difficult and perennially debated. It would require a response to Descartes's objections, explaining how a material object has been given purpose, meaning, normativity, consciousness, and that contact with realness that Descartes held so elusive.

Strong AI is an elusive goal, and people who are invested in that goal are cautious about predicting its advent. It is ineluctable that computational machines are going to continue radically changing our society in the next ten to twenty years. The progress continues to accelerate, and as the advent begins to feel more inevitable, it also feels exigent to undertake the project wisely and responsibly. It is not obvious that this project will translate into a profound understanding of the nature of the mind or finally certify a Cartesian or Hobbesian worldview.

AI researchers fall on both sides of this issue. Many people in the professional AI business think that Hobbes is ultimately right although a sizable minority share Descartes's view about the primacy of consciousness. If they are good scientists, all AI researchers take Descartes's challenge seriously. For many people, Descartes's view preserves a more religious orientation, and the possible immortality of soul while Hobbes's represents an absolute desacralization of human life and soul.

However, Descartes's solution has an existential cost. The Cartesian view takes mind and matter as essentially different. Mind moves on purpose, according to values, meaning, and qualia. It pursues the truth and has a contact with itself that no material thing has. Matter, on the other hand, is extended in space and time. It displays force and transfers energy. Each has the properties lacked by the other; mind is a completely immaterial substance while matter is a completely material substance.

Here is the problem. If mind and matter share no properties, how do they causally interact? When I am thirsty, I desire water. In the state of thirst, water is good. I move on purpose toward the goal.

Notice these mental terms: desire, want, value and purpose. When I move and pour some water, my mind has effected a change in matter.

But how is that possible? Mind has no energy. It does not take up space. It does not have any force. What about the reverse? Can matter cause mind? When I drink the water, my thirst is satisfied, and I become able to focus on things other than my thirst. A completely material event has become a completely mental event. My quenched thirst is a qualia about the value of my experience.

But how much does it weigh? What color is it? What is its electromagnetic radiation? What is its chemical structure? Your experience is moment-to-moment, whereby mind and matter seem to intimately interact in a bidirectional manner. Yet Descartes's response to Hobbes made it impossible for these to interact. He maintained a scientific gap between matter and mind, but the gap undermined our whole existence and cut us off from ourselves. In the Cartesian paradigm, the relationship between mind and body remains a complete and utter mystery. The most intimate aspects of your experience, like the taste or texture of water, are absurd; there is no way that the taste, a mental phenomenon, and the water, a physical phenomenon, could in any way be related to each other.

This problem takes on a more severe dimension when we consider the relational implications. Do you know what goes on in another person's mind? Can you perceive it directly? How do you know it exists at all? The person utters words, you might say, and I can make sense of them. But according to Descartes, the person does not utter words. He makes sounds, and nothing in the sounds is inherently meaningful.

We mentally construct the meaning. We pick up gestures, tones, and facial expressions, but if we cannot assume any essential link between these bodily, physical signs and a person's presence of mind, then we have no way of knowing a person's mental state. In fact, we have no way of knowing if they have a mental state at all. This is called the *problem of other minds* in philosophy. How do I know that the rest of you are not just mindless automatons, or zombies? Descartes was very worried about this problem. If the mind can only touch itself, it is stranded from contact with all other minds.

From Descartes, we were left with two different standards of realness: subjective consciousness and objective math. Our culture and society have since careened back and forth between them. The empiricists and the positivists turn to science for realness but have no answer for how their version of rationality fits into mathematical certitude or accounts for purpose or truth.

The Romanticism of the nineteenth century would prioritize subjective experience, but it could not make meaningful contact with the world or other people. In either case, we were disconnected, vacillating between meaningful isolation and meaningless contact. Each of these seemed to impoverish us. Descartes, despite his own best intentions, left us with an unstable grammar of realness, and we have languished ever since with the ambiguous relationship between mind and body as well as between mind and mind.

After Descartes, there was a still more profound loss of perspectival and participatory knowing, a gradual loss of contact with the world, with tradition and history, with our own bodies, with other people, with other minds, and with reality. Even the island of certainty that he left us, the sure contact with our own minds, were not so sure at all. If we are to be Cartesian and logical, we should also be Socratically consistent.

With his famous cogito ergo sum, Descartes affirmed his existence, but he also implicitly invoked a historical, cultural notion of the self. If I try on his pronouncement, what is this "I" I find existing? Is it all of John Vervaeke? I cannot be just anything I introspect; a lot of my introspections are false. Is it based on my memories? My memory also makes all kinds of mistakes. What about my history? What access do I have to this history? How do I measure it mathematically? All I have contact with is this current moment of self-awareness. If I take this moment as something atomic and isolated, contentless, without autobiography, without contact with its body, without contact with the world or other minds, and I place it inside Pascal's infinite spaces, it is a great and empty horror. By the close of the nineteenth century, the Meaning Crisis had finally arrived in the West.

The Spirit of Geometry and the Spirit of Finesse

As we briefly discussed in the previous chapter, Pascal had a deep awareness of the Meaning Crisis. He too was a great mathematical genius and participated in the Scientific Revolution. He recreated Euclidean geometry as an adolescent, and he invented the barometer to measure air pressure. But he also had a transformative experience, which convinced him that Cartesian certainty was not possible to achieve.

Pascal made a distinction between what he called the *spirit of geometry*, the knowledge that describes the world, and the *spirit of finesse*, which teaches us to interact with it meaningfully—the knowing how, and knowing what it is like, the gnosis of mutual transformation and revelation. To be with finesse involves these other elements of knowing that cannot be captured by mathematical propositions, the kind that involve the kairos of right time and placement, that are essential to ritual and relationships, arts and athletics, and the sensibility transcendence that occurs when we begin to know by means of another mind.

Pascal knew that the Scientific Revolution had suppressed the spirit of finesse and with it our capacities for truth and knowing. His transformative experience was, for him, also a religious experience, and he grieved loss of this domain of life. The Protestant Reformation had removed the emphasis on self-transcendence in Christian life, and Descartes had assured the early modern world that we needed computation, not transformation, to come into contact with ultimate reality. We were now stuck where Socrates was at the beginning of the Axial Revolution, faced with an impossible choice between an objective scientific truth that lacked personal relevance and a subjective personal relevance that lacked any shareable truth. Neither of these ways promised any meaningful wisdom or self-transcendence.

23

ROMANTICISM, NIHILISM, AND THE WILL TO POWER

The early modern world was afflicted by disconnection—from our own bodies and minds, from other people, from the world, from history, from culture, and from the sapiential institutions that were now slowly disappearing below the horizon. The religious psychotechnologies that gave such transformation in the Axial period had not vanished altogether, but their warmth and power was now set low in the sky.

The heritage of Descartes, the Scientific Revolution, and the ongoing fragmentation that followed the Protestant Reformation made for an increasingly secularized world. Meanwhile, there was a countervailing movement against this secularization, a nostalgic effort to return to a prescientific world. But this movement was trapped inside the same propositional paradigm as its scientific opponent.

Religious fundamentalism would not provide the poetry, complexity, or plausibility required to revive the three orders of meaning or the multivariate transformation needed to meet so many new and complex crises—existential, political, and ecological. We will always live in a post-scientific world, and whatever a revival of religious sacredness looks like, it will have to harmonize with this reality. Ideally, of course, it would strive to complement the scientific world, rather than persist in spite of it.

The modern mind is trapped in a glass pane between inner and outer kingdoms. The religious worldview has flattened in the West. It no longer seems like a world we can plausibly inhabit. But the scientific world, for all its descriptive acumen, is also not a world we can live out or find ourselves meaningfully reflected in. We cannot be completely secular, but many people cannot bring themselves to be religious.

It is rather like the existential inertia we feel when despairing over our identity, lingering on the cusp of transformative experience; we are trapped between who we are and who we aspire to be, but we cannot bring ourselves to go backward or forward. This paradoxical tension and contradiction is a hallmark of the Cartesian legacy and the post Reformation world. There would be many visceral cultural reactions to this collective existential inertia throughout the modern period.

These would not resolve the condition but set it aflame. As we will discuss in the next chapter, the secular, pseudo-religious ideologies that flooded in to replace the sacred canopy of Christianity would not bring resolution but titanic warfare and genocidal bloodshed. They would evince the potency of our hunger for meaning, reduce the margin of error, and provide an indelible warning of what happens when the longing for religious participation is vented without the care of wisdom.

Kant and the Romantics

We have been moving briskly through many colossal philosophical figures. Each of the figures has made for their own volumes and scholarly traditions. It is important that the profiles provided in this book not be taken as exhaustive summaries of any one of these figures but for the roles they played in this specific genealogy. Their relevance to this argument should not be mistaken for an exhaustive account of their relevance. Indeed, the thing that makes each so important is that their contributions, and our understanding of their ideas, continue to evolve in the hands of new and discerning scholars. This is certainly true for the Greeks, and it is also true for the next pivotal figure in our story, the German philosopher Immanuel Kant.

Kant tried to deal with this fracture in realness that Descartes left behind—the inner subjective mind touching itself, set against the outer mathematical objectiveness. Kant was not content to leave certain Cartesian assumptions unquestioned. For instance, how is it that math is so good at describing reality? Should we just accept Galileo's claim that it is the language of the universe?

In the Neoplatonic worldview, reality was ultimately grounded in the eidos; those intelligible forms were abstract and eternal, not spatiotemporal. They could therefore be expressed mathematically and musically. But modern Cartesian math did not involve the same ontology, so its emphasis on math could not rest on the same reasoning. How did the two aspects of Descartes fit together? How could math have primacy when all I really had access to was my own mind?

Kant came up with a radical proposal, another kind of Copernican Revolution. The categories of mathematics, he proposed, and the patterns of intelligibility we find in the world, were not actually in the world—at least not in the sense we thought they were. Kant made use of Ockham's razor. These patterns of intelligibility that appeared as features in the world were actually features of mind, specifically of the way that mind organized our experience.

Imagine that the world is blurry. There is too much information to process, so it has to be filtered with lenses. The filter helps fit the blurry mass of the world to my eye so my brain can make sense of it. Kant proposed that structures in the mind acted as these filtering frames. They imposed a structure of intelligibility on our experience. This view was a striking reversal to the Platonic worldview.

We were not discovering patterns of intelligibility that structurally functionally organized the world. The patterns we perceived were imposed on the information entering our senses, an inner mold into which reality was poured. This was the basis of our capacity for reasoning. I could reason about the world not because it was rationally structured—as Ockham said, the world was absurd in itself—but because I had filtered the world according to my mind's internal grammar.

This was indeed another Copernican reversal, and a subversion of Platonic realism. Math was not discovering reality. Rather, math was a function of the mind's structure. Mind was *making* sense of reality. Our contact with the world was already withdrawn in the minds of Luther and Descartes. In Kant, not only was the mind withdrawn, it was also imprisoned.

Everything we knew and sensed had to pass through this filtering frame. That meant we could never know the world as it was, as a *thing in itself*. The Cartesian search for certainty was thus undermined. The mind was trapped within itself and only touched itself. It lost contact with the world. For Kant, math worked so well because it was a property of our mental schematic, the *transcendental* conditions of experience. It did not really reveal the structure of the world, but only the structure of thought.

This was the price we paid for merging the two sides of Descartes. You might imagine why it was simultaneously so compelling and threatening. Information about the world flowed in from the world, and our mental filter processed it and gave it a certain structure. This Kantian model is still the most prevalent in most cognitive psychology and cognitive science. One way of understanding the Kantian model is to understand the contrast between *bottom-up processing* and *top-down processing*. The concept of bottom-up processing starts in perception and moves towards cognition. Top-down processing starts in cognition and moves down into perception.

We already discussed this difference in relation to attention: top-down processing allows you to read a cluster of letters as a word, or cluster of words as a phrase (e.g., "The Cat"). If the "H" and "A" are made to look identical, you use the knowledge of the word to disambiguate the letters, and you use the knowledge of the letters to reconstruct the word.

The two are interpenetrating in a self-organizing manner, outside of your cognitive awareness. This kind of cognitive processing is a condition of your thinking. It is what makes reading possible. This is the same model in Kant's proposed filter frames. They impose structure on the information coming into your mind, and they make it intelligible. In the first direction—from the world to mind—the world becomes intelligible to the mind as the mind filters and frames the information. In the second direction—from mind to the world—the intelligible structure is found in the world.

The Kantian model is pervasive through all of cognitive science, and for good reason. It turns out to be a very powerful way of looking at the structure of thought and experience. As I move into the mind and inside the framework, my cognition becomes more rational, mathematically and logically intelligible. But notice this: as my processing becomes more rational, logical and mathematical, I get farther away from being in contact with the world.

The reversal of Platonic structure is also bringing a reverse consequence. For Plato, as you pursue rationality, you move deeper and deeper into reality. But for Kant, the opposite is true. If I stray from the mind to the outer layers of my mental filters and to the frontier between my mind and reality—if I open the mind up to these more irrational, less processed parts of cognition, straddle the boundary between the conscious and the unconscious aspects of my experience, and stray into the imaginary, irrational dreamlike aspects of myself—I will begin to lose rationality. But in losing my rationality, I shall gain back my lost contact with the world.[1]

The pursuit of the irrational, imaginary, and absurd as an attempt to regain contact with reality became a defining feature of *Romanticism*. While I consider this response to be ultimately unwise, it is certainly not without value. The Romantics, like Pascal before them, were trying to recapture perspectival and participatory knowing. However, the Kantian framework required them to forfeit rationality to advance this project. The combined Romantic strategy and Kantian paradigm would frame the early psychoanalytic theories of Freud and Jung; for each of these men, the exploration of the psyche inevitably led to confrontation with irrational forces and

---

1.   Gary Lachman, *Lost Knowledge of the Imagination* (Floris Books, 2017).

movements that stood on the far side of its tenuously rational structure.[2]

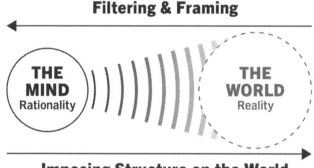

Filtering & Framing

THE MIND
Rationality

THE WORLD
Reality

Imposing Structure on the World

Figure 23.1: A diagram depicting the Kantian framework in which the world is filtered to the mind and the mind is imposing a structure on the world. Notice that the outer layers of processing, which are the less refined initial stages of making sense, represented by the thicker lines, are simultaneously closer to reality and farther from rationality. This is the basis of the Romantic idea that the irrational aspects of the mind put us more in direct contact with reality.

Romanticism, in its original meaning, is not just the mood of lovers. It is the idea that we can recapture contact with reality by moving away from the rational layers of cognition. How, then, did it become associated with love? The Romantics, in their own refracted way, were trying to return to Neoplatonic gnosis and participatory knowing. In the Neoplatonic and Christian tradition, love was the quintessential form of this knowing, a force of creation and realization. It combined invention and discovery.

The Romantics remembered that; for them, love was an irrational force that powered the faculty of imagination, which stood between reason and perception, between sensuous experience and mathematical intelligibility. For the Romantics, imagination was not

---

2. Jung repeatedly tells his readers that he is a Neo-Kantian. One way to understand Jung is by taking Kant's epistemology and putting it into dialogue with Gnostic mythology.

merely mental images moving in our heads. This was among their greatest insights.

The Romantics made a distinction between imagination and the faculty they called *fancy,* the ability to generate phantasm. Through imagination, the mind imposed structure on raw data, making it available to reason. Imagination was therefore the place where human beings could transcend reason and gain deeper access to reality. Music and art, as works of imagination, were the places where meaning was made.

By the early nineteenth century, two views were now coming into opposition. One was paradigmatic of the Enlightenment and the Scientific Method. In this view—represented by philosophers like John Locke—the mind was an empty canvas overwritten by sense experience. This view was called *empiricism.*

The Romantics held the opposite view. We did not know what the world was in itself. The world was an empty canvas on which imagination *expressed*—pressed itself out onto the world. Expression was therefore central to the Romantics, and it would inform the psychoanalytic concept of *projection.* The empiricists, by contrast, thought the mind was a blank slate onto which the world impressed itself. All of our knowledge and ideas were derived from these impressions.

Both of these views—an empty world subject to our expressions, or an empty mind subject to the world's impressions—are significantly mistaken. Both have shown themselves to be philosophically dissatisfying and erroneous when set against our current cognitive science. However, Romanticism was a deeply attractive response to the frustrations of the Cartesian worldview, and it became a pan-European movement of art and thought. This movement produced some of the most celebrated artists of the time —Goethe,[3] Blake, and Wordsworth in literature and Beethoven in music.

The German theologian Schleiermacher understood

---

3. Johann Wolfgang von Goethe, *The Sorrows of Young Werther and Selected Writings* (Penguin Publishing Group, 2005).

Romanticism as a way of trying to renew the function of religion, integrating music, art, and literature while using imagination to make meaning inside the scientific worldview. Romanticism was the forerunner to most pseudo-religious ideologies that would emerge in the twentieth century. It provoked a significant transformation in culture, cognition, and consciousness; people started experimenting with ASCs, and spiritualism became more prolific. Both poets and scientists began to experiment with different substances and practices, like hypnosis (in the case of Freud), and opium (in the case of Coleridge and others).

As with many others, the legacy of Romanticism is ambivalent. It lent a profound poetic voice to the nature of the human spirit and the perennial longing for sacredness. However, we have paid a devastating price for the pseudo-religious ideologies it inspired. Strains of Romanticism remain alive in our culture, especially in our ideas of love, which we often paint as an irrational force of cosmic destiny with no intrinsic ties to agency, reason, decision or virtue.

Contemporary romantic comedies are emblematic of these metaphysical perversions, a bullshit of salience trapped inside a chamber of fantasy and imagination, trying to carry all the Neoplatonic weight that religion, tradition, philosophy, and history carried. No romantic partner or human relationship can bear that burden. We often enter our romantic relationships with salvific expectations, and when the fatality occurs in separation, we no longer have the Stoic resilience to refocus our perspective. Consequently, our romantic relationships are often the most profound sources of meaning in our lives and therefore cause us the greatest suffering.

One of the most powerful aspects of the Romantic legacy was the mysticism of its poetic form. Since the loss of Lectio Divina in the Middle Ages, human beings had been increasingly trapped inside a petrified, propositional way of using language. But figures like Blake and Coleridge turned language on itself to break free of its cognitive strictures and invite transformative experience ("to see the world in a grain of sand...").

Unfortunately, this mystical movement was available to few; it was not grounded in any sapiential traditions or spiritual exercises. Most people were not William Blake, and they could not poetically bend the world to make it more vulnerable to participation. While the Romantics provided some of the most beautiful words and images, they did not provide enduring practices, institutions, or systemic psychotechnologies.

Their gnostic longing involved religious beliefs and expressions, but it was loose, undisciplined and improvisational. It did not provide the orders of worldview of the Axial religions. It provoked raw spiritual appetite without the reason to constrain and manage it properly. It was more of a mood than a religion, and it could be appropriated for idiosyncratic ends. Ironically enough, this expressive, pseudo-religious mood became dangerously impressionable as it swept through Europe in the second half of the eighteenth century.

Romanticism played a significant role in the rise of the French Revolution and Napoleonic Wars. Napoleon's imperial conquest was a powerful demonstration of Romantic sensibility; he attempted to paint a new order over the world by force of will and imagination. Beethoven was initially inspired by Napoleon, at least until the famous commander crowned himself emperor.

Schopenhauer, Nietzsche, and the Primacy of Will

Napoleon was defeated, of course, and the scientific project continued to advance. Romanticism had failed to replace Christianity, but it did not fade away entirely. People continued to probe the irrational aspects of the psyche and its world-making capacity. The priority of will that began with Ockham and Aquinas persisted into modernity.

Romanticism passed into the hands of Schopenhauer, the godfather of *nihilism,* one of many German thinkers—including Nietzsche, Hegel, and Marx—who would respond to the decadent Romanticism and angst of Cartesian isolation. Germany had become the center of these movements. Schopenhauer internalized the worlds of Ockham, Luther, and Kant. He proposed a model of the mind that separated it into the irrational part (which was in touch with reality) and the rational part (which was out of touch with reality).

Schopenhauer concentrated on the idea of *arbitrary will* within the irrational mind.[4] For him, the will to live was a drive that structured, filtered, and framed all of our experience. The drive itself was irrational, relentless, and pointless. Unlike in Kant, the will to live was not in service of the rational mind although it did make reasoning possible. Schopenhauer inverted Kant the way Kant inverted Protestantism. The irrational mind was now in charge. The will was the most potent force, and the ego—the rational mind— merely sat on its shoulders (see Figure 23.2). This new model of the self would become a significant influence for Nietzsche, Jung, and many other thinkers of the modern period.

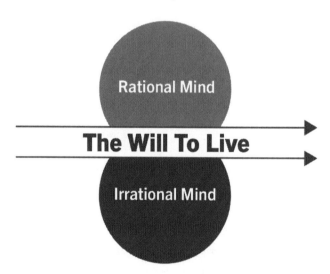

Figure 23.2: Schopenhauer's model of the irrational and rational mind, in which the will is primary.

Schopenhauer's thoughts on sexuality were exemplary of his existential paradigm, and they prefigured Freud in a powerful way. Sex was a cruel joke that our species played on individuals. It was the

---

4. It is like that God that we get after Ockham. It is a purely absurd force of will moving things.

source of our irrational will to live, filtering and framing our experience. It longed for meaning and fulfillment—everything that God, religion, and history had always promised. But once a person experienced it, the meaning was withheld. God was not revealed. We were moved by a drive that was unconscious and irrational. It hailed from the same place to which our arbitrary God had withdrawn.

In Schopenhauer, the Lutheran, Cartesian, Kantian sense of isolation now turned properly into nihilism. With the human self confined to such a winnowed, meager place, it would be easier for twentieth century positivists and scientistic atheists—most famously Richard Dawkins—to profess a reductive view of human meaning. Nothing was essential or intrinsically valuable anymore about human experience. Our lives could be restyled as replicator machines for our selfish genes.

Freud would eventually propose that our spiritual aspirations were neurotic projections, epiphenomenal pretexts for our libido. Schopenhauer saw that once we removed the connection between meaning-making and rationality, we paid a devastating price: a meaningless existence, contactless and egocentric, irrational and unconscious, and arbitrary. Schopenhauer was enough a Romantic himself to believe that art offered momentary respite from the restless, pointless will to live, but the unsatisfiable drive would inevitably overpower us and shake us loose from our rational projects. In him, the ideas of Romanticism and nihilism become inextricably linked, each responding to the conditions of the other.

Friedrich Nietzsche was among Schopenhauer's greatest readers. He reacted seismically to the loss of the infinite aspect of man. Like Pascal, Nietzsche peered keenly into the existential vacuum of the cosmos, into the spiritlessness and isolation that had come to roost in the human heart. He saw the declension of orders and values in the West, and he thought our nihilistic condition was a consequence of the worldview we had erected. Its values and moral framework, he declared, had diminished our spiritual vitality by inhibiting our ability to participate properly in our own nature.

The worldview had been fashioned on poor foundations, and now that it was decadent, its arbitrariness and self-deception was patent, and our fall was proportional to the scope of our historical foolishness. The highest values were now "devaluing themselves." Human beings were paying for our historical presumptions.

Nietzsche also understood the human will as the way beyond this predicament, though he took a very different approach than Schopenhauer. His writings and thoughts would be claimed by many movements in the twentieth century, ideologies that would call traditional metanarratives into question (like postmodernism) or that would seek—as Napoleon had—to revive the power of human will by expressing its force through conquest (like fascism).

Nietzsche was a disciple of Wilhelm Richard Wagner, the famous German composer. Wagner's compositions relieved German music of the influence of Romanticism. He broke the connection to the *home key*,[5] gradually untethering his form from its traditions. Wagner's antisemitism also became a significant influence on the German ethos. It attached itself to the undercurrent of Gnosticism inherited through the Rhineland Mystics and recalled Luther's treatise *On the Jews and Their Lies*.

The treatise argued for burning Jewish books, synagogues, and homes, and drafting Jews into forced labor. Many people have characterized Luther's views as a prelude to the atrocities of the twentieth century, though it is important to understand their theological context: the Jews, in Luther's mind, were followers of the law, and Luther—inspired by Augustine and Paul—interpreted followers of the law to be striving for their salvation.[6]

In Luther's Christian paradigm, no person was capable of earning his salvation by lawful merit, and the Jews who rejected Jesus, faith, and salvation in the name of law were therefore evil by this measure. Coincidentally, Luther and Nietzsche are two figures who are most directly credited with creating the modern German style.

Nietzsche did not give up completely on Schopenhauer's model,

---

5. Most music is written in a particular key. This means that one of the twelve notes sounds like the home note. When the piece finishes, it normally comes to rest on this home note.

6. See Martin Luther, *On the Jews and Their Lies*, trans. Thomas W. Marrs (Austin: The University of Texas Press, 1971).

but he tried to invert it. He held to the notion of will and its primacy over rationality. However, he rejected much of Kant and Plato. For him, the schools of wisdom that began with the Socratic tradition as well as the Christian tradition that emerged from it had created a life-denying asceticism that repressed something essential and primordial in human beings, diminishing human vitality. In a fragment from 1875, he famously wrote: "Socrates, to confess it frankly, is so close to me that almost always I fight a fight against him."[7]

Nietzsche quarreled with the Axial Revolution. His response to the Nihilism of Schopenhauer was a different articulation of will, the *will to power*.[8] For Nietzsche, everything had a will to power. Everything pressed itself out into being. This was not merely a feature of our minds but a feature of reality itself. For Schopenhauer, the will to live put us in contact with our own driving force, the irrational part of us that was most in touch with reality. However, the will to live was also pessimistic; it was wearying, relentless, meaningless.

Nietzsche turned this around. He declared that we needed to abandon the self-negation of the Christian worldview. The will to power was a pre-Christian movement to extend, create, and master oneself in the world. For Nietzsche, this was what humanity needed. Our spirits were suffocating from the nihilism of having the ancient orders fall before our eyes. There was no longer a higher world to draw our ascent. The lower world was now colorless. "No longer can your Self do that which it desireth most," he famously wrote: "create beyond itself."[9]

The will to power was a way of recovering the self-transcendence that began receding in the late Middle Ages and still more rapidly with the scientific and industrial revolutions. Nietzsche's father was a

---

7. Walter Kaufmann, *Nietzsche: Philosopher, Psychologist, Antichrist, 4th ed*, (Princeton, N.J.: Princeton University Press, 1974), 398.
8. It shares some features with somebody we will talk about in another book, another important Cartesian thinker, Spinoza and the notion of *conatus*.
9. Friedrich Nietzsche, *Thus Spoke Zarathustra: A Book for Everyone and No One* (Penguin Books Limited, 1974).

Lutheran pastor, and he understood Christianity from within a Lutheran paradigm. As we discussed in the previous chapter, Lutheran Christianity suppressed the dimension of self-transcendence that had been so critical to the Neoplatonists, and Nietzsche's Lutheran interpretation of Christianity seemed to cloud his appreciation of its transcendent aspects.

Nietzsche expressed disdain for the two-worlds mythology of the Axial project, but he was also deeply influenced by the Stoics and other thinkers of antiquity. His writings are gnomic and poetic, filled with ambiguity and ambivalence. He folded philosophical rigor into the florid style of the Romantics, which would be a significant influence for twentieth-century philosophy. If he could break through Christianity's modern repressions and glorified meekness, perhaps Nietzsche could transmute the pessimistic, world-weary will to live into the creative act of self-transcendence, a response to the modern crisis that looked no further than what was already accessible in humanity's deepest nature.

There was a brilliant, intuitive vitality to Nietzsche's works, but they came with certain dangers. It is difficult to critique Nietzsche because he did not write with a single voice. His style was as artistic as it was philosophical, and his many voices undermined and criticized each other. He defies a single interpretation; reading Nietzsche is like reading the Bible. His famous work *Thus Spake Zarathustra* was a conscious, Romantic exercise in religious myth-making. While his writings are singularly impressive and insightful, they draw from me a certain Socratic criticism. Nietzsche understood how self-deceptive human beings were and criticized them accordingly.

His famous diagnosis of the modern Meaning Crisis was perhaps more pointed and stirring than any other philosopher of his or any other era. But his own axioms inhibited his capacity for a coherent response. He was still living in a world that had been framed by Luther, Descartes, and Kant, and he too reduced the function of reason to a mere device of logical framing.

Nietzsche strove for transcendence without rationality, without psychotechnologies that could carefully address the perennial problem of self-deception. The volatile combination of self-transcendence and self-deception evinced itself in Nietzsche's thoughtful attraction to the concept of tragedy. This dramatic mood became the overtone to his life and legacy, just as it did for the Meaning Crisis itself; human beings had led ourselves into darkness by mistaking our own nature, and we were trapping ourselves in a worldview of value and reality that suffocated our own selfhood.

24

HEGEL AND THE HISTORICAL CULMINATION

Friedrich Nietzsche is one of the great prophets of the Meaning Crisis and perhaps its most iconic modern herald. Just like the Hebrew prophets of the Axial period, he noticed a pattern in the fault lines of our culture. He beheld the gradual fall of the sacred canopy, the loss of value itself, the all-engulfing darkness of nihilism that was creeping over civilization from the inside out.

He named this nihilism with great alarm, like Cassandra pronouncing the fall of Troy. Like Pascal, he saw the cosmic scale of the crisis, and he inflected it with stricken desperation, the horror that foresaw the magnitude of its stakes. This horror is most famously depicted in a passage of *The Gay Science,* when Nietzsche sent his madman into the village to proclaim the death of God.

> "Where has God gone?" he cried. "I shall tell you. We have killed him—you and I. We are his murderers. But how have we done this? How were we able to drink up the sea? Who gave us the sponge to wipe away the entire horizon? What did we do when we unchained the earth from its sun? Whither is it moving now? Whither are we moving now? Away from all suns? Are we not perpetually falling? Backward, sideward, forward, in all directions? Is there any up or down left? Are we not straying as through an infinite nothing? Do

we not feel the breath of empty space? Has it not become colder? Is it not more and more night coming on all the time? Must not lanterns be lit in the morning? Do we not hear anything yet of the noise of the gravediggers who are burying God? Do we not smell anything yet of God's decomposition? Gods too decompose. God is dead. God remains dead. And we have killed him. How shall we, murderers of all murderers, console ourselves? That which was the holiest and mightiest of all that the world has yet possessed has bled to death under our knives. Who will wipe this blood off us? With what water could we purify ourselves? What festivals of atonement, what sacred games shall we need to invent? Is not the greatness of this deed too great for us? Must we not ourselves become gods simply to be worthy of it? There has never been a greater deed; and whosoever shall be born after us—for the sake of this deed he shall be part of a higher history than all history hitherto."[1]

As scholars take great pains to point out, nothing is celebratory about Nietzsche's elegiac proclamation. He was not simply an atheist, rejoicing in the loss of divinity. He was sounding an alarm in the town square. Our two-thousand-year gambit had proven foolish; we had bet on the wrong world, and now that world had absconded with the infinite aspect of man. It left us barren. The religious worldview of Plato and Christianity had failed to bring self-transcendence, and now it somehow had to be rescued from the broken vestiges of the Axial world.

Hegel: Absolute Idealism and the Historical Geist

As we move toward concluding this phase of our argument, we must trace another important line of our genealogy that unspooled from Kant and the Romantics. This time, the line brings us to another titanic German philosopher, Georg Wilhelm Friedrich Hegel. Many philosophers of the nineteenth century—like Fichte and Schelling—

---

1. Friedrich Nietzsche, *The Gay Science*, trans. Walter Kaufmann (New York: Vintage Books, 1974), 181.

took up the lineage of Kant. But Hegel's contribution was singularly influential. For Kant, you will recall, the mind framed reality to produce its rational structure.

The Romantics inverted the structure; the closer one came to reestablishing contact with reality, the more he reversed this process of rationalization. Our contact with reality was deepened through irrational states of mind. Reality out in the world, the thing in itself, was something we could not access directly. We could only interact with our experience. Meaning existed within a self-constructing, self-enclosed activity of the mind.

Hegel presented an alternative view to Kant's. He was aware of both the Kantian framework and its Romantic response, but he rejected the idea that we could not interact with reality. If reality were completely unknowable, he argued, it would be indistinguishable from the nonexistent, and we should not bother thinking about it at all. If you removed the thing in itself, reality could be found squarely within the structure of the mind.

This was Hegel's *idealism*, the notion that reality was first and foremost a creation of mind. For him, in continuity with the entire Greek tradition, being was identical to intelligibility. Rationality was the method by which things were made intelligible. For Hegel, we did not move closer to reality by means of the irrational. Instead, rationality enhanced one's self-consciousness. It brought irrational filters into consciousness and made them rationally apprehensible. Hegel made the famous claim that the real *was* the rational, that rationality and reality were actually identical. If you got rid of "the thing in itself," you were left with this: the real was the rational, and the rational was the real.

Hegel's insight was inspired by many classical Greek philosophers, including Parmenides, Plato, and the Neoplatonists. He saw the deep connection between being and being known, between reality and sensibility.[2] Hegel took the Platonic inspiration and wed it to a critique of the "thing in itself." For him, the mind was not

---

2. For an excellent account of this, refer to Perl in his book, *Thinking Being: Introduction to Metaphysics in the Classical Tradition.*

structuring the rational experience of reality. It was structuring reality itself.

Hegel reinterpreted the irrational aspects of the Romantic mind as developmental potential, the beginnings of rational awareness. The rational faculties and experiences were not fully developed, not fully self-actualized. The Aristotelian influence in Hegel becomes clear in this idea; the irrational aspects of experience were our encounters with the unformed potential of reality prior to becoming fully rational.

The idea of "mind" must be treated carefully here. Hegel was not referring to *your* individual mind. He invoked an extended sense of mind, the entire human system of intelligible patterns that structured everyday space and experience. The room you are sitting in, all of your other surroundings are, in a deeply metaphysical sense, the activity of these patterns of intelligibility, this extended sense of mind.

These patterns were not simply experience. They formed a living system, and like the individual person, they traveled through a process of self-actualization. The irrational elements were constantly transformed into more rational intelligible elements. The Germans had a name for this living system: *Geist*. The term does not have a simple English translation. It covers word, mind, and spirit.

If Kant's unknowable reality could not be a reality, the patterns of making sense were identical to those patterns by which reality itself was structured. This was first expressed as an individual idealism, but it would eventually become *absolute idealism*: a self-realization of the patterns of intelligibility, as though all of reality—all of our combined thoughts and perceptions—gathered in the cognizance of a single cosmic mind as it gradually matured through time.

It is difficult not to become abstruse when talking about Hegel's idealism. How does one study something so abstract? How do we observe this living system of patterns, the rhythms of intelligibility that structure experience and reality? Here, Hegel was inspired by the influence of Judaism and Christianity.

We track the patterns through time, he thought, via those processes by which reality—and our understanding of reality—have unfolded together. In other words, we study the patterns of history. You can see the influence of Hegel's historical genealogy in this very book. These are the patterns we *realize*, experience, and make real. We look at history to discover the development of intelligibility, this grammar of human thinking, human being, human living, and the creation of worldview.

If you look at this history, Hegel said, you will see that it is not static. It reflects a developmental process, and that development is driven by two opposing forces. One is a process of *differentiation*. We must grasp the differences between things, the contrast, in order to comprehend them. The term *articulation* is a helpful way of thinking about this. Articulation means to speak and to make sense, but it also means to find all the joints, the division points between things.

Meanwhile, we also pursue *integration*. We gather things together to realize systematic connections between entities. In realizing these connections, we not only become aware of them, but we also constitute them. We are making them, again, not as individual agents imposing our will on the world but as participants; the patterns of intelligibility are working themselves out through our thought and behavior, through our ways of living and being in the world. You are likely noticing some Neoplatonic influences resurfacing through Hegel's idealism.

For Hegel, the process of understanding is the creation of a system—*systematization*. Remember the opponent process we discussed in earlier chapters. When I simultaneously differentiate things and integrate them together, I put them into a systematic relationship. You may recall the model of childhood development we discussed in chapter 10.

Children have ways of making sense of the world, and their sense-making discloses and structures their reality in certain ways. But as they grow through stages of development, that system sharpens and improves. Things that were conflated become differentiated, articulated, and then reintegrated into a more sophisticated, systematic understanding. For Hegel, this same developmental process unfolded across history.

The living system of intelligible patterns evolved through time, articulated by differentiation and then integrated into a more coherent and systematic model. The history of ideas, Hegel proposed, followed this pattern. An idea was proposed, a particular way of understanding the world. This idea was inevitably refuted and contrasted with an opposing view. The contrast clarified and distinguished it from other ideas. Eventually, however, the idea and counter idea were drawn together into a higher integration. This dynamic is often explained using terms that Hegel himself did not actually use. The idea is called the thesis, the counter idea is the antithesis, and the higher integration is referred to as the *synthesis*.

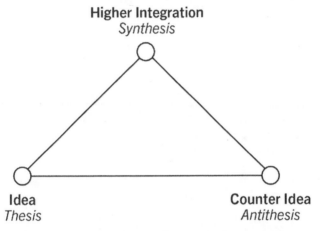

Figure 24.1: *A diagram depicting the connection between the idea and counter idea as they are drawn together to form a higher integration. Thesis and antithesis are drawn together to form the synthesis.*

For Hegel, this process unfolded repeatedly across time. The new, higher integration served as a new idea, drawing new contrast, and the whole process began again. The graduating form of articulation and integration continued to clarify the patterns of reality and intelligibility. These patterns produced ongoing complexification, providing emergent capacities for understanding and being in the world. Hegel called this process *dialectic*.

Hegel's idea is far from ridiculous. Even a cursory look at the history of ideas reveals profound and evolving patterns of mind. Parmenides, for instance, proposed that reality was changeless. After all, how could we grasp the truth if it was constantly changing from under us? Yet this claim was countervailed by equally compelling ideas. If we write off all change as illusion, then there is no content to experience at all.

So Heraclitus argued the opposite: that all reality was change. These alternating perspectives of reality—changing and unchanging—drew a powerful tenson. Both seemed true; we talk about immutable eternity, and we talk about reality as an ongoing process. Then Plato, as we have seen, proposed a way of integrating them together: *eternal patterns* (related to the real world) structurally organize *changing processes* (related to the everyday world).

The same dynamic plays out in our scientific enterprise. Science is built around the idea that eternal patterns and laws constrain and interact with forces of change. Science is a synthesis of these two dimensions. We use math to talk about the eternal patterns, and we use experiments to talk about the changing processes.

Hegel's "dialectic" was inspired by Plato, but his interpretation was different. Hegel's dialectic was the historical process of the gathering Geist, its emergence and self-transcendence. Hegel proposed that in the history of dialectic, we can come to a stage where this living system of understanding and realization becomes aware of itself, becomes conscious of itself through our participation. There is arguably some hubris in this claim: Hegel argued that his philosophy was the means by which the Geist attained realization—a systematic understanding of its own principles—and became reflectively self-aware. This brought about what Hegel called the *absolute Geist*. This was the telos of rationality and philosophy. For Hegel, all of history moved to this moment of Absolute Idealism.

When the process of sense-making passed into self-understanding, and when the living process of rationality evolved into systems of ideas that could grasp this pattern of dialectic, the *Geist* moved from understanding to reason. Everything was integrated into a reflective, systematic understanding, and this understanding also understood itself.

This was a powerful way of thinking, especially when combined with the original premise of idealism: the real was the rational, and in the process of the rational, reality realized itself. Human beings were host to this process. It moved in us and through us, in and through history. We can see why Hegel understood philosophy as the rational successor to religion. The mythological form of sense-making in religion was now transmuted into rational self-awareness. Hegel adopted and secularized a Hebrew and Christian idea. We developed and created the world with God. He was the very process of our teleological movements.

Hegel's God did not intervene through the words of prophets. He was realized through the reflective action and contemplation of a philosopher. Hegel understood his project in religious terms, but he always translated those religious terms into the philosophical concepts of rational development. In the *Oldest System Program of German Idealism* (generally attributed to him), Hegel proposed a new mythology in the service of the ideas, a "mythology of reason."[3]

Hegel used the term mythology in much the same way we have used it. He goes on to say: "In the end, enlightened and unenlightened must clasp hands...mythology must become philosophy in order to make the people rational and philosophy must become mythological in order to make philosophers sensible." This was simultaneously a philosophical proposal and a social-cultural program for how to transform religion, people, and society. It was novel and powerful. It drew from the religious past without forsaking the scientific, secular present. Its influence, just like its ambition, was colossal.

Hegel went on to say: a "higher spirit, sent from heaven, must found this new religion among us. It will be the last, greatest work of mankind." This, for Hegel, was the culmination of history, the final utopia, the last religion. The Geist, this living system of the patterns of intelligibility, the evolving structure of reality, would finally understand itself, and all previous works, movements, and dilemmas would become intelligible. Hegel tried to synthesize mythology and

---

3. H.S. Harris, *Hegel's Development Towards the Sunlight* (Oxford: The Clarington Press, 1972), appendix titled "The Oldest System Program of German Idealism."

philosophy in order to create a religion beyond all other religions. To do this, he also made use of existing mythological structures.

Hegel sought to secularize the Christian symbolic language to fit it into his system of thinking. For example, the Father in Christian Trinity represented for Hegel the undifferentiated, the unarticulated, the unactualized. The Son, of course, was the incarnation. He drew contrast. In the Son, our understanding could differentiate, and articulate. It settled into particular things. In the Son, we could begin to understand the world and its components and to identify ourselves within them.

Now we see the application of Hegel's pattern: the Son is the counter idea, the antithesis of the Father. When the Son is sacrificed, He reconciles with the Father. That is the moment of higher integration. A new, higher kind of identity is created by the realization of identity between Father and Son. The Father and Son are different, but they are also one; the integration and the differentiation are brought together in understanding, and a higher order self-awareness emerges. The reconciliation of the Son with Father creates the Holy Spirit.

There is a great elegance to Hegel's Christian interpretation. Geist is one way of translating the Holy Spirit. In the New Testament, we come to the idea that God is agape. He is identical to the very process by which we create, personify, and poeticize one another. Human beings do not each possess agape, individually, in our minds. Agape is something we dwell within. It is a process of making sense, making persons, and making the body of community. The Holy Spirit, Hegel's Geist, dwells within its self-awareness. God has always been agape, even before we realized it. But in realizing it, we bring Him to consciousness, and His destiny to fruition.

Hegel has been called the Thomas Aquinas of Protestantism, and it is easy to see why. He did in post-reformation Germany what Aquinas attempted in the medieval period, when the systems of scholastic thought first encountered Aristotelian science. Hegel took all of the theological and mythic machinery at his disposal and attempted to integrate it with the philosophical and scientific understanding that had fallen so powerfully upon the European psyche.

He tried to restructure the Christian worldview in the image of the Scientific Revolution and Protestant Reformation. His philosophical system, his grand synthesis, was an attempt to reunify all of reality in the midst of its great fracture. It was a total explanation of reality, mind, being, God, religion, philosophy, and history. He thought the system exemplified itself. The dialectic in the system's propositions reflected the dialectic in the philosophical process, which reflected the dialectic in the history of ideas, which reflected the dialectic in reality's unfolding.

Every scale of reality was present in this system. Each participated in the same pattern and recreated it. For Hegel as well as his students and followers this gave the system a powerful, undeniable plausibility. He made a formidable attempt to save the meaning-making machinery, salvage the Axial Legacy, recapture the contact with reality, and rediscover the axis between spirituality and rationality.

The Critique of Hegel, and the End of History: Kierkegaard and Marx

Hegel's German idealism spread rapidly across Europe and became the prevailing vocabulary for philosophical discourse. It was also adopted by pivotal figures like Josiah Royce in the early intellectual history of America. Nearly two centuries later, however, Hegel's German idealism has all but faded. There are many ardent students of Hegel today, but it no longer has traction as a generally viable worldview. The critical response Hegel inspired would decisively affect the development of the Western worldview and the intensification of the Meaning Crisis.

Hegel set up a pattern that secularized religion into systems of ideas. He sought to *totalize* our understanding of self and world. He is, in this sense, the godfather of totalitarian ideologies. There were three significant sources of response to Hegel's ideas. We already addressed one of these critics, Schopenhauer, who understood the relationship to being as a matter of will, not an evolving system of reason or ideas. Nietzsche, of course, took this up as the will to power, a movement to recapture self-transcendence. Hegel's idealism had not accounted for this primacy of will that became so central to modern thought.

The most enduring critique of Hegel, however, came from the Danish philosopher and Christian thinker, Søren Kierkegaard, who famously remarked that Hegel had made a system of ideas and then sat down beside it. Kierkegaard saw a certain impersonalism in Hegel's thought, a weightless objectivity. His system lacked a certain vitality, a genuine and visceral connection to reality and to oneself. For Kierkegaard, a Socratic spirituality, and especially a Christian one, could not be an exercise in dispassionate contemplation. It must invoke the felt character of our existence, our most personal suffering, our experience of absurdity, and our intense relationship with the inherent limits of our comprehension.

Though Socratic reason could awaken us to false beliefs and ways of life, making contact with reality—like Plato's anagoge—could not fundamentally be reasoned. It was accessed only through a radical change of self, personal transformation, and self-transcendence. This conviction connected Kierkegaard to the Platonic and Augustinian traditions as well as to the Lutheran one. Theology under Hegel had become purely conceptual and propositional. It was not engaged with projects of transformative experience—any process by which we grew, overcame egocentrism, or became capable of agapic love.[4]

As Kierkegaard famously proposed, moving through those transformative experiences required an intense confrontation with our own existence, and with it, a certain responsibility for our relationship to God. Assenting to this relationship, and consummating it, famously involved a powerful shift in consciousness and character—a leap into faith.

Discussing Kierkegaard's idea of faith and its ties to the Socratic

---

4. Merold Westphal, in his book entitled *Transcendence and Self-Transcendence,* echoes this critique and points out that while Hegel is proposing epistemic self-transcendence, he lost Plato's deep connection to what Westfall calls ethical self-transcendence.

tradition is a discussion for another day.[5] For now, it suffices to remember what we have already observed in the works of L. A. Paul, Agnes Callard, and others: there is a significant dimension to wisdom that cannot be reasoned. Kierkegaard is perhaps most known as the father of existentialism. The conditions of our experience appear absurd and contradictory, and each of us inherits the lonely responsibility of committing to that existence and becoming a self before God. Confronting this predicament requires us to undertake a process of agapic transformation. For all its grandeur, Hegel's system did not account for this predicament or for the finite nature of human beings. Kierkegaard was a Socratic figure, and he found in his own philosophical tradition the same failing Socrates had found in the natural philosophers: a collection of profound, persuasive ideas that had no existential relevance to the solitary individual, who was desperate to know what he must do.

Karl Marx was the other great critic of Hegel. Unlike Schopenhauer or Kierkegaard, his critique did not concentrate on will, absurdity, self-transcendence or transformative experience. Recall Plato's idea of the man, the lion, and the monster; for Marx, history was driven by the monster, by the appetitive dimension of human beings, and by the socioeconomic activity produced by the striving of our material existence.

Marx was deeply influenced by the German philosopher and anthropologist Ludwig Andreas von Feuerbach[6], who proposed—contrary to Hegel's Geist—that religion was a *projection*.[7] When we think about God, Feuerbach argued, we are projecting an ideal model of our own humanity. Feuerbach believed that this projection distorted, distracted, and deluded us, ultimately alienating human beings from our rightful role in the historical process.

Marx took up this critique of religion; he did not see religion the way Hegel did, as a mythic vessel for reason's development. Instead

---

5. "Socrates Meets Kierkegaard: Philosophy's Greatest Dialogues" in *After Socrates* (YouTube series, Mar 31, 2023)
6. Marx said that you could not understand him unless you had passed through the "fire stream" of Feuerbach's work.
7. Inspiring Freud.

he saw it as a noxious projection that deluded people and distracted them from their roles in the authorship of history. Marx proposed that once we removed the religious distortion and shifted to the material monster, we could see the real dialectic at work. His dialectic was a dialectical materialism not a dialectical idealism.

The clash was not between ideas contrasting and integrating. It was a process of political struggle between opposing ways—classes—of socioeconomic life. Marx retained some of Hegel's scaffolding. The economic classes were systematically related, and interdependent. They relied on one another, and defined one other. History was a dialectic of political clash and conflict, a tension between the classes as they worked through self-contradictions in socioeconomic life.[8] Marx was a utopist. He believed that this process of political struggle and violence would resolve the self-contradictions, leading to a political state of peace and freedom, a promised land.

Marx tried to complete the secularization that was already implicit in Hegel's system. He strove to bring it to fruition and supply the missing axis of participation. Philosophers only talked about the world, but *The Communist Manifesto* was a call to arms. ("Workers of the world unite!") Dialectic and participation came together in the quest for socioeconomic revolution. The force of will held over from early modernity, and as the nineteenth century turned into the twentieth, it turned to new, violent, totalizing ideologies that promised secular utopia as the culmination of history's pendulous dialectic. The search for kairos transfigured itself into political revolution.

This was the decisive turning point in history, and you were compelled to participate in it, to fall on the right side of it, to help bring about the desired utopia. Hegel's idea of historical culmination broke like white light through the prism of his critics. Kierkegaard's critique was the beginning of a new religious existentialism. Schopenhauer's critique, through Nietzsche, developed into an anti-religious existentialism. Marx's critique, of course, led to Marxism.

---

8. This is the core of Marx's critique of capitalism that contains all these inherent self-contradictions.

There is some irony to this outcome: the desperate search for conclusion, for historical finality, the appetite to re-devour all of reality into a single narrative—all of this would shape the events that shattered the lofty ambitions of secular progress and alert us to the consequences of utopic ambition.

25

CLASH WITHOUT CONCLUSION

Though it perhaps risks recency bias, it is not unreasonable to say that the Meaning Crisis only revealed its true catastrophic dangers by dawn of the twentieth century, like an infection that grew steadily in the body before it suddenly produced life-threatening symptoms. What began in Romanticism had now come to fruition: the fall of a sacred canopy, the loss of the normative, narrative and nomological orders, the disappearance of the higher world, the radical schisms of the church, the isolation of the individual, and the severance of sacredness from reason and rationality. All of this left us in an impossibly lonely position.

We could not find ourselves in the lifeless, inertial world, but we had not lost our spiritual longing to be connected to ourselves, to others, and to reality. So this longing, and its attendant will, inevitably found its expression in other forms of life, such as idols of worship that masqueraded as transformative symbols and domains of experience that could never satisfy our spiritual appetites but pulled them compulsively in unexpected directions—the very directions that the existential prophets, like Nietzsche and Kierkegaard, had dreaded.

Secularized ideologies had begun to emerge in the devastating aftermath of the Black Plague, but by the twentieth century, they were manifest. Whether political, economic, environmental, or drawn along the lines of social identity, they were religious in their engagement and orientation. They wanted to envelop the world into a single, unchanging salience landscape, a static mode of agent-arena relationship.

Social and political identity became the arenas where agency was found and where meaning was made. Here, at last, we could participate in the world and conspire in its recreation. For Marx, the participation was spurred by class, but for others, it was spurred by nation. In nationalism, the nation-state took the role of God. It became the arbiter of normativity, the highest, most integrated form of realness. It ceded the individual her identity, organized her everyday life, and drew commitment, passion, participation, and sacrifice. It was marked by ritual and understood itself to be the culmination of the historical development that preceded it.

Millions of people had given their lives for nationhood over the centuries, of course, often with religion as a backgrounding force. But the rise of fierce, secular national identity became prominent in the nineteenth century around the same time as continental philosophy was emerging, when Marx, Nietzsche, and Kierkegaard were undertaking their seminal works.

The Twentieth Century: The True Stakes of the Meaning Crisis

Nationalism, energized by unbridled will, wedded to the emerging socioeconomic, technological power driven by the Scientific and Industrial Revolutions in Europe. It also quickly wedded to imperialism, which became a kind of secular evangelism, a lesser god of nationhood. This too was Romantic way of expressing the spiritual will, a quest to totalize the world and steer its course with a decisive hand of agency.

The rise in nationalism was particularly evident in Germany. Since Luther, it had been the site of Europe's most influential philosophy and the first big proponent of secularization. Yet as a political entity, Germany was young; it did not come into existence until 1871. The Germans had been fragmented for centuries, but through the efforts of Bismarck, Germany was crafted and united into a nation-state. Germany had finally transitioned from a cultural leader to a political entity with tremendous economic industrial power and scientific production in its grasp. It was locked in competition with the other nation-states, like England and France, that had a head start in their imperial self-promotion. So nationalism and imperialism in Germany become both urgent and paramount.

As we know, the rising nationalism and imperialism in Europe erupted into catastrophe at the beginning of the twentieth century. The attempt to secularize progress and to measure it by material, scientific, and technological advancement came to disaster in the first World War. The machinery that was supposed to bring us to utopia, that tacitly took the place of God and our spiritual traditions, drenched Europe in a wave of blood and destruction. An entire generation was decimated, and the continent of Europe was traumatized. Germany, as the defeated party, was left stricken. Its national, imperial, and cultural ambitions had been thwarted. The victors, especially France and England, pressed their advantage. Their postwar reprisals weakened the German economy and crippled its military.

This history is complex, and it is not our task to do it justice here. We must simply understand that post-World War I Germany, the Weimar Republic, was a destitute entity. German idealism, already weakened by Marx and the proto-existentialists, had collapsed. The dialectic, whether one of economy, science, or ideas, had failed to deliver salvation. Meanwhile, the undercurrents of gnosticism—carried over from the Romantics and Rhineland Mystics—began to resurface, and Luther's anti-Semitism remained latently present.

Nietzsche's idea of will to power was refracted through this state of destitution and the resentment of its gnostic character. The collapse of German idealism and the Romantic tradition left a gaping philosophical vacuum. Nationalism and imperialism, the advocacy of a will to power, emerged as a way for human beings to recapture their lost self-transcendence and produced a reactionary sense of cosmic exceptionalism. The nationalism integrated with a racist interpretation of history, replacing Hegel's idealistic interpretation of history and Marx's socioeconomic interpretation of history. All of these influences, it would seem, drew together in Adolph Hitler, and the autodidactic vortex of his convictions. We already discussed the dangers of a fragmented, autodidactic approach to addressing the Meaning Crisis.

The Meaning Crisis came to a fever pitch in the Weimar Republic. All of these forces were spun inside a decadent Romanticism. *Mein Kamp*, beyond its moral abhorrence, reflects the scattered incoherence of a fractured worldview and the narcissism of taking one's own personality to be the only measure of reality. Hitler saw his own personal struggle as emblematic of all German experience and, indeed, all of Western Civilization.

You misunderstand Nazism if you see it only as a political system or a pure expression of fascism or racism. These elements served the mythology of a gnostic nightmare: a master race of true, authentic selves, etched into the blood and soil of a nation, trapped within a worldwide conspiracy that obfuscated their divine heritage. Only by opposing the demiurgic, evil overlords could they recover this heritage and attain the needed transcendence. Luther's anti-Semitism and his radical self-isolation mixed with the ancient strain of Gnosticism that held the Jewish God of the Old Testament as the evil demiurgic force.

When these influences constellated in Hitler, they produced a bizarre admixture: a totalitarian, pseudo-religious ideology that confused and distorted myth, mysticism, and nationalism fused with decadent Romanticism and Gnostic mythology as well as a misappropriated understanding of Nietzsche's will to power. Consequently, the great propaganda film of Nazis was entitled *Triumph of the Will*.

The two prevailing pseudo-religious ideologies of the twentieth century, Marxism and Nazism, were diametrically opposed to one another, but they shared a totalitarian utopic spirituality and gnostic quest. Hitler proposed his history of race against the communist history of class. Both understood themselves as the kairos and culmination of their histories. These two ideologies met in the most titanic military struggle in history, on the Eastern front in World

War II. In 1943, their engagement met its climax at the Battle of Kursk.

This was the biggest battle in recorded world history, involving millions of men, thousands of tanks, and thousands of airplanes. It was unfathomably violent, and it stretched from horizon to horizon. Individual acts of brutality fell against a background of titanic technology, a machine of mass destruction. The Battle of Kursk ended in a Russian victory. It spelled the beginning of the end for the Nazis and the ascendance of the Soviet Union into the military superpower that would dominate Eastern Europe. It is difficult to imagine the sheer amount of technology and material put to use and the immeasurable death it caused.

The Battle of Kursk was a summation of the stakes of the Meaning Crisis: two imperialist powers, tyrannically charged with will, unhesitant to sacrifice millions of lives for their self-promotion. Both sides were fixated on belief systems, totalitarian systems of ideology that forced secular alternatives to religion to explain history and reality as well as achieve utopia and recapture the Axial legacy. The politicized mythology had snared the human quest for meaning. Perspectival knowing was reduced to a political viewpoint. Participatory knowing was reduced to a political identity. This titanic struggle of wills and ideologies marshaled tremendous physical resources—eventually, of course, the Soviet Union also collapsed.

The Twenty-First Century: When Everything Is Permitted

The ideologies not only symptomatized the Meaning Crisis but exacerbated it. Now, we find ourselves facing a *meta-crisis*[1]—intertwining crises of ecology, socioeconomy, and mental health that intensify our spiritual despair. Our capacity to respond wisely to these crises has been disarmed by existential exile. Addressing the meta-crisis would require a comprehensive change in consciousness,

---

1. Thomas Bjorkman has referred to the Meaning Crisis in this way. You can watch my discussion with Thomas on my *Voices with Vervaeke* YouTube series. The video is entitled: "Understanding the Meta-Crisis and Metamodernism with Tomas Bjorkman."

cognition, character, and culture—the way we cultivate virtue and wisdom, compassion and self-transcendence, and how our communities structure distributed cognition and create systemic psychotechnologies.

Historically, religion is the only system that has reliably fulfilled these functions. The pseudo-religious alternatives we concocted in the nineteenth and twentieth centuries succeeded only in traumatizing us and drenching the world in blood. Consequently, many people now pursue a nostalgic return to religious belief. But without the three orders of worldview, it is difficult for many of us to access the symbolic vitality of Axial religions.

We settle for a truncated form of participation, a propositional tyranny that leads into fundamentalism. As I argued, popular forms of atheism are a species of pseudo-religious fundamentalism, subject to the same misframing as the objects of their ridicule.[2] Both sides attempt to totalize the world with propositions. In doing this, they lose the mysterious, invisible dimension—present in ritual—that cannot be intoned or expressed but can only be known in meaningful relation, lived through the opening of personal transformation.

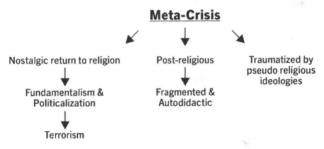

Figure 25.1: A depiction of the three current responses and effects of the meta-crisis.

When the fundamentalism of religious nostalgia meets the politicization of nation and class, it produces something horrific. In 2001, the Western paradigm of the twenty-first century was

---

2. A good case for this is made by Chris Hedges. For further reading, see *When Atheism Becomes Religion: America's New Fundamentalists* (New York: Free Press, 2008).

christened with this horror. The specter of terrorism continues to loom as a force of chaos, a dissociative menace in humanity's spiritual will. It can erupt unsuspectingly at any moment and in any place. Our disorientation has become more manifest with globalization and the rise of the internet and smart technology.

Many have written expertly about the impacts of these technologies, so there is no need for me to do so here. It seems evident that the condensation of space and time, an *all-at-once-ness* that Marshall McLuhan observed,[3] has added to this disorientation and created a sense of historical discontinuity, a loss of primordial memory—of anamnesis—that afflicts both individual and society.

As Jung put it, we cannot access the "lower stories" of our spiritual life and identity, and we are left with superficial adornments of ego that envelop us in the narcissism of small differences. The Platonic continuity between time and eternity seems all but inaccessible. German philosopher Byung-Chul Han has remarked that the atomization of time has also atomized the individual, and we have lost the sense of wonder in our encounter with beauty.[4] The gradual dissolution of the family has also eroded the structures that symbolized our sense of place and relation to the sacred.[5]

Postmodernists have taken pains to point out that the loss of meta-narrative has created an all-pervading relativism, where attention is vectored by illusion and assertion. The post-religious individual finds himself fragmented and autodidactic. He is therefore vulnerable to politicization and social tribalism. We are desperate to play with our identities, to seek ourselves out in this hall of mirrors and find a final place where we belong. These corners of belonging self-segregate into tribes of race, or gender, or sexuality, fall into fixations with personal health and wellness, or niche mythologies that try to recreate Bronze Age and Axial myths. These ever-

3. Marshall McLuhan and Quentin Fiore, *The Medium Is the Massage: An Inventory of Effects* (Gingko Press, Incorporated, 2017) p. 63.

4. Byung-Chul Han, *The Scent of Time: A Philosophical Essay on the Art of Lingering* (Polity Press, 2017).

5. Mary Eberstadt, *How the West Really Lost God: A New Theory of Secularization* (Templeton Press, 2013).

multiplying pseudo-religious ideologies subdivide our attention and identity ever further, isolating us inside worlds of self-reference that become more willful and esoteric, refusing to be penetrated by compromise or comprehension.[6]

The COVID-19 pandemic that began in 2020 caused a fraction of the death inflicted by the Black Plague or Spanish Flu, but it too was a revelation of the Meaning Crisis. It exposed the fault lines in our cultural and individual lives: our fragmented worldview, the lack of existential instruction, the absence of a superordinate value system to resolve ethical dilemmas, and a lattice of rituals to keep us anchored when our material comforts and institutions are called into question.

The impotence of our wisdom traditions is a critical disability. We have physicians for the body but not for the soul, and we have little training—like the Epicureans or Stoics did—to tend the health of the spirit. The vertigo of dilemmas that COVID presented, the paranoia caused by the sudden change in the significance landscape of the world, the polluted space between bodies, exacerbated the atomization of both time and person. It also stoked the neo-gnostic longing, the desperate search for narrative coherence in a disordered ontology; there must be a story behind all of this chaos, we insisted, if only we could uncover it.

Searching for a Response

The loneliness, atomization, and ontological uncertainty of COVID was personally revealing for many people. It forced people to live with decisions they had made and showed which of our relationships were vital. It proved that the world outside our window could become gray and inhospitable at a moment's notice. It revealed the tenuousness of the scaffolding that many people in the West unthinkingly took for granted. Most of all, it showed that people could be possessed by irrational forces of conviction and ideology—of every kind—when faced with fear and domicide.

---

6. Christopher Mastropietro and John Vervaeke, "Diagnosing the Current Age: A Symptomology of the Meaning Crisis," *The Side View* 2, no. 1(2020): 78–93.

This was a modest taste of the domicide that the Hellenes experienced after the death of Alexander, but it was enough to lay bare the vacuum of wisdom and connection in our culture. Many people looked to politicians for answers, but the political arena was not equipped to provide us with existential guidance. We cannot deal with the Meaning Crisis by pursuing pseudo-religious ideologies or political advocacy.

If traditional religious worldviews are no longer viable, secular ideologies are dangerous, and the scientific enterprise cannot provide the connection to sacredness and a spiritual life, we face a cultural aporia. People like Nietzsche, Jung, and Tillich understood that our sacred symbols could die. They needed to evolve and transform along with humanity itself. The Axial symbol of God was like a dying star, growing colder and more distant. Somehow, God had to be raised again from the horizon and reborn into the psyche of humankind. A new sacred canopy must be lifted to the sky, a God beyond the gods of tradition.

For many of us, this seems an unimaginable prospect, a living contradiction. We are thrown upon the horns of this dilemma, and the wound has bled us into an ashen state. Consequently, the myth of the zombie has now become a symbol for the domicide of the Meaning Crisis. It is the loss of sapience and spiritual vitality, the corruption of personhood, the gradual decay of cognition, consciousness, character, and community.[7]

This new symbol draws a contrast to the many nineteenth- and twentieth-century elegies—from Fyodor Dostoevsky, Joseph Conrad, and Herman Melville, among others—who depicted the madness that grips human beings when our primordial spirituality resurfaces without a symbolic container to tame it. They illustrated the horror of will without wisdom, the realization that we lack an ultimate measure of realness, of goodness, some higher order that can guide the course and direction of our lives. Pure will revealed itself to be

---

7. For more information on this, read the book I wrote with Christopher Mastropietro and Filip Miscevic entitled *Zombies in Western Culture: A Twenty-First Century Crisis*.

destructive, so we call out for some new cosmic constraint, something to tell us what the world is and who we are within it. What must we do? How must we live? We cry these questions into a vacuum. "If there is no God," Dostoevsky famously wrote, "then everything is permitted."

I have endeavored to trace the genealogy of the Meaning Crisis, to make an argument—if not a comprehensive one, at least a plausible one—for the primacy of meaning-making in human cognition and culture. I have attempted to show how a series of historical conditions induced powerful shifts in human activity, thought, and practice, leading to the emergence of powerful orders of meaning.

These orders told us what reality was, where it was going, and how we could interact with it. I have tried, in broad historical strokes, to show how the Axial Revolution gave birth to these orders of meaning and how the revolutions of the modern period have gradually disempowered them. No one person, or group of people, bears responsibility for the Meaning Crisis. It is, by its very definition, a collective problem, a disorder of distributed cognition. I have certainly tried to identify figures of critical influence, people whose inventions and ideas led to pivotal shifts of worldview, of consciousness and character. But these people, just like us, were embedded in their times. No matter their brilliance, their perspectives were finite, and they could not predict the future. Our predicament does not rest on their shoulders. It rests squarely on our own.

It is time now, therefore, to move on from the historical analysis and turn to the other side of the argument that we need to make: a cognitive scientific analysis of the cognitive machinery of meaning-making itself. This will be the topic for the book that follows. If we hope to respond and awaken from the Meaning Crisis without burying ourselves deeper in the problem or delivering ourselves into the hands of utopic totalitarian ideologies, I propose that we must undertake to understand, using our best science, the machinery of meaning-making.

If we understand the dynamics of worldview, the significance of states of consciousness, and the different kinds of knowing, we can develop our understanding of how meaning is made, and we can begin building a theoretical structure—and an ecology of practice—for recovering what we can of the Axial legacy. Our scientific acumen, combined with literacy in our wisdom traditions, can help give new perspectives on the past and reorient us to the possibilities of how we engage with the world. It can afford the engineering of new, systemic sets of psychotechnologies and help slowly recover the connectedness lost in the three cosmic orders.

The task before us is monumental. The first part of this argument is complete, but the work is far from finished. We must endeavor to continue this project, to find a wise and virtuous way of responding to this moment of impasse. With patience and effort along with support for one another, I believe genuinely in our capacity for awakening, our resourcefulness, and our penchant for learning. We can evolve ourselves beyond the confines of this Meaning Crisis, but we must begin by deepening our knowledge of our own cognitive processes, the perennial parts of our nature as well as our potential for growth. This is the task for the forthcoming book.

Until then, I humbly thank you for your time and attention.

BIBLIOGRAPHY

CHAPTER 1

Anderson, Michael L. *After Phrenology: Neural Reuse and the Interactive Brain*. The MIT Press, 2014.

Chomsky, Noam. *Language and Mind*. Cambridge University Press, 2006.

Clark, Andy. *Natural-Born Cyborgs: Minds, Technologies, and the Future of Human Intelligence*. Oxford University Press, 2003.

Csikszentmihalyi, Mihaly. *Flow: The Psychology of Optimal Experience*. Harper & Row, 1990.

Doidge, Norman. *The Brain's Way of Healing: Remarkable Discoveries and Recoveries from the Frontiers of Neuroplasticity*. Penguin Random House, 2015.

Eberstadt, Mary. How the West Really Lost God: A New Theory of Secularization. West Conshohocken, PA: Templeton Press, 2014.

Frankfurt, Harry G. *On Bullshit*. Princeton University Press, 2005.

Jung, C. G. *Psychology and Religion*. New Haven: Yale University Press, 1927.

Kabat-Zinn, Jon, Daniel Siegel, Thich Nhat Hanh, Jack Kornfield, Jan Chozen Bays, Ellen Langer, Michael Carroll, Daniel Goleman, and Madeline Bruser. *The Mindfulness Revolution: Leading Psychologists, Scientists, Artists, and Meditation Teachers on the Power of Mindfulness in Daily Life*. Edited by Barry Boyce and Shambhala, 2011.

Krediet, Erwin, Tijmen Bostoen, Joost Breeksema, Annette van Schagen, Torsten Passie, and Eric Vermetten. "Reviewing the Potential of Psychedelics for the Treatment of PTSD." *International Journal of Neuropsychopharmacology* 23, no. 6 (2020): 385–400. https://doi.org/10.1093/ijnp/pyaa018.

Kuss, Daria J. and Mark D. Griffiths. "Online Social Networking and Addiction—A Review of the Psychological Literature." *International Journal of Environmental Research and Public Health* 8, no. 9 (2011): 3528–3552. https://doi.org/10.3390/ijerph8093528.

Lewis-Williams, J. David. *The Mind in the Cave: Consciousness and the Origins of Art*. Thames & Hudson, 2002

MacLean, Katherine A., Matthew W. Johnson, and Roland R. Griffiths. "Mystical Experiences Occasioned by the Hallucinogen Psilocybin Lead to Increases in the Personality Domain of Openness." *Journal of Psychopharmacology* 25, no. 11 (2011): 1453–1461. https://doi.org/10.1177/0269881111420188.

Oehen, Peter, Rafael Traber, Verena Widmer, and Ulrich Schnyder. "A Randomized, Controlled Pilot Study of MDMA (±3,4-Methylenedioxymethamphetamine)-Assisted Psychotherapy for Treatment of Resistant, Chronic Post-Traumatic Stress Disorder (PTSD)." *Journal of Psychopharmacology* 27, no. 1 (2013): 40–52. https://doi.org/10.1177/0269881112464827.

Paul, L. A. *Transformative Experience*. 1st ed. Oxford University Press, 2014.

Pigliucci, Massimo. *How to Be a Stoic: Using Ancient Philosophy to Live a Modern Life*. Basic Books, 2017.

Rossano, Matthew J. *Supernatural Selection: How Religion Evolved*. Oxford University Press, 2010.

Schindler, D. C. *Plato's Critique of Impure Reason: On Goodness and Truth in the Republic*. Notre Dame, IN: University of Notre Dame Press, 2015.

Siegel, Daniel J. *Mindsight: The New Science of Personal Transformation*. Random House Publishing, 2010.

Taylor, Charles. *The Malaise of Modernity*. Toronto: Harvard University Press, 1991.

Taylor, Steve. *Waking from Sleep: Why Awakening Experiences Occur and How to Make Them Permanent*. Hay House, 2010.

Vervaeke, John, Chistopher Mastropietro, and Filip Miscevic. *Zombies in Western Culture: A Twenty-First Century Crisis*. Open Book Publishers, 2017.

Winkelman, Michael. *Shamanism: A Biopsychosocial Paradigm of Consciousness and Healing*. 2nd ed. Praeger, 2010.

Winkelman, Michael. "Shamanism and Cognitive Evolution." *Cambridge Archaeological Journal* 12, no. 1 (2002): 71–101. https://doi.org/10.1017/S0959774302000045.

Yaden, D. B., K. D. Le Nguyen, M. L. Kern, N. A. Wintering, J. C. Eichstaedt, H. A. Schwartz, A. E. K. Buffone, L. K. Smith, M. R. Waldman, R. W. Hood and A. B. Newberg. "The Noetic Quality: A Multimethod Exploratory Study." *Psychology of Consciousness: Theory, Research, and Practice* 4, no. 1 (2017): 54–62. https://doi.org/10.1037/cns0000098.

CHAPTER 2

Bellah, Robert N. "What Is Axial about the Axial Age?" *European Journal of Sociology* 46, no. 1 (2005): 69–89. https://doi.org/10.1017/S0003975605000032.

Bellah, Robert N. and Hans Joas. *The Axial Age and Its Consequences*. Harvard University Press, 2012. https://doi.org/10.4159/harvard.9780674067400.

Camus, Albert. *The Myth of Sisyphus*. Penguin, 2005.

Cline, Eric. *1177 BC: The Year Civilization Collapsed*. Princeton: Princeton University Press, 2014.

Colwell, John, Sadi Schröder, and David Sladen. "The Ability to Detect Unseen Staring: A Literature Review and Empirical Tests." *British Journal of Psychology* 91, no. 1 (2000): 71–85. https://doi.org/10.1348/000712600161682.

Csikszentmihalyi, Mihaly. *Flow: The psychology of optimal experience*. 1st ed. Harper & Row, 1990.

Csikszentmihalyi, Mihaly. *Finding Flow: The Psychology of Engagement with Everyday Life*. Basic Books, 1998.

Drews, Robert. *The End of the Bronze Age*. Princeton: Princeton University Press, 1993.

Hogarth, Robin M. *Educating Intuition*. University of Chicago Press, 2010.

Kashdan, Todd B. and Michael F. Steger. "Curiosity and Pathways to Well-Being and

Meaning in Life: Traits, States, and Everyday Behaviors." *Motivation and Emotion* 31, no. 3 (2007): 159–173. https://doi.org/10.1007/s11031-007-9068-7.

King, Laura A., Joshua A. Hicks, Jennifer L. Krull, and Amanda K. Del Gaiso. "Positive Affect and the Experience of Meaning in Life." *Journal of Personality and Social Psychology* 90, no. 1 (2006): 179–196. https://doi.org/10.1037/0022-3514.90.1.179.

Lakoff, George and Mark Johnson. *Metaphors We Live By*. University of Chicago Press, 1980.

Lobach, Eva and Dick J. Bierman. "The Invisible Gaze: Three Attempts to Replicate Sheldrake's Staring Effects." *The Parapsychological Association Convention*, 2004.

Reber, Arthur S. "Implicit Learning and Tacit knowledge." *Journal of Experimental Psychology: General* 118, no. 3 (1989): 219–235. https://doi.org/10.1037/0096-3445.118.3.219.

Rossano, Matthew J. *Supernatural Selection: How Religion Evolved*. Oxford University Press, 2010.

Struck, Peter T. *Divination and Human Nature: A Cognitive History of Intuition in Classical Antiquity*. New Jersey: Princeton University Press, 2016.

Vervaeke, John, and John M. Kennedy. "Conceptual Metaphor and Abstract Thought." *Metaphor and Symbol* 19, no. 3 (2004): 213–231. https://doi.org/10.1207/s15327868ms1903_3.

Vervaeke, John, Leo Ferraro, and Arianne Herrera-Bennett. "Flow as Spontaneous Thought: Insight and Implicit Learning." *The Oxford Handbook of Spontaneous Thought: Mind-Wandering, Creativity, and Dreaming*. Oxford University Press, 2018.

Vervaeke, John, and John M. Kennedy. "Metaphors in Language and Thought: Falsification and Multiple Meanings." *Metaphor and Symbolic Activity* 11, no. 4 (1996): 273–284. https://doi.org/10.1207/s15327868ms1104_3.

Winkelman, Michael. *Shamanism: A Biopsychosocial Paradigm of Consciousness and Healing*. 2nd ed. Praeger Publishers, 2010.

CHAPTER 3

Conford, F. M. Principium Sapientiae: *A Study of the Origins of Greek Philosophical Thought*. Edited by W. K. C. Guthrie. Harper Torchbooks, 1965.

Costa, Paolo. "A Secular Wonder." *The Joy of Secularism* 11 (2011): 134–54.

DeConick, April D. *The Gnostic New Age: How a Countercultural Spirituality Revolutionized Religion from Antiquity to Today*. New York: Columbia University Press, 2019.

Holland, Tom. *Dominion: How the Christian Revolution Remade the World*. New York: Basic Books, 2019.

McDonald Cornford, Francis. *From Religion to Philosophy: A Study in the Origins of Western Speculation*. Princeton University Press, 1992.

Nietzsche, Friedrich W., R. J. Hollingdale, Michael Tanner. *The Twilight of the Idols and the Anti-Christ: How to Philosophize with a Hammer*. Penguin Books, 2003.

Taylor, Charles. "What Was the Axial Revolution?" *The Axial Age and Its Consequences*. Cambridge, MA and London, England: Harvard University Press, 2012: 30–46.

Taylor, Mark. *After God*. University of Chicago Press, 2009: xi.

Vervaeke, John, Christopher Mastropietro, and Filip Miscevic, *Zombies in Western Culture: A Twenty-First Century Crisis.* Open Book Publishers, 2017.

CHAPTER 4

Frankfurt, Harry G. *The Reasons for Love.* Princeton University Press, 2004.

Frankfurt, Harry G. *On Bullshit.* Princeton University Press, 2005.

Moore, Christopher. *Socrates and Self-Knowledge.* Cambridge University Press, 2015.

Schindler, D. C. *Plato's Critique of Impure Reason: On Goodness and Truth in the Republic.* Notre Dame, IN: University of Notre Dame Press, 2015.

CHAPTER 5

Ainslie, George and Nick Haslam. "Hyperbolic Discounting." In *Choice over Time.* Russell Sage Foundation, 1992: 57–92.

Versluis, Arthur. *Platonic Mysticism: Contemplative Science, Philosophy, Literature, and Art.* State University of New York, 2017.

CHAPTER 6

Gerson, Lloyd P. *From Plato to Platonism.* Cornell University Press, 2014.

Juarrero, Alicia. *Dynamics in Action: Intentional Behavior as a Complex System.* First paperback edition, MIT Press, 2002.

Perl, Eric D. *Thinking Being: Introduction to Metaphysics in the Classical Tradition.* Brill, 2014.

Thompson, Evan. "Life and Mind: From Autopoiesis to Neurophenomenology. A Tribute to Francisco Varela." *Phenomenology and the Cognitive Sciences* 3(2004). 381–398.

Vervaeke, John, Ryan Wu, and Anderson Todd. *Scale Invariant Mutual Modelling Theory of Consciousness.* Unpublished manuscript.

CHAPTER 7

Armstrong, Karen. *The Great Transformation: The Beginning of Our Religious Traditions.* 1st ed. Knopf, 2006.

Buber, Martin. *I and Thou.* Translated by Walter A. Kaufmann, Simon & Schuster, 1970.

Collingwood, R. G. *The Principles of Art.* Oxford University Press, 2010.

Dreyfus, Hubert and Charles Taylor. *Retrieving Realism.* Harvard University Press, 2015.

Fromm, Erich. *To Have or to Be?* Rev. ed. New York: Continuum, 2005.

Geertz, Clifford. *The Interpretation of Cultures: Selected Essays.* Basic Books, 1973.

Kierkegaard, Søren. *Concluding Unscientific Postscript.* Translated by David F. Swenson and Walter Lowrie. Princeton: Princeton University Press, 1941

Lewis, Marc. https://memoirsofanaddictedbrain.com/connect/addiction-narrowing-opportunities-in-brain-and-environment/.

Marcus Aurelius. *Meditations.* Translated by Martin Hammond, Oxford University Press, 2011.

Perl, Eric D. *Thinking Being: Introduction to Metaphysics in the Classical Tradition.* Brill, 2014.

Vervaeke, John, Christopher Mastropietro, and Filip Miscevic. *Zombies in Western Culture: A Twenty-First Century Crisis.* Open Book Publishers, 2017.

CHAPTER 8

Batchelor, Stephen. *Alone with Others: An Existential Approach to Buddhism.* 1st Evergreen ed. Grove Press, 1983.

Batchelor, Stephen. *Buddhism without Beliefs: A Contemporary Guide to Awakening.* New York: Riverhead Books, 1997.

Batchelor, Stephen. *The Awakening of the West: The Encounter of Buddhism and Western Culture.* Berkeley, CA: Parallax Press, 1994

Buber, Martin. *I and Thou.* Translated by Walter A. Kaufmann, Simon & Schuster, 1970.

Bruno, Giordano. *Ars Memoriae.* In *The Art of Memory*, translated and interpreted by Frances A. Yates, 200-250. Chicago: University of Chicago Press, 1966.

Carse, James P. *Finite and Infinite Games: A Vision of Life as Play and Possibility.* New York: Free Press, 1986.

Cicero, Marcus Tullius. *De Oratore.* Translated by E. W. Sutton and H. Rackham. Cambridge, MA: Harvard University Press, 1942.

Eysenck, Michael W. and Mark T. Keane. *Cognitive Psychology: A Student's Handbook.* 6th ed. Psychology Press, 2010.

Langer, Ellen J. *Mindfulness.* 4th print., 1st paperback printing. Addison-Wesley, 1992.

Mole, Christopher. *Attention Is Cognitive Unison: An Essay in Philosophical Psychology.* Oxford University Press, 2010.

Russon, John. *Bearing Witness to Epiphany: Persons, Things, and the Nature of Erotic Life.* SUNY Press, 2009.

Vervaeke, John and Leonardo Ferraro. "Reformulating the Mindfulness Construct." In *Hypnosis and Meditation: Towards an Integrative Science of Conscious Planes*, edited by Amir Raz and Michael Lifshitz. Oxford University Press, 2016. 241–268.

Vervaeke, John, Christopher Mastropietro, and Filip Miscevic. *Zombies in Western Culture: A Twenty-First Century Crisis.* Open Book Publishers, 2017.

CHAPTER 9

Apter, Michael J. "Metaphor as Synergy." *Metaphor: Problems and perspectives* (1982): 55–70.

Baker-Sennett, Jacquelyn and Stephen J. Ceci. "Clue-Efficiency and Insight: Unveiling the Mystery of Inductive Leaps." *Journal of Creative Behavior* 30 (1996): 153–172.

Forman, Robert K. C., ed. *The Problem of Pure Consciousness: Mysticism and Philosophy*. Oxford University Press, 1990.

Huxley, Aldous. *The Perennial Philosophy*. Harper & Row, 1970.

Knoblich, Günther, Stellan Ohlsson, Hilde Haider, and Detlef Rhenius. "Constraint Relaxation and Chunk Decomposition in Insight Problem-Solving." *Journal of Experimental Psychology: Learning, Memory, and Cognition* 25 no. 6 (1999): 1534–1555.

Langer, Ellen. *Mindfulness*. Addison-Wesley, 1992.

Miller, William R., and Janet C'de Baca. *Quantum Change: When Epiphanies and Sudden Insights Transform Ordinary Lives*. Guilford Press, 2001.

Polanyi, Michael. *The Tacit Dimension*. Anchor Books, 1967.

Taylor, Steve. *The Leap: The Psychology of Spiritual Awakening*. New World Library, 2017.

Watzl, Sebastian. *Structuring Mind: The Nature of Attention and How It Shapes Consciousness*. First edition. Oxford University Press, 2017.

CHAPTER 10

Baars, Bernard J. A Cognitive Theory of Consciousness. Cambridge University Press, 1988.

Baars, Bernard J. "In the Theatre of Consciousness: Global Workspace Theory, a Rigorous Scientific Theory of Consciousness." *Journal of Consciousness Studies* 4, no. 4 (1997): 292-309.

Bor, Daniel, and Anil K. Seth. "Consciousness and the Prefrontal Parietal Network: Insights from Attention, Working Memory, and Chunking." *Frontiers in Psychology* 3 (2012). https://doi.org/10.3389/fpsyg.2012.00063.

Broadway, James M. and Randall W. Engle. "Validating Running Memory Span: Measurement of Working Memory Capacity and Links with Fluid Intelligence." *Behavior Research Methods* 42, no. 2 (2010): 563–570. https://doi.org/10.3758/BRM.42.2.563.

Chalmers, David J. "Facing Up to the Problem of Consciousness." Journal of Consciousness Studies 2, no. 3 (1995): 200–219.

Conway, Andrew R. A., Michael J. Kane, and Randall W. Engle. "Working Memory Capacity and Its Relation to General Intelligence." *Trends in Cognitive Sciences* 7, no. 12 (2003): 547-552.

Gibson, James J. *The Ecological Approach to Visual Perception*. Houghton Mifflin, 1979.

MacLean, Katherine A., Matthew W. Johnson, and Roland R. Griffiths. "Mystical Experiences Occasioned by the Hallucinogen Psilocybin Lead to Increases in the Personality Domain of Openness." *Journal of Psychopharmacology* 25, no. 11 (2011): 1453–1461. https://doi.org/10.1177/0269881111420188.

Merleau-Ponty, Maurice. *Phenomenology of Perception*. Translated by Colin Smith. Routledge, 2005.

Miller, William R., and Janet C'de Baca. *Quantum Change: When Epiphanies and Sudden Insights Transform Ordinary Lives*. New York: Guilford Press, 2001.

Newberg, Andrew B., and Mark Robert Waldman. *How Enlightenment Changes Your*

Brain: The New Science of Transformation. Avery, an imprint of Penguin Random House, 2016.

Piaget, Jean. *The Child's Conception of Number.* Routledge, 1997.

Schopenhauer, Arthur. On the Fourfold Root of the Principle of Sufficient Reason. Open Court Publishing Company, 1997.

Shanahan, Murray, and Bernard Baars. "Applying Global Workspace Theory to the Frame Problem." *Cognition* 98, no. 2 (2005): 157–176. https://doi.org/10.1016/j.cognition.2004.11.007.

Taylor, Steve. *Waking from Sleep: Why Awakening Experiences Occur and How to Make Them Permanent.* Carlsbad, CA: Hay House, 2014.

Tononi, Giulio. "Integrated Information Theory." Scholarpedia 10, no. 1 (2015): 4164. https://doi.org/10.4249/scholarpedia.4164.

Vervaeke, John, Richard Wu, and Anderson Todd. *Scale Invariant Mutual Modelling Theory of Consciousness.* Unpublished manuscript.

Yaden, David B., Khoa D. Le Nguyen, Margaret L. Kern, Nancy A. Wintering, Johannes C. Eichstaedt, H. Andrew Schwartz, Anneke E. K. Buffone et al. "The Noetic Quality: A Multimethod Exploratory Study." *Psychology of Consciousness: Theory, Research, and Practice* 4, no. 1 (2017): 54–62. https://doi.org/10.1037/cns0000098.

Zelazo, Philip David, Morris Moscovitch, and Evan Thompson, eds. *The Cambridge Handbook of Consciousness.* Cambridge University Press, 2007.

CHAPTER 11

Dreyfus, Hubert, and Charles Taylor. *Retrieving Realism.* Harvard University Press, 2015.

Griffiths, Roland R., Matthew W. Johnson, William A. Richards, Brian D. Richards, Robert Jesse, Katherine A. MacLean, Frederick S. Barrett, et al. "Psilocybin-Occasioned Mystical-Type Experience in Combination with Meditation and Other Spiritual Practices Produces Enduring Positive Changes in Psychological Functioning and in Trait Measures of Prosocial Attitudes and Behaviors." *Journal of Psychopharmacology* 32, no. 1 (2018): 49–69. https://doi.org/10.1177/0269881117731279.

Heintzelman, Samantha J. and Laura A. King. "Life Is Pretty Meaningful." *American Psychologist* 69, no. 6 (2014): 561–574. https://doi.org/10.1037/a0035049.

Heintzelman, Samantha J., and Laura A. King. "(The Feeling of) Meaning-as-Information." *Personality and Social Psychology Review* 18, no. 2 (2014): 153–167. https://doi.org/10.1177/1088868313518487.

Heintzelman, Samantha J., Jason Trent, and Laura A. King. "Encounters with Objective Coherence and the Experience of Meaning in Life." *Psychological Science* 24, no. 6 (2013): 991–998. https://doi.org/10.1177/0956797612465878.

Irving, Zachary and Evan Thompson. "The Philosophy of Mind-Wandering." In *The Oxford Handbook of Spontaneous Thought: Mind-Wandering, Creativity, and Dreaming.* Oxford University Press, 2018.

Jung-Beeman, Mark, Edward M. Bowden, Jeffrey Haberman, Jennifer L. Frymiare,

Stella Arambel-Liu, Richard Greenblatt, Paul J. Reber, and John Kounios. "Neural Activity When People Solve Verbal Problems with Insight." *PLoS Biology* 2, no. 4 (2004): e97. https://doi.org/10.1371/journal.pbio.0020097.

Kaplan, Craig A., and Herbert A. Simon. "In Search of Insight." *Cognitive Psychology* 22, no. 3 (1990): 374–419. https://doi.org/10.1016/0010-0285(90)90008-R.

McKee, Patrick, and Claire Barber. "On Defining Wisdom." The International Journal of Aging and Human Development 49, no. 2 (1999): 149–164. https://doi.org/10.2190/8G32-BNV0-NVP9-7V6G.

Merleau-Ponty, Maurice. *Phenomenology of Perception*. Translated by Colin Smith. Routledge, 2005.

Newberg, Andrew and Mark Robert Waldman. *How Enlightenment Changes Your Brain: The New Science of Transformation*. Avery, an imprint of Penguin Random House, 2016.

Oppenheimer, Daniel M. "The Secret Life of Fluency." *Trends in Cognitive Sciences* 12, no. 6 (2008): 237–241. https://doi.org/10.1016/j.tics.2008.02.014.

Ratner, Kaylin, Anthony L. Burrow, and Frank Thoemmes. "The Effects of Exposure to Objective Coherence on Perceived Meaning in Life: A Preregistered Direct Replication of Heintzelman, Trent & King (2013)." *Royal Society Open Science* 3, no. 11 (2016): 160431. https://doi.org/10.1098/rsos.160431.

Rosch, Eleanor, Carolyn B. Mervis, Wayne D. Gray, David M. Johnson, and Penny Boyes-Braem. "Basic Objects in Natural Categories." *Cognitive Psychology* 8, no. 3 (1976): 382–439. https://doi.org/10.1016/0010-0285(76)90013-X.

Segal, Eliaz. "Incubation in Insight Problem Solving." *Creativity Research* Journal 16, no. 1 (2004): 141–148.

Stephen, Damian G., Rebecca A. Boncoddo, James S. Magnuson, and James A. Dixon. "The Dynamics of Insight: Mathematical Discovery as a Phase Transition." *Memory & Cognition* 37, no. 8 (2009): 1132–1149. https://doi.org/10.3758/MC.37.8.1132.

Stephen, Damian G., and James A. Dixon. "The Self-Organization of Insight: Entropy and Power Laws in Problem Solving." *The Journal of Problem Solving* 2, no. 1 (2009). https://doi.org/10.7771/1932-6246.1043.

Stephen, Damian G., James A. Dixon, and Robert W. Isenhower. "Dynamics of Representational Change: Entropy, Action, and Cognition." *Journal of Experimental Psychology: Human Perception and Performance* 35, no. 6 (2009): 1811–1832. https://doi.org/10.1037/a0014510.

Topolinski, Sascha and Rolf Reber. "Gaining Insight into the 'Aha' Experience." *Current Directions in Psychological Science* 19, no. 6 (2010): 402–405. https://doi.org/10.1177/0963721410388803.

Williamson, Eric. "Finally, the Real Answer Why Your Best Ideas Come While Showering." UVA Today, October 5, 2022. https://news.virginia.edu/content/finally-real-answer-why-your-best-ideas-come-while-showering.

Yaden, David B., Khoa D. Le Nguyen, Margaret L. Kern, Nicole A. Wintering, Johannes C. Eichstaedt, H. Andrew Schwartz, Enneke E. K. Buffone, et al. "The Noetic Quality: A Multimethod Exploratory Study." *Psychology of Consciousness:*

Theory, Research, and Practice 4, no. 1 (2017): 54–62. https://doi.org/10.1037/cns0000098.

CHAPTER 12

Baltes, Paul B., and Ursula M. Staudinger. "Wisdom: A Metaheuristic (Pragmatic) to Orchestrate Mind and Virtue Toward Excellence." American Psychologist 55, no. 1 (2000): 122–136. https://doi.org/10.1037/0003-066X.55.1.122.

Carhart-Harris, Robin L., Robert Leech, Peter J. Hellyer, Murray Shanahan, Amanda Feilding, Enzo Tagliazucchi, Dante R. Chialvo, and David Nutt. "The Entropic Brain: A Theory of Conscious States Informed by Neuroimaging Research with Psychedelic Drugs." *Frontiers in Human Neuroscience* 8 (2014). https://doi.org/10.3389/fnhum.2014.00020.

Claxton, Guy. "Neurotheology: Buddhism, Cognitive Science and Mystical Experience." In *The Psychology of Awakening: Buddhism, Science, and Our Day-to-Day Lives*, edited by Gay Watson, Stephen Batchelor, and Guy Claxton. 1st ed. Samuel Weiser, 2000.

Grossmann, Igor, and Ethan Kross. "Exploring Solomon's Paradox: Self-Distancing Eliminates the Self-Other Asymmetry in Wise Reasoning about Close Relationships in Younger and Older Adults." *Psychological Science* 25, no. 8 (2014): 1571–1580. https://doi.org/10.1177/0956797614535400.

Jung, Rex E., and Richard J. Haier. "The Parieto-Frontal Integration Theory (P-FIT) of Intelligence: Converging Neuroimaging Evidence." *Behavioral and Brain Sciences* 30, no. 2 (2007): 135–154. https://doi.org/10.1017/S0140525X07001185.

Kelso, J. A. Scott. "Multistability and Metastability: Understanding Dynamic Coordination in the Brain." *Philosophical Transactions of the Royal Society B: Biological Sciences* 367, no. 1591 (2012): 906–918. https://doi.org/10.1098/rstb.2011.0351.

Kross, Ethan, and Igor Grossmann. "Boosting Wisdom: Distance from the Self Enhances Wise Reasoning, Attitudes, and Behavior." Journal of Experimental Psychology: General 141, no. 1 (2012): 43–48. https://doi.org/10.1037/a0024158.

Lipton, Peter. *Inference to the Best Explanation*. Routledge, 1991.

Millgram, Elijah. *Practical Induction*. Harvard University Press, 1997.

Newberg, Andrew B., and Mark Robert Waldman. *How Enlightenment Changes Your Brain: The New Science of Transformation*. Avery, an imprint of Penguin Random House, 2016.

Novak, Philip. "Buddhist Meditation and the Consciousness of Time." Journal of Consciousness Studies 3, no. 3 (1996): 267–277.

Rescher, Nicholas. *Plausible Reasoning: An Introduction to the Theory and Practice of Plausibilistic Inference*. 1976.

Sui, Jie, and Glyn W. Humphreys. "The Integrative Self: How Self-Reference Integrates Perception and Memory." *Trends in Cognitive Sciences* 19, no. 12 (2015): 719–728.

Tognoli, Emmanuelle, and J. A. Scott Kelso. "Brain Coordination Dynamics: True and False Faces of Phase Synchrony and Metastability." *Progress in Neurobiology* 87, no. 1 (2009): 31–40. https://doi.org/10.1016/j.pneurobio.2008.09.014.

Woodward, Alexander, Tom Froese, and Takashi Ikegami. "Neural Coordination Can Be Enhanced by Occasional Interruption of Normal Firing Patterns: A Self-Optimizing Spiking Neural Network Model." *Neural Networks* 62 (2015): 39–46. https://doi.org/10.1016/j.neunet.2014.08.011.

CHAPTER 13

Batchelor, Stephen. *Alone with Others: An Existential Approach to Buddhism.* Grove Press, 1983.

Batchelor, Stephen. *The Awakening of the West: The Encounter of Buddhism and Western Culture.* Parallax Press, 1994.

Batchelor, Stephen. *Buddhism without Beliefs: A Contemporary Guide to Awakening.* Riverhead Books, 1997.

Batchelor, Stephen. *After Buddhism: Rethinking the Dharma for a Secular Age.* Yale University Press, 2015.

Lewis, Marc D. "Brain Change in Addiction as Learning, Not Disease." New England Journal of Medicine 379, no. 16 (2018): 1551–1560. https://doi.org/10.1056/NEJMra1602872.

Lewis, Marc D. *Memoirs of an Addicted Brain: A Neuroscientist Examines His Former Life on Drugs.* Anchor Canada, 2011.

Smith, Steven M., Arthur Glenberg, and Robert A. Bjork. "Environmental Context and Human Memory." *Memory & Cognition* 6, no. 4 (1978): 342–353. https://doi.org/10.3758/BF03197465.

Vervaeke, John, and Leonardo Ferraro. "Relevance, Meaning and the Cognitive Science of Wisdom." In *The Scientific Study of Personal Wisdom: From Contemplative Traditions to Neuroscience*, edited by Monika D. Ferrari and N. Weststrate, 21–51. Springer, 2012.

Wittenborn, Andrea K., Hossain Rahmandad, John Rick, and Narges Hosseinichimeh. "Depression as a Systemic Syndrome: Mapping the Feedback Loops of Major Depressive Disorder." *Psychological Medicine* 46, no. 3 (2016): 551–562. https://doi.org/10.1017/S0033291715002044.

CHAPTER 14

Beck, Aaron T. *Cognitive Therapy and the Emotional Disorders.* Penguin, 1979.

Greenberg, Jeff, Tom Pyszczynski, Sheldon Solomon, Abram Rosenblatt, , Mitchell Veeder, Shari Kirkland, and Deborah Lyon. "Evidence for Terror Management Theory II: The Effects of Mortality Salience on Reactions to Those Who Threaten or Bolster the Cultural Worldview." *Journal of Personality and Social Psychology* 58, no. 2 (1990): 308–318. https://doi.org/10.1037/0022-3514.58.2.308.

Greenberg, Jeff, Tom Pyszczynski, Sheldon Solomon, Linda Simon, and Michael Breus. "Role of Consciousness and Accessibility of Death-Related Thoughts in Mortality Salience Effects." *Journal of Personality and Social Psychology* 67, no. 4 (1994): 627.

Kierkegaard, Søren. *The Concept of Anxiety: A Simple Psychologically Oriented*

Deliberation in View of the Dogmatic Problem of Hereditary Sin. WW Norton & Company, 2014.

Porteous, J. Douglas and Sandra E. Smith. *Domicide: The Global Destruction of Home.* McGill-Queen's University Press, 2001.

Rosenblatt, Abram, Jeff Greenberg, Sheldon Solomon, Tom Pyszczynski, and Deborah Lyon. "Evidence for Terror Management Theory: I. The Effects of Mortality Salience on Reactions to Those Who Violate or Uphold Cultural Values." *Journal of Personality and Social Psychology* 57, no. 4 (1989): 681–690. https://doi.org/10.1037/0022-3514.57.4.681.

Stanovich, Keith E. *What Intelligence Tests Miss: The Psychology of Rational Thought.* Yale University Press, 2009.

Stanovich, Keith E., and Richard F. West. "Individual Differences in Reasoning: Implications for the Rationality Debate?" Behavioral and Brain Sciences 23, no. 5 (2000): 645–665. https://doi.org/10.1017/S0140525X00003435.

Tillich, Paul. *The Courage to Be.* Yale University Press, 1952.

Vervaeke, John and Leonardo Ferraro. "Relevance, Meaning and the Cognitive Science of Wisdom." In *The Scientific Study of Personal Wisdom: From Contemplative Traditions to Neuroscience.* Dordrecht: Springer Netherlands, 2013: 21–51.

Vervaeke, John, Christopher Mastropietro, and Filip Miscevic. *Zombies in Western Culture: A Twenty-First Century Crisis.* Open Book Publishers, 2017.

Walsh, Brian J. "From housing to homemaking: Worldviews and the Shaping of Home." *Christian Scholar's Review* 35, no. 2 (2006): 237.

CHAPTER 15

Barnes, Julian. *A History of the World in 10 1/2 Chapters.* 1st Vintage international ed. Vintage Books, 1990.

Hadot, Pierre. *Philosophy as a Way of Life: Spiritual Exercises from Socrates to Foucault.* Wiley, 1995.

Hadot, Pierre. *What Is Ancient Philosophy?* Harvard University Press, 2002.

Hadot, Pierre, and Arnold I. Davidson. *Philosophy as a Way of Life: Spiritual Exercises from Socrates to Foucault.* Blackwell, 1995.

Marcus Aurelius. *Meditations.* Translated by Martin Hammond. Oxford University Press, 2011.

Trope, Yaacov, and Nira Liberman. "Construal-Level Theory of Psychological Distance." Psychological Review 117, no. 2 (2010): 440–463. https://doi.org/10.1037/a0018963.

Visser, Margaret. *Beyond Fate.* House of Anansi Press, 2002.

CHAPTER 16

Camus, Albert. *The Plague.* Translated by Stuart Gilbert. London: Penguin Books, 2001.

Holland, Tom. *Dominion: How the Christian Revolution Remade the World.* Basic Books, 2019.

Paul, L. A. *Transformative Experience*. Oxford University Press, 2014.

CHAPTER 17

Frankfurt, Harry G. *The Reasons of Love*. Princeton University Press, 2004.

Hopkins, Jasper. *Nicholas of Cusa on Learned Ignorance: A Translation and an Appraisal of De Docta Ignorantia*. A.J. Benning Press, 1981.

Murdoch, Iris. *The Sovereignty of Good*. Reprint. Routledge, 2006.

Paul, L. A. *Transformative Experience*. 1st ed. Oxford University Press, 2014.

Plato, *Phaedrus,* 247c–247d.

Wright, J. R. "Transcendence without Reality." *Philosophy* 80, no. 3 (2005): 361–384. https://doi.org/10.1017/S0031819105000343.

CHAPTER 18

Costa, Paolo. "A Secular Wonder." *The Joy of Secularism* 11 (2011): 134–54.

DeConick, April D. *The Gnostic New Age: How a Countercultural Spirituality Revolutionized Religion from Antiquity to Today*. Columbia University Press, 2016.

Hedges, Chris. *American Fascists: The Christian Right and the War on America*. Free Press, 2006.

Hedges, Chris. *I Don't Believe in Atheists*. 1st Free Press hardcover ed. Free Press, 2008.

Jonas, Hans. *The Gnostic Religion: The Message of the Alien God and the Beginnings of Christianity*. 2nd ed., rev. Beacon Press, 1991.

Murdoch, Iris. The Sovereignty of Good. Reprint. Routledge, 2006.

Perl, Eric D. *Thinking Being: Introduction to Metaphysics in the Classical Tradition*. Brill, 2014.

Plotinus. *Ennead V.1: On the Three Primary Levels of Reality*. Translated by Eric D. Perl. Parmenides Publishing, 2015.

Tillich, Paul. *The Courage to Be*. Yale University Press, 1952.

CHAPTER 19

Augustine, St. *Confessions*. Translated by Henry Chadwick. Oxford World's Classics. Oxford: Oxford University Press, 1991.

Casey, Michael. *Sacred Reading: The Ancient Art of Lectio Divina*. Triumph Books, 1996.

Cheetham, Tom. *The World Turned Inside Out: Henry Corbin and Islamic Mysticism*. Spring Journal Books, 2003.

Cheetham, Tom. *Imaginal Love: The Meanings of Imagination in Henry Corbin and James Hillman*. 1st ed. Spring, 2015.

Clarke, W. Norris. *Explorations in Metaphysics: Being-God-Person*. University of Notre Dame Press, 1992.

Illich, Ivan. *In the Vineyard of the Text: A Commentary to Hugh's Didascalicon*. University of Chicago Press, 1993.

Lewis, Marc. https://memoirsofanaddictedbrain.com/connect/addiction-narrowing-opportunities-in-brain-and-environment/.

Morello, Sebastian. *The World as God's Icon: Creator and Creation in the Platonic Thought of Thomas Aquinas*. United States: Angelico Press, 2020.

Taylor, Mark C. *After God*. Chicago: University of Chicago Press, 2007.

Chapter 21

Adorno, Theodor W. *The Jargon of Authenticity*. Northwestern University Press, 1973.

Hobbes, Thomas. *The Elements of Law, Natural and Politic*. United Kingdom: Cass, 1969.

Pascal, Blaise. *Pensées*. Penguin Publishing Group, 1995.

Weber, Max. *The Protestant Ethic and the Spirit of Capitalism*. Translated by Talcott Parsons. London: Routledge, 2001.

Chapter 22

Damasio, Antonio R. *Descartes' Error: Emotion, Reason, and the Human Brain*. Penguin, 2005.

Descartes, René. *Descartes: Philosophical Letters*. Clarendon Press, 1970.

Chapter 23

Kaufmann, Walter. *Nietzsche: Philosopher, Psychologist, Antichrist*, 4th ed. Princeton University Press, 1974. 398.

Lachman, Gary. *Lost Knowledge of the Imagination*. Floris Books, 2017.

Luther, Martin. *On the Jews and Their Lies*. Translated by Thomas W. Marrs. Austin: The University of Texas Press, 1971.

Nietzsche, Friedrich. *Thus Spoke Zarathustra: A Book for Everyone and No One*. Penguin Books Limited, 1974.

Von Goethe, Johann Wolfgang. *The Sorrows of Young Werther and Selected Writings*. Penguin Publishing Group, 2005.

Chapter 24

Callard, Agnes. *Aspiration: The Agency of Becoming*. Oxford University Press, 2018.

Harris, H.S. *Hegel's Development Towards the Sunlight*. Oxford: The Clarington Press, 1972.

Nietzsche, Friedrich. *The Gay Science*. Translated by Walter Kaufmann. New York: Vintage Books, 1974.

Paul, L. A. *Transformative Experience*. 1st ed., Oxford University Press, 2014.

Perl, Eric D. *Thinking Being: Introduction to Metaphysics in the Classical Tradition*. Brill, 2014.

Westphal, Merold. *Transcendence and Self-Transcendence: On God and the Soul*. Indiana University Press, 2004.

Chapter 25

Eberstadt, Mary. *How the West Really Lost God: A New Theory of Secularization*. Templeton Press, 2013.

Han, Byung-Chul. *The Scent of Time: A Philosophical Essay on the Art of Lingering*. Polity Press, 2017.

Hedges, Chris. *When Atheism Becomes Religion: America's New Fundamentalists*. New York: Free Press, 2008.

Mastropietro, Christopher and John Vervaeke. "Diagnosing the Current Age: A Symptomology of the Meaning Crisis." *The Side View 2,* no. 1 (2020): 78-93

McLuhan, Marshall and Quentin Fiore. *The Medium Is the Massage: An Inventory of Effects*. Gingko Press, Incorporated, 2017. 63.

Vervaeke, John, Chistopher Mastropietro, and Filip Miscevic. *Zombies in Western Culture: A Twenty-First Century Crisis*. Open Book Publishers, 2017.

ACKNOWLEDGMENTS

I'm grateful to many friends and colleagues who, directly and indirectly, helped bring this work to fruition:

Madlene Abramian; her tireless efforts and conscientious work contributed significantly to the production of this book.

Alan Kian and his crew; his offer to film this course sparked the YouTube series on which the book is based, and therefore made the whole project possible.

Rafe Kelley, Paul VanderKlay, Alexander Beiner and David Fuller of *Rebel Wisdom*, and Jonathan Pageau of *The Symbolic World*. Each of these friends engaged thoughtfully with this argument and offered creative insights, questions and commentaries that enriched it.

My friend and colleague, Jordan Peterson, who led the way in bringing philosophy and psychology onto social media, and galvanized the culture about the Meaning Crisis.

Finally, the argument in this book owes a debt of gratitude to my students, those on YouTube and at the University of Toronto. For the latter, I refer specifically to students in the following courses, *Introduction to Cognitive Science, the Psychology of Wisdom, the Psychology of Thinking and Reasoning, and Buddhism and Cognitive Science*. Their boundless passion and curiosity continues to inspire and improve this work.

ABOUT THE AUTHORS

John Vervaeke is an Associate Professor in the University of Toronto's Department of Psychology, and former director of its Cognitive Science Program. He teaches courses on thinking, reasoning, rationality, the nature and function of the self, the psychology of wisdom, and the cognitive science of consciousness. He directs the Consciousness and the Wisdom Studies Laboratory at the University of Toronto, and has won or been nominated for several teaching awards, including the 2001 Students Administrative Council and Association of Part-time Undergraduate Students Teaching Award for the Humanities, and the 2012 Ranjini Ghosh Excellence in Teaching Award. He has published articles on relevance realization, general intelligence, mindfulness, flow, metaphor, and wisdom. He is the author and presenter of the popular YouTube series, *Awakening from the Meaning Crisis* and *After Socrates,* and coauthor of *Mentoring the Machines* (Story Grid, 2023).

Christopher Mastropietro is a writer and former public policy advisor. He is a co-author of several publications related to philosophy, dialogue, and meaning, including *Zombies in Western Culture: A Twenty-First Century Crisis* (Open Book Publishers, 2017) and *Dialectic into Dialogos and the Pragmatics of No-thingness in a Time of Crisis* (Eidos: A Journal for Philosophy of Culture, 2021).

Made in the USA
Coppell, TX
19 November 2024

40556727R00247